EXPLAINING INTERNATIONAL RELATIONS SINCE 1945

EXPLAINING INTERNATIONAL RELATIONS SINCE 1945

Edited by Ngaire Woods

OXFORD UNIVERSITY PRESS
1996

Oxford University Press, Walton Street, Oxford OX2 6DP
Oxford New York
Athens Auckland Bangkok Bombay
Calcutta Cape Town Dar es Salaam Delhi
Florence Hong Kong Istanbul Karachi
Kuala Lumpur Madras Madrid Melbourne
Mexico City Nairobi Paris Singapore
Taipei Tokyo Toronto
and associated companies in
Berlin Ibadan

Oxford is a trade mark of Oxford University Press

Published in the United States
by Oxford University Press Inc., New York

British Library Cataloguing in Publication Data
Data available

Library of Congress Cataloging in Publication Data
Data available

ISBN 0-19-874195-2
ISBN 0-19-874196-0 (Pbk)

Typeset by Graphicraft Typesetters Ltd., Hong Kong
Printed in Great Britain
on acid-free paper by
Bookcraft (Bath) Ltd
Midsomer Norton, Avon

CONTENTS

II. Other Regions and States

III. International Institutions

LIST OF FIGURES AND TABLES

NOTES ON CONTRIBUTORS

PETER BARSOOM is a graduate student in the Department of Politics at Princeton University and is currently working on his doctoral dissertation and a book (with George Downs) on the role of enforcement in international regulatory institutions.

BRUCE BUENO DE MESQUITA is Senior Fellow at the Hoover Institution at Stanford University and has published extensively on issues such as decision-making, forecasting, and war. His most recent books include *War and Reason* (co-authored with David Lalman) and *European Community Decision Making* (jointly edited with F. Stokman).

JOHN DARWIN is a Fellow of Nuffield College Oxford, and has written extensively about the history of decolonization. He is author of *Britain, Egypt and the Middle East* and *Britain and Decolonization*.

ANNE DEIGHTON is a Fellow of St Antony's College Oxford, undertaking research about Europe, Britain, and the early origins of the cold war. She is author of *The Impossible Peace* and has edited *Britain and the First Cold War* and *Building Postwar Europe*.

GEORGE DOWNS is the Class of 1942 Professor of Peace and War at Princeton University. His recent books include *Tacit Bargaining, Arms Races, and Arms Control: Collective Security Beyond the Cold War* and *Optimal Imperfection? Domestic Uncertainty and Institutions in International Relations*.

JOHN DUFFIELD is Assistant Professor of Government and Foreign Affairs at the University of Virginia and has published work on NATO and European security. He is author of *Power Rules: The Evolution of NATO's Conventional Force Posture* and is currently working on German security policy after unification.

ROSEMARY FOOT is the John Swire Senior Research Fellow in International Relations of East Asia at St Antony's College Oxford. She has written about the Korean War, United States foreign policy and East Asia. Her most recent book is *The Practice of Power: US Relations with China since 1949*.

JOHN LEWIS GADDIS is Distinguished Professor of History at Ohio University in Athens, Ohio, and has published many books about the cold war and its origins, the most recent of which include *The Long Peace: Inquiries into the History of the Cold War* and *The United States and the End of the Cold War: Reconsiderations, Implications, Provocations*. He is now writing a reassessment of cold war history, based on recently opened Soviet and Chinese sources, and a biography of George Kennan.

ANDREW HURRELL is a University Lecturer in International Relations and Fellow of Nuffield College Oxford, and writes on the theory of international relations and the international relations of Latin America. He has recently edited *The International Politics of the Environment* (with Benedict Kingsbury) and *Regionalism in World Politics* (with Louise Fawcett).

TAKASHI INOGUCHI is Senior Vice-Rector of the United Nations University, on leave from his post as Professor at the University of Tokyo. He has published extensively on Japanese foreign policy and international relations, and his most recent book on the subject is *Japan's Foreign Policy in an Era of Global Change*.

YUEN FOONG KHONG is the John G. Winant University Lecturer in American Foreign Policy and Fellow of Nuffield College Oxford, and writes on issues of United States foreign policy and the international relations of East Asia. He is author of *Analogies at War: Korea, Munich, Dien Bien Phu, and the Vietnam Decisions of 1965*.

MARK KRAMER is Fellow of the Russian Research Center at Harvard University and Research Fellow at the Institute for International Studies at Brown University. He is currently completing books on Soviet policy in Eastern Europe, 1945–91, and the 1968 crisis in Czechoslovakia, and is editing a volume on the role of blue-collar workers in the post-Communist transitions in Eastern Europe and the former Soviet Union.

ADAM ROBERTS is Montague Burton Professor of International Relations and Fellow of Balliol College Oxford. His published work on issues of war, collective security, and international relations includes *Nation in Arms: The Theory and Practice of Territorial Defence* and *United Nations, Divided World: The UN's Roles in International Relations* (co-edited with Benedict Kingsbury).

AVI SHLAIM is the Alastair Buchan Reader in International Relations and Fellow of St Antony's College Oxford. He has written about British and American foreign policy and, most recently, about the Middle East, including *The Politics of Partition* and *War and Peace in the Middle East: A Critique of American Policy*.

PAUL TAYLOR is Reader in International Relations at the London School of Economics and Political Science. He has published work on both European integration and international organizations. His most recent book is *International Organization in the Modern World*.

NGAIRE WOODS is Fellow and Lecturer in Politics at University College Oxford. She writes about international relations theory and international political economy and is at present completing a book on the impact of the international financial institutions on the politics of economic policy-making in Mexico, 1982–94.

ANDREW WYATT-WALTER is a University Lecturer in International Relations and Fellow of St Antony's College Oxford, and writes about international political economy. He is author of *World Power and World Money: The Role of Hegemony and International Monetary Order* and is at present working on issues of regionalism in the world economy, and technology policy in the United States, Japan, and Europe.

INTRODUCTION

Ngaire Woods

History and theory are often treated separately in the study of international relations. History is left for historians to ponder on, while scholars of international relations plunder the 'facts' that historians uncover. The facts, it would seem, are fed into theoretical approaches, developed rigorously to explain and to produce models which predict events in international affairs. Yet this is a distorted view of international relations, both the practice and the study of which reflect a continuing exchange between history and theory.

This volume was conceived as a small step in the direction of drawing history and theory together, so as better to comprehend the ways in which each relies on, or informs, the other. To sceptics of theory, the book demonstrates that theories can powerfully illuminate issues and episodes of international relations. To those who would leave history to the historians, the book seeks to show that history can not be left to others and used merely as a data set. Good theory requires good historical scholarship. There is no easy way out of properly exploring history. Nor, however, should those more comfortable with a historical approach ignore the sharp and sophisticated tools social science offers to the study of international relations.

The book is divided into two Parts. The first, comprising three chapters, addresses questions of methodology and approach: what we might expect theory to do in international relations; what we seek to 'explain'; and how we might best go about it. The second part, itself divided into three sections on broad thematic lines, comprises thirteen chapters which offer new interpretations of events and analyses of the strengths and weaknesses of prevailing theories used to explain them.

Throughout the book the aim is to make both the history and the theoretical arguments readily accessible, and to this end two particular devices have been used. At the end of each chapter in Part Two a chronology is provided which serves both as a background to the discussion and as a reminder of key events and their timing. Also, many chapters in both parts of the book include a table which offers a simplified summary of the theoretical arguments. These tables are not intended to be read separately from the text; they will be fully comprehensible only to those who have read the chapters in which they occur.

The first chapter, by Ngaire Woods, offers a new framework for thinking about the different ways in which theory is used in the study of international relations. Contemporary theoretical approaches draw on many disciplines and concepts, including classical political theory, modern analytical economics, and post-modernism. Analytical tools from each have been borrowed to enrich the study of international relations. Yet this eclecticism has also brought confusion about the nature and purposes of theory. This first chapter seeks to allay this confusion, presenting five categories of theory and explicitly noting how and where the different types of theory are linked.

Chapters 2 and 3 explore the debate at the heart of method in international relations: will a historical or a social-scientific approach reveal the most? In Chapter 2 John Gaddis defends the historical approach, challenging the view that it is 'unscientific' and presenting its analytical strengths. Conversely, in Chapter 3 Bruce Bueno de Mesquita argues that there are great benefits in a more social-scientific approach, because it offers both greater analytical rigour and a capacity to predict. Ultimately these two scholars are prepared to admit that the historical and social-scientific approaches are complementary. Nevertheless, their arguments suggest different starting-points for research in international relations.

Part two of the book moves from the discussion of theory to its application. Each chapter explores a particular episode or issue in international relations since 1945. Unsurprisingly, we start with the Cold War, which has perhaps shaped the course of international relations since 1945 more than any other phenomenon. In Chapter 4 Anne Deighton analyses the origins of the Cold War, deploying critically the traditional approaches which focus respectively on ideology, decision-making, and geostrategic factors. Although she offers an explanation of both the origins and the course of the Cold War, ultimately she concludes that, in the 1990s, scholars must collaborate more with historians from both East and West.

One scholar who has used Eastern sources is Mark Kramer, who in Chapter 5 explores the Soviet Union's control over Eastern Europe, and the dramatic loss of that control. Theories of spheres of influence assist Kramer in identifying the military, political, and economic instruments used by the Soviet Union to maintain hegemony in Eastern Europe for forty years. His analysis explains both the extent of Soviet control in the years 1945–85 and the limitations on that control, and hence the process by which it was relinquished.

Chapters 6, 7, and 8 expose the very different natures of three vital sets of relations, between the United States and, respectively, Western Europe, Latin America, and East Asia. Scholars of international relations have deployed very different types of theory to explain these relations, reflecting in part their own very different preoccupations and purposes.

Economic relations are the focus of hegemonic stability theory, which is often used to explain the stable relationship between the United States and Western Europe since the Second World War. In Chapter 6 Andrew Wyatt Walter critically evaluates the theory and, by carefully re-examining history, demonstrates that security concerns were at least as important as economic relations in the evolution of the transatlantic relationship.

In Chapter 7 Andrew Hurrell discusses neorealism and its strengths and weaknesses in explaining four distinct phases of relations between the United States and Latin America. Neorealism, he demonstrates, although very popular in the United States as a theory of international relations, offers little explanation of the overall evolution of US–Latin America relations, or of the sources of domestic political change on both sides of the relationship. More illuminating, suggests Hurrell, is an analysis which draws upon both liberal and dependency theories.

Systemic theories of international relations suggest that US policy towards East Asia in the early Cold War period was defined by the policy of containment: a policy which reflected a bipolar world in which no countries were peripheral to superpower interests. Yuen Foong Khong challenges this view in Chapter 8. The systemic view rests on the US responses to Korea in 1950 and Vietnam in 1965; yet, as Khong argues, the United States did not respond to China in 1949, nor to Dien Bien Phu in 1954. In order to explain US policy we need to look more closely at history and at the way in which each US response conditioned the next.

Chapters 9, 10, 11, and 12 discuss regions and states all too often treated simply as extensions of the Cold War. Africa and decolonization are discussed by John Darwin in Chapter 9, where the author rightly points out that most theories of international relations neglect both the region and the phenomenon. Yet decolonization brought about a 'seismic change' in world politics, both in Africa and in the (formerly colonial) international system. In his explanation of Africa and world politics Darwin draws on theories of dependency, nationalism, and modernization, as well as on historians' accounts of decolonization, leaving us with a deeper understanding of the region, of the nature of decolonization, and of its implications for the international system.

In Chapter 10 Avi Shlaim illuminates the causes of war in 'one of the most volatile and violent subsystems' of the post-war international system: the Middle East. Arab–Israeli wars, he argues, have been spurred on by the Arab–Israeli conflict, inter-Arab tensions, and great power involvement. The relative weighting of these factors can be ascertained in part by identifying three levels of analysis: the individual level, the domestic political level, and the international level. Wars in the Middle East have been caused by reverberations of regional and international tensions in politics at all three levels.

Chapter 11 shifts to Japan and to the relationship between power and wealth in international relations. Takashi Inoguchi challenges the traditional characterization of power which casts wealth as a trade-off, requiring states to opt either for 'guns' or for 'butter'. Japan has been heavily constrained in its foreign policy since the end of the Second World War and unable to build and rely upon military might. Yet a careful examination of Japan's recent history reveals that the pursuit of wealth has enabled Japan to achieve its goal of securing honour, prestige, position, and status in the international system.

China, in contrast to Japan, has pursued a seemingly inconsistent foreign policy in the post-war period. In Chapter 12 Rosemary Foot explains the sources of China's international behaviour. Although realist and neorealist accounts offer attractively simple explanations, she argues that they leave too much unexplained. Delving into domestic political changes within China, she presents an analysis which makes sense of China's behaviour as it occurred, rather than offering, as realist analyses do, a neat *ex post facto* rationalization of foreign policy.

The final four chapters address four different types of institutions which have emerged in international relations since 1945. The emergence of the European Union is often invoked by scholars of international relations to demonstrate the dynamics of economic interdependence and cooperation among states. In Chapter 13 Paul Taylor assesses the 'neofunctionalist' and 'federalist' theories which make this case and argues that neither accounts for either the processes or the end results of integration. Rather, he argues, we need to analyse more thoroughly relations between élites and domestic constituencies in each European state. He presents 'consociationalism' as a theoretical account which does this and thereby offers a more accurate analysis of integration in Western Europe since 1945.

Broader than European cooperation is the ambitious scheme of collective security created by the Charter of the United Nations. In Chapter 14 Adam Roberts discusses the tensions which arise from attempts to reconcile state sovereignty with collective security. His analysis of the operation of the United Nations since 1945 highlights the impediments to collective security, yet also illuminates the various manifestations of the principle which have been achieved, such as peacekeeping operations and regional security arrangements.

The most successful post-war regional security institution is examined by John Duffield in Chapter 15. The North Atlantic Treaty Organization, initiated in 1949, is distinctive in its longevity, its popularity, and the high level of security cooperation achieved by its members. Theories of alliances, based on realist or balance-of-power theories, usefully point to key factors which explain the success of NATO. Yet beyond these factors, Duffield argues, internal threats, ideology, and the institutional character of NATO have each played a crucial role. To explain burden-sharing within the alliance he deploys economic approaches, but shows that here too the theories are too narrow and fail adequately to take account of factors such as different perceptions of threat in member states.

Chapter 16 addresses the fourth and final institution to be examined in the book: arms control. This chapter, more than any other, offers an application of the social-scientific approaches discussed in Chapter 3. George Downs and Peter Barsoom explain several variations of game theory, or different 'games,' which depict arms control and arms races. Non-cooperative game theory highlights the potential of arms control for reducing the likelihood and destructiveness of war by reducing the attractiveness to states of initiating conflict and of increasing defence spending. The unique strength of the game-theoretic approach is that it offers decision-makers advice as to which strategy will best bring about and maintain meaningful arms agreements.

Overall this book is not intended as a comprehensive survey of all international relations history and theory since 1945. Subjects such as nationalism, self-determination, and international law have not been dealt with; nor have many key institutions been discussed, such as the GATT, the international financial institutions, the Group of Seven, multinational enterprises, and non-governmental organizations. The book is, however, one of the very few existing attempts to bring together recent theoretical advances in international relations with careful, scholarly history. The resulting analysis of major events and episodes in international relations since 1945 seeks to further debate both about the issues and episodes themselves and, more broadly, about the methods and approaches appropriate to explaining international relations.

PART ONE: THEORIES, HISTORY, AND SOCIAL SCIENCE IN THE STUDY OF INTERNATIONAL RELATIONS

CHAPTER ONE

THE USES OF THEORY IN THE STUDY OF INTERNATIONAL RELATIONS

Ngaire Woods

International relations involves the study of a great number of 'facts' about the world. Yet these facts are only relevant when there is a framework to put them in. In E. H. Carr's words, 'a fact is like a sack, it won't stand up till you've put something in it'.[1] It is theory that provides the framework for the study of international relations. Yet different theories call upon 'facts' in different ways. The same facts can tell a number of stories and lead to any one of a variety of conclusions. Hence, theories need to be carefully chosen and their purposes and limitations carefully identified. Herein lies the task of this chapter, which seeks to distinguish the different types of theorizing which provide frameworks for the study of international relations, highlighting their various assumptions, goals, and weaknesses.

The first part of the chapter discusses the basic yet crucial business of defining terms and concepts. Theory is used to define what we are studying in international relations, our purposes in studying it, and categories within which we might set about analysing the behaviour of international actors. The second section of the chapter discusses theory as 'perspectives' or the exercise of conceptually 'mapping' the international landscape. Four particular perspectives are discussed: 'economic interdependence' (liberalism), 'world capitalism' (radicalism), 'law and collective security' (international society), and 'power politics' (realism). Each perspective highlights a different set of core actors, preferences, and interactions. Such perspectives are crucial for generating hypotheses about the forces which drive international relations. The third part of the chapter discusses model-building or formal theory. Formal theory permits better explanation, testing, and prediction in international relations. This section also highlights the ways in which formal theory must depend for strength upon the two previous types of theorizing. The fourth section of the chapter looks at quantitative analysis. Statistical analysis and the rules of inference lie at the heart of quantitative analysis and some would argue that such rules should also apply to qualitative analysis (a claim that is discussed and endorsed only in a limited way). The fifth section of the chapter discusses the contribution of reflectivism or theories of knowledge to the study of international relations. This section distinguishes postmodernists, critical theorists, and constructivists, highlighting the different levels of challenge that each poses to the other types of theory discussed in the chapter. The final section draws some conclusions, noting the relationships between different theoretical approaches and different purposes and assumptions.

1.1. Definitions, Purposes, and Categories

One of the first functions theory performs is to define the terms and concepts used to describe, explain, or predict in the study of international relations. Definitions and categories (or 'taxonomies'—a term used by Gaddis in Chapter 2) are crucial to social science, as they are to all science, for we can not study 'war' or 'states' unless we first know what falls (or does not fall) into such a category. Useful definitions will specify both what a term is and, just as importantly, what it is not and what its opposite or a contrasting term might be. The more closely connected any two terms are, the more useful it is to specify and distinguish them. This is true even of the terms used to describe the object of the study of international relations (what we are studying) and our purposes in studying it.

The object of the study of international relations is variously described as the 'international system' and 'international society'. Yet the two terms describe very different enterprises. This becomes clear if we adequately define and distinguish the terms. Hedley Bull defines an international system as comprising two or more states which have sufficient contact between them and sufficient impact on one another's decisions to cause them to behave as parts of a whole. In such an international system, states behave 'strategically', making their decisions on the basis of what they think other states will do. By contrast, an 'international society' is defined as a group of states which knowingly share common interests and values and 'conceive themselves to be bound by a common set of rules in their relations with one another and share in the working of common institutions'.[2] If we choose to define international relations as the study of the 'international system', our study becomes one highly amenable to game theory and to formal theorizing about strategic interaction among players. On the other hand, if we define international relations as that which goes on in an international society, we would want to draw on much more traditional tools of analysis including history, philosophy, and traditional political science. The definitions we use do not simply clarify but also reflect the purposes of our study. So, too, definitions crucially shape what we study and the methods we use to study it.

Our purposes in studying international relations are often described by either of the terms 'explaining' or 'understanding'. Yet these terms, as Martin Hollis and Steve Smith point out, are worth distinguishing, for they embody very different purposes.[3] 'Explaining' is concerned with identifying what caused a particular event or state of affairs. In order rigorously to assert that a particular factor caused a particular outcome, a number of cases must be studied so as to test whether the factor singled out was indeed the likely cause or whether it was merely a coincidental occurrence. Scholars who seek to 'explain' are in the business of generating and testing hypotheses such as 'a change in x caused y'. By contrast, 'understanding' involves a search not so much for the cause of an event as for its meaning. Scholars seeking to 'understand' will prefer to investigate a particular event or a state of affairs, rather than a set of cases, delving into history not as a bank of information which might falsify a theory, but as a narrative which permits a greater appreciation of the origins, evolution, and consequences of an event. The 'understanders', however, may well be prone to drawing out conclusions about the causes of an event without subjecting such conclusions to the more rigorous appraisal of the 'explainers'. At this point in research understanding and explanation become complementary. This point underpins the debate in Chapters 2 and 3 of this book, where John Gaddis and Bruce Bueno de Mesquita argue the respective strengths of the more historical 'understanding' approach and the more scientific 'explaining' approach.

Theorizing is important in establishing even the core concepts and categories used in international relations. Yet no matter how carefully they are defined, concepts will always be subject to modification and 'reinvention'. Here theorizing plays a dynamic role. Levels of analysis, for example, are created by scholars of international relations to categorize and conceptually to separate at least three different arenas of politics: individual decision-makers; domestic political factors; and the influence of the workings of the international system on states' behaviour. The conceptual separation is useful for it allows a scholar to ignore two (or more) arenas of politics and to focus on one. For example, at the individual level, the role of ideologies, ideas, and the psychology of decision-makers can be examined; at the level of the state, bureaucratic decision-making structures and procedures, interest groups, and coalitions of interests can be analysed; and at the systemic level, the distribution of power among states and its impact on their behaviour can be assessed. Thus these three levels of analysis can help us to think about international relations; but there are several problems we must face if we use categories defined in this way.

In the first place, it is not necessarily the case that there are only three levels of analysis. One could equally focus on other levels, such as that between the level of individuals and that of state structures—domestic groupings—or, alternatively, the regional level between state structures and the international system. A guide to defining levels of analysis might be to ask whether a particular level captures an arena which has a distinct logic of its own. A second problem with levels of analysis is knowing where to start. Just as skipping from one level of analysis to another risks producing a rather ad hoc mixture of causes, so too starting at one particular level of analysis will inevitably bias one's conclusions. In her excellent analysis of the individual-level factors which influenced the origins of the Cold War, Larson suggests that we use a 'composite strategy'. This strategy involves using all levels of analysis as checks against one another, with the result that we can more effectively fill out historical explanation.[4] The composite approach is perhaps satisfactory for scholars aiming better to understand, but it is not adequate for those wishing to explain. Scholars wanting to identify causal relationships need to be able to identify, for a given issue, that level on which the most important cause is to be located. Here, alas, there is no easy solution. The research itself needs first to identify the 'right' level of analysis. But how much research is required to arrive at one's method of research?

Finally, distinguishing three or more levels of analysis artificially separates 'units' (whether individuals or states) from the 'structure' (the international system), whereas in fact the two are in constant interaction with each other.[5] Where states interact at the international level, their interactions affect decision-makers' beliefs and attitudes, domestic political pressures, and conceptions of national interest. For example, once Reagan and Gorbachev started to negotiate disarmament, the two leaders engaged in a process which changed not only their own aspirations and perceptions but also those of interest groups, political institutions, and public opinion in their own countries. A different way to think about the relationship between 'structure' and 'units' is to focus on bargaining among states and to analyse its impact on individuals and domestic politics as well as on international relations. Some scholars do this using a 'two-level game analogy' or what has been called 'double-edged diplomacy'.[6] The problem with 'double-edged diplomacy' is that it addresses only the decision-making process; the questions of how states come to form their preferences and how they go about implementing policies on which they have agreed are neglected. These questions are not just questions of 'understanding'; they also bear on what it is that scholars set out to explain. Using the two-level game analogy, scholars will analyse particular negotiations, perhaps wrongly neglecting the other processes affecting politics.

Levels of analysis, along with other categories and definitions in international relations, assist scholars in identifying what they are analysing and distinguishing this from what they are holding constant or choosing not to analyse. Academic debates about categories and definitions are crucial in ensuring that important aspects of international relations are not neglected. Definitions and categories must be subject to continual scrutiny, not just to achieve precision but also to check the purposes and ambit of the research.

1.2. Perspectives, or Mapping the International Landscape

Theory is used in international relations not only to define concepts and categories but also to draw concepts together so as to outline perspectives or build up 'maps' of the international arena. The 'international system', as defined above, is the basis of one such map: the 'international society' provides an alternative map.

Maps, of course, are not straightforward depictions of a given terrain; they offer a simplified depiction of the terrain with a specific purpose in mind. A map of the London Underground is of little use to a tourist wishing to walk from Trafalgar Square to Buckingham Palace. Similarly, a realist map of the international system is of little use to a scholar wishing to trace the rise of pacifist ideas in Europe. The realist map was drawn to trace out power relations, not the rise of ideas. It is worth emphasizing here that by focusing on particular actors, actions, and motivations, and by neglecting others, so-called 'maps' don't just simplify but in fact construct the terrain of international relations (more on this in section 1.5 below). For this reason the term 'perspective' is used in the rest of this section.

The four perspectives outlined below are, of course, not post-1945 inventions. Each has long historical roots and each was used to inform debates in the aftermath of the First World War about why states go to war and what might prevent them from doing so, and more generally about the nature of international relations. The different views are captured by the labels 'economic interdependence' (or liberalism), 'world capitalism' (or radicalism), 'law and collective security' (or international society), and 'power politics' (or realism). Each perspective offers very different specifications of the *core actors* in international relations; how it is that core actors *formulate their preferences*; how it is that actors *interact*; and which *capabilities* affect the implementation and achievement of preferred outcomes. The perspectives are outlined to highlight their importance in formulating questions and hypotheses. Their weaknesses as an approach to theorizing about international relations are discussed at the end of the section.

'Economic Interdependence'

A first perspective focuses on the web of interests which lie behind the state in its foreign policy. Hence Norman Angell argued, prior to the First World War, that war was unlikely: economic interdependence had reduced the likelihood of war by reducing the gains to be made from war. Any government wanting to undertake a war for gain or conquest faced severe pressure from bankers and businessmen not to do so. These bankers and businessmen would know that in the new 'complex financial interdependence of the capitals of the world' any war-like activities which affected banking and business in another major country risked bringing about financial collapse which would affect their own economy.[7] In other words, domestic interests would ensure that governments did not under-take actions which might jeopardize their capital or bring about a financial collapse.

The general argument is that growing interdependence creates similar eco-nomic interests across all states and thus a community of interests which will facilitate cooperation among states. From this perspective, states' preferences in international relations are strongly influenced by domestic economic interests. States will interact with an eye to their own potential economic gains and losses, and will seek to maximize their economic gains. Implementation of state policies is assumed to be assured by the rational interests that underpin them.

The concept of economic interdependence was revived in the late 1960s and early 1970s, as global capital markets expanded and international trade and investment increased. US scholars such as Cooper, Morse, and Keohane and Nye theorized that growing economic interdependence would alter the agenda and behaviour of states.[8] As economic interdependence grew, so too, it was argued, the utility of military power among states would be reduced. With the end of the Vietnam War and the emergence of detente, concepts of economic inter-dependence provided the language of linkage and economic incentives which came to shape US foreign policy in this period.

In contemporary debates, economic interdependence is still an important vantage-point from which work is undertaken on cooperation among states and on the dynamics of economic and political integration. Theories have been enriched by a variety of methods including rational choice, collective action, interdependent decision-making, and game theory. However, the basic purpose of the economic interdependence map has remained the same: it was drawn in search of forces that might lead states away from war and into more cooperative relations. To this purpose it is still put. At the same time, the economic inter-dependence perspective not only reflects a growing interdependence among states but also constructs a view of international relations which focuses on this element of change and produces a language and a set of justifications for policy-makers wishing to pursue particular policies.

'World Capitalism'

As with the economic interdependence perspective, the focus of the 'world capital-ism' perspective is economic relations; yet here a very different map is specified for a very different purpose. In the inter-war years 'world capitalism' was power-fully invoked by Lenin and other scholars to explain the outbreak of the First World War. While others focused on poor diplomacy and a lack of cooperation as causes of the war, for Lenin the war of 1914–18 was imperialist (that is, an annexationist, predatory war of plunder) on the part of both sides; it was a war for the division of the world, for the partition and repartition of colonies and spheres of influence of finance capital.[9] Far from facilitating cooperation, eco-nomic interests forced states into conflict.

The world capitalism perspective focuses on the ownership and control of the means of production in the world economy. The central actors are the owners of productive capital (whether states or multinational enterprises) who seek to compete in the world economy. The interests of these actors shape states' pre-ferences and strategies. States in the so-called 'core' of the world economy act so as to maximize the opportunities of the owners of capital or to drive capitalism. In the 'periphery' or 'South', states in which owners of capital do not reside are weak and vulnerable to the core states. The weak states have little capacity to act except in the interests of capitalists in the core. In many ways, the influence of economic interests on the behaviour of states is similar to that specified in the economic interdependence perspective. Here, however, the South is not ignored and the purpose is altogether different. The world capitalism map was drawn not to highlight the possibilities of cooperation among states but to examine the sources of world inequalities.

In the 1950s and 1960s three theories sprung up within the world capitalism perspective to challenge the view that the expansion of capitalism would positively transform the Third World. The focus of modern world capitalism theories shifted away from Lenin's preoccupation with the European centres of capital to the countries to which capital was being exported. 'World systems' theorists argued that the world capitalist system perpetuated underdevelopment in the South.[10] 'Dependency theorists' focused on the distortionary consequences of world capitalism in the South, and examined the dynamic of change within the South.[11] 'Structuralists' sought ways to reform the international economic system in such a way as to overcome the obstacles to development being faced by developing countries.[12]

All three variants of the world capitalism perspective highlighted the disadvant-aged position shared by all countries in the South and in doing so constructed 'the South' as a group with a particular identity and a shared interest—as was expressed in the early 1970s when developing countries passed a resolution in the United Nations General Assembly calling for the adoption of special measures to enable countries of 'the South' better to overcome structural barriers to development. In the 1990s, as the world capitalism perspective has declined in popularity, so too the cohesiveness of a 'Southern coalition' has diminished.

In the 1990s various competing perspectives depict diverging possibilities and interests in the countries of the South. Two central themes which run through the world capitalism perspective have been re-examined. First, the role of the state in development has been reassessed by scholars who now focus on the differences in experience among countries of the 'South' and ask questions about the distribution of the benefits of development; the consequences of economic change for political regimes; and the relation between industrialization and political democracy. Secondly, the question of how the international capitalist system constrains development is being reassessed. The influence of the international system on the South is now analysed by assessing the different impacts of international constraints, pressures, and shocks on countries. Countries such as Korea are examined by economists, anthropologists, and political economists in search of an explanation of how one state overcame the barriers to growth and rapid development in the world economy. Furthermore, scholars have started to apply to developing countries theories developed in analyses of the North, be they comparative historical analysis; the application of a rational choice approach to politics in Africa; or the application of 'Northern' economic theory to Africa.[13]

The world capitalism perspective was drawn by Lenin to highlight the processes of capital expansion across the world and was developed by subsequent theorists to highlight the negative impact of world capitalism on developing countries. The perspective constructs a world divided into the North (where capital is plentiful) and the South (where development is hindered). In the 1990s the world capitalist perspective is no longer fashionable, however, it remains the only perspective in international relations which highlights questions of inequality and development.

'Law and Collective Security'

A wholly different map of international relations is provided by the law and collective security perspective. Here the preferences of states are assumed to be influenced by public opinion which, given free expression, will oppose war and support institutions for collective security. Hence US President Woodrow Wilson argued that the First World War broke out because there was no effective and openly accountable diplomacy and no appropriate laws and institutions among states to ensure peace. In Wilson's view, the League of Nations was the type of institution that could ensure peace. States would give up some of their sovereignty to the League, which would derive its strength from public opinion in member countries. This 'map' of international relations was drawn to find ways to ensure peace among nations; however, the failure of the US Congress to ratify the Covenant of the League of Nations and the failure of the League more generally discredited the law and collective security perspective for many decades.[14]

One of the implications of the law and collective security view is that democracies are unlikely aggressively to cause wars (a proposition which has been much studied since 1918 and subjected to ever more formal theorizing and investigation). The international system is conceived as a society both of states and of the citizens they represent, so that agreements reached among states reflect the preferences of their citizens. In states' interactions with other states it is assumed that states mutually recognize and respect certain international norms. States exist not so much in an anarchic system as in a society in which they recognize and constrain each other. This proposition has been developed in a body of literature on regime theory, where 'regimes' are defined as 'sets of principles, norms, rules, and decision-making procedures around which actor expectations converge in a given issue-area'.[15] Finally, on the question of 'implementation', the law and collective security perspective does not ask whether states are capable of implementing what they promise other states they will do; it is simply assumed that leaders will not be hindered by domestic institutions.

There are two areas in which the law and collective security perspective has continued to be used in international relations. In the first place, advocates of world order and world government have developed a view of 'ground-up' world order based on the premiss that world politics must be rooted in public opinion.[16] In the second place, both regime theorists and constructivists (see section 1.5 below) have developed the notion that rules and norms constrain international relations.[17] Perhaps the most prominent re-emergence of the law and collective security perspective occurred in 1990 when the end of the Cold War brought forth arguments astonishingly similar to those advanced by Woodrow Wilson in 1918. For some, the US–UN intervention in the Persian Gulf in 1990 spelt out the possibilities of a 'new world order' based on international law, an effective system of collective security, and democracy. Such a system would be based on the increasing number of democratic governments in the world and their openness to public opinion.

International institutions lie at the heart of the law and collective security perspective, perceived as a way to draw states and peoples of the world into a community of peace and cooperation for collective mutual gain. Unlike the economic interdependence view, cooperation among states is conceived as reliant not on specific economic interests across nations but rather on enlightened world opinion expressed through the actions of states. This perspective constructs a new, additional dimension in international relations: the society of states which exists beyond the domestic politics of the state and outside of the world capitalist system. Within the international society, states as representatives of their peoples are capable of forming norms and laws which constrain their foreign policies.

'Power Politics'

Power politics or realism describes the fourth and final perspective on international relations considered here. This perspective emerged with a critical purpose on the eve of the Second World War, when hostilities loomed in spite of Wilson's League of Nations, in spite of the rationality of Angell's economic interdependence, and in spite of Lenin's Third International. In this context E. H. Carr wrote a trenchant critique of the idealism of collective security and economic interdependence. In *The Twenty Years Crisis* Carr presented international relations as a struggle among states for power. He debunked the proponents of the League of Nations for their belief that international law and order were in the interests of mankind. Such beliefs, according to Carr, were the 'unconscious reflexions of national interests at a particular time'. Supporters of the League or of free trade were simply clothing their national interests (as 'satisfied powers') in internationalist rhetoric.[18]

Several aspects of Carr's views were later to be picked up by scholars in the United States such as Hans Morgenthau in order to attack four categories of idealists who were, at the end of the Second World War, offering advice on US foreign policy: 'Utopians', who were wrong in conceiving the United Nations as the foundation for a new world order; 'legalists', who were wrong in assuming that the UN could be a foundation of international law; 'sentimentalists', who framed prudent and necessary policies, such as intervention in Greece and Turkey, in wide moralistic terms (e.g. the Truman Doctrine) and were dangerous since they left no room for the distinction between what is desirable and what is possible (a lack of distinction which led the United States into Vietnam a decade or so later); and the 'neoisolationists', who misguidedly believed the United States to be omnipotent and wrongly disparaged traditional diplomacy, believing that the United States could deal with the rest of the world on its own terms (a view very similar to that emerging in the US Congress in 1995).[19]

More recently, theorists have projected the assumptions underpinning classical realism into a more formal conceptualization in which states are depicted as functionally alike within the international system. The system itself is defined by stable ordering principles and an unchanging specification of functions of formally differentiated parts. What changes in the anarchic international system is the distribution of power, with shifts in this distribution producing ever-changing balances of power.[20]

Three crucial assumptions about international relations underpin the power politics perspective: first, that the 'international system' is the level of analysis which determines state policies; secondly, that states are rational, unitary actors which have stable, power-maximizing preferences; and thirdly and finally, that the balance of power is the ordering mechanism in the international system. In other words, the preferences of states are formulated by state leaders on the basis of their perceptions of the national interest. The national interest is shaped by the state's power relative to other states. Successful decision-makers act prudently in their relations with other states, at all times using strategies that maintain or extend their power relative to other states. That is to say, foreign policies are dictated by the logic of the international system and the distribution of power among states. It is assumed that, in implementing foreign policies, leaders are relatively unhindered by their domestic political systems.

The power-political map constructs international relations as a continuous struggle for power by states. States' ultimate ends are not discussed; rather, states are assumed to seek to maintain their power, to extend their power, or to demonstrate their power (in the pursuit of maintaining or extending it). Only power, it is assumed, can restrain power. Hence the only mechanism which provides some modicum of order in international relations is the balance of power. The only effective way to manage the balance of power is through a developed and sophisticated diplomacy. Diplomacy is an arena of concern only for decision-makers and is presented as a virtually autonomous sphere of action. Public opinion and domestic constraints on foreign policy are virtually ignored.

The Weaknesses of 'Perspectives'

The four maps of international relations depicted above each focus on different actors, different motivations, and different outcomes in international relations. Each has been created for a given purpose and each constructs a different terrain of international relations. Although these perspectives are often described as 'theories', they are not theories in the formal sense of the term; rather, they are conceptualizations which assist us in defining actors and formulating hypotheses about international relations.

Maps or perspectives can only suggest generalizable patterns which might seem to be confirmed by history. They do not, on the whole, present us with hypotheses that are falsifiable.[21] Furthermore, analysts propounding perspectives are sometimes accused of interpreting history so as always to confirm their theory. Morgenthau is explicitly guilty of this. He defines his theoretical enterprise as to 'bring order and meaning to a mass of phenomena which without it would remain disconnected and unintelligible'.[22] His own test of a theory is simple: Do the facts lend themselves to this interpretation? And do the conclusions of the theory follow logically from its premises? Not for Morgenthau concerns about whether or not his theory might be falsified.

An alternative approach is to be more 'scientific'. This means two different things in international relations. On the one hand, the term 'scientific' is used to refer to rigorous deduction in international relations: formal modelling and the use of theoretical tools such as game theory. On the other hand, 'scientific' is used to refer to inductive methods in international relations, namely quantitative methods. It is to these other approaches that we will now turn.

1.3. Model-building, or Formal Theory

Formal theorizing in international relations makes use of tools such as game theory and expected utility theory to build models which explain and predict outcomes. This method contrasts both with historical methods, such as those discussed above, and with quantitative methods, which will be discussed below. Both historical and quantitative approaches are inductive in the sense that they build generalizations from the evidence. Historical methods use case studies, looser theories, and intuition; quantitative methods use data sets and regression. Formal models, on the other hand, are deductive and use logic to develop generalizable hypotheses.

A formal model is developed from a simple, abstract depiction of some aspect of the real world. A set of theorems or statements is then logically derived from the abstract depiction. From these theorems, predictive statements are constructed which can be tested against empirical observations. In a good theory, predictive statements will correspond with observations based on an identifiable universe of cases in the real world. To give an example, a model may posit the proposition that 'if x increases by a particular amount, then y will change in the following way'. This proposition can then be tested against the real world. If actual events belie the claim, then the theory is refuted and clearly needs rethinking. If events support the theory, it is not 'proven correct' because we still do not know whether the theory holds for all cases; nevertheless, each time a theory is supported by the evidence, the case for the theory is strengthened.

Formal models are not intended to make sense of or describe the rich details and texture of events. In the words of Bruce Bueno de Mesquita in this volume (see Chapter 3), they sacrifice details for breadth, specificity for generality. In this sense, as defined above, formal models are wholly aimed at explanation and not at understanding. In the post-war period, models have been used in international relations to deal with a number of issues.

Game theory has been variously used to analyse the arms race between the superpowers, nuclear deterrence and brinkmanship, arms control, trade negotiations, and cooperation among states.[23] Theories of games assist in structuring the theorems and hypotheses which form the heart of the formal models described above. The main insight of game theory is that actors do not make decisions independently of one another: rather, decisions are made *interdependently*. That is to say, a leader (or a state) will take into account what he or she believes other actors will do before deciding to pursue a particular policy.

The implications of game theory for international relations are important both for analysis and for prescription. The abstract logic of game theory adds hypotheses to our analysis of international relations, some of which are counter-intuitive. The analysis forces us to consider the possibility that states' motivations may be strategic (based on a perception of what other states will do), or that outcomes are the unintended consequences of policies undertaken either without considering other parties' actions or by mistaking their intentions. A second implication of game theory is prescriptive. Game theory suggests what states should do, highlighting the rational strategy for any particular situation, given probabilities about what other parties may do. For example, a game-theoretic analysis may prescribe defecting from an agreement where there is a probability that other parties may defect.

Expected utility theory is another tool which assists in formulating hypotheses in a formal model.[24] Drawn from microeconomics, this theory propounds that in choosing among alternative policies a decision-maker will choose the policy which carries the highest expected utility. In order to understand what is meant by expected utility, we need to clarify that it is assumed that decision-makers have preferences which are stable and transitive. In other words, we assume that a policy-maker will always prefer *a* to *b* and *b* to *c* and hence will also always prefer *a* to *c*. On the basis of these preferences, policy-makers are able to rank potential strategies in order of desirability. The value they assign to a particular strategy is described as the 'utility' of that strategy. *Expected utility* is the utility associated with a particular strategy designed to achieve an outcome multiplied by the probability that this outcome will be achieved. As stated above, policy-makers in an expected utility model will always choose a strategy with the highest expected utility.

The implications of both expected utility theory and game theory in international relations are manifold. As mentioned above, formal theories shed all complex historical and social details from the analysis, and enable us to arrive at a range of outcomes and alternatives, including some which are counter-intuitive. A second strength of formal theory is that assumptions and 'intuitions' are not buried within the analysis but are, to some extent, laid out as a priori assumptions, enabling others to assess or alter them. A third strength of formal theory is that it enables prediction. International relations has traditionally been concerned with understanding and explaining events, yet formal theory permits an attempt to go one step further towards science and to attempt to predict outcomes. Finally, because formal theories attempt prediction, they permit us to adjudicate more rigorously among competing theories. That is to say, the results of formal theory can be readily and transparently tested against actual outcomes which they are supposed to have predicted.

Although there are many advantages to be gained from using formal theory, it is also worth stating that formal theories can not achieve any of the tasks listed above without relying heavily on the other types of theorizing which are discussed in this chapter. At the most fundamental level, it is not possible to formulate hypotheses about particular events, such as wars, without adequately defining the event or the categories of events. Furthermore, both game theory and expected utility theory are theories of *decision*. They rely upon an a priori knowledge of what the preferences and the goals of actors are. The theories themselves do not tell us how states or decision-makers formulate preferences or about the difficulties of implementing strategies. In this respect formal theories rely heavily on broader conceptualizations of international relations such as those discussed above. It is the broader 'perspectives' or 'maps' of international relations which specify who are the core actors, how it is that core actors formulate their preferences, and which capabilities affect actors' implementation of decisions.

Finally, a further limitation of formal theories lies in their predilection towards particular types of perspectives and assumptions. It is unsurprising that most game theorists and expected utility theorists have used the power politics or realist perspective on international relations as their starting-point. As we saw above, within the power politics perspective core actors are states whose pursuit of self-interested goals is defined as rational within an anarchic international system. Power politics lends itself easily to models of rational decision-making. It is important, however, to recall that the power politics perspective has a particular purpose and, furthermore, 'constructs' a particular terrain for international relations. Formal theorists who build from this perspective inherit both the purposes of realism and the limited terrain it has constructed for international relations.

1.4. Statistical Methods

We have seen that formal theories use logic to deduce propositions about international relations. By contrast, statistical methods or quantitative analysis derive general propositions about international relations from the aggregation of particular instances. Quantitative research is inductive in that it starts with the data, analyses it using the rules of statistical inference, and then offers statistical probabilities about the correlation of particular events.

Quantitative methods became particularly popular in international relations in the 1960s as behaviouralists argued that it was wrong to deduce grand theories from intuitive beliefs about human nature. Rather, scholars ought first to collect data, then to frame and to test scientific hypotheses, and only then to construct theories. The 1960s behaviouralists were able to tap into several collections of data which dealt with the causes of war,[25] and in the 1990s much quantitative research continues. Furthermore, some scholars have extrapolated the methods of statistical testing and have suggested that the rules applied to quantitative analysis should be applied equally to other types of research,[26] arguing that applying the rules of statistical inference to other forms of research will force scholars to be more rigorous and self-conscious about the conclusions they draw from case studies and history. It is further argued that research which follows the methods of quantitative analysis will be both more transparent (initial as-sumptions will be clearer) and more replicable: in brief, other scholars will be able to pick up and work with the same hypotheses.

Several problems and reservations arise in respect of both quantitative research and the application of the rules of statistical inference to other research. In the first place, simplification is a problem. In order to aggregate data one has to simplify vastly complex human interactions so as to create classes of 'identical' events such as wars or revolutions. Yet it is not easy to define and quantify such things as wars or revolutions. Such simplifications suggest two important caveats for quantitative analyses of international relations. In the first place, simpli-fications or biases inherent in definitions, categories, or hypotheses can all too easily be forgotten or set aside in the pursuit of rigour in the more formal parts of analysis. At worst, there is a temptation to define concepts in such a way as to fit the data, creating from the start a biased analysis. In the second place, statistical analysis requires a very large number of cases or events in order for any finding to be significant; and yet, at the same time, it requires that all events within a sample be as nearly identical as possible. In international relations the two requirements are impossible to satisfy simultaneously. Either one finds a very small number of events which are highly similar or one is forced to define a broad class of events in which similarity is sacrificed.

Aside from problems inherent within statistical analysis, it is also the case that quantitative research cannot be undertaken without relying on the other types of theory discussed in this chapter. In the first place, the strength of quantitative research will depend upon the quality of its initial concepts, definitions, and data. Furthermore, quantitative analysis relies on other types of theory to provide hypotheses and explanations. Statistical analysis will tell us to what extent x and y occur together. Before we can conduct that analysis we need a method for choosing x and y. We then also need an explanation as to why it is that they occur together. While statistical testing tells us about correlation, it does not explain causation: for generating both initial hypotheses and explanations, other types of theorizing, such as broader 'perspectives' and formal theories, are crucial.

1.5. Reflectivism and Theories of Knowledge

One major criticism levelled at virtually all the above forms of theorizing is that they neglect the relationship between language, knowledge, and power. Definitions, categories, maps, formal theories, and data sets are not just ways of representing 'the facts'. Rather, as was mentioned in section 1.1, definitions and theories are also ways of constructing 'facts'. In international relations the term 'reflectivism' has been used to cover at least three different critiques of the way in which explanations of international relations are constructed: these include post-modernism, critical theory, and constructivism. Although all share a concern with the language and discourse of international relations and with the bases upon which we interpret the world around us, the three strands are worth separating carefully, for in international relations each has something distinctive to say about the questions we ask and how we might set about answering them.

Post-modernists

The post-modern approach to international relations is perhaps the most radical challenge to the approaches that have so far been discussed in this chapter. Attempts to theorize, to define, and to create taxonomies are all deprecated as modernist throw-backs. Post-modernism draws on the ideas of discourse analysis, genealogy, deconstructionism, and textuality of a group of mainly French thinkers such as Foucault, Lacan, Barthes, Lyotard, Derrida, Kristeva, and Baudrillard, in order to challenge our most fundamental premises about 'meaning' and 'knowing'.[27] At the core of post-modernism lies the assumption that all social reality is constructed: just as we interpret texts in literature, so too texts create social and political realities in international relations.

The implication of post-modernism is that the definitions, perspectives, and theories used both to identify subjects and objects in international relations, and to frame particular questions and hypotheses, are misleading. They do not lead us closer to understanding or explaining the 'real world'. Rather than using texts to try to research the world, we should be examining texts so as better to understand the historical, cultural, and linguistic practices which lie behind our construction of the world.

The post-modern challenge is a powerful and instructive one when deployed to question the ways in which our categories and perspectives 'construct' and 'define' identities, peoples, and political processes. It is this challenge, for example, that Edward Said laid down in his influential exposure of the extent to which 'orientalism' has perpetuated a particular type of understanding of identity and politics in the Middle East. Orientalism, argues Said, is a construction which echoes the mindset of colonialism and domination and which has shaped most Western scholarship about the Middle East. Silenced in this so-called 'understanding' have been identities or processes which the variety of peoples who have been defined as 'orientals' themselves describe.[28] In theories of international relations, post-modernists remind us that although the assumptions underpinning realism and neorealism are deemed timeless and unchanging, it is in fact our way of understanding which is fixed. Concepts of sovereignty and diplomacy are in fact contested, and change over time.[29]

The strength of post-modernism lies in its critical voice: it is a rebellion against hegemonic ways of thinking. Yet post-modernists do not offer international relations much beyond this rebellion. The logic of post-modernism undercuts the validity of virtually any other form of academic research: no category of knowledge is stable enough to yield knowledge. Yet, if we were *all* to take on the post-modern agenda, post-modernism would have nothing left to feed on. International relations would become nothing more than the study of texts and discourses: ultimately a barren research agenda, not to mention a somewhat self-indulgent one. In the end fruitful critical research must return to examine the origins of the inequalities of power which underpin the hegemonic discourse which the post-modernists expose. Indeed, although some post-modernists invoke the political theorist Gramsci as their source for thinking about cultural and linguistic hegemony, they would do well to recall that material inequalities were Gramsci's own starting-point.

Critical Theorists

Like post-modernism, critical theory challenges the way in which international relations is 'constructed' by the language, concepts, and categories we use. Critical theory, however, is based on critical sociology (from Marx to Horkheimer), not on linguistics and deconstructionism.[30] The core of critical theory was established by the inter-war scholars at the Frankfurt School of Social Research who declared that knowledge was not about explaining sets of facts but rather about understanding that the so-called 'facts' are social and historical products. Critical theorists set out to uncover the social and historical origins of our 'knowledge' of international relations, and to move beyond it—with an explicitly normative purpose. Critical theorists believe that social theory is a vehicle of social and political emancipation. Through social theory, humans can come better to understand and to counter the ways in which the dominant culture constrains their autonomy.

Critical theorists attack realism, neorealism, and other state-centred perspectives on international relations by highlighting that the questions they pose automatically limit the types of 'knowledge' we might acquire about international relations. For example, realists and neoliberal institutionalists ask questions such as: How can there be cooperation under anarchy? This question 'constructs' the world as anarchic, and as a world in which states, first and foremost, must protect themselves and interact strategically. An alternative world, such as one in which societies concerned about their own identities interact, is excluded by the very way in which the question is formulated. By 'silencing' other depictions of the world, the dominant state-centred depictions of international relations bolster the structure of power that exists: that is to say, they reinforce the élites within states who control foreign policy and justify existing policies.[31] In order to move to a more just international system, critical theorists argue, we must uncover the power and interests behind dominant forms of 'knowledge' and move beyond them.[32] However, this is where we find a real weakness in critical theory: How exactly do we move 'beyond'? A rather fuzzy set of assumptions connects *theorizing about* the world (in a new way) and *changing* that world. Ultimately the critical theorists make a Kantian assumption that individuals will change in the light of new reason. Yet new ways of thinking do not always lead to new ways of acting—a reality unexplained by the critical theorists.

Constructivists

A third and final category of reflectivism is sometimes labelled constructivism. This strand of thinking draws on social theory and does not attack the foundations of mainstream international relations so much as build on the view that world politics takes place in an international society, not just in an international system. This society, constructivists argue, is constituted by rules and norms. By examining these rules and norms, these scholars examine in a more practical way than either post-modernism or critical theory how it is that the social and political worlds of international relations are 'constructed'.

Other so-called mainstream approaches to international relations (discussed earlier in this chapter) treat norms and rules as reflections of the rational interests of states. Constructivists argue that rules and norms are the parameters within which interests are formulated. Rules and norms *constitute* the international game by determining who the actors are, what rules they must follow if they wish to ensure that particular consequences follow from specific acts, and how titles to possessions can be established and transferred.[33] In other words, norms do not *cause* a state to act in a particular way, but rather *provide reasons* for a state to do so. Language is important for the constructivists, not for textual analysis but because language is action, which is to say it does not reflect meaning but *is* in fact practice and behaviour. For example, when a state threatens another state, it is not just using words but is committing an act.

Constructivists, like other reflectivists, emphasize the changing, contested nature of the bases upon which international relations proceed. They stress that one cannot separate international relations from domestic politics, for the two are interacting processes which construct international society. Our theorizing itself is a product of history and of our own position in the world, and shapes (or excludes) future possibilities for change.

The challenge of the constructivists is the least threatening of those mounted by the reflectivists, for they do not set out completely to undercut existing approaches to and methods of study of international relations, nor are they completely committed to producing an emancipatory social theory. Rather, they point to a wider range of possibilities for change in world politics than more state-centred perspectives on international relations. Hence constructivists provide a bridge between those who treat international relations as a set of facts and those who argue that social and political life in the international arena is entirely constructed.

1.6. Conclusions

This chapter has discussed the different ways in which theories are used in international relations (see Table 1.1). Definitions, concepts, and taxonomies are as crucial to the social sciences as they are to the natural sciences. Yet in international relations the challenge is not just to seek clear and unambiguous definitions, it is also to analyse the extent to which concepts and categories do more than define a group of events or processes. As reflectivism reminds us, definitions both reflect and construct the terrain of international relations.

So, too, the various dominant perspectives on international relations reflect not only different assumptions but different purposes and puzzles. While interdependence theorists set out to find reasons and processes which enhance cooperation among states, the realist purpose is a critical one: to expose idealism. Before taking up categories, perspectives, and assumptions we should be sure to examine the context within which they have been created and the interests and purposes which lie behind them. *Caveat emptor!* (let the buyer beware!).

Examined more closely, the difference between defining the facts and reflecting on their meaning separates distinct purposes in the study of international

Table 1.1. The uses of theorizing

Type of theorizing	Uses	Example
Concepts and definitions	To define the objects and subjects of study; to create taxonomies of events and processes; to reflect but also to construct the terrain of international relations	Definitions of: international system/society, explaining/understanding, and levels of analysis
Maps or perspectives	Highlight actors; explain relations among variables; provide deductive explanations	Economic interdependence; world capitalism; law; collective security and international society; power politics (realism)
Formal theories	Permit models to be built on logic; open up analysis to possibility of counter-intuitive outcomes; used to predict	Game theory; expected utility analysis
Quantitative methods	Base theories in empirical facts; allow for rigorous testing of relationship between variables	Rules of statistical inference
Reflectivism	To challenge theory; to demonstrate that the so-called 'facts' are actually 'constructions' based on our own theorizing, language, culture, and power	Post-modernism; critical theory; constructivism

relations: some express this as the difference between 'understanding' the processes of international relations and 'explaining' outcomes. Different types of theory give higher priority to one or other of these aims. While some scholars of international relations are engaged in constructing theories which will forecast events in the international arena, others carefully sift through historical documents in order to piece together an understanding of events gone by. Hence, some inquiries are labelled 'social-scientific' while others are labelled 'historical'.

In certain phases in the study of international relations, exponents of social-scientific approaches have claimed a higher status. Following theoretical economists who claim the higher rungs of the hierarchy of social science, the more scientific scholars of international relations have at times laid claim to doing a more difficult and 'more rigorous' type of theory. These claim are misguided. As this chapter has shown, both formal theories and quantitative approaches to international relations rely heavily on the other types of supposedly 'softer' theorizing. The so-called 'soft theory' produces the concepts and typologies upon which any more rigorous theory must proceed. Yet, of course, the looser forms of theory must be used appropriately. Most particularly, these forms of theorizing are not amenable to 'testing' and 'falsification' as are the more formal theories: hence, to speak of 'testing realism' is to misunderstand both 'realism' and the notion of 'testing'. Testing, prediction, and modelling require careful specifications of hypotheses and it is here that both formal theories and quantitative analysis come into their own.

The challenge for scholars of international relations is critically to examine the way in which the various types of theory that inform their approach fit together. Particular methods or approaches will tend to draw on particular perspectives. An obvious example is the way in which most formal theorizing tends to rely upon state-centred and realist perspectives in order to define rational actors (states) and to generate assumptions upon which their behaviour can be hypothesized. However, once transformed into a formal theory, stripped of its rhetoric, the basic purposes and normative outlook of realism are all too easily forgotten. Yet they will still shape the world as seen and depicted by the theorist. The lesson here is that although theories can improve the ways in which we understand and explain phenomena in international relations, they can also be deployed as unlabelled ingredients in potent yet anonymous brews. Here, to the recipients we must repeat: *caveat emptor!*

Notes

1. Edward Hallett Carr, *What is History?* (Harmondsworth, 1961), 11.
2. Hedley Bull, *The Anarchical Society: A Study of Order in World Politics* (London, 1977), 13.
3. Martin Hollis and Steve Smith, *Explaining and Understanding International Relations* (Oxford, 1990).
4. Deborah Welch Larson, *Origins of Containment: A Psychological Explanation* (Princeton, 1985).
5. This argument is particularly clearly discussed in Barry Buzan, Charles Jones, and Richard Little, *The Logic of Anarchy: Neorealism to Structural Realism* (New York, 1993).
6. Peter B. Evans, Harold K. Jacobson, and Robert D. Putnam, *Double-edged Diplomacy: International Bargaining and Domestic Politics* (Berkeley and Los Angeles, 1993).
7. Norman Angell, *The Great Illusion* (London, 1914).

8. Richard Cooper, *The Economics of Interdependence* (New York, 1968); Edward L. Morse, 'The Transformation of Foreign Policies: Modernization, Interdependence and Externalization', *World Politics*, 22/3 (1970), 371–92; Robert Keohane and Joseph Nye, *Power and Interdependence* (Boston, 1977).

9. V. Lenin, *Imperialism: The Highest Stage of Capitalism* (Moscow, 1968).

10. Paul Baran, *The Political Economy of Growth* (London, 1957); André Gunder Frank, *Capitalism and Underdevelopment in Latin America* (New York, 1967); Immanuel Wallerstein, *The Capitalist World Economy* (Cambridge, 1979). See also John Darwin's discussion in Chapter 9 of this volume.

11. Fernando Henrique Cardoso and Enzo Faletto, *Dependency and Development in Latin America* (Berkeley and Los Angeles, 1979). See also Andrew Hurrell's discussion in Chapter 7 of this volume.

12. Raul Prebisch, *Change and Development: Latin America's Great Task* (New York, 1971).

13. Examples of each are, respectively: Theda Skocpol, *States and Social Revolutions: A Comparative Study of France, Russia, and China* (Cambridge, 1979); Robert Bates, *Markets and States in Tropical Africa* (Berkeley and Los Angeles, 1981); David Bevan, Paul Collier, and Jan Willem Gunning, *Controlled Open Economies: A Neoclassical Approach to Structuralism* (Oxford, 1990).

14. See Adam Roberts's discussion of collective security in Chapter 14 of this volume.

15. This now 'classic' definition is Stephen Krasner's, expressed in the very useful reader Stephen Krasner (ed.), *International Regimes* (Ithaca, NY, 1983), 1.

16. See Richard Falk, Samuel Kim, and Saul Mendlovitz, *Toward a Just World Order* (Boulder, Colo., 1982).

17. See Krasner, *International Regimes*.

18. E. H. Carr, *The Twenty Years Crisis: 1919–39* (London, 1946; first publ. 1939).

19. Hans Morgenthau, *In Defense of the National Interest* (New York, 1951).

20. For a critical discussion of this view see Robert Keohane (ed.), *Neo-realism and its Critics* (New York, 1986); David Baldwin (ed.), *Neorealism and Neoliberalism: The Contemporary Debate* (New York, 1993).

21. See Bruce Bueno de Mesquita's discussion of 'falsifiable hypotheses' in Chapter 3 of this volume.

22. Hans Morgenthau, *Politics among Nations: The Struggle for Power and Peace* (New York, 1948; repr. 1993), 3.

23. See Chapter 3 by Bruce Bueno de Mesquita and Chapter 16 by George Downs and Peter Barsoom in this volume. On the arms race between the superpowers see Steven J. Brams, *Superpower Games: Applying Game Theory to Superpower Conflict* (New Haven, 1985). On nuclear deterrence and brinkmanship the classic is Thomas Schelling, *The Strategy of Conflict* (Cambridge, Mass., 1960). On cooperation among states the classic is Robert Axelrod, *The Evolution of Cooperation* (New York, 1984).

24. See Bruce Bueno de Mesquita, *War and Reason* (New Haven, 1992) and 'The Contribution of Expected-utility Theory to the Study of International Conflict', in Manus Midlarsky (ed.), *Handbook of War Studies* (Boston, 1989), 143–69. See also Irving Janis and Ralph Mann, *Decision Making* (New York, 1977).

25. These included such works as Quincy Wright, *A Study of War* (Chicago, 1947), Lewis Fry Richardson, *Statistics of Deadly Quarrels* (Pittsburgh, Pa., 1960). A major later work collecting data on war is David J. Singer (ed.), *The Correlates of War: Testing some Realpolitik Models* (New York, 1980).

26. Gary King, Robert Keohane, and Sidney Verba, *Designing Social Inquiry: Scientific Inference in Qualitative Research* (Princeton, 1994).

27. A useful reader is James Der Derian and Michael Shapiro, *International/Intertextual Relations: Postmodern Readings of World Politics* (Lexington, Mass., 1989).

28. Edward Said, *Orientalism* (New York, 1979). For a post-modern critique of Said see Robert Young, *White Mythologies: Writing History and the West* (London, 1990).

29. On sovereignty see Robert B. J. Walker, *Inside/outside: International Relations as Political Theory* (Cambridge, 1993); on diplomacy, James Der Derian, *On Diplomacy: A Geneaology of Western Estrangement* (Oxford, 1987).

30. For an overview see Mark Hoffmann, 'Critical Theory and the Inter-Paradigm Debate', *Millennium*, 16/2 (1987), 231–50.

31. See Richard Ashley, 'Untying the Sovereign State: A Double Reading of the Anarchy Problematique', *Millennium*, 17/2 (1988), 265.

32. Hence the title of Andrew Linklater's book, *Beyond Realism and Marxism: Critical Theory and International Relations* (London, 1990).

33. See Friedrich V. Kratochwil, *Rules, Norms and Decisions: On the Conditions of Practical and Legal Reasoning in International Relations and Domestic Affairs* (Cambridge, 1989).

Further Reading

CARR, E. H., *The Twenty Years Crisis: 1919–39* (London, 1946; first publ. 1939). A classic and very readable statement of the nature and purposes of thinking about international relations.

HOFFMANN, STANLEY, 'International Relations: The Long Road to Theory', *World Politics*, 11 (1959), 346–77. A short, inspirational reminder of some of the perils and purposes of international relations theory.

HOLLIS, MARTIN, and SMITH, STEVE, *Explaining and Understanding International Relations* (Oxford, 1990). A very useful discussion of the philosophical and theoretical under-pinnings of modern theories of international relations.

KING, GARY, KEOHANE, ROBERT, and VERBA, SIDNEY, *Designing Social Inquiry: Scientific Inference in Qualitative Research* (Princeton, 1994). A highly persuasive account of one way in which research into social science might proceed.

NICHOLSON, MICHAEL, *Formal Theories of International Relations* (Cambridge, 1989), or *Rationality and the Analysis of International Conflict* (Cambridge, 1992). Either of these texts gives a good overview of more formal, social-scientific approaches to the study of international relations, including a defence from critics of this approach.

CHAPTER TWO

HISTORY, SCIENCE, AND THE STUDY OF INTERNATIONAL RELATIONS

John Lewis Gaddis

'When I was very young,' the historian E. H. Carr once wrote, 'I was suitably impressed to learn that, appearances notwithstanding, the whale is not a fish. Nowadays these questions of classification move me less; and it does not worry me unduly when I am assured that history is not a science.'[1] If one were to deconstruct that statement, it would appear to have three possible meanings. One is that, appearances to the contrary notwithstanding, history is indeed a science. The second is that it isn't. The third is that Carr, like many English dons, developed the habit of sweeping away ambiguities, rather in the way Oxford and Cambridge college waiters, at high table, sweep away crumbs.

The habit may be catching, for historians generally have been reluctant to specify whether what they do is science or not. All would claim to practise some kind of 'historical method' with scientific attributes, but they can be extraordinarily imprecise in characterizing it. David Hackett Fischer had it right years ago when he pointed out the tendency of historians, when asked about their methodology, 'to respond as Fats Waller (or maybe Louis Armstrong) did, when asked to explain the nature of jazz. "Man," he said, "if you don't know what it is, don't mess with it."'[2]

Political scientists operate very differently. Not only do they insist that there is such a thing as a 'scientific' approach to the study of world politics; most of them pride themselves on rigorously applying it. Methodological issues preoccupy,

I am grateful to students and colleagues in the Contemporary History Institute at Ohio University, as well as to Ngaire Woods and Bruce Bueno de Mesquita, for comments on earlier versions of this paper.

fascinate, and at times transfix practitioners in this field: indeed, one critic has complained, rather rudely, that the political scientists spent so much time arguing about how to study the Cold War that the Cold War itself ended before they had resolved the matter.[3]

Where political scientists are imprecise is with respect to the kind of 'science' they do. They tend to assume that reductionist, systemic, and quantitative approaches constitute good science, despite the fact that physical and biological scientists are less and less certain of that. They seek to apply, within the realm of politics, methods that produced impressive results in the so-called 'hard' sciences from the days of Isaac Newton through to the end of the nineteenth century. But the political sciences have been slow to acknowledge that the sciences on which they modelled themselves have not, since that time, stood still.

Students of international relations therefore face a dilemma. They can follow the methods of historians, but without any confidence that what they are doing qualifies as a 'science' at all: they may simply wind up producing interesting stories. They can follow the methods of political scientists, but without any assurance that today's 'hard' scientists would regard these as valid: they may simply wind up propounding labour-intensive platitudes. Or they can attempt to navigate the slippery slopes of post-modernism, which sees all approaches to knowledge, in whatever field, as 'constructed': each person's mode of investigation is as good as any other.[4]

2.1. What is a Science?

Perhaps it would help, in trying to work our way out of this dilemma, to get back to the question of what it is to be a 'science' in the first place. Neither historians nor political scientists give this issue as much attention as they should. They take it for granted that a scientific approach is a good thing, without specifying why that is so or what we should expect from such a methodology.

We generally require, of any science, that it should do two things: (1) it should *explain*, which is to say that it should help us to understand why things happen in the way that they do; and (2) it should *forecast*, which is to say that it should provide us with at least some means of anticipating how things will happen in the future. The two tasks go hand in hand. There would be little point in explaining anything if one did not expect some future benefit from the explanation. But there can hardly be an anticipation of the future without some understanding of what it is that is being anticipated, and that in turn requires explanation.

Now, science is hardly the only method of explanation and forecasting: throughout most of human history, a wide variety of non-scientific means have been used, ranging from the examination of animal entrails and the reading of tea leaves up through claims of divine revelation. They all had pretty much the same purpose, though: accounting for things that had happened, and attempting to foresee things that were going to happen. The problem with these earlier methods was not so much that they failed to produce results, for they certainly did do that; it was rather that they did not produce widespread agreement on the validity of the results.

The scientific method, in contrast, has shown itself capable of generating agreement across cultures, in different languages, and among highly dissimilar observers as to the validity of explanations and the probable accuracy of the forecasts that emerge from them. This is not to say that scientists agree on everything; if that were so, there would be little point in continuing to pursue scientific investigation. I mean only that science comes closer than any other method we have, or are likely to have, to building a consensus with regard to explanation and forecasting, in whatever field.[5]

Examples of scientific consensus pervade modern life. The structure of the DNA molecule appears much the same to researchers in Switzerland, Singapore, and Sri Lanka. Aircraft wings bear stress similarly whether the airlines that rely upon them operate as subsidized state monopolies or adventurous entrepreneurial enterprises. Astronomers of Christian, Muslim, and Buddhist persuasions have little difficulty in agreeing on what causes eclipses or how galaxies move.

The key here is reproducibility: observations made under equivalent conditions, no matter who makes them, are expected to produce closely corresponding results.[6] When they don't, as was the case not long ago with experiments on 'cold fusion',[7] the theories that lie behind the observations are simply not regarded as credible.

2.2. Scientific Method and Human Affairs

Unfortunately, the scientific method does not work with equal precision, or command anything like universal assent, when it comes to the study of human affairs. The reason is obvious: consciousness—perhaps one should say wilfulness—can override the kinds of laws that govern the behaviour of molecules, or air flows, or celestial objects. People, the political scientist Stanley Hoffmann once reminded his colleagues, are not 'gases or pistons'.[8] That fact considerably complicates the task of explaining and forecasting human behaviour.

The social sciences have often sought to deal with this problem by denying its existence. They have viewed the realms of politics, economics, and society as not all that different from the physical world; they have operated from the conviction that consciousness and the behaviour that results from it are subject, at least in general terms, to the workings of laws whose existence we can detect and whose effects we can describe. Once this has been done, social scientists have assumed, we will then be able to accomplish in the realm of human affairs at least some of the tasks of explanation and forecasting that the natural sciences routinely perform.

Examples of this approach include: (1) 'rational choice' assumptions in economics, which maintain that people calculate their own best interests objectively and on the basis of accurate information about the circumstances within which these exist; (2) 'structural functionalism' in sociology, which sees institutions as necessary components of the particular social structures within which they are embedded; (3) the 'where you stand depends on where you sit' argument in organizational studies, which explains the behaviour of bureaucracies, large and small, in terms of an overriding concern with self-perpetuation; (4) Freudian psychology, which seeks to account for the behaviour of individuals by invoking a set of unconscious impulses and inhibitions inherited—by everyone—from childhood; and, of course, (5) 'realist' and 'neorealist' theories of international relations, which claim that all nations seek, in all situations, to maximize their power.

These are, to be sure, gross oversimplifications. They may stand, though, as rough approximations of how introductory university courses teach these subjects; and because these are hierarchically arranged disciplines which proceed from fundamental principles to more complex applications, such assumptions do still influence more sophisticated practices in the fields to which they pertain—not least in the training of graduate students.

All of these assumptions, it is worth noting, have certain features in common. They tend to be reductionist, attributing human behaviour to one or two basic 'causes' without recognizing that people often do things for complicated combinations of reasons. They tend to be static, neglecting the possibility that human behaviour, individually or collectively, might change over time. And they tend to claim universal applicability, thereby failing to acknowledge that different cultures—to say nothing of different individuals—respond to similar situations in different ways.

The social sciences make these assumptions of reductionism, stability, and universality for a specific reason: if they were to allow for multiple causes, or for the passage of time, or for cultural and individual diversity, explanations would proliferate and forecasting might become impossible. Social scientists, were they to proceed in this manner, would be functioning like historians; for although historians are good at explanation, they tend to resist making forecasts and they are notoriously inept in presenting their findings in such a way as to make them useful to policy-makers.[9] And what is policy-making, after all, but a kind of forecasting? How can one undertake it if constantly facing backwards?

Social scientists, when they face forwards, have to make their own compromises, though, and one result is that they wind up operating like teaching assistants in undergraduate physics laboratories. We were all told, when seeking to demonstrate Newton's laws of motion, not to worry about friction, or air resistance, or other inconveniences whose effects would be difficult to calculate. Instead we were supposed to visualize ideal pendulums swinging in perfect vacuums, featureless balls rolling down impossibly smooth inclined planes, and feathers and stones that always fell to earth at the same rate—even if our eyes told us that things never quite happened that way. We were taught to make these assumptions to facilitate calculation: it was too hard to measure the effects of friction or air resistance, or to predict the variations in the results these might cause with each repeated experiment. So we were instructed just to 'smooth out the data' until they illustrated the basic law of physics that was being demonstrated. It didn't matter if the actual results were a little messy: what was important was to understand the underlying principles.

But look what was happening here: the requirement to be 'scientific' meant that we were asked to reject what our own powers of observation were telling us. It drove us towards a Platonic realm of ideal forms that had little to do with the real world. It didn't even come close to predicting the actual arrival, on the floor or on our feet, of those feathers and stones we kept being told to drop. One of the basic *techniques* of sciences—calculation—had taken precedence over one of the basic *objectives* of science—the anticipation of what is actually going to happen. The forecasts that emerged from this scientific process, predictably enough, never quite worked out.

2.3. The Social Sciences and 'Physics Envy'

Something like this has happened in the social sciences, and for similar reasons. Actual economic history, it turns out, is filled with examples of people making irrational rather than rational choices on the basis of inaccurate rather than accurate information;[10] sociologists themselves have questioned structural functionalism because of its bias in favour of social stability and its failure to explain social change;[11] organizational history shows repeated instances of bureaucracies and the bureaucrats that run them acting in ways that do not perpetuate their interests;[12] Freudian psychology has been shown to provide a less than adequate explanation of human behaviour, especially when it is projected across cultures and through time, or—increasingly frequently—when it is compared with physiological explanations;[13] and, of course, international relations theory, which organized itself around the study of power, failed utterly to explain why the two most powerful nations of the modern era chose, at certain points during the twentieth century, to relinquish power rather than retain it—the United States in 1919–20, and the Soviet Union in 1989–91.[14]

But why are the social sciences operating—not in all instances, but in many— at roughly the level of undergraduate physics experiments? Why don't the forecasts they make more frequently correspond with the reality we subsequently encounter? And why don't we get the kind of consensus—among individuals, across departments, throughout universities, and in the wider world—that botanists who deal with such lowly organisms as the slime mould regularly achieve?

It is not just that social scientists deal with molecules that have minds of their own, although that is certainly part of the problem. I think a tendency has also developed within these disciplines to allow a preoccupation with technique— based on what I will argue is an outdated view of the scientific method—to overshadow what they are really supposed to be doing, which is explaining and forecasting social reality. To put it bluntly, and in Freudian terms, the social sciences suffer from physics envy.

The malady is nicely documented in M. Mitchell Waldrop's book *Complexity*, in which he describes a meeting between physicists and economists that took place at the Santa Fe Institute a few years back:

As the axioms and theorems and proofs marched across the overhead projection screen, the physicists could only be awestruck at [the economists'] mathematical prowess— awestruck and appalled. 'They were almost too good,' says one young physicist, who remembers shaking his head in disbelief. 'It seemed as though they were dazzling themselves with fancy mathematics, until they really couldn't see the forest for the trees. So much time was being spent on trying to absorb the mathematics that I thought they often weren't looking at what the models were for, and what they did, and whether the underlying assumptions were any good. In a lot of cases, what was required was just some common sense.'[15]

Remember, this is a physicist talking about economists; but, as anyone who has tried to read the *American Political Science Review* or the *International Studies Quarterly* or the *Journal of Conflict Resolution* lately will understand, he could as easily have been talking about political scientists. The passage suggests that social scientists might do well to reacquaint themselves with the so-called 'hard' sciences, where a quiet revolution has been taking place in the conception of what it is to be a science in the first place.

2.4. The Historical Sciences

Can there be a science that does not attempt to boil things down to a few simple variables? That does allow for change over time? That accommodates, rather than trying to gloss over, particularities and peculiarities? And that would still accomplish those tasks of explanation and forecasting that a science is supposed to perform? The answer, of course, is yes. Two excellent examples are modern geology and biology. Although both operate within a dominant overall paradigm—plate tectonics and natural selection—neither of these sciences would insist upon a rigorous specification of independent and dependent variables in assessing causation, or upon quantification as the most authoritative way of characterizing it. Both would allow multiple causes for what takes place; both certainly take into account the passage of time; both have ways of accounting for, even if they cannot always anticipate, the role of contingency.

It is true that a good deal is sacrificed along the way. Geologists and biologists are strong on explaining the past, but much more modest in their claims to forecast the future. They do not rule out that possibility by any means: geologists can tell us with some precision where earthquakes will occur and with what approximate frequency; biologists can say with confidence that species will either adapt to changing environments or eventually die out. But they find it much more difficult to specify precisely when, how, and to whom these things will happen, or what the consequences will be.

Within their respective paradigms of plate tectonics and natural selection, moreover, geologists and biologists allow for the impact—literally—of unpredictable events. We know now that comets and asteroids have frequently hit the Earth, with profound ecological effects.[16] We know that the Atlantic Ocean has opened and closed several times, but that it does not do so in each instance in just the same way.[17] We know that natural selection may work as much by luck—who was in the right place at the right time—as by the old principle of 'the survival of the fittest'. The palaeontologist Stephen Jay Gould has pointed out that the bilateral symmetry we all inherited through hundreds of millions of years of evolution was not the only way we could have evolved: if things had happened slightly differently in the Cambrian era, we could as easily have wound up looking like elaborate vacuum cleaners.[18]

Nor do geology and biology depend heavily on quantification. One still has to go out into the field, look at rocks or fossils, describe them and classify them in a way not greatly different from how it was done in Darwin's day. Taxonomy—careful comparative description—is still the accepted means of communication in these disciplines, and the basis upon which consensus is built.[19]

Geologists and biologists, therefore, function largely without the capacity for controlled reproducible experiment, without the reductionism, and without the propensity for quantification that provides the basis for verification in the other 'hard' sciences; but few people would conclude, because of this, that geology and biology are not themselves sciences. They are in fact, as Gould has pointed out, 'historical sciences', whose strength lies in explaining in great detail where we are and how we got there, but whose pretensions to forecasting are confined to much less specific observations about the overall framework within which certain known processes will occur. These sciences of *process* are not always valued as highly as the static *structural* sciences,[20] probably because of the tendency to confuse some of the techniques of the latter—especially quantification and rigorous calculation—with those larger functions of explanation and forecasting that are characteristic of all sciences. But Gould's 'historical sciences' are still sciences, none the less.

If that is the case, then there is no reason why the traditional historical approach to the study of human affairs cannot be at least as 'scientific' as our more conventional, but increasingly questioned, social-scientific approaches. For in history too, multiple causes intersect, time passes, patterns coexist with singularities, quantification is not required, and explanation is far more precise—and more reliable—than forecasting. It might even be that sciences of process provide the more appropriate model for studying human behaviour, despite the fact that the social sciences have sought far more often to emulate sciences of structure; they certainly accommodate more easily the phenomenon of learning. Since both are equally valid approaches in the 'hard' sciences, it is worth at least asking why the social sciences have tilted towards one, at the expense of the other, to the extent that they have (see Table 2.1).

2.5. History and the New 'Hard' Sciences

There is yet another reason for not valuing structure over process, and that is that the structural sciences themselves have been changing over the course of this century. Even as the social sciences have sought to emulate the physical and natural sciences, those disciplines have been moving away from the rigorously quantifiable reductionism to which the social scientists so keenly aspire. There has been a methodological passing of ships in the night, with the result that 'hard' scientists are beginning to think more and more like historians.

In order to see this, it might be useful to revisit the old debate between traditional social scientists and historians, and to examine why the first group tends not to regard the second as scientists at all. History, it is alleged: (1) fails to achieve objectivity, because its practitioners make no effort to free themselves

Table 2.1. History and social science: a comparative summary

	History	Social science
Actors	Often irrational, wilful, ill-informed	Assumed to be rational and predictable
Events	Multiple causes, role of contingency important	Strict causation
Patterns	Some singular, some generalizable	Generalizable
Objectives of study	Explanation always; forecasting where possible	Explanation and forecasting

from their own biases and preconceptions; (2) fails to agree on uniform standards by which to measure phenomena; (3) fails to build sophisticated models, or even any models at all; (4) fails to take into account the extent to which its preference for description over quantification makes its findings unreproducible; (5) fails to lift itself above a preoccupation with contingencies and a corresponding neglect of generalization; (6) fails to collect evidence systematically, relying instead largely on intuition; and (7) fails to approach rigorous standards of proof, relying instead only on the use of rhetoric to persuade.

Let me take these criticisms one by one, comparing them with what is happening today in the 'hard' structural sciences. I will also suggest, along the way, some possible implications for international relations theory in the post-Cold War world.

Objectivity

All science, we now realize, operates within paradigms that cause preconceptions to interfere with the assessment of reality. As Thomas Kuhn has shown, these can persist long after sufficient evidence has accumulated to undermine them; but once that happens—and it can happen very quickly—the old approaches stand exposed as little more than reflections of their proponents' limited perspectives. There is no reason to think, therefore, that the physical or social sciences have any less of an objectivity problem than do historians;[21] indeed, given the commitment of energy, resources, and time required to construct a rigorous scientific paradigm,[22] it is probably easier for 'unrigorous' historians to liberate themselves from an outdated intellectual framework than it is for 'hard' scientists or social scientists.

This point was brought home to me with considerable force several years ago when I ran into a prominent 'neorealist' and asked him how well that theory of international relations had held up under the events surrounding the end of the Cold War. 'Terribly,' he immediately acknowledged. Then he added: 'I'm still firmly committed, though, to neorealist theory.'

How come? At the time I was so astonished that I didn't ask, but I suspect he was reluctant to give up the precision, clarity, and calculability that came from picturing the great powers as featureless billiard balls, while neglecting altogether what was happening inside them. Apples and oranges might have been a better metaphor: at least it would have allowed for the possibility of asymmetry, irregularity, and internal rot.

Measurement

Historians long ago repudiated the alleged view of Leopold von Ranke and his followers that observations in history can and should be separated from the observer who is making them. Relativism in history arose simultaneously with relativity in physics, and not by accident: the most influential historical relativist, Charles A. Beard, was well aware of Albert Einstein.[23] Whether Beard knew about Werner Heisenberg is less likely, but the physicists' discovery of the uncertainty principle—that attempts to measure phenomena can actually alter phenomena[24]—would have come as no particular surprise to him or to most other historians.

With the development of the new sciences of complexity, it is becoming clear that this problem of observation affecting reality extends throughout the physical world: that the results one gets when one measures something depend upon the instrument of measurement used. 'How long is the coastline of Britain?' the English meteorologist Lewis Richardson once asked. It depends: measurements in miles, kilometres, metres, feet, inches, and centimetres will all produce different results, and the same problem would extend down to the levels of molecules and atoms.[25] It is a commonplace now to observe that history has been 'measured', for centuries, with instruments that pick up the activities and influence of white males, while missing altogether those of women and of non-white males, rather in the way that measuring the British coastline in miles would leave quite a lot out.[26]

I wonder whether international relations theory, in its preoccupation with measuring and quantifying military and economic power, did not leave out certain other forms of power that helped to bring the Cold War to an end and are already defining the nature of the post-cold war world—namely the power of ideas, whether they relate to human rights or to human rivalries. Who would have thought that, at the end of the twentieth century, given the opportunity some people would choose to fight and even die in the defence of what appear to many others to be trival, esoteric, even medieval arguments about religion, ethnicity, language, culture, and race?[27] Obviously our 'rational choice' models have not been measuring 'rationality' on a sufficiently precise scale;[28] obviously our understanding of 'power' as well as of its limits has been too general.

Modelling

What is the purpose of having a model in the first place? No scientific model does more than approximate reality; for to replicate reality would be to defeat the purpose of having a model in the first place. It would be like trying to fold an entire country, rather than a map of it, into the glove compartment of your car. Models are therefore metaphors, and their sophistication is assumed to depend upon how well they balance accuracy against utility in yielding insights.

Certainly this is true in the 'hard' sciences. When we speak of the famous Newtonian 'clockwork' universe, we are calling to mind the actual models—orreries—that were built to represent it. For many years, the relationship between the atomic nucleus and the electrons whizzing around it was assumed to be 'like' a tiny solar system; our understanding of nuclear physics advanced significantly when it became clear that electrons can shift their orbits instantly, while planets cannot. And what are we to make of the discovery of the subatomic particles now known as 'quarks' (a term coined not by the physicist Murray Gell-Mann but by the author James Joyce[29])—objects no one has ever seen, but which regularly have such qualities assigned to them as 'colour', 'strangeness', and 'charm'?

Historians operate in much the same way. When they say that Pickett's charge failed because the Union troops mowed down the Confederates like a scythe cutting through stalks of dry wheat, or that Franklin D. Roosevelt had a 'flypaper' mind, historians are not just trying to keep their students, or their readers, awake. These too are metaphors: they are ways of representing complex realities in forms we can more readily grasp than if we were to employ less vivid methods of description.

The point of having a model in science or a metaphor in history, is much the same: it is a way of coping with complexity. In this respect scientists and historians, as well as novelists, poets, psychologists, sociologists, economists, and even political scientists, are in the same methodological boat: we all resort to models, or metaphors, not just for convenience, but because it is the only way we can understand reality ourselves, or try to communicate it to others. The historical narrative has exactly identical purposes to those of the scientist's model; indeed, because it need not depend upon reductionism, because it does incorporate the passage of time, and because it accommodates and even relishes particularity, it may be—if thought of in this way—the most sophisticated model of all.[30]

Language

Language is itself a kind of model, a way of approximating reality. Apart from the ease with which quantification allows communication across the boundaries posed by spoken and written languages, there is—precisely because of the problems of measurement and modelling mentioned above—no reason to assume that mathematical expression comes any closer to performing the function of language than does taxonomy, with its reliance upon careful observation and precise verbal description.[31]

It is also worth remembering that there are in mathematics many problems for which there are no single solutions. Whole classes of equations produce unpredictable results, depending upon sensitivity to initial conditions, the number of variables in the system, and the phenomenon of feedback. And then there is something truly subversive called Gödel's theorem, which calls into question the very basis of proof in mathematics even where it is predictable, forcing us to take the whole thing largely on faith.[32] The distance back to divine revelation— or to witch doctors if you prefer—may not be so great after all.

Contingency

No science that seeks to describe the real world—as opposed to the laboratory world—can divorce itself from the problem of contingency. The concept of sensitive dependence on initial conditions, as it has emerged from the sciences of chaos and complexity, demonstrates that immeasurable perturbations at the beginning of a process can produce immense results at its end.[33] Any system that operates with more than a couple of variables—and surely most social systems do—is going to produce unpredictable reactions among those variables, a proposition easily illustrated with the simple three-magnet pendulum toys anyone can pick up at airport gift shops. The only way one can describe the behaviour of such a system is to trace its history.

What this suggests is that the whole basis of forecasting in the social sciences may need to be rethought. Certainly we ought to embark upon that enterprise with much greater humility than in the past. But we may also need to realize that what we should be trying to forecast is not so much what is going to happen as what *categories of phenomena* we are likely to confront: some of these will lend themselves to prediction but many—because of sensitive dependence on initial conditions or an excessive number of variables, or both—simply will not. A major task for the 'new' social sciences should be to sort out which problems are which, and then to confine our forecasts to those where we can expect at least some possibility of success.

Intuition

No science really works in the way that most textbooks on the scientific method describe it as working, namely through the patient accumulation of evidence, only after which insights emerge. Rather, the compilation of information and the emergence of insights are simultaneously occurring and mutually interactive aspects of the process, in which hypotheses determine the evidence one seeks, while the evidence one finds in turn reshapes hypotheses.[34]

Ask yourself this question: why did it prove easier to end the Cold War itself than to redesign the various massive data-collection projects, growing out of the events-data movement some quarter of a century ago, that were supposed to tell us how to formulate the policies that might bring about an end to the Cold War?[35] It was, I think, because those projects tried to operate as empirical black holes, sucking in data without sufficient mechanisms for assessing standards of significance—one of the functions, after all, of theory. No wonder so few insights emerged. There is no such thing as a purely inductive or a purely deductive research enterprise, and we might as well acknowledge this too as we contemplate the post-Cold War era.

Persuasion

All 'hard' science has a rhetorical purpose, in that it seeks to persuade its 'consumers' that its conclusions are valid.[36] That is how one achieves the consensus that makes the scientific method work. The same is certainly true in the social sciences and in history; indeed, a scientific, social-scientific, or historical account that is totally free from rhetoric of one kind or another is probably as unattainable as a purely 'objective' historical study would be.

2.6. Rediscovering Narrative

None of this is to claim that one can or should try to do history, social science, and 'hard' science in exactly the same way. For although the phenomenon of 'feedback' probably exists in all sciences,[37] the possibility of *conscious* responses to circumstances confronts historians and social scientists with tasks of explanation and forecasting considerably more complex than anything physical and biological scientists face. I am suggesting, though, that if problems of objectivity, measurement, modelling, language, contingency, intuition, and persuasion exist in the 'hard' sciences, then it is difficult to see why we should regard either the social or the historical sciences, where these same problems also exist, as any less 'scientific'. The 'scientific method', if understood in up-to-date terms, is capable of providing a common rationale, and hence a common basis for a new and valuable dialogue, across the entire spectrum of the natural, social, and historical sciences. It can, for this reason, provide us with a sounder intellectual justification than we have had, until now, for an eclectic, imaginative, and interdisciplinary approach to the study of world politics. The post-Cold War world is already proving to be an extraordinarily complex place. Our tools for understanding it should be appropriate to the task.

The historical narrative may well serve as a kind of bridge between the 'new' hard sciences of chaos and complexity and the 'old' social sciences. By sticking with narratives, the historians, who never bought into the 'old' social sciences in the first place, have achieved something rather remarkable: they have come out on the cutting edge of a revolution by persisting in a reactionary stance. They find themselves, at least in metaphorical terms, somewhat in the position of Molière's bourgeois gentleman, who was astonished to discover that he had been speaking prose all his life.

Whether historians will recognize the central position they now occupy in the Great Interdisciplinary Chain of Being, though, I am not sure: they are an inward-looking community who have rarely suffered from 'physics' or any other kind of methodological envy. Fortunately, they have no monopoly over the uses of narrative: in addition to being the most sophisticated model available, it is also the most accessible. A rediscovery of narrative by social scientists could move us back towards that pre-professional era when intelligent people could comfortably involve themselves in, and learn from, multiple disciplines without being regarded as dilettantes. That, I think, would be no bad thing.

This promise will materialize only if we can advance our thinking beyond the bounds imposed on it over three centuries ago by the followers of Isaac Newton, who sought to persuade us—falsely, as it has turned out—that science necessarily has to be reductionist, static, and universal in its applications. That particular view of science was itself the reflection of a particular time, if not a specific place; and time itself, as it does tend to do, has now most assuredly moved on.

Notes

1. Edward Hallett Carr, *What is History?* (New York, 1961), 70.
2. David Hackett Fischer, *Historians' Fallacies: Toward a Logic of Historical Thought* (New York, 1970), p. xii.

3. John Lewis Gaddis, 'International Relations Theory and the End of the Cold War', *International Security*, 17 (Winter, 1992/93), esp. 25–6.
4. For an acrid critique see Gertrude Himmelfarb, *On Looking into the Abyss: Untimely Thoughts on Culture and Society* (New York, 1994).
5. John Ziman, *Reliable Knowledge: An Exploration of the Grounds for Belief in Science* (Cambridge, 1978), 3.
6. Ibid. 42–3.
7. Gary Taubes, *Bad Science: The Short Life and Weird Times of Cold Fusion* (New York, 1993).
8. Stanley Hoffmann, 'International Relations: The Long Road to Theory', in James N. Rosenau (ed.), *International Relations and Foreign Policy: A Reader in Research and Theory* (New York, 1961), 429.
9. For some of the difficulties involved see Ernest R. May, *'Lessons' of the Past: The Use and Misuse of History in American Foreign Policy* (New York, 1973); Richard E. Neustadt and Ernest R. May, *Thinking in Time: The Uses of History for Decision Makers* (New York, 1986).
10. W. Brian Arthur, 'Competing Technologies, Increasing Returns, and Lock-in by Historical Events', *Economic Journal*, 94 (March 1989), 116–31. See also M. Mitchell Waldrop, *Complexity: The Emerging Science at the Edge of Chaos* (New York, 1992), 15–51.
11. Peter Burke, *History and Social Theory* (Cambridge, 1992), 104–9.
12. The most obvious recent example is, of course, the peaceful relinquishment of power by Communist Parties in the former Soviet Union and Eastern Europe. But there are also several interesting US examples: for example, the Defense Department's strong resistance, prior to the outbreak of the Korean War in 1950, to having its own budget increased, while the State Department was strongly advocating that course of action; also the Pentagon's obvious reluctance to endorse the use of military force over the past decade, as against the frequency with which State Department and other civilian advisers have recommended it.
13. Burke, *History and Social Theory*, 114–15; also, for an example of new (and still controversial) physiological findings, see Simon LeVay and Dean H. Hamer, 'Evidence for a Biological Influence in Male Homosexuality', *Scientific American*, 270 (May 1994), 44–9.
14. I have discussed some of the reasons for the latter event in John Lewis Gaddis, *The United States and the End of the Cold War: Reconsiderations, Implications, Provocations* (New York, 1992). For the failure of theory see Gaddis, 'International Relations Theory and the End of the Cold War', passim.
15. Waldrop, *Complexity*, 140.
16. Walter Alvarez and Frank Asaro, 'What Caused the Mass Extinction? An Extraterrestrial Impact', *Scientific American*, 263 (Oct. 1990), 78–84.
17. R. Damian Nance, Thomas R. Worsley, and Judith B. Moody, 'The Supercontinent Cycle', *Scientific American*, 258 (July 1988), 72–9.
18. Stephen Jay Gould, *Wonderful Life: The Burgess Shale and the Nature of History* (New York, 1989).

19. Ziman, *Reliable Knowledge*, 43–56.
20. Gould, *Wonderful Life*, 280–81. I see the Bueno de Mesquita forecasting model, discussed in Chapter 3 in this volume, as based upon the identification of certain decision-making *processes*, into which specific variables are inserted. Despite its reliance upon quantification and calculation, it incorporates the passage of time and allows for the repeated interactions that structural approaches often exclude. It resembles, in this respect, the work of Robert Axelrod (*The Evolution of Cooperation*, New York, 1984), and I suspect that their incorporation of process is why these two computer-based methods have a better record of successful forecasting than do most static structural models.
21. For the historians' problem see Peter Novick, *That Noble Dream: The 'Objectivity' Question and the American Historical Profession* (New York, 1988).
22. Thomas S. Kuhn, *The Structure of Scientific Revolutions*, 2nd edn., enlarged (Chicago, 1970), 23–4.
23. See Charles A. Beard, 'Written History as an Act of Faith', *American Historical Review*, 39 (January 1934), 225.
24. One of the best brief summaries of the Heisenberg uncertainty principle that I have seen occurs in Jack Cohen and Ian Stewart, *The Collapse of Chaos: Discovering Simplicity in a Complex World* (New York, 1994), 44–5.
25. James Gleick, *Chaos: Making a New Science* (New York, 1987), 94–6.
26. One of the best discussions is Joyce Appleby, Lynn Hunt, and Margaret Jacob, *Telling the Truth about History* (New York, 1994), 146–97.
27. Robin Wright and Doyle McManus, *Flashpoints: Promise and Peril in a New World* (New York, 1991), was one of the first books to examine this trend; but see also Robert Kaplan, *Balkan Ghosts: A Journey Through History* (New York, 1993).
28. Bueno do Mesquita suggests in Chapter 3 that one can find rational explanations for such behaviour. I agree, as long as one views such 'rationalities' as embedded within particular cultures, contexts, and circumstances.
29. Murray Gell-Mann, *The Quark and the Jaguar: Adventures in the Simple and the Complex* (New York, 1994), 180–1.
30. This is what I had in mind when I suggested, in a now somewhat notorious article, that we might have done better, in seeking to anticipate the end of the Cold War, to have relied upon carefully crafted historical narratives rather than the structural systemic perspective with which the traditional approach to the study of international relations provided us ('International Relations Theory and the End of the Cold War', 56–8). Certainly in thinking about the post-Cold War world we ought not to neglect the importance of narratives—not least because they can help us to understand certain aspects of the pre-Cold War world that it may resemble. See also, on the inseparability of narrative and science, Donald N. McCloskey, 'Once Upon a Time There Was a Theory', *Scientific American*, 272 (February 1995), 25.
31. Ziman, *Reliable Knowledge*, 55–6.
32. Waldrop, *Complexity*, 328–9. See also Douglas R. Hofstadter's highly adventurous *Gödel, Escher, Bach: An Eternal Golden Braid* (New York, 1979).
33. Gleick, *Chaos*, 11–31.

34. Gould, *Wonderful Life*, 244. See also Steven Weinberg, *Dreams of a Final Theory: The Search for the Fundamental Laws of Nature* (New York, 1992), esp. 128, 180.
35. Gaddis, 'International Relations Theory and the End of the Cold War', 26.
36. Ziman, *Reliable Knowledge*, 21.
37. Note especially recent work on the capacity of both animate and inanimate systems for self-organization, in apparent violation of the second law of thermodynamics. There is a good discussion in Waldrop, *Complexity*, 272–87.

Further Reading

CARR, E. H., *What is History?* (New York, 1961), and MARC BLOCH, *The Historian's Craft* (New York, 1953) are the classic primers on the historical method that implicitly anticipate more recent developments in the 'new' sciences of chaos and complexity.

GADDIS, JOHN LEWIS, 'International Relations Theory and the End of the Cold War', *International Security*, 17 (Winter 1992–3), 5–58, expands on the argument made in this chapter, that international relations theorists have been practising outdated science.

GLEICK, JAMES, *Chaos: Making a New Science* (New York, 1987) and M. MITCHELL WALDROP, *Complexity: The Emerging Science at the Edge of Chaos* (New York, 1992). These two volumes, together, provide the best introduction for social scientists to the new developments in the 'hard' sciences that are creating the basis for a convergence of methods.

GOULD, STEPHEN JAY, *Wonderful Life: The Burgess Shale and the Nature of History* (New York, 1989). A brilliant palaeontologist's exploration of historical processes, making the case that history is indeed a science, but also that scientists need to think more like historians.

KUHN, THOMAS S., *The Structure of Scientific Revolutions*, 2nd edn. (Chicago, 1970) and PETER NOVICK, *That Noble Dream: The 'Objectivity' Question and the American Historical Profession* (New York, 1988) make the point that both scientists and historians find 'objectivity' an elusive concept.

ZIMAN, JOHN, *Reliable Knowledge: An Exploration of the Grounds for Belief in Science* (Cambridge, 1978). An excellent introduction to the scientific method based on how it's used in the physical and biological sciences; quite possibly the single most useful introduction for social scientists.

CHAPTER THREE

THE BENEFITS OF A SOCIAL-SCIENTIFIC APPROACH TO STUDYING INTERNATIONAL AFFAIRS

Bruce Bueno de Mesquita

International affairs, like all human interaction, invites study from a multiplicity of perspectives. The end of the Second World War brought with it a natural proliferation of international relations research methods. Philosophical, historical, and scientific methods have been applied to security issues and to questions of international economic exchange, with each approach providing some important insights and each failing to unravel the mysteries of how states relate to one another.

My purpose here is to discuss some of the benefits of a scientific approach to the study of international relations. By 'scientific approach' I mean one that emphasizes making assumptions explicit, deriving logically consistent implications from those assumptions, and systematically testing those implications through controlled comparisons across cases. The scientific approach, then, is concerned with specifying causal explanations and with ascertaining how well the proposed causal explanation predicts patterns across observations. In focusing on the scientific method I do not mean to suggest that other methods are not equally appropriate or more appropriate for some research strategies. I only mean to help the reader gain a greater appreciation of the application of scientific methods to the study of international affairs.

Most essential features of the scientific method, of course, are not different in

I am grateful to James Morrow, James Ray, Duncan Snidal, Ngaire Woods, and Barry Weingast for helpful comments on earlier versions of this paper.

the social sciences from in other fields, although controlled experiments are clearly problematic in social enquiry. There is nothing about international relations research that makes it unusually well suited or ill suited for scientific enquiry. The method of science imposes only a few crucial requirements on research. These are that the explanation of a phenomenon be based on a logically consistent and explicit argument and that the empirical evaluation of an argument rely on testable, falsifiable claims whose assessment is replicable by independent researchers. Occasionally people confuse falsifiability with questions of whether a hypothesis is true or false. That is, sometimes people seem to think that a true argument is not falsifiable. Of course, falsifiability has to do with the ability to state a priori conditions under which one would conclude that an argument was false. Those conditions may never be satisfied, because the argument is true; still the argument was falsifiable. The ability to predict classes of events or phenomena is often held up as a critical standard in tests of hypotheses. I share the view that prediction is critical and so give it a prominent role here as well.

Enquiries into international affairs that are more or less based on the scientific method proceed from a multiplicity of substantive and theoretical perspectives. Structural, behavioural, and psychological approaches are especially likely to be well known to the reader. Perhaps less familiar among 'scientific' perspectives are those that rely on rational choice models. I place 'scientific' in quotation marks here to remind the reader that many theoretical perspectives can be compatible with the scientific method. Science addresses issues of how to evaluate arguments and evidence; the scientific method is agnostic with regard to particular substantive foci. Rational choice theories, therefore, are not inherently more or less scientific than other theories. Still, in this essay I focus especially on rational choice approaches to the study of international relations that rely upon game theory. I do so for several reasons.

First, game theory is a body of reasoning designed explicitly to attend to the logic of strategic interaction. Strategic interaction, in which decision-makers select a course of action taking into account expectations about how others will respond, is central to all of international affairs. It is difficult to imagine constructing any explanatory theory of international relations without thinking explicitly about the interdependencies between events and individual choices. Non-game-theoretic points of view often assume away or greatly simplify the most interesting features of strategic interaction in international affairs. This is sometimes done by assuming that all foreign policy decision-makers wish to maximize the same thing (e.g. security) and wish to gain as much of that thing as possible before considering other types of benefits. That is, many such approaches assume lexicographic preferences. Lexicographic preferences are characterized by the condition that no amount of one good can compensate for even a minuscule amount of another, lexicographically preferred good. Game theory models rarely make assumptions that eliminate strategic manœuvring. In that sense, game theory seems an approach particularly well suited to the subject of concern.

Second, game theory provides tools for dealing with many of the concerns and assumptions of structural, behavioural, and psychological theories and so can help to integrate the important knowledge derived from these other approaches. Structure is a central element in games of sequential decision-making in which choices are constrained by the situation in which decision-makers find themselves. Through a strategic analysis of preferences and beliefs, game theory provides a means to examine attitudes, perceptions, uncertainties, and learning on the part of decision-makers. At the same time, game theory provides a systematic means of analysing and predicting behaviour across large classes of events, whether they involve sincere behaviour, bluffing, or other forms of strategic acts. These all seem to be crucial elements in the study of international affairs. Other approaches may take these features into account, but game theory is the only method with which I am familiar that explicitly requires attentiveness to all of these concerns. Having said that, we should keep in mind that there is not a single game theory of international relations. Rather, game theory is a mathematical foundation on which different, even competing theories of international relations may be constructed. As such, game theory is an axiomatically based theory of decision-making. In international relations, game theory provides a method of explaining and analysing strategic behaviour. The quality of any given theory, of course, depends on the insights of the researcher. Game theory as a method only ensures that certain crucial factors, including the ones I have enumerated, are taken into account.[1]

A third reason for focusing on game-theoretic approaches to international relations is that they have enjoyed particular success in the area of prediction. As John Gaddis has noted, structural, behavioural, and psychological perspectives have failed to yield clear, specific, and detailed predictions of important events. Regrettably, he did not review the accomplishments or predictions based on rational choice theories, including game theory models.[2] I will here try to fill that lacuna in his otherwise generally compelling assessment. In doing so, I enumerate examples of detailed predictions about important international events that were made using game theory methods and document the predictive character of these assessments and their rate of accuracy. I hope in this way to give the reader a better understanding of the potential this particular body of social science literature has for explaining and predicting international affairs.

The emphasis on game theory perspectives on international affairs should not be taken as a criticism of other approaches. Space does not permit me to attend to all types of scientific analysis; and, in any event, I aim here not so much to review an approach as to explain its scientific foundations and accomplishments in general. My central concern is to highlight the ways in which the scientific method can help correct certain common limitations in other approaches, especially those grounded in the methods of the historian.

3.1. Are Social Scientists and Historians Competitors?

One might legitimately mark the modern beginning of scientific enquiry in the West with the fall of Constantinople in 1453. The flow of Christian Byzantine scholars to Rome seeking the assistance of the Catholic church included several who brought with them original Hellenic manuscripts. The much broadened exposure of Europeans to these manuscripts accelerated an ongoing eagerness for learning that stimulated the further resurgence of independent thought in Europe. This growth of humanist enquiry contributed to the decline of the authority of the Catholic church and made room for such revolutionary thinkers as Copernicus, Galileo, and Newton.

The upsurge of humanist enquiry eventually contributed to the development of both modern historical research and modern social science. It is peculiar, then, that these two branches of knowledge, growing from a common origin, should today be thought of as competing modes of thought. Despite the core commitment to critical thinking and empirical knowledge, there is room, of course, among humanists for epistemological and methodological differences. Still, it is puzzling that historians and social scientists sometimes seem to be at odds regarding what constitutes appropriate methodologies. With few exceptions, the methods of the historian and the methods of the social scientist are complementary, not competitive. Each seems interested in resolving different and important aspects of our understanding of international relations. Perhaps the source of the seeming competition is confusion over what each is interested in accomplishing, and in particular what the role of the scientific method is in understanding history and future international affairs.

Historians and social scientists share a common interest in the context, sequence, and meaning of events. They differ, however, in the emphasis placed on and the interpretation of context, sequence, and meaning. And, of course, historians and social scientists differ in the methods used to evaluate evidence and to reach conclusions. At the risk of speaking for historians, which I certainly am not qualified to do, I express my view that many historians—certainly not all—are primarily interested in explanations that emphasize particularistic factors that distinguish one event, one sequence, one location from another. The meaning or explanation of events and actions is often assumed to be revealed through culturally and temporally bounded interpretations. Such a perspective naturally draws the scholar towards a close examination of particular events and actions. The historian's focus on particularistic factors inspires the belief that little can be gained from explanations rooted in conjectures about motives for actions that are presumed to be quite general, if not universal. A common and perhaps correct claim is made, for instance, that medieval social, political, and economic relations cannot be understood through the application of modern notions of individual interests or welfare maximization.[3] Here the differences between social scientists and historians is rather explicit.

The belief in the existence of broadly applicable generalizations is at the core of scientifically orientated social enquiry. Social scientists, including game theorists, do not deny the relevance of cultural, temporal, or contextual considerations as means to understand past or future events; rather, such factors are embedded within theoretical constructs in which they serve as variables.[4] Social scientists tend to be more concerned with how variables relate to each other than with explaining particular events or actions. Social science emphasizes the causation behind recurrent phenomena, while historical analysis seems more to emphasize the particular agents of causation for singular events. Put differently, the social scientist is more likely to emphasize general explanations of social phenomena, while the historian is more likely to emphasize particularistic, unique features of individual episodes of social phenomena. The distinction should not be drawn too sharply as there surely is a continuum of interests among researchers rather than a dichotomy. Still, the differences are sufficiently real for history departments rarely to hire people trained as social scientists and social science departments rarely to hire people trained as historians.

For the social scientist the events of history are a laboratory in which to test their claims about how variables are associated with each other; to test their theoretical propositions about causation. As such, the social scientist's task is not so much to explain particular events as to identify relations among critical variables that explain classes of events or phenomena. For the historian, the search is for an evaluation of which variables were of relevance in a particular past case or sequence of events. The historian is more likely to be concerned with giving meaning to the events rather than with defining the relations among variables. These are not logically equivalent exercises, though they are undoubtedly two important aspects of understanding human interactions.

The differences in the interests of these two groups of scholars have led to considerable confusion about appropriate methods. Historians emphasize discourse, meaning, context, and complexity; internal validity, if you will. Social scientists tend to emphasize regularities, replication and parsimony; external validity, if you will. For many historians, path dependence, or the way in which one set of events influences another, is crucial to understanding historical events.[5]

For many social scientists, sequence and path dependence are important because they help us understand the endogeneities—how the logic of the situation
leads decision-makers to choose strategically the values on key variables—behind the evolution of circumstances. The circumstances, then, are not treated as
primarily exogenous elements (that is, elements whose value is dictated by factors outside the logic of the situation) in the evolution of human interaction.
For the historian, sequences of events set the stage for future developments, but
often appear not to be shaped consciously by the expectations of decision-
makers about how those future developments may benefit or harm particular
interests. Path dependence and its implications are very different for the historian and for the game-theoretically orientated social scientist.

In the remainder of this chapter I focus attention on four aspects of the study
of international affairs from a game-theoretic perspective. These four aspects
are endogenous choices and their implications for path dependence; selection
effects in theory and in data, and how they can distort inferences from historical
analysis; the importance of independence between arguments and the evidence
used to evaluate their merits if we are to distinguish description, explanation,
and prediction; and prediction as a means of evaluating the potential of scientific
enquiry to help influence future international affairs. These four items—endogeneity, selection effects, independence between argument and evidence, and
prediction—represent areas where scientific enquiry into international affairs
has proven helpful in clarifying problems that frequently arise in other modes
of analysis. A summary of my main claims is found in Table 3.1.

3.2. Situations and Strategic Choices

In his otherwise outstanding analysis of the issues underlying the emergence
during the medieval centuries of the concept of the king's two bodies, Ernst
Kantorowicz suggests that the evolution of institutions in the Catholic church
and in Europe's nascent states followed similar but essentially independent paths.[6]
For instance, he argues: 'When in the twelfth century the Church, including the
clerical bureaucracy, established itself as the "mystical body of Christ," the secular
world sector proclaimed itself as the "holy Empire." This does not imply causation,
either in the one way or the other. It merely indicates the activity of indeed inter-
related impulses and ambitions . . . [that] happened to emerge simultaneously—
around the middle of the twelfth century.' This perspective, which is representative
of much historical and social-scientific analysis of international relations, whether
contemporary or from the distant past, treats the flow of events as exogenous.[7]
Nature or circumstances, in essence, are believed to throw up stumbling-blocks

Table 3.1. Historical and game-theoretic approaches: a comparative summary

	Inductive or historical approach	Social-scientific (especially game-theoretic) approach
Flow of events	Taken as given or as the product of 'exogenous' developments	Endogeneity is analysed; events are linked to strategic interaction
Selection of cases	Sampling on the dependent variable; cases are chosen in which similar outcomes seem to be caused by similar factors; cases with the same factors but without similar outcomes may be overlooked	Sampling on the independent variables; cases are chosen to evaluate whether similar factors occur with similar outcomes when variation in factors and outcomes are both represented in the cases analysed
Evidence	Often drawn from the same events as provided the basis for the hypotheses	Evidence should be independent of the information used to derive hypotheses
Objective of study	To describe and explain specific events and actions in terms of contextual factors	To make and test claims about causation as indicated by the proposed relations among variables

around which people must find their way. The solutions are not thought of as strategic in the sense that they might be forward-looking and designed to stymie manœuvres by rivals; rather, solutions are thought to be backward-looking, designed to address the problem of the moment which was created by forces treated essentially as outside the control of any individual. Because problems and sequences are regarded as exogenous, small deviations in circumstances or chance developments are thought to be capable of producing, in time, radically different realities. Those who take such a path-dependent perspective find solace in the apparent complexity suggested by the mathematics of chaos theory and by the theory of evolution. They view cultural and temporal differences as fundamental barriers that are contextually imposed and are not easily altered or subject to choice.

One might maintain, alternatively, that many of the important sequences of history are endogenous. From this perspective, the evolution of many events and choices is shaped by the logic of the situation and the interests of decision-makers rather than being shaped primarily by happenstance. Instead of thinking of the international system, the nation-state, alliances, and other constructs as given, one might think of each as a phenomenon to be explained by the motivations behind individual choices and the logic of the context within which such choices are made. From this point of view, choices are forward-looking and are designed to gain advantages over competitors as the sequence of events plays itself out. In contrast to the viewpoint suggested by Kantorowicz, one might, for instance, think of the evolution of church institutions and the evolution of sovereign state institutions as strategic manœuvres designed by each side to try to gain a political or economic advantage over the other side.

I have in mind as examples of strategic choices of church institutions the replacement of electors of the Holy Roman Empire by the College of Cardinals as the means of giving the church greater independence from temporal authorities; the identification of the Pope as the Vicar of Christ as a means of asserting church hegemony over kings; the promotion by the church of the concept of inalienable lands in order to weaken the ability of kings to raise money; papal infallibility, excommunication, interdiction, and coronation as further assertions of the Pope as superior to kings. Examples of endogenously chosen monarchical institutions include hereditary rather than elective monarchy as an institution to tie together the interests of a king as an individual and the interests of a king as head of state; rights to revenues from regalian sees during the interregnum between bishops to gain control over church appointments; divine right monarchy as a means to assert equality with the Pope; and schismatic papacies to bring the church under temporal control. Naturally, these and other examples could be elaborated upon if space permitted.

Endogeneity is a central theme in rational choice arguments that assume individuals are motivated to do as well as they *believe* they can. Endogeneity immediately implies that sequence or path dependence is important and that evolutionary processes are essential elements in understanding how circumstances, nations, alliances, systems, and the like change. Endogeneity can be seen in the contemporary international environment, for instance, in the re-emergence of nationalist rivalries in central Europe. While some suggest that the fighting in Bosnia and elsewhere is the product of longstanding nationalist or ethnic feuds—without explaining why these feuds lay dormant for decades and then suddenly erupted—some game-theoretic treatments suggest that such fighting is a policy chosen in the face of evolving political institutions. The problem, according to some theorists, is that evolving political institutions are not reliable enough to protect the minority from a tyranny of the majority. This may be true even, or perhaps especially, when the institutions are democratic.[8] Game-theoretic applications suggest reasoning of the following sort.

The anticipation that self-interested decision-makers may choose to exploit minorities if given a chance can be sufficient to encourage resistance by those very minorities even before any exploitation has occurred. Promises not to exploit them lack credibility once the minorities have accepted the legitimacy of new institutions that, for instance, assign decisive authority to the majority viewpoint. Therefore, it is plausible to hypothesize that minorities are likely to rebel against the majority when political institutions undergo significant changes even though no outward (clear) evidence of their exploitation may yet exist. Notice that this argument states relations among variables in its effort to arrive at causation and does not focus on the specific details of any case. Changes in political institutions under conditions of uncertainty are proposed as sufficient to raise the risk of political rebellion. Ethnicity is an incidental factor in this hypothesis that is correlated with fears by a minority that new institutions will result in their oppression.

Of course, one does not need game theory to arrive at this particular hypothesis, but game theory does compel one to think about the endogeneity of choices and beliefs in a way that can suggest testable and falsifiable hypotheses. James Fearon, Francine Friedman, and Robert Bates and Barry Weingast provide examples of just such hypothesis formation based on the rejection of the notion that nationalist fury erupts spontaneously and more or less randomly through time.[9] The latter explanation, with its appeal to longstanding animosities and cultural differences, is a way of dealing with such events common among those who view the symbols and interpretation of culture as exogenously determined. Still, this explanation also appeals to relations among variables and so can be subjected to scientific scrutiny and comparison with alternative explanations.

The research by game theorists on nationalist and ethnic conflict nicely accentuates the distinctions I have tried to draw between the approaches of a historian and a social scientist. In the cases of Fearon, Friedman, and Bates and Weingast, each has constructed a somewhat different theory to explain these conflicts. In each case the author(s) evaluate theory by applying it to the current fighting in the former Yugoslavia. Friedman, a specialist on Yugoslav affairs, is particularly interested in disputes in that part of the world, but she is explicitly using a general theory developed to analyse interest-group politics, not Yugoslav affairs. Fearon and Bates and Weingast are specifically concerned to explain features of nationalist or ethnic conflict: Yugoslavia serves as a test case for the implications of their theories. They are not specifically interested in Yugoslavia per se, but rather turn to Yugoslavia as a site of current events which can serve to help test their hypotheses. This is quite different from the detailed examination of relations among the peoples of the former Yugoslavia that one would expect to be undertaken by a historian or by an area specialist. Both forms of enterprise, of course, can be illuminating.

Concern for path dependence naturally turns attention to evolutionary models. Although adaptations of the theory of evolution have proven useful in trying to understand the complexity of history, sometimes historians and social scientists mistakenly maintain that evolution teaches us that path dependence, while critical, leads to unpredictable consequences. It is this presumed unpredictability that leads some to reject scientific approaches out of hand.

The notion seems to be that the evolution of specific characteristics (whether of events or of species) is inherently unpredictable and that, therefore, the theory of evolution (or its social applications) is not falsifiable. Because evolution is clearly an explanatory theory, it appears to be an exemplar of theory-building that explains but cannot predict. This view has led some to believe that evolutionary theory demonstrates that explanation can readily be decoupled from prediction and that the scientific method, with its reliance on falsification, is inadequate for path-dependent, evolutionary problems. These arguments seem to me to be misinformed, at least when it comes to the application of such theories to problems of international relations.

To be sure, a powerful case can be made that social interaction is path-dependent or subject to evolutionary forces of selection and change (mutation). However, such an assertion is not inconsistent with the application of the scientific method. The path dependence of social interaction is consistent with an approach to international affairs that emphasizes strategic interaction and rational choice. Evolutionary or path-dependent perspectives within a game-theoretic framework are, as all scientific theories are, susceptible to testing and, in principle, to falsification.

To clarify, let me begin with the claim made by some that evolutionary theory is not falsifiable. This claim confuses evolutionary theory's focus on time and the emergence of specific characteristics with the belief that predictions must therefore be about timing and those characteristics. While genetic research certainly points to predictability on these dimensions, evolutionary theory contains many testable (and falsifiable) hypotheses that have to do with population equilibria that follow from, but are not about, timing and characteristics.[10] That is, falsifiable predictions about population characteristics follow directly from the axiomatic basis of evolutionary theory despite the theory's focus on timing and characteristics.

For instance, key parts of evolutionary theory would be falsified if we found that, over time, predator populations stabilized at levels that exceed the supply of prey. In fact, one reason evolutionary theory has been so influential is that it provides well-supported predictions like the predator–prey predictions in an elegant explanatory structure that relies on little more than four central axioms. Changes in population sizes and relatively small variance around observed population equilibria given fixed environmental conditions represent just a few sources of important, falsifiable hypotheses.

Since the development of atomic and nuclear weapons, there has been considerable debate and discussion about the harmful or beneficial effects of offensive or defensive arms races. Predator–prey evolutionary models instruct us that arms races should be expected to produce fairly stable equilibria in which offensive and defensive capabilities remain generally in balance. If offensive technology should outpace defensive technology, then predatory states will expand at the expense of weaker neighbours. Such expansion, however, is likely to be self-containing as the international environment increasingly is altered to include a disproportionate number of predatory states. Thus we expect and generally observe that the development of offensive and defensive weapons oscillates narrowly around an equilibrium that generally preserves existing states. In this way we can understand that the great longevity of states is itself endogenous to the evolutionary process of arms racing between offensive and defensive capabilities.[11]

Some game theory models capture critical comparative static elements found in the dynamic theory of evolution. Rational actors choose efficiently, maximizing their prospects, and therefore do better on average than those who choose on some other basis.[12] Of course, as with any species with an advantage in survivability, the performance of any individual rational chooser is subject to probabilistic failure. But, on average, efficient choosers do better than inefficient choosers. Consequently, and in accordance with the fundamental axioms of evolution, we should expect a concentration of rational actors in the population of decision-makers. This should be increasingly true as the cost of inefficient decision-making rises, as when the stakes are high—as they usually are when it comes to matters of foreign policy and international affairs. It is not surprising, then, that evolutionary models of choice seem to yield results over time that are consistent with the expectations derived from theories of choice that assume rational action.

The dismissal of the scientific method is unwarranted for reasons that go beyond mistaken claims about the non-predictive nature of evolutionary theories. It is also important to recognize that some of the complexity underlying arguments about path dependence may be more apparent than real. If people are trying to choose efficiently then they are always trying to construct, or at least constrain, the future circumstances in which they will find themselves. This can be very difficult to do successfully, of course, because rivals are trying to do exactly the same thing. What is more, everyone knows that everyone else is trying to gain an advantage and everyone knows that everyone else knows that. Sometimes, researchers think that this principle of common knowledge about the desire to 'play the game as well as it can be played' leads to an infinite regress that makes social-scientific enquiry all but impossible. To escape the presumed infinite regress, they propose variants on path dependence intended to simplify the problem.

The most common such effort is to assume that individuals are not fully rational but are, instead, subject to bounded or limited rationality. Yet such perspectives open a Pandora's box. While theories of rational choice provide a rigorous basis for predicting the choices individuals will make given particular, explicitly assumed constraints, theories of bounded rationality do not. In sequential games with rational actors it is a straightforward matter to see what choices can be made and what choices cannot be made. Those that are expected to lead to inferior outcomes for a player are avoided by that player. In models of bounded or limited rationality, by contrast, the sequence in which options present themselves determines actions, yet no theory of what governs the sequence of choices is provided: a fundamental factor—the order in which options are presented to players—is taken as exogenous rather than as strategically shaped by rivals. Theories of bounded rationality, then, are capable only of weak, vague predictions rather than the more precise predictions possible with game theory. Even when game-theoretic predictions are somewhat vague, as in cases of multiple equilibria, bounded rationality models are vaguer, with even more equilibria. Theories of bounded rationality, rather than simplifying or clarifying expectations, lead to a proliferation of equilibria beyond those supported in rational choice models.[13]

Equilibrium here refers to Nash equilibria and their refinements. A Nash equilibrium is a set of strategies for all players such that no player can improve his or her expected welfare by a unilateral switch in actions at any choice point in the game. While normal or strategic form games are usually solved by finding their Nash equilibria, extensive form games take advantage of the greater structural details of a game tree to use refinements of Nash equilibria. These refinements help eliminate equilibria lacking credible commitments and other implausible conditions. Most common among these refinements are subgame perfect equilibria, Bayesian equilibria, and universal divinity. All these refinements are Nash equilibria, but not all Nash equilibria satisfy the requirements of the refinements.

By turning away from theories in which choices about crucial variables are endogenous, some historians and social scientists have imposed complexity where there may be greater simplicity and regularity than has been recognized. This is likely to be one reason why such approaches have not proven to be effective in prediction. But notions about exogenously determined path dependence, evolution, and complexity are not the only factors restricting the prospects for developing predictive theories of international affairs.

3.3. Selection Effects and Mis-stated Hypotheses

A consequential flaw in much research by historians and social scientists stems from the way researchers choose their cases. In particular, researchers often wrongly ignore endogenous choices or the extent to which situations arise as a result of strategic decisions of actors. By doing so, researchers increase the risk that they will draw incorrect inferences from their empirical observations. Studies of alliance reliability, deterrence, the effects of bipolarity or multipolarity on stability, and many other topics in social science enquiries about international politics seem to highlight the non-predictability of foreign affairs. Indeed, a common selection problem in the social sciences and in historical research is likely to yield inaccurate inferences and wrong predictions. That problem is a consequence of selection effects that result from a failure to take adequately into account the impact that strategic interaction has on behaviour.

Consider the following mind experiment. Suppose there is a nation called *A*. That nation has a rival, an enemy state called *B*. That rival has an ally called *C*. Many observers have concluded that alliances are worth no more than the paper on which they are written; that is, they claim that alliances are unreliable. The evidence they offer in support of their argument consists of historical examples or statistical analyses which show that, most of the time, when a nation like *A* attacks a nation like *B*, *C* does not help *B*.[14] That is, the alliance apparently proved to be unreliable. Now let us think about this observation a bit more carefully. The inference that alliances are unreliable does not necessarily follow from the empirical observation. In fact, the observation is exactly what we should expect if some alliances are formed for security purposes, and are reliable, and others are formed for other purposes. Consider the following two cases: *A* attacks *B* or *A* does not attack *B*. In either case we stipulate that *A*'s motivation to attack is the same. Suppose *A* believes it can defeat *B* and gain a benefit that exceeds the anticipated costs of the fight. Suppose, however, that *A* does not believe the benefits warrant the expected costs of a fight against both *B* and *C*. Then, if *A* believes the alliance is reliable, *A* does not attack *B*. If *A* believes the alliance is unreliable, *A* does attack *B*. Naturally, some of the time *A*'s beliefs will be mistaken, but in general we expect that *A*'s beliefs will be consistent with the subsequent behaviour of *C*.

By examining only cases of attack we fail to test the reliability of alliances properly. Indeed, a focus on strategic interaction instructs us to anticipate that we should expect that the applicable alliances will generally prove to be unreliable *if* an attack has taken place. *A*, after all, has already taken into account the anticipated reliability of *C*'s commitment as part of *A*'s strategic decision-making about whether to attack B or not. A has considered what is known in game theory as 'behaviour off the equilibrium path': that is, A has estimated the consequences both of attacking and of not attacking B. If A believes that C will come to B's assistance, then attacking B is not as desirable for A as not attacking. Therefore, A does not attack. The response by C to the contingent attack never takes place, then, because A, contemplating what would happen if it did attack, chooses instead to live with the existing state of affairs. C's response is placed off the equilibrium path by A's decision not to attack. C has successfully deterred A by signalling that it is a reliable ally to B. Our empirical expectation, then, is that the most reliable alliances do not get tested because they succeed in deterring attacks, while the relatively less reliable alliances are more likely to be tested and prove wanting. These other alliances may serve other functions than to provide deterrence, but they are not evidence that alliances in general are unreliable.[15]

By thinking of choices in the way just described, we see how strategic interaction can lead to important insights into behaviour. By studying only what has happened, as is the nature of inductive or empirical research, we are drawn to make conclusions that reflect selection effects of the type just described. Historical research is focused on interpreting 'what really happened'. But a part of what really happened is often calculations about what would have happened had a different course been followed. The path chosen is unlikely to be determined without consideration of the counterfactual consequences of actions not taken.[16]

Almost all historical research on such topics as the causes of big wars suffers from selection effects. Scholars concerned with such wars almost never examine events that threatened to become big wars but did not escalate beyond low levels of dispute. Similarly, there is surprisingly little research about wars with dramatic consequences that were not themselves big events. Scientific analyses, with a strong concern for control groups, and especially game-theoretic analyses, with their emphasis on actions expected off the equilibrium path, help reduce errors of inference that prevail in other forms of investigation. Again, a mind experiment regarding war can help to focus on the problem.

Consider which events in history, all else being equal, were probably expected to yield bigger costs if they escalated to violence: those that became wars or those that were resolved peacefully through negotiations. One important reason for finding a negotiated resolution to an international dispute is that the costs of fighting are expected to be too high. When the costs of war are expected to be relatively low, however, then fighting becomes more attractive. It immediately follows that we cannot understand the causes of big wars without examining many crises that had the potential to become big wars but were averted by reaching a negotiated settlement beforehand. The Cuban Missile Crisis is the most obvious example of such an event, but one can see similar patterns in as minor a dispute as that between Bavaria and Prussia over Hesse in 1850. In the latter case, there is little historical research—perhaps because, in the end, almost nothing happened. Yet contemporaneous newspaper accounts of the dispute in 1850 were dominated by fears that the conflict would erupt into a general war in Europe. Fear of just such a war prompted Prussia to grant concessions that might otherwise not have been given to as weak a rival as Bavaria, or even to Bavaria's Austrian allies.

In these examples, the selection effect is of a different type. Researchers are sampling on the dependent variable, the thing to be explained, and so are unwittingly biasing their inferences by failing to identify whether relationships are spurious or meaningful. That is, they are picking only cases where a particular outcome has occurred, as opposed to choosing cases where a particular set of variables are relevant. In the case of war, historians tend to ignore the bulk of disputes which had the potential to become cataclysmic but were resolved peacefully. Many of the events expected to be the costliest wars remain unstudied because, having anticipated the costs, the parties to the dispute resolved their differences before a war erupted. As a result, the event fails to fall within the purview of the military or diplomatic historian. The war was selected out 'in reality' by expectations off the equilibrium path and was ignored by researchers who sampled on the dependent variable.

Arguments about bipolarity and multipolarity suffer from just such a selection bias, as does much writing on the rise or the decline of great powers. A careful examination of the arguments why bipolar or multipolar systems are likely to promote stability shows, for instance, that the logic behind these arguments depends on specific assumptions about how people respond to uncertainty. Kenneth Waltz's bipolarity argument implicitly assumes that decision-makers are risk-acceptant in the face of uncertainty and are more risk-averse as uncertainty diminishes. Those, like Deutsch and Singer, who have argued that multipolar systems are stable and bipolar systems are unstable, implicitly assume that decision-makers are risk-averse in the face of uncertainty, but become more risk-prone as uncertainty diminishes. Historical and statistical research produces very mixed results, lending strong support to neither hypothesis. Again, this is what we should expect if decision-makers are not selected on the same risk-proneness criteria in all societies at all times. By turning a variable (i.e. the response to uncertainty) into a constant, the accompanying investigations have selected out the cases that belie their hypotheses. That is, only cases in which policy-makers have chosen in a particular way are examined.[17]

3.4. Distinguishing Arguments from the Evidence Supporting Them

A third area in which rational choice models, including especially game theory models, help advance our understanding of international relations concerns the nexus between argument and evidence. Historical research and much empirical social science enquiry are concerned with describing events or the sequence of events. In doing so, scholars are frequently tempted to step beyond description and to portray their observations as explanations or even predictions. When they do so, they sometimes conflate description, explanation, and prediction.

An example may help illustrate the point. Although Paul Kennedy is careful to avoid this error, many scholars who rely on his research infer from his observations that great powers enter into decline as a result of overspending on the military. Kennedy, however, does not provide a benchmark basis against which to evaluate what constitutes large or small defence expenditures. Instead, this assessment is made subjectively, perhaps being influenced by the fact that the state in question did or did not decline. His cases, therefore, do not by themselves constitute a valid test of the hypothesis. When expected military expenditures are estimated independently of the state's subsequent rise or decline, it appears that defence expenditures are unrelated to the phenomenon studied. That is, larger than expected defence expenditures apparently are not associated with hegemonic decline, contrary to the selection argument inferred from Kennedy's research.[18]

Inductive research typically does not keep tests separate from the source of hypotheses. This is true whether the empirical research is qualitative or quantitative. Deductive modelling is much less likely to conflate argument and evidence. Let us consider the problem a bit more carefully.

One objection frequently raised by historians to social science enquiry is its failure to attend to the nuances and details of historical circumstances. The method of 'thick analysis' is designed specifically to address this apparent need to get at the details of what really happened in a given event. Here we see most clearly the epistemological difference between historical research and social science research. Thick analysis is exactly what one would want to do if the object were to describe or interpret particular, individual events as accurately as possible. Thick analysis is exactly what one would *not* want to do if the object were to evaluate an explanation of how variables relate to one another across cases of a social phenomenon. When the objective is to explain general phenomena, the causality implied by a theory of how variables relate to each other, thick analysis serves to distort and mislead. The individual nuances of a particular case are, of course, likely to be unique to that case. As such they may provide important clues about an individual episode (which is why thick analysis is so important for historical research on events or their sequences), but they are not part of the general explanation that the social scientist is interested in providing. Therefore, it is a mistake to take such idiosyncratic factors into account, except as control variables, as part of the social scientist's explanation or test of general hypotheses. One might wish to control for idiosyncratic factors, but to incorporate them into an explanation is to eschew the prospect of evaluating a general explanation for a class of events and, instead, to account for what happened in a singular event. As I noted at the outset, this is a worthy enterprise; it just is not the objective of social science as I understand it.

When the relationship between variables is apparently derived from observation, as in the case of the hypothesized association between military expenditures and declining hegemony, then it is important that we distinguish carefully between the evidence from which the inference is derived and evidence suitable for testing the proposition. To assess the credibility of a hypothesis it is necessary to acquire unbiased evidence that is independent of the statement of the hypothesis. Most statistical studies fail to do this, as also do most case analyses and historical assessments. In the case of quantitative analyses, it is common for the analyst to examine coefficients—that is, statistically derived associations— and to provide an explanation of why the coefficients have the signs they do. The analyst will frequently point to the statistical significance of the coefficients as evidence in support of the explanation he or she suggested. The coefficients, however, do not test the proposed explanation. After all, the coefficients are the basis on which the explanation was derived. Therefore, while a replication of the coefficients on an independent data set can serve as a test of the hypothesized explanation, the original data set cannot. Moreover, the pattern of coefficients must be tested in their *exactly specified form* on the second, independent data set. Here it is a mistake to take new factors into account, except as control variables, or to alter the precise specification of the relationship expected, because it is the relationship that is being tested. The object is not to maximize the 'goodness of fit' between data and test, but to evaluate the 'goodness of fit' between the stated hypothesis and the evidence.

The same is true for a qualitative analysis. If a hypothesis is derived from a case history, for instance, then that case history cannot possibly serve as an independent test of the hypothesis. Yet this is how much case-analytic literature proceeds. Here it is important to remember that the social scientist is generally interested in using the case to test some hypothesized relationship among variables, not to explain as accurately as possible the details of the particular case. The latter seems to me to be closer to the worthy objective of the historian.

3.5. Prediction and International Relations

Perhaps the most difficult test for any theory is to apply it to circumstances in which the outcome events have not yet occurred. Prediction is demanding exactly because the researcher cannot fit the argument to the known results. This is a fundamental difference between real-time prediction and so-called post-diction. Not surprisingly, few theories of international relations have been routinely exposed to the demands of real-time prediction. Some game-theoretic models, however, have been. Consequently, I turn to the evidence regarding predictability in this body of literature. Gaddis has already made the point that behavioural, structural, and psychological approaches to international relations do not appear to fare very well when it comes to prediction.[19] I disagree with the fervour with which some ring the death knell of a body of research that is in as early a stage of development as the literatures to which he refers; still it cannot be denied that these literatures do not thus far have an enviable record in producing reliable predictions. As with so many theoretically promising lines of enquiry, including, among others, research on artificial intelligence, social evolution, prospect theory, chaos models, and catastrophe models, I hope the research community has the patience to see these approaches more fully developed and more carefully tested before determining whether they should be discarded. At the moment all scientific enquiry into international relations is still in a nascent, immature state of development.

In discussing predictability in international relations I focus on my own research rather than that of others. As doing so is rather embarrassing for me, allow me to provide three reasons. First, I have set out to build a track record of real-time predictions. I view this as an important test of the credibility of my particular approach (or, for that matter, of any approach). Consequently, there are numerous published tests against which to assess accuracy. This is less true of other research programmes. Secondly, the predictions I have made over the years have been subjected to scrutiny and evaluation by others, making it possible for me to report scientific evidence developed by disinterested parties regarding the accuracy of literally thousands of predictions made using a model I developed. Finally, I do not want to risk mis-stating or misinterpreting the evidence for other research programmes that have been less explicitly focused on developing evidence about real-time predictions.

Let me begin with a little background. In 1981, A. F. K. Organski, Jacek Kugler, and I, together with non-academic business partners, established a company whose purpose was and is to utilize certain game theory models to make predictions about foreign and domestic policy decision-making, as well as to assist businesses in preparing to cope with the strategic environment within which they operate.[20] The details of the models have been presented in the academic literature,[21] and so I do not repeat them here. The models used by Decision Insights Incorporated have been applied to many more than a thousand specific policy questions within the context of US government intelligence assessments, as well as having been used in a wide variety of private-sector applications. Consequently, there is a substantial base of evidence on which to base an evaluation of the predictive accuracy of the method. The Central Intelligence Agency has specifically tested the reliability of predictions made using these models (called Policon in their business setting and called FACTIONS within the CIA) against alternative methods. In the pages that follow, I summarize their findings, as well as pointing to other evidence readily available in the political science literature.

In 1989 Dr Stanley Feder of the CIA gave a speech reported on by the *Salt Lake City Tribune* (1 March 1989) in which he said that 'the "Spatial Theory of Politics" has been gaining increased acceptance at the agency and has resulted in accurate predictions in 90 per cent of the situations in which it has been utilized.' In response to that article, Professor James Ray contacted Dr Feder to ascertain more about the claim of predictive accuracy. On 22 October 1991 Dr Feder wrote to Professor Ray, making the following statements:

The article correctly reports that I said that political forecasts made with a model based on the 'spatial theory of voting' were accurate about 90 per cent of the time. . . . The forecasting model about which I lectured at the University of Utah was developed by Professor Bruce Bueno de Mesquita, now at Stanford University. . . . Since 1982 a colleague and I have used Bruce's models to analyze and identify policy choice scenarios for over, 1,000 issues in scores of countries around the world. . . . At the end of 1985 we did a systematic analysis of the accuracy of forecasts made with the policy choice model. That assessment showed the policy decision model *with inputs provided by recognized country or issue experts* correctly identified the configurations of political forces that would lead to specific, well defined policy decisions over 90 per cent of the time. The model made it possible to identify easy-to-observe differences among alternative political situations and to forecast correctly the policy decision associated with each. . . . [The models] provide specific forecasts, something few other methods or pundits can do with more than a moderate degree of accuracy.

A similar view was expressed by Charles Buffalano, Deputy Director of Research at the Defense Advanced Research Projects Agency, in a letter dated 12 June 1984. He said:

One of the last (and most successful projects) in the political methodologies program was the expected utility theory work of Professor Bruce Bueno de Mesquita of the University of Rochester. The theory is both exploratory and predictive and has been rigorously evaluated through post-diction and in real time. Of all quantitative political forecasting methodologies of which I am aware, the expected utility work is the most useful to policy makers because it has the power to predict *specific* policies, their nuances, and ways in which they might be changed. (Emphasis in original)

Feder referred in his letter to a systematic assessment, but that assessment was not available at the time as it was classified. However, the analysis to which he referred was declassified in March 1993 and now is readily available. As that article contains many specific, detailed examples, I take the liberty of examining it in depth.[22]

What types of issues has the CIA analysed using the models offered by Decision Insights? A sample, taken from table 2 in the declassified article, includes the following questions:

- What policy is Egypt likely to adopt towards Israel?
- How fully will France participate in SDI?
- What is the Philippines likely to do about US bases?
- What stand will Pakistan take on the Soviet occupation of Afghanistan?
- How much is Mozambique likely to accommodate with the West?
- What policy will Beijing adopt toward Taiwan's role in the Asian Development Bank?
- How much support is South Yemen likely to give to the insurgency in North Yemen?
- What is the South Korean government likely to do about large-scale demonstrations?
- What will Japan's foreign trade policy look like?
- How much Islamization will the Sudanese government promote?
- What stand will the Mexican government take on official corruption?
- How much austerity can the Egyptian people tolerate?
- When will presidential elections be held in Brazil?
- How much autonomy will be granted to Sudan's southern province?
- What form will cooperation between France's Socialist president and the non-Socialist parliamentary majority take?
- How will a new head of government be chosen in Paraguay?
- How fair are elections likely to be in Panama?
- Can the Italian government be brought down over the wage indexing issue?
- How open will the political system be in Turkey?

As is evident from this sample, the modelling method is capable of addressing very diverse questions. Analysts have examined economic, social, and political issues; they have dealt with routine policy decisions and with questions threatening the very survival of particular regimes. Issues have spanned a wide variety of cultural settings, economic systems, and political systems.

The CIA assessment compares the forecasts based on this so-called expected utility model to those generated by more conventional approaches used by the intelligence community. Feder notes that the model makes specific, detailed predictions 60 per cent of the time. Such specificity is found only 33 per cent of the time in 'traditional' intelligence analyses.[23] He goes on to remark that 'while traditional and Policon-based analyses both scored well in terms of forecast accuracy, Policon offered greater detail and less vagueness,' noting further that the Policon predictions hit what he calls 'the bull's eye' twice as often as standard intelligence analyses. Perhaps more importantly, he observes that while the data for the model generally are obtained from area experts, the predictions frequently differ from those made by the very experts who provide the data. That is, the model is not a Delphi technique that asks experts what they believe will happen and then reports back that information. Rather, the experts provide best estimates of data on a few key variables (namely the relative potential influence of each player, the preferred outcome of each player, and the salience of the issue for each player); the model's method of processing that information, based on a spatial analysis within a limited information game setting, provides more reliable predictions than do the experts whose data have been used. Indeed, Feder reports that every time the model and the intelligence community made different predictions, the model proved correct, and he offers many detailed examples.[24]

The CIA assessment is not the only basis on which to evaluate predictions from this rational actor model. In our book *European Community Decision Making* Frans Stokman and I examine five competing models, including an improved version of the expected utility model (a more advanced, dynamic version of the static Policon/FACTIONS model examined by the CIA in 1987) as well as models developed by James Coleman, Frans Stokman, Reinier Van Osten, and Jan Van Den Bos.[25] All the models were tested against a common database of policy decisions taken by the European Community over the past few years. Statistical tests were used to compare the predictive accuracy of the alternative models relative to the now-known actual outcomes on the issues we examined. The various network analysis and log-rolling models of Coleman, Stokman, and others produced predicted values that, when compared to the actual outcomes, had probabilities of being correct varying from a low of 10 per cent to a high of 62 per cent. The expected utility model's results had a 97 per cent probability of being the same as the actual outcome on the same issues.

Additional evidence can be found in the published articles that contain predictions based on this rational actor model. In 1984, for instance, I predicted in print that Ayatollah Khomeini would be succeeded by Rafsanjani and Khameini as leaders of Iran following Khomeini's death.[26] At the time of publication, Khomeini had designated Ayatollah Montazari as his successor, so the predictions were contrary to expectations among Iran specialists. Khomeini died five years later, in 1989. He was succeeded by Rafsanjani and Khameini.

In 1991 Chae-Han Kim and I wrote an article in which we predicted that both North and South Korea would be admitted to the United Nations. At the time the prediction was made this was considered an unlikely outcome by Korea specialists. The article was actually published after the UN voted to admit both Koreas, but, as the editor notes in the journal, it was completed and accepted well before the UN decision took place. In 1982, in an interview with *US News and World Reports*, I predicted that a war between Iraq and Saudi Arabia or between Iraq and the Gulf states was likely within a few years after the Iran–Iraq War ended. Within three years of the end of that war, of course, Iraq invaded Kuwait (August 1990) and then fought the broader Gulf War in January–March 1991. That article also predicted that a war between Greece and Turkey over Cyprus was likely, an eventuality that has not materialized.[27] Other predictions over the years can be found in articles dealing with, among other topics, the prospects of a peace agreement in the Middle East, prospects of political instability in Italy over the budget deficit, the dispute over the Spratly Islands, the likelihood that Taiwan will develop a nuclear weapons capability, the outcome of the Maastricht referendum in Europe, and others.[28]

To be sure, some predictions have been wrong or inadequate. The Policon model successfully predicted the breaking away of several East European states from the Soviet Union, but failed to anticipate the fall of the Berlin Wall. The model predicted that the August 1991 Soviet coup would fail quickly and that the Soviet Union would unravel during the coming year, but it did not predict the earlier, dramatic policy shifts introduced by Mikhail Gorbachev. Indeed, the model was not applied to that situation so that such predictions could not have been made. That, of course, is an important difference between prediction and prophecy. The first step to a correct—or incorrect—prediction is to ask for one. Alas, no one sought from me or my colleagues any predictions about the demise of the Soviet Union before critical events had begun to unfold. More recently, the model incorrectly predicted that in July 1994 the UN Security Council would approve a resolution to permit Turkey to flush its oil pipeline pursuant to a return of Iraqi oil to the market. The decision to permit Turkey to flush the pipeline was made in August 1994, a month later than anticipated with the model. Still, the decision in the UN came as a surprise to the oil market when it happened. The price of West Texas Intermediate crude oil fell sharply during trading right after the UN vote, not before.

3.6. Limitations

The model just discussed has many limitations. It is inappropriate for predicting market-driven events not governed by political considerations. It is imprecise with respect to the exact timing of decisions and outcomes. (The model can have timing elements incorporated into it by including timing factors as contingencies in the way issues are constructed, but the model itself is imprecise with regard to time: the dynamics of the model indicate whether a decision is likely to be reached after very little give and take or after protracted negotiations, but it cannot say how long in clock-time a round of negotiations will last.) The model by itself is of limited value without the inputs from area or issue experts. They, of course, are quite valuable without the model. Still, the combination of the two is substantially more reliable than the experts alone. These limitations remind us that scientific and predictive approaches to international relations are in their infancy. Nevertheless, some encouragement can be taken from the fact that in many domains it has already proven possible to make detailed, fairly accurate predictions.

Game theory in general, while adding many benefits, also contributes add-itional limitations to the process of analysing international relations. Game-theoretic analyses are abstract. They represent great simplifications of reality. As such, it can be difficult to apply game-theoretic analyses convincingly to a precise study of an individual event. The use of game theory almost assures that a thick analysis cannot be undertaken. That is not surprising, given that the objective is to investigate the logic of general causation. Still, it is a limitation for those, like many historians, who want to understand the complexity of individual events. Game-theoretic analyses also tend not to be user-friendly. They often rely—sometimes to excess—on mathematical notation and a highly specialized vocab-ulary that is not readily accessible to scholars who use other methods. This is a fault more of game theory practitioners than of the theory itself. We can hope that in time game theorists will show greater sensitivity to the requirements of the audience. Ultimately, the objective is to understand key social phenomena, whether one is a game theorist, a behaviouralist, a historian, or an ordinary citizen concerned about our future welfare. Game theory should be a tool in the arsenal of those trying to advance understanding and not a barrier to all but a select few.

3.6. Conclusion

International relations is appropriately studied from a multiplicity of perspec-tives. Historical research sheds important light on how events unfold, providing detailed explanations of unique, significant circumstances. In this way historians contribute important knowledge about the causal mechanisms that transform international affairs.

Scientific approaches contribute knowledge that is complementary to the insights provided by historical research. Researchers in the scientific vein add insights into general causal mechanisms that operate to a greater or lesser extent across events. The observation, for instance, that liberal democratic states apparently do not fight wars with one another, coupled with logical explanations for why this might be so, exemplifies the scientific concern with how variables (government type, dispute resolution) relate to one another across time and space. Among the currently plausible explanations of the 'democratic peace' are arguments that depend on institutional constraints and others that depend on societal norms. Each dispute between states undoubtedly is influenced by factors other than institutional constraints or societal norms, while many disputes are likely to be given partial shape by these factors. In this way, the concerns of the historian and the social scientist together are likely to approximate a complete explanation of the democratic peace and resolutions of specific disputes.

A game-theoretic approach proves especially helpful in addressing certain common problems in research on international relations. These problems relate to endogenous choices, selection effects, independence between argument and evidence, and predictive ability. Of course, game theory is not necessary to deal with these issues and using game theory is no guarantee that the issues will be addressed successfully. But the use of game theory, especially with extensive form games, ensures that these issues must be addressed and facilitates seeing whether they have been attended to successfully or not. In the end, game theory is a mathematical theory, not a political theory. For the political analyst, game theory serves as a method, a tool for discovering the logical implications of the researcher's assumptions in an environment of strategic interaction. The political analyst must add a theory of politics to the game-theoretic framework to provide the content within which the logic of game theory is applied. No method, of course, can substitute for good theory and good empirical research; but scientific methods can make more transparent whether problems have been dealt with adequately or not.

There is a growing body of evidence that indicates that prediction is possible in international relations. Although the project is at a primitive state of development, some encouragement can be taken from the fact that a 90 per cent accuracy rate has been achieved in predicting significant events in real time during the 1980s and 1990s. Much remains to be done; but we can begin to see the possibilities of joining together the fruitful research of the historian and the social scientist as we progress towards a general understanding of international affairs.

Notes

1. A non-exhaustive sample of game-theoretic approaches to international relations includes S. J. Brams and D. M. Kilgour, *Game Theory and National Security* (New York, 1988); B. Bueno de Mesquita and D. Lalman, *War and Reason* (New Haven,

1992); J. Fearon, 'Domestic Political Audiences and the Escalation of International Disputes', *American Political Science Review*, 88 (1994), 577–92; W. Kim and J. D. Morrow, 'When Do Power Shifts Lead to War?', *American Journal of Political Science*, 36 (1992), 896–922; J. Kugler and F. Zagare, 'The Long-term Stability of Deterrence', *International Interactions*, 15 (1990), 255–78; J. D. Morrow, 'Modeling the Forms of International Cooperation', *International Organization*, 48 (1994), 387–423; M. Nicholson, *Formal Theories in International Relations* (Cambridge, 1989), E. Niou, P. Ordeshook, and G. Rose, *The Balance of Power* (Cambridge, 1989); R. Powell, *Nuclear Deterrence Theory* (Cambridge, 1990); R. H. Wagner, 'The Theory of Games and the Problem of International Cooperation', *American Political Science Review*, 77 (1983), 330–46.

2. An article especially relevant to the issues raised by J. Gaddis, 'International Relations Theory and the End of the Cold War', *International Security*, 17 (1992), is J. L. Ray and B. Russett, 'The Future as Arbiter of Theoretical Controversies: Predictions, Explanations, and the End of the Cold War,' paper presented at the Annual Meeting of the American Political Science Association, 1994.

3. I personally, however, am not convinced of that point of view. See B. Bueno de Mesquita, 'Counterfactuals and International Affairs: Some Insights from Game Theory', paper presented at the conference on Counterfactual Thought Experiments in World Politics (Berkeley, 13–15 Jan. 1995).

4. Examples of rational choice theories that, for instance, subsume cultural factors as different values on specific variables include A. Rabushka and K. Shepsle, *Politics in Plural Societies* (Columbus, Oh., 1972); B. Bueno de Mesquita, *The War Trap* (New Haven, 1981); R. Bates and B. Weingast, 'A New Comparative Politics: Integrating Rational Choice and Interpretivist Perspectives', unpublished manuscript (Stanford, Calif., Hoover Institution, 1994).

5. Path dependence is certainly evident, for instance, in the arguments of John Gilchrist, *The Church and Economic Activity in the Middle Ages* (New York, 1969); Giorgio de Santillana, *The Crime of Galileo* (Chicago, 1955); or William H. McNeill, *The Pursuit of Power* (Chicago, 1982), to name but a very few examples.

6. E. Kantorowicz, *The King's Two Bodies* (Princeton, 1957), 197.

7. Numerous other examples of the assumption that the evolving sequence of critical events is exogenous can be cited. A small sample representing otherwise quite different historical concerns includes J. Keegan, *A History of Warfare* (New York, 1993); J. W. Baldwin, *The Government of Philip Augustus* (Berkeley, 1986); and B. Tuchman, *The March of Folly* (New York, 1984). Some notable exceptions include F. Braudel, *The Structures of Everyday Life* (New York, 1981); W. McNeill, *Plagues and Peoples* (Garden City, NY, 1976); and A. Waldron, *The Great Wall of China* (Cambridge, 1990).

8. For interesting rational choice perspectives on this issue see J. Fearon, 'Ethnic Wars as a Commitment Problem', paper presented at the American Political Science Association Meeting (New York, 1994); F. Friedman, 'To Fight or Not to Fight: The Decision to Settle the Croat–Serb Conflict', Proceedings, Indiana Political Science Association Meetings (1994) and Bates and Weingast, 'A New Comparative Politics'.

9. Ibid.

10. The literature on biological evolution contains many examples of the application of

game theory and tests of its predictability in evolutionary settings. For an excellent summary of some biological games with evolutionarily stable strategies and supporting empirical evidence see D. P. Barash, *Sociobiology and Behavior*, 2nd edn. (New York, 1982). For a clear discussion of falsifiable hypotheses about predator-prey relations based on the axioms of evolutionary theory see A. Rosenberg, *The Structure of Biological Science* (Cambridge, 1985).

11. J. D. Morrow, 'A Twist of Truth: A Reexamination of the Effects of Arms Races on the Occurrence of War', *Journal of Conflict Resolution*, 33 (1989), 500–29, Keegan, *History of Warfare*.

12. Choosing efficiently, of course, does not mean that rational actors always end up with desirable results. As Creasy wisely observed, 'We thus learn not to judge of the wisdom of measures too exclusively by the results. We learn to apply the juster standard of seeing what the circumstances and the probabilities were that surrounded a statesman or a general at the time he decided on his plan': E. Creasy, *The Fifteen Decisive Battles of the World* (New York, 1851), preface. Creasy was a wise historian who provided an early warning against judging people's choices by outcomes rather than by what made most sense given what they knew at the time they had to choose. Hindsight is never available when decisions must be made; but fallible foresight is.

13. See K. Binmore, *Essays on the Foundations of Game Theory* (Cambridge, Mass., 1990); T. Sargent, *Bounded Rationality in Macroeconomics* (Oxford, 1993). For a fairly non-technical description of game theory concepts as applied to politics see J. D. Morrow, *Game Theory for Political Scientists* (Princeton, 1994).

14. A. Sabrosky, 'Interstate Alliances: Their Reliability and the Expansion of War', in J. D. Singer (ed.), *The Correlates of War II* (New York, 1980), reports that 73% of allies did not come to their partner's defence in the event of war between 1816 and 1965.

15. Some studies that explain alliance formation and that suggest reasons for variations in alliance reliability include J. D. Morrow, 'Alliances and Asymmetry', *American Journal of Political Science*, 35 (1991), 904–33; D. Lalman and D. Newman, 'Alliance Formation and National Security', *International Interactions*, 16 (1991), 239–54; B. Berkowitz, 'Realignment in International Treaty Organizations', *International Studies Quarterly*, 27 (1983), 77–96; M. Altfeld, 'The Decision to Ally', *Western Political Quarterly*, 37 (1984), 523–44; R. Siverson and J. King, 'Attributes of National Alliance Membership and War Participation, 1815–1965', *American Journal of Political Science*, 24 (1980), 1–15; M. Altfeld and B. Bueno de Mesquita, 'Choosing Sides in Wars', *International Studies Quarterly*, 23 (1979), 87–112; A. Smith, 'A Theory of Alliances', Ph.D. dissertation (University of Rochester, 1994).

16. J. Fearon, 'Counterfactuals and Hypothesis Testing in Political Science', *World Politics*, 43 (1991), 169–95.

17. P. Kennedy, *The Rise and Fall of the Great Powers* (New York, 1987); K. Waltz, 'The Stability of a Bipolar World', *Daedalus*, 93 (1964), 881–909; K. Waltz, *The Theory of International Politics* (Menlo Park, Calif., 1979); K. Deutsch and J. D. Singer, 'Multipolar Power Systems and International Stability,' *World Politics*, 16 (1964), 390–406.

18. I have supervised several undergraduate and graduate research projects designed to evaluate the association between defence expenditures and hegemonic decline.

Expected defence expenditures were based on various regression models that examine defence expenditures relative to measures of national wealth and, sometimes, the magnitude of external threats. Positive residuals were taken as indicators of 'large' defence expenditures, while negative residuals were taken to indicate 'small' expenditures. Despite variations in methods, variables, and data sets, none of my students has found support for a causal (or correlational) association that supports the hypothesis that larger than expected defence expenditures are associated with hegemonic decline.

19. J. Gaddis, 'International Relations Theory and the End of the Cold War', *International Security*, 17 (1992), 5–58.
20. I thank Decision Insights Incorporated, for permitting me to make use of some corporate materials.
21. See e.g. B. Bueno de Mesquita, D. Newman, and A. Rabushka, *Forecasting Political Events: The Future of Hong Kong* (New Haven, 1985); B. Bueno de Mesquita and F. Stokman, (eds.), *European Community Decision Making* (New Haven, 1994).
22. S. Feder, 'Factions and Policon: New Ways to Analyze Politics', *Studies in Intelligence*, Spring 1987, 41–57.
23. Ibid. 42.
24. Ibid. 57.
25. Bueno de Mesquita and Stokman, *European Community Decision Making*.
26. B. Bueno de Mesquita, 'Forecasting Policy Decisions: An Expected Utility Approach to Post-Khomeini Iran', *PS* (1984), 226–36. This article contains several other predictions that also have been borne out by subsequent events.
27. B. Bueno de Mesquita and C.-H. Kim, 'Prospects for a New Regional Order in Northeast Asia', *Korean Journal of Defense Analysis*, 3 (1991), 65–82; 'A Conversation with Bruce Bueno de Mesquita: Where War is Likely in the Next Year or Two', *US News and World Report*, 3 May 1982, 30.
28. B. Bueno de Mesquita and B. Berkowitz, 'How to Make a Lasting Peace in the Middle East', *Rochester Review* (1979), 12–18; B. Bueno de Mesquita, 'Multilateral Negotiations: A Spatial Analysis of the Arab–Israeli Dispute', *International Organization*, 44 (1990), 317–40; B. Bueno de Mesquita and D. Beck, 'Forecasting Policy Decisions: An Expected Utility Approach', in S. Andriole, ed., *Corporate Crisis Management* (Princeton, 1985), 103–22; S. Wu and B. Bueno de Mesquita, 'Assessing the Dispute in the South China Sea: A Model of China's Security Decision Making', *International Studies Quarterly*, 38 (1994), 379–403; J. D. Morrow, B. Bueno de Mesquita, and S. Wu, 'Forecasting the Risks of Nuclear Proliferation: Taiwan as an Illustration of the Method', *Security Studies*, 2 (1993), 311–31; A. F. K. Organski and B. Bueno de Mesquita, 'Forecasting the 1992 French Referendum', in R. Morgan, J. Lorentzen, and A. Leander (eds.), *New Diplomacy in the Post-Cold War World* (New York, 1993), 67–75. The executive summary of a study predicting the shape of a peace agreement in Cambodia is available from the author. That study was completed for the State Department in November 1989. The peace agreement was reached in November 1991 and fitted quite well with the predictions that were made, including the holding of successful elections and Khmer Rouge participation. Even days before the election these events were considered unlikely by the *New York Times*.

Further Reading

Bueno de Mesquita, Bruce, 'The Game of Conflict Interactions: A Research Program', in Joseph Berger and Morris Zelditch (eds.), *Theoretical Research Programs: Studies in Growth of Theories of Group Process* (Stanford, Calif., 1993). Applies the principles laid out in my chapter to an ongoing research programme in international relations.

—— and Lalman, David, *War and Reason* (New Haven, 1992). Uses game theory, statistical analysis, and historical case studies to develop and test propositions about the necessary and sufficient conditions for a variety of events in international affairs, while distinguishing between a realist view and a view that is attentive to the role of domestic politics in shaping foreign policy choices.

Fearon, James, 'Domestic Political Audiences and the Escalation of International Disputes', *American Political Science Review*, 88 (1994), 577–92. Uses game theory to show that states with larger political audience costs (e.g. democracies) are always less likely to back down in a crisis than are states with lower audience costs, which means that democracies can probably signal their intentions in a crisis more credibly than can non-democratic states, thereby facilitating the amelioration of the security dilemma between democratic states.

Morrow, James, 'Arms vs. Allies: Tradeoffs in the Search for Security', *International Organization*, 47 (1993), 207–33. Presents a simple argument of how domestic political factors affect choices between arming and forming alliances and examines the resultant propositions using three historical cases.

—— *Game Theory for Political Scientists* (Princeton, 1994). Explains game theory in non-technical terms and offers many examples of its use in studying problems in international relations.

Riker, William H., 'Political Science and Rational Choice', in J. Alt and K. Shepsle (eds.), *Perspectives on Positive Political Economy* (New York, 1990). Explains the logical foundations behind the use of a rational choice perspective in studying politics.

PART TWO: EXPLANATIONS OF INTERNATIONAL RELATIONS SINCE 1945

I The Cold War, the Superpowers, and Beyond

CHAPTER FOUR
THE COLD WAR IN EUROPE, 1945–1947: THREE APPROACHES

Anne Deighton

The collapse of the iron curtain and of the Soviet Union has made the study of the Cold War both easier and harder. It is easier because the Cold War can now be studied as a period of history which is not entangled with future policy judgements. But as Cold War fears and passions die, other frameworks for analysis and new concerns are taking over: the Cold War is relatively diminished as scholars reach beyond it to make sense of the century as a whole.[1] However, it was the major reference point for an understanding of the configuration of global power for over forty years after the Second World War, and its shadow lay across every significant area of international politics during that period. Key characteristics of the Cold War were a broadly bipolar global system typified by bloc-building; political rivalry and confrontation; military competition; and a lack of free economic interaction—all of which were marked by strong ideological distinctiveness.[2] How to analyse the transition from war to Cold War has been a major concern for historians, as well as for international relations specialists who have been able to deploy the slow and specific archival research of historians in their own quests for generalized explanation. The problems of when and where the Cold War began; whether it was inevitable; and why states and individuals acted in the way that they did, remain as important as ever.

This chapter takes as its starting-point the unconditional surrender by the Germans in May 1945. Europe had been liberated by the efforts of the Allies, led by the United States, the Soviet Union, and Britain. Some progress had been made at Bretton Woods, Dumbarton Oaks, Yalta, and San Francisco towards planning for the post-war world, but how the transition from war to peace would develop was unclear, and there already existed much tension among the Allies themselves. In Europe, millions had died (perhaps as many as twenty million in the Soviet Union alone) and the problem of refugees was acute. Food and fuel were in short supply; communications were disrupted. In the United States, by contrast, gross GNP had almost doubled during the war.

The Potsdam meeting between the US, Soviet, and British leaders in July and August 1945, failed to make headway beyond confirming principles for an Allied control of Germany that also included a French zone. The armies of liberation remained in Europe, and the future of East European countries, as well as Italy and the North African littoral, remained undecided. In August, the Americans detonated two atomic weapons over Hiroshima and Nagasaki, and the Japanese surrendered. During the autumn of 1945, foreign ministers again failed to make progress in their meetings, as tensions between the Soviet Union and Britain (especially over the Mediterranean), and between Britain and the United States (over atomic questions and aid), continued to mount.

The key areas of difficulty between the major victorious powers were control and management of the defeated and the liberated territories—Germany and Poland in particular—and aid for reconstruction. These problems were exacerbated by growing mutual suspicions, fuelled by a re-emergence of ideological distinctiveness between East and West that had been masked during the fight against Nazism and Fascism. By the spring of 1946, it was proving impossible to manage Germany cooperatively on a quadripartite basis, because of French and Russian obstructionism and because of divergent long-term aims on the part of the Allies; there was also rising tension over the eastern Mediterranean, Greece, and the Straits: national attitudes were hardening. Despite the successful completion of some of the minor peace treaties, it seemed clear by 1947 that the post-war world would be marked by East–West tension and conflict rather than by effective international cooperation. The Truman Doctrine rather than Roosevelt's Four Policemen characterized the emerging political climate. Further, deteriorating economic prospects, particularly in Britain, France, Italy, and the western zones of Germany, were exacerbated by the harsh winter of 1946–7. The Moscow foreign ministers' conference of March–April 1947 seemed to confirm the breakdown of Soviet–Western dialogue over Germany (especially on reparations), and was followed quickly by the US offer to Europe of long-term aid for reconstruction. By July 1947, when the Russians walked out of the Paris meeting and rejected Marshall Aid, British Foreign Secretary Ernest Bevin reflected that he was witnessing the birth of the Western bloc. The failure of the December foreign ministers' conference clinched the end of the wartime alliance; the rapid political and economic rehabilitation of the western zones in Germany, intensification of Soviet controls over eastern Europe, military alliance formation, and a furious international propaganda war all followed. By 1949, the Cold War was institutionalized by the European Recovery Programme, by the creation of NATO and of West and East Germany, and by the formation of blocs which gave broad if not total or willing allegiance to one superpower or the other: the diplomatic revolution known as the Cold War was in place.

From 1945 to 1947, the running sore of Germany—the division of which was the touchstone of the beginning and of the end of the Cold War—lay at the centre of the diplomatic and ideological hostilities. The problem of what to do about Germany aggravated other sources of conflict in Europe, in the Mediterranean, and in Asia. Yet the framework of 1945–7 is an arbitrary one: the origins of the Cold War reach back far beyond 1945, and the subsequent timing, focus, and intensity of the 'mischief' continually shifted, ebbed, and flowed.

In 1983 historian John Lewis Gaddis wrote a major article which drew together a mass of literature on the Cold War.[3] He highlighted three explanatory categories of Cold War scholarship: orthodoxy, revisionism, and post-revisionism. Orthodox writers included some Americans who were 'present at the creation', and many orthodox works were memoirs or eye-witness accounts. According to orthodox writers, the Soviet Union's desire to expand its borders and influence drove a reluctant United States to develop a defensive policy that would encircle the Soviet Union. Revisionists, however, levelled their criticisms at US capitalism and, in a mirror image of orthodoxy, blamed US rather than Soviet expansionism. Whether the focus was on economic expansionism and the desire to secure and retain markets, or devious atomic diplomacy, it was the capitalist, expansionist, and dishonest side of US policy that came under fire. Gaddis argued that these two antithetical approaches were synthesized by post-revisionism. The post-revisionists, who began writing during the period of detente after the trauma of the Vietnam War, sought not to attribute blame but rather to understand cause and process. They were helped by the increasing availability of primary source material to which early scholars had not generally had access. Gaddis's explanation of how Cold War scholarship had developed chronologically has given rise to a generation of scholars who have been happy to call themselves post-revisionist, although post-revisionism has subsequently been considered both as orthodoxy with documents and as revisionism without teeth.[4]

Meanwhile, the levels-of-analysis approach to the beginning of the Cold War has been the one generally adopted by international relations specialists, although little of the levels-of-analysis literature deals specifically with the beginnings of the Cold War. The three levels normally depicted are those of the international system, in which the existence of conflict is predicated on structural factors, although this does not elucidate the character and depth of conflict; the societal or state domestic level, at which the decision-making cultures and domestic pressures upon governments are examined; and the individual level, which reduces explanation to the specific—Stalin's paranoia, or Truman's fear of US isolationism, for example.[5]

This chapter will illuminate debates by historians and international relations specialists about the beginning of the Cold War by using three explanatory approaches which draw upon the historical and international relations frameworks referred to above. The three approaches adopted here focus respectively on the roles of ideology; decision-making factors; and geostrategic factors. They accommodate a conceptual distinction between the historian's interest in understanding and explaining specific problems and the international relations scholar's quest for generalized theoretical frameworks. None of these approaches alone offers a total explanation of the beginning of the Cold War. Ideological conflict was a powerful motivating factor, and was not just a cloak for power politics, although ideology was also used for advantage by politicians. Analysis of the perceptions and motivations of decision-makers who were frequently influenced as strongly by the domestic environment as by the international adds to our understanding of ideology, as well as casting doubt upon the inevitability of the Cold War. Geostrategic explanations, while important, can lead to a deterministic attitude to policy as being driven by analyses of power measurement.

3.1. Ideology

The concept of ideology is a highly contested area, and those who took the view that the Cold War was caused by ideological conflict used the word in a way that was intended to carry explicit criticism and delegitimization of the other side's system. Ideological explanation underpins Gaddis's two categories of orthodoxy and revisionism. Early Western analysts saw the Cold War as rooted in the Marxist–Leninist ideology of the Soviet Union.[6] The fact that the Soviet Union was a closed system fuelled fears about its intentions and drove both policy-makers and scholars to examine what they knew of Stalin's record and to draw their own conclusions. Stalin's Soviet Union was no 'ordinary' state, but a rogue, totalitarian state with which it was impossible to do normal diplomatic business. The particularly distasteful character of its leader combined with Communist ideology, which preached that the eventual collapse of capitalism and the triumph of socialism was historically inevitable, to entrench this view.

The misunderstandings and conflicts of 1945–6 were interpreted as giving credence to this stance. In particular, Soviet behaviour over eastern Europe and Germany after the Yalta conference, at Potsdam, and at the London Council of Foreign Ministers in the autumn of 1945 was held up as evidence not only that the Soviet Union was not prepared for the give and take of peacetime international politics, but that Soviet behaviour indicated a 'forward', aggressive stance which would undermine the status quo and lose it the goodwill of its former allies. Stalin's Bolshoi Theatre speech of 9 February 1946 came to be seen as the prime example of a public indication of a new offensive against the West, and the leader was seen as being impervious to external influences. The crises over the Straits and Iran only served to confirm Western fears. Kennan's famous 1946 telegram and the 'X' article of 1947, the dispatches of Frank Roberts from the British Embassy in Moscow, the establishment of the Russia Committee in Britain, and the language of the Truman Doctrine, Marshall's Harvard speech, and NSC 68 are all evidence of the ideological cast of Western policy in response to new threats. American principles of universalism, self-determination, equality, and freedom, together the antithesis of Marxism–Leninism, were part of the foreign-policy-making fabric of the United States, and were also drafted in to balance the ideological threat from the East.[7]

We are much less well informed about Soviet scholarly perceptions of the role of ideology, although it is clear that Soviet thinking also reflected deep fears about the nature of the capitalist system, the Western desire to encircle (contain) the Soviet Union, to weaken it rather than work with it, and ultimately to clear the decks for winning world domination.[8] These fears were tempered only by a belief that capitalism held within it the seeds of its own destruction.

The ideological approach taken by most writers between the 1940s and the 1960s reflected the general difficulties of writing contemporary history. Academic work became overshadowed by debates which frequently deployed a worst-case analysis of early Soviet policy. The mid-1940s was the first time that the United States had adopted a hands-on approach to peacetime international diplomacy. Hands-on diplomacy required the continuing consent both of public opinion and of Congress for expensive policies, from Marshall Aid to NSC 68 and beyond. In mirror fashion, the Soviet Union's new role demanded a continual domestic allegiance which was reflected in public statements and justifications that worked against any opening up of the Soviet system, or even of demobilization and reconstruction after the horrendous losses of the Second World War.

A less partisan way of approaching the ideological component of the Cold War is to interpret it as a system-level conflict with the main players in serious and very real competition at the state level and the societal–economic level. This implies that the post-war international system could not accommodate both communism and capitalism. There was, therefore, a dynamic of conflict in which one system had to prevail over the other, and the whole Cold War period was underpinned by continuous international social and ideological struggle. Ideology was far more than just an aspect of the domestic environment; it was at the centre of the conflict between the two blocs. In other words, the intrinsic nature of capitalism and of communism fuelled international as well as domestic conflict in the socio-economic, ideological–cultural, and military–political spheres.[9]

Ideology clearly has an important role in our understanding of the beginning of the Cold War. Both Marxism–Leninism and capitalist imperialism were perceived by their opponents as inherently expansionist, and both also came to be used as cohesion-building elements within states. But ideology alone is not a sufficient explanation for the beginning of the Cold War. Western states had found themselves in an ideological bind during the early stages of the Second World War, but the decision to work with Communists to defeat Nazis was nevertheless made, as was the supremely 'realist' percentages agreement struck between Churchill and Stalin in 1944. Ideological factors alone do not explain why the period after 1945, rather than that after 1917, marked the beginning of what we call the Cold War. Moreover, ideological conflict tells us very little about where the Cold War began or the diplomatic complexities of the first eighteen months immediately following the end of the Second World War. It is to the internal functioning of the state and of society, to the domestic environment, and to decision-making factors in particular that we should now turn, as the interweaving of domestic and international history is another remarkable feature of the Cold War.

3.2. Decision-making Factors

The second perspective lies at the level of the domestic environment of state actors. Research on foreign policy analysis, the cybernetics of decision-making, perception and misperception, belief systems and operational codes, has not been exclusively concerned with the beginnings of the Cold War, but is relevant to the decision-making environment in which Cold War decisions were made. Such work, by breaking down the assumption that governments respond in a rational and coherent fashion to clearly understood international problems, reinforces a view that the transition from war to Cold War was uncertain and not inevitable, incremental and not predetermined. Decisions taken were not simply driven by inexorable external forces.

Work on perception and misperception as determining factors in decision-makers' international political choices thus raises many new questions about the years 1945–7, in particular the question about whether what happened was inevitable.[10] Scholars who work on perception emphasize the possibilities of incremental processes of misperception among actors. For example, the predisposition of individuals to the processing of certain ideas and actions in the international sphere through a so-called operational code helps in arriving at an understanding of how actions were interpreted and decisions reached.[11] At the Potsdam conference there appeared to be a strong disposition towards distrust of the Soviet Union by the US and British teams. This, coupled with alarming reports on the need to rehabilitate Germany, particularly to address the acute need of

German coal for European reconstruction, and fears about what the Soviet Union wanted in Germany, had a powerful influence on the perceptions of the US and British teams at Potsdam. For their part, the Soviet team were worried about any planning for German recovery before the scores of the war were settled, so that attempts at rehabilitation by the British and US delegations were perceived as a retrograde step from military victory over the Germans. Soviet 'ideological romanticism' may well have contributed to an assumption that they would continue to be warmly welcomed as 'liberators' in eastern Europe, and they therefore lacked a clear early policy towards their zone, to Germany as a whole, or to the region.[12] Thus, while it is often argued that the Potsdam conference inevitably reinforced the geopolitical status quo over Germany that had been arrived at by May 1945, it is arguable that the resulting zonal demarcation, regional divisions, and accompanying antagonism were not all necessarily inevitable.

An engrossing study which combines historical and social–psychological interpretations is that by Deborah Welch Larson, who draws out her ideas on containment with new intellectual tools drawn from the discipline of social psychology. Larson's work focuses directly upon the beginnings of the Cold War, and she deploys detailed archival material to elaborate her arguments. Among her many insights are the reflection that enormous uncertainty dominated US decision-making during the late 1940s, which contradicts the view that there was a coherence or inevitability in US foreign policy-making. US policy shifts were gradual and ragged, and she points out that if policy-makers interpret events differently, then state behaviour cannot be explained solely as a response to geopolitical restraints. She paints convincing portraits of the contrasting world-views of Byrnes, Acheson, and Truman which reveal their different perceptions of the Soviet Union and shows how these influenced particular policy outcomes. She argues that many historians have imposed retrospectively and inaccurately a coherence on American foreign policy that did not exist at the time.[13] Equivalent work on the Soviet Union, and in particular on the personality and aims of Stalin, is long overdue.

The 'lessons of the past' that decision-makers carry with them, from a fear of appearing to appease hostile powers to stereotypical images of the totalitarian 'enemy', also bring new insights into decision-makers' mindsets. As the Cold War began, analogies between Nazi totalitarianism and Communism were frequently drawn. As President Truman said, 'A totalitarian state is no different whether you call it Nazi, Fascist, Communist or Franco Spain.'[14] The offensive comparison between Stalin and Hitler made by the British Foreign Secretary Ernest Bevin to the Soviet Foreign Minister Molotov during the September 1945 Council of Foreign Ministers severely soured their already fragile relationship, but was indicative of how deeply Bevin's mindset was influenced by the experience of two wars against the Germans, a distrust of Communism that stretched back to the 1920s, and a personal dislike of Molotov.[15] 'Lessons of the past' apply to key political leaders and to whole bureaucracies, which necessarily carry a stronger collective memory than do Cabinets or parties in power.[16]

If the processes that inform decision-making add to our understanding of Cold War beginnings, so do analyses which set those policies within the context of appealing to domestic audiences and, indeed, of maintaining and strengthening loyalty within the state. The nature of early Cold War decisions and the timing of policy shifts can be explained in part by domestic political constraints. Within the United Kingdom, it is possible to argue that until the Soviet Union had been demonized in the public's mind, that is by mid-1947, it was not possible to carry through overtly anti-Soviet policies, in part because admiration of the Soviet Union's war effort remained a potent force in public opinion. The French dilemma over its Soviet policy made inevitable a similar 'dual policy' because indigenous support for Communism in France remained high throughout this period. Likewise, the debate about the Truman Doctrine shows that it was written with appeal to a domestic audience in mind—'the greatest selling job in US history'—rather than in consideration of the impact that such language would make upon the Soviet Union.[17] Thus timing and presentation, as well as content of policy, may be explained by domestic political considerations. What was going on within the state (or, later, within a bloc) was as important to the development of the Cold War as the relations among states. An elaborate exposition of this view is the 'two dungeons' thesis, in which it is claimed that internalist factors played the key part in determining foreign policy.[18]

The importance of the domestic context of policy has also been emphasized, but in a completely different way, in the work of some American economic historians who draw upon the United States' own economic history, in particular its experiences after the First World War, and the New Deal, thus avoiding questions about the beginning of the Cold War. In this context 'the years 1947–54 appear in retrospect as a historical transition', as they closed an interval of turmoil and international instability that had begun before the First World War, 'the longest period of crisis since the seventeenth century'.[19] Corporatism and geo-economics drive analyses that assume that the United States *had* to manage the global economic system as the careers of American political leaders depended upon being able to deliver continued growth, prosperity, and stability at home after 1945. It was this domestic demand that led the United States into its postwar role of leadership and hegemony. This is the position taken by Michael Hogan, whose study roots the Marshall Plan in its American domestic environment 'as an outgrowth of organizational, economic and political forces that had been working to forge an American brand of corporatism long before the second postwar era'.[20] The effect of the work of these specialists, although driven by the domestic economic environment, ironically comes close to a geostrategic argument about the inevitability and necessity of a world role for the United States.

3.3. Geostrategic Factors

By 1945 the Versailles system in eastern Europe had collapsed; there was a power vacuum created by the Allied decision to insist upon the unconditional surrender of Germany and Japan; Britain was bankrupt and unable to finance its global commitments. This disruption of the inter-war and wartime balance of power marks a decisive moment for geopolitical accounts of the period. Although there had been intense ideological conflict between capitalism and Marxism–Leninism since 1917, the Cold War as a phenomenon of international politics emerged with the dislocation of old power centres after the Second World War.

Realists and neorealists are not primarily concerned with causality and process, but concentrate on interests and outcomes and their relationship to the structure of the international system. They deliberately seek to play down the ideological and to emphasize concepts of power and balance. Hans Morgenthau's *Politics among Nations: The Struggle for Power and Peace* provided, in its many editions, a realist theory of international politics that avoided equating the foreign policies of statesmen with their ideological beliefs, or deducing the former from the latter, although many statesmen may 'make a habit of presenting their foreign policies in terms of their philosophic and political sympathies in order to gain support for them'. International politics was, starkly, about the maximizing of power by individual states. So at the end of the Second World War, the superpowers 'faced each other like two fighters in a short and narrow lane', or like 'a scorpion and a tarantula together in a bottle'.[21]

Neorealists also emphasize the salience of state power. Kenneth Waltz views the actions of the state as overwhelmingly determined by the system itself; for, as water seeks to find its own level, so states will seek to find as secure a place as they can in an anarchic international system. His analysis fits well with a view of a tight, bipolar global system. As soon as their wartime alliance ended, the great powers became locked in a Cold War, for each was bound to focus its fears on the other, and to impute offensive intentions even to defensive measures. International conflict was thus structurally ordained.[22] Many historians have also emphasized the structural relationship between the two superpowers and their allies in the international system. Anton DePorte places the origins of the Cold War in the context of policy towards Germany and argues that the demand for unconditional surrender created a power vacuum subsequently filled by the new powers: 'There should have been no need to postulate demon motivations on either side to account for the friction which developed between them as they undertook to define their relations with each other.'[23] The by-product of their rivalry was a divided Europe.

John Lewis Gaddis's work on the Cold War has been deeply influential but, in part because his work is constantly developing and not merely seeking to defend a position, it is hard to place. On the specific issue of the beginnings of the Cold War, Gaddis has shown a remarkable ability to break down some of the assumptions about the importance of 1945, looking as he does back to the early 1940s and forward to the Korean War, as well as inwards into the structure of American political life, to build a more subtle presentation of the shifts in the international system. In the 1980s his interest in Soviet imperialism and the inevitable strategic response of US containment policies indicated a drift away from the concentration on the pressures of domestic policies that marked his *The United States and the Origins of the Cold War*. His later work, of which *The Long Peace* is the most striking example, has, with a sophisticated neorealist understanding of the issues, reworked the traditionalist standpoint into a geo-political narrative centred on the concept of security.[24] But more recently Gaddis argued that the way the Cold War ended was directly related to the way it began. He has now travelled full circle to an ideological position, apparently sidestep-ping the geopolitical and domestic considerations on which he worked for twenty years, arguing that the way the Cold War ended serves 'to remind us of a fact that many of us had become too sophisticated to see, which is that the Cold War really was about the imposition of autocracy and the denial of freedom'.[25]

Other writers who emphasize geopolitical factors assume that unavoidable economic imperatives—the economic foundations of geopolitical success—determined early post-war American policy, which gives reason to assign as much of the responsibility for the origins of the Cold War to the United States as to the Soviet Union. Melvyn Leffler dwells on the long-term US policy of coopting friendly powers in the Eurasian heartland. American leaders thought that 'if the United States could successfully co-opt the industrial core of Eurasia, it would establish a magnet to attract the Kremlin's satellites westward . . . How-ever nastily the Soviets might respond in the short run, they would bow to power realities in the long run. They would learn to acclimatize themselves to a configuration of power that ensured America's preponderance.' Over Europe, diplomatic alternatives were therefore not open to the United States, although whether Soviet fears about the post-war world would have been alleviated by a sensible deal on reparations remains one of the interesting counterfactual ques-tions about the years 1945–7.[26]

Neorealism is deterministic: the Cold War bipolar divide was inevitable and ideology was irrelevant to the new balance within the system. This proposition is suggestive, simple, parsimonious, and elegant. The conflict created by the need to fill the vacuum left by the collapse of German power was indeed a key feature of the beginning of the Cold War, although, of course, this proposition is not pertinent in the case of the collapse of Japan. Neorealism is however inadequate for the student of the years 1945–7 as neorealist analysis is weakest at explaining change. It does not, for example, address the significant problem about whether dividing Germany up actually influenced the future stability of the bipolar system, or the question whether the outcome for the next forty years would have been the same if one side or the other had gained complete control of the collapsed unit. It implies that the division of Germany and Europe was inevitable. Further, it does not deal with the real fear of Germany's power that continued to influence international policies after 1945. Neorealists also fail to explain how a unit's own, or its adversary's, power is perceived and measured, an important question for the European great powers as well as the superpowers; nor do they adequately address the question of the relations between power, influence, capability, and political will. They give little space to the role and perceptions of the introduction of nuclear weaponry.[27] In short, neorealism is strong on structures but weak on politics.

Neorealism in general pays scant attention to the policies of lesser powers, beyond their desires to form alliances with those powers that would bring them the most security. The role of West European countries in the emerging Cold War is now being extensively examined by historians. Such work approaches the beginnings of the Cold War from a non-American perspective and raises many new issues about the interactions between old and new great powers in a changing international system, concerning for example whether major policy errors were made, whether conflicts in particular areas were causes or consequences of superpower disharmony, and whether different aspects of the Cold War coincide chronologically. This new perspective has also focused on the kind of relationship that the smaller countries themselves wished to create with the United States, with the Soviet Union, and with East European countries, rather than seeing them solely as objects of US and Soviet policy. It also emphasizes the distinctions made between economic, military, and political intentions, as well as the relationship between the superpowers, and their attitudes to Germany.[28]

Some of this scholarship fits well with the overall assumptions about bloc-formation, although it gives a more nuanced picture of how this process took place, emphasizing uncertainty and contingencies in the policies of all players. The drive for nuclear weaponry in Britain and France displayed a continued quest for national power and quasi-independence as well as a desire to enhance security within an alliance system. Work on the 'third force' concept also undermines some of the conceptual simplicity of neorealism and of US-dominated geostrategic work. In the late 1940s, the idea of a third force first embraced the hope that socialists in Europe could form a distinct grouping between Communism and capitalism, then shifted to embody transient aspirations to create a third world power by combining the imperial inheritance of Britain and France. It also existed as an undercurrent in Western Europe during the debate on European integration in the 1950s.[29]

One example will show how nuanced policies were at the beginning of the Cold War. It is now clear that Britain played a major role in the years between 1945 and 1947, not least because British decision-makers were aware of the many conflicting opinions about the direction post-war policy should take. The British kept up the pressure for the radical policy of a divided Germany, thinking in geopolitical terms that western Germany would, with US backing, be able to contribute to a very favourable balance of power against the Soviet Union in Europe. This was an audacious policy, because the post-war tensions between the United States and Britain were considerable, exemplified by the row over the December 1945 loan and the McMahon Act of 1946. Further, the Cold War began for Britain before it began for the United States; Britain was the prime focus of hostile diplomacy from the Soviet Union during the early post-war months. Despite this, Bevin concurrently retained very strong ideas about securing a post-war role for Britain as a third force, a great power occupying 'the middle of the planet', despite the country's bankruptcy, even if this stance fuelled more hostility and fear of residual British imperialism.

3.4. The End of the Cold War and the Beginning of the Cold War

The *Wende* of 1989–91 threw down a major intellectual challenge to both historians and international relations scholars. Thereafter, even were a perceived overriding threat to international security from Russia to return, this would not mean that the Cold War had also returned, for its origins, ideological base, geopolitical and psychological environment, and technological characteristics would not be the same. There have been many publications about the end of the Cold War, reminiscent in a way of the rash of American analyses in the 1950s on the early Cold War. Lively debate has taken place both on the interface between policy and scholarship (although some international relations scholars have run for cover—caught out like everyone else by the capacity of history to surprise) and on an examination of how the end of the Cold War has affected earlier historical research.[30] Yet it is not at all clear that the way in which the Cold War ended has definitively illuminated the debate about its beginnings, although its end has changed the debate over how to date the Cold War and whether the period 1917–91 (the broadest option), or 1948–53 (the narrowest) is the more accurate. The labels of first and second Cold Wars have often been used conventionally since the mid-1980s, but these categories now need refinement, as the first and second Cold Wars begin to look more like jousts in one long tournament than they did a decade ago.[31]

It is a quest for an elusive goal to try to achieve an all-embracing theoretical or historical explanation of the beginnings of the Cold War. No one of the three sets of factors adopted here, whether ideological, decision-making, or geopolitical, is, alone, a sufficient explanation. It is clear that ideological factors were perceived to be important to policy-makers still reeling from the onslaught upon Nazism and Fascism, and ideological competition seeped into political relations within and between the blocs. Geopolitical considerations consciously and unconsciously drove much policy-making, although neorealism tells us little about which events were of most importance in a chronologically narrow but politically important period of history. Studies of the actions of and influences upon decision-makers bring challenging perspectives that, with their proximity to post-revisionist writing, enable historians to disaggregate monolithic approaches to policy decisions. The three approaches are not incompatible with one another, and are open-ended enough to continue to illuminate historical research. But for historians, the sheer quantity of new archival material from Eastern archives, while changing some preconceptions, now ironically also raises questions about whether a total international history that recounts and explains the beginning of the Cold War could be written at all, unless by a multilingual team of historians.[32] Both the end of the Cold War itself and historical research since then have thus complicated rather than simplified our interpretations of the beginning of the Cold War. This should in time stimulate a dynamic research relationship between historians and international relations scholars. Nevertheless, it may well also be that the Cold War itself will increasingly be seen as what D. C. Watt has mischievously called 'the invention of categories based on the use of metaphors, rather than the study of reality'.[33] Meanwhile, the debate on beginnings continues.

Chronology

Aug.–Oct. 1944	Dumbarton Oaks conference on a United Nations
Sept. 1944	Quebec conference on Germany
Oct. 1944	'Percentages' agreement between Stalin and Churchill on Eastern Europe
Feb. 1945	Yalta conference (USA, UK, Soviet Union)
Apr. 1945	Death of Roosevelt; Truman President of USA

May 1945	End of war in Europe; unconditional surrender to Allies; four-power Allied control over Germany and Austria
June 1945	UN charter signed in San Francisco
July–Aug. 1945	Potsdam conference (USA, UK, Soviet Union)
July 1945	Attlee becomes UK Prime Minister
Aug. 1945	Atomic bombs dropped on Hiroshima and Nagasaki; Japan capitulates
Sept. 1945	Fourth Republic established in France
Sept.–Oct. 1945	Council of foreign ministers (London)
Dec. 1945	Foreign ministers' meeting (Moscow)
Mar. 1946	Churchill's 'iron curtain' speech in Fulton, Mo.
Mar. 1946	Straits and Azerbaijan crises
Apr. 1946	Socialist/Communist parties merge in Soviet German zone
Apr.–July 1946	Council of foreign ministers (Paris)
Sept. 1946	US Secretary of State Byrnes' Stuttgart speech
Dec. 1946	Council of foreign ministers (New York)
Jan. 1947	UK/US zones in Germany merged
Feb. 1947	Peripheral peace treaties signed
Mar. 1947	Treaty of Dunkirk (UK/France)
Mar. 1947	Truman Doctrine
Mar.–Apr. 1947	Council of foreign ministers (Moscow)
June 1947	Secretary of State George Marshall's 'Marshall Aid' speech
July 1947	Soviet walk-out from Marshall Aid talks
Oct. 1947	Creation of Cominform
Nov.–Dec. 1947	Council of foreign ministers (London)
Feb. 1948	Czech coup
Mar. 1948	Brussels Treaty signed between UK, France, Benelux
Apr. 1948	Organization of European Economic Cooperation established to administer Marshall Aid

Notes

1. See e.g. Eric Hobsbawm, *Age of Extremes: The Short Twentieth Century, 1914–1991* (London, 1994); John Gerard Ruggie, 'Territoriality and Beyond: Problematizing Modernity in International Relations', *International Organization*, 47/1 (Winter 1993), 139–73.
2. This definition does not deny other themes of the international politics of these years, notably decolonization, nationalism, the expansion of the size of economic enterprises, and the salience of other great powers (particularly China) in world politics.

3. John Lewis Gaddis, 'The Emerging Post-revisionist Thesis on the Origins of the Cold War', *Diplomatic History*, 7 (Summer 1983).

4. See the symposium on the origins of the Cold War, *Diplomatic History*, 17/2 (1993).

5. Joseph S. Nye, Jr., *Understanding International Conflicts: An Introduction to Theory and History* (New York, 1993), 110–12; Kenneth Waltz, *Man, the State and War* (New York, 1959); see also J. David Singer, 'The Level of Analysis Problem in International Relations', in Klaus Knorr and Sidney Verba (eds.), *The International System: Theoretical Essays* (Princeton, 1961).

6. For a bibliographic list see Anne Deighton, *The Impossible Peace: Britain, the Division of Germany and the Origins of the Cold War* (Oxford, 1990; pb 1993), 1–3.

7. See e.g. US Senate Committee on Foreign Relations on the North Atlantic Treaty, 81st Congress, 1st Session (Washington, 1949), part 1, 97, in which NATO was described as seeking to shift not the balance of power, but the balance of principle.

8. The best recent overview of Soviet thinking is Vladislav Zubok and Constantine Pleshakov, 'The Soviet Union', in David Reynolds (ed.), *The Origins of the Cold War in Europe* (New Haven, 1994), 53–76. They state that 'there is no proper historiography of the Cold War in Russia': 55. Nikolai Novikov, 'US Foreign Policy in the Postwar Period', 27 Sept. 1946, reproduced in *International Affairs* (Moscow), 12 (Dec. 1990), 123–9.

9. Fred Halliday, *Rethinking International Relations* (London, 1994).

10. Robert Jervis, *Perception and Misperception in International Politics* (Princeton, 1976); John D. Steinbruner, *The Cybernetic Theory of Decision* (Princeton, 1974); Irving L. Janis, *Crucial Decisions: Leadership in Policy-making and Crisis Management* (London, 1989).

11. Alexander George, 'The Operational Code: A Neglected Factor in the Study of Political Decision-making', *International Studies Quarterly*, 12 (1969); Daniel Yergin, *The Shattered Peace: The Origins of the Cold War and the National Security State* (Boston, 1977), on US decision-makers' mindsets which Yergin called the Riga and Yalta axioms; see also Avi Shlaim, 'Truman's Belief System', in Richard Little and Steve Smith (eds.), *Belief Systems and International Relations* (Padstow, 1988).

12. John Lewis Gaddis, 'Rethinking Cold War History', The Klaus Knorr Memorial Lecture in International Security (Center of International Studies, Princeton University, 8 Dec. 1994).

13. Deborah Welch Larson, *Origins of Containment: A Psychological Explanation* (Princeton, 1985), 329, 355. The introduction lucidly explains her approach.

14. Margaret Truman, *Harry S. Truman* (New York, 1973), 359–60; Beatrice Heuser, 'Stalin as Hitler's Successor: Western Interpretations of the Soviet Threat', in Beatrice Heuser and Robert O'Neill (eds.), *Securing Peace in Europe, 1945–62* (London, 1992).

15. Alan Bullock, *Ernest Bevin: Foreign Secretary, 1945–1951* (London, 1983), 90, 105–6.

16. Richard Neustadt and Ernest R. May, *Thinking in Time: The Uses of History for Decision-makers* (New York, 1986).

17. Melvyn Leffler, *A Preponderance of Power: National Security, the Truman Administration and the Cold War* (Stanford, Calif., 1992), 145–6.

18. Noam Chomsky, *Towards a New Cold War* (New York, 1982).

19. Charles Maier, 'The Presence of the Superpowers in Europe (1946–54): An Overview', in Antonio Varsori (ed.), *Europe 1945–1990s: The End of an Era?* (London, 1994), 142. See also Charles Maier, 'The Two Postwar Eras and the Conditions for Stability in Twentieth Century Western Europe', *American Historical Review*, 86 (Spring, 1981); Michael Hogan, *The Marshall Plan: America, Britain and the Reconstruction of Western Europe, 1947–1952* (Cambridge, 1987); Robert A. Pollard, *Economic Security and the Origins of the Cold War, 1945–1950* (New York, 1985).

20. Hogan, *The Marshall Plan*, xii.

21. Hans J. Morgenthau, *Politics among Nations: The Struggle for Power and Peace* (New York, 1973 edn.), 688, 352–3 (first publ. 1948). See also Louis Halle, *The Cold War as History* (London, 1967); Henry Kissinger, *Diplomacy* (New York, 1994), ch. 17.

22. Kenneth Waltz, *Theory of International Politics* (New York, 1979); Glenn H. Snyder and Paul Diesing (eds.), *Conflict among Nations: Bargaining, Decision Making and System Structure in International Crises* (Princeton, 1977), esp. 420.

23. A. W. DePorte, *Europe between the Superpowers: The Enduring Balance* (New Haven, 1979; 2nd edn 1986), 59.

24. John Lewis Gaddis, *The United States and the Origins of the Cold War, 1944–1947* (New York, 1972); 'Was the Truman Doctrine a Real Turning Point?', *Foreign Affairs*, 52 (1974); *Strategies of Containment* (New York, 1982); *The Long Peace: Inquiries into the History of the Cold War* (New York, 1987).

25. John Lewis Gaddis, 'The Cold War, the Long Peace and the Future', in Michael J. Hogan (ed.), *The End of the Cold War: Its Meaning and Implications* (Cambridge, 1992), 24, 28.

26. Leffler, *Preponderance of Power*, 501, 506, 515. On reparations see Anders Stephanson, *Kennan and the Art of Foreign Policy* (Cambridge, Mass., 1989). For the difficulties involved in 'placing' Leffler's work see the perceptive review article by Lynn Eden, 'The End of US Cold War History?', *International Security*, 18/1 (Summer 1993), 174–207.

27. John Lewis Gaddis, 'Great Illusions, the Long Peace and the Future', in Gaddis (ed.), *The United States and the End of the Cold War: Implications, Reconsiderations, Provocations* (New York, 1992), argues that this is rightly so: 173. See however David Holloway, *Stalin and the Bomb* (New Haven and London, 1994), who argues that the events of August 1945 led to a quicker breakdown of the wartime alliance. For a theoretically based realist critique of neorealism and the early Cold War see R. Harrison Wagner, 'What was Bipolarity?', *International Organisation*, 10/47 (Winter 1993), 77–105.

28. See e.g. Geir Lundestad, 'Empire by Invitation? The United States and Western Europe, 1945–1952', *Journal of Peace Research*, 23 (Sept. 1986), 263–77; Ennio di Nolfo (ed.), *L'Italia e la politica di Potenza in Europa, 1945–1950* (Milan, 1988); Deighton, *The Impossible Peace*; Olaf Riste (ed.), *Western Security: The Formative Years* (New York, 1985); Lawrence Aronsen and Martin Kitchen, *The Origins of the Cold War in Comparative Perspective: American, British and Canadian Relations with the Soviet Union, 1941–1948* (London, 1988). Historians await similar new work from East–Central Europe.

29. Wilfried Loth, *The Division of the World* (London, 1988); John Young and John Kent, 'British Policy Overseas: The Third Force and the Origins of NATO—In Search of a New Perspective', in Heuser and O'Neill (eds.), *Securing Peace in Europe*; René Girault, 'On the Power of Old and New in Europe', in Ennio di Nolfo (ed.), *Power in Europe? II, 1952–1957* (Berlin, 1992), 46–49, 553–61; Philippe Vial and Claude d'Abzac Epezy, 'In Search of a European Consciousness: French Military Elites and the Idea of Europe, 1947–54', in Anne Deighton (ed.), *Building Postwar Europe: National Decision-makers and European Institutions, 1948–1963* (London, 1995).

30. e.g. Hogan, *The End of the Cold War*; Gaddis, *United States and the End of the Cold War*; Reynolds, *Origins of the Cold War in Europe*; Vojtech Mastny, 'Europe in the Aftermath of the Second World War (1945–7): An Overview', in Antonio Varsori (ed.), *Europe 1945–1990s: The End of an Era?* (London, 1994).

31. Fred Halliday, *The Making of the Second Cold War* (London, 1983); Anne Deighton (ed.), *Britain and the First Cold War* (London, 1990); David Reynolds, 'Introduction', in Reynolds (ed.), *Origins of the Cold War in Europe*, 2.

32. The Cold War International History Project, run from the Woodrow Wilson International Center for Scholars, Washington, DC, USA, has the largest collection of publications drawn from recently released material.

33. D. C. Watt, 'Notes Towards a Synthesis', in Norbert Wiggershaus and Roland G. Foerster (eds.), *The Western Security Community, 1948–1950* (Oxford, 1993), 422.

Further Reading

DEIGHTON, ANNE, *The Impossible Peace: Britain, the Division of Germany and the Origins of the Cold War* (Oxford, 1990; pb 1993).

DEPORTE, A. W., *Europe between the Superpowers: The Enduring Balance*, 2nd edn (New Haven, 1986).

HALLIDAY, FRED, *Rethinking International Relations* (London, 1994), ch. 8.

HOLLOWAY, DAVID, *Stalin and the Bomb* (New Haven, 1994).

LARSON, DEBORAH WELCH, *Origins of Containment: A Psychological Explanation* (Princeton, 1985).

LEFFLER, MELVYN, *A Preponderance of Power: National Security, the Truman Administration and the Cold War* (Stanford, Calif., 1992).

REYNOLDS, DAVID (ed.), *The Origins of the Cold War in Europe* (New Haven, 1994).

WALTZ, KENNETH, *Theory of International Politics* (New York, 1979).

CHAPTER FIVE

THE SOVIET UNION AND EASTERN EUROPE: SPHERES OF INFLUENCE

Mark Kramer

This chapter will examine Soviet policy toward Eastern Europe from 1945, when the Soviet Union emerged as the dominant power in the region, until 1991, when the last vestiges of Soviet hegemony were dissolved.[1] The chapter is divided into six sections. The first section will lay out an analytical framework for the rest of the chapter. The second will provide a brief historical overview of Soviet–East European relations between 1945 and 1985. The third will examine the military, political, and economic factors that contributed to Soviet hegemony in Eastern Europe. The fourth will discuss the limits of Soviet power in Eastern Europe between 1945 and 1985. The fifth will highlight the fundamental changes in Soviet–East European relations after 1985. The final part will determine what broad analytical conclusions can be drawn from these four-and-a-half decades of Soviet–East European relations.

5.1. Spheres of Influence and Asymmetrical Power Relationships

For analytical purposes, it is useful to compare the post-war Soviet–East European relationship with other highly unequal inter-state relationships that have existed in various parts of the world. One way of approaching this task might be through the use of 'dependency theory', a neo-Marxist perspective developed in the 1970s as an outgrowth of earlier theories of economic imperialism.[2] The original proponents of dependency theory were interested solely in studying relationships between developed capitalist states and underdeveloped countries (e.g.

US–Latin American relations), rather than devising a comparative framework that would also encompass relations among Communist states. Subsequently, a few scholars specializing in the study of Communist systems applied the main tenets of dependency theory to Soviet–East European relations.[3] Their efforts were useful in underscoring the shortcomings of dependency theory, but their research shed relatively little light on the broad dynamics of Soviet policy in Eastern Europe.

A more fruitful approach to the study of Soviet–East European relations (and of other highly asymmetrical relationships) has emerged from work done in the late 1970s and 1980s on 'spheres of influence' and interactions between 'preponderant and subordinate states'.[4] These concepts have facilitated cross-regional comparisons of unequal power relationships over broad periods of history. It is now possible, for example, to compare post-1945 Soviet–East European relations with post-1933 US–Central American relations, with the pre-1990 relationship between South Africa and its neighbours, or with the post-1991 relationship between Russia and the newly independent Central Asian republics. The differences among these cases may be at least as great as the similarities, but that is precisely what a comparative framework is designed to show.

As used in this chapter, a sphere of influence can be defined as a region of the world in which a preponderant external actor (state A) is able to compel the local states to conform with state A's own preferences. Other outside powers may also have some leverage over the countries in state A's sphere of influence, but that leverage is relatively circumscribed and is greatly eclipsed by the power that state A exerts. By this definition, Eastern Europe was clearly a sphere of influence for the Soviet Union after the Second World War. Although Western countries had some effect on the behaviour of the East European states, the dominant external influence in the region came from the Soviet Union. The Soviet sphere of influence was never formally recognized as such by Western governments, but the de facto existence of the sphere was widely understood. The Soviet sphere of influence in Eastern Europe was simultaneously a buffer zone for Moscow against West Germany and other members of NATO. In that sense, the East European sphere was quite different from the US sphere of influence in Central America, which never had to serve as a buffer zone for the preponderant external actor (i.e. the United States).

A further specification is needed to distinguish the various possible ways in which the preponderant state can exploit its political, economic, and military leverage to gain influence or control over the group of weaker states. Despite the peculiar nature of the Soviet bloc (especially in the ideological sphere), the post-1945 Soviet–East European relationship fits well into a broad typology devised by Hedley Bull of relationships between a preponderant state and a group of subordinate states. His typology included the three alternatives of 'dominance', 'hegemony', and 'primacy', which are best conceived of as points on a continuum, ranging from the most coercive to the least coercive.[5] Only the first two alternatives can truly be regarded as descriptive of a 'sphere of influence'. In a relationship of *dominance*, the preponderant state exercises tight and pervasive control over the subordinate states, often paying little heed to modern norms of international law. In a relationship of *hegemony*, the preponderant state exercises looser control and usually abides by most norms of international law, but still seeks—if necessary, through the use of armed force—to ensure that the internal and external orientation of the subordinate states is in accord with its own preferences. In a relationship of *primacy*, the preponderant state makes no recourse to the threat or use of force in its dealings with the weaker states, and instead relies solely on standard means of diplomatic and economic influence.

At any given time, a highly unequal relationship in the modern state system, including all sphere-of-influence relationships, will approximate one of these three ideal-types. No such relationship, however, is static over the longer term. Even the Soviet Union's sphere of influence in Eastern Europe, as will be shown in the discussion below, was more dynamic and variable than is often assumed. What began as outright Soviet 'dominance' over Eastern Europe during the Stalin era evolved after the mid-1950s into a 'hegemonic' and more complex relationship.

Even so, the changes in Soviet–East European relations over time, important though they may have been, were never far-reaching enough to prevent the whole structure from collapsing in 1989–90. If at some point long before 1989 the transition from 'dominance' to 'hegemony' had been carried further to leave the Soviet Union with something closer to 'primacy', the Soviet–East European relationship might have proven more durable. No such transition was ever forthcoming. The basic structure of the relationship that was imposed on the East European countries just after the Second World War—a structure requiring them to maintain Marxist–Leninist systems at home and to pursue 'socialist internationalist' policies abroad—was left essentially intact even after pressures for drastic change had set in. Those pressures occasionally burst into the open, forcing the Soviet Union to defend and restore its sphere of influence, though at ever greater cost and with ever greater difficulty. When the Soviet Union itself finally became intent on abolishing the old order, the pressures that had been building for so long in Eastern Europe came rapidly to the surface, leaving the whole Soviet bloc in tatters.

5.2. Historical Overview, 1945–1985

In the closing months of the Second World War, Soviet troops occupied most of Eastern Europe. Over the next few years, the establishment of Communism in Eastern Europe proceeded at varying rates. In Yugoslavia and Albania, the indigenous Communist parties led respectively by Tito and Hoxha had obtained sufficient political leverage and military strength through their role in the anti-Nazi resistance to eliminate their opposition and assume outright power as the war drew to a close. In the Soviet zone of Germany, the Soviet occupation forces enabled the Socialist Unity Party (SED) to gain pre-eminent power well before the East German state was formally created in 1949. Similarly, in Bulgaria and Romania Communist-dominated governments were imposed under Soviet pressure in early 1945. Elsewhere in the region, events followed a more gradual pattern. Not until the spring of 1948 were 'People's Democracies' in place all over East–Central Europe. Moreover, only a few months after the Soviet sphere of influence was finally consolidated, a significant breach was opened. A bitter rift with Yugoslavia in 1948 nearly provoked Soviet military intervention, but in the end Stalin refrained from using military force. From then on, Yugoslavia was able to pursue a more or less independent course.

Despite the 'loss' of Yugoslavia, Soviet influence in Eastern Europe came under no further threat during Stalin's time. From 1947 through to the early 1950s, the East European states embarked on crash industrialization and collectivization programmes, causing vast social upheaval yet also leading to rapid short-term economic growth. No conflict between 'viability' and 'cohesion' yet existed, for Stalin was able to rely on the presence of Soviet troops, a tightly woven network of security forces, the wholesale penetration of the East European governments by Soviet agents, the use of mass purges and political terror, and the unifying threat of renewed German militarism to ensure that regimes loyal to Moscow remained in power.[6] By the early 1950s Stalin had established a degree of control over Eastern Europe to which his successors could only aspire.

Following Stalin's death in March 1953 a shift began in Soviet–East European relations, as the new Soviet leaders encouraged the East European governments to loosen economic controls, adopt 'new courses' of development, and downgrade the role of the secret police. The severe economic pressures that had built up on workers and farmers during the relentless drive for industrialization and collectivization were gradually eased, and many victims of the Stalinist purges were rehabilitated, often posthumously. As a result, the socio-economic turmoil that had earlier been contained now began to surface, rendering all but impossible a full-scale return to the pervasive control of the Stalinist years. Thus from 1953 until the late 1980s the fundamental problem for the Soviet Union in Eastern Europe was how to preserve a fully fledged sphere of influence while adapting to the changed social and political conditions that made such a sphere far more difficult to maintain.

In the first few months after Stalin's death the situation in Eastern Europe was greatly exacerbated by the initial stages of the succession struggle in the Soviet Union and the analogous struggles in several of the East European countries. The pronouncements and recommendations about reform that emanated from the Soviet Union in the spring of 1953 were erratic and haphazard, enabling several of the East European governments to retrench and avoid any real movement away from Stalinism. Only after the outbreak of riots in Plzeň in early June 1953, stemming from the Czechoslovak regime's harsh 'currency reform', did the urgent need for greater economic liberalization become apparent. This need was demonstrated even more vividly two weeks later by a workers' uprising in East Germany. Coming at a time of profound uncertainty and leadership instability in both Moscow and East Berlin, the uprising threatened the very existence of the SED regime and, by extension, vital Soviet interests in Germany. Although the Soviet army put down the rebellion rather easily and with relatively little bloodshed—roughly two dozen demonstrators were killed, several hundred wounded, and many thousands arrested—the military intervention was crucial both in forestalling an escalation of the violence and in reasserting Soviet control.

Despite the resolution of the June 1953 crisis, the use of Soviet military power in East Germany did not impart greater consistency to Soviet policy or eliminate the prospect of further turmoil in Eastern Europe. Most Soviet leaders were preoccupied with domestic affairs, and they failed to appreciate the implications of the changes taking place in the Eastern bloc. They hoped that the events in Plzeň and East Germany were an aberration, rather than a portent of more explosive unrest to come. Not until the events of October and November 1956 did a modicum of direction finally return to Soviet policy. The peaceful outcome of the crisis with Poland demonstrated that some Soviet flexibility would continue and that a return to fully fledged Stalinism was not in the offing. At the same time, the Soviet Union's armed intervention in Hungary in early November 1956 made clear to all the Warsaw Pact countries the bounds of Soviet restraint and the limits of what could be changed in Eastern Europe. Far more than the uprisings of 1953 in Czechoslovakia and East Germany, the events in Hungary posed a fundamental threat to Soviet hegemony in the region. By re-establishing military control over Hungary and by exposing—more dramatically than in 1953—the emptiness of the 'roll-back' and 'liberation' rhetoric in the West, the Soviet invasion stemmed any further loss of Soviet power in Eastern Europe.

By the time the next major challenge to the Soviet sphere of influence emerged, in 1968, Soviet–East European relations had undergone several notable changes. Certain developments had facilitated greater Soviet control over Eastern Europe and better cohesion among the Warsaw Pact states. On balance, though, most developments since 1956 had pointed not towards an increase of Soviet control but towards a loosening of that control. In part, this trend reflected the growing heterogeneity of the East European societies and the continued impact of the 'thaw' under Soviet leader Nikita Khrushchev, but it was also due to the schism in world Communism that had been opened by the Sino-Soviet conflict. Less than a year after the Sino-Soviet split became public knowledge in 1960, Albania sparked a crisis with the Soviet Union by openly aligning itself with China—a precedent that caused deep concern in Moscow. To compound matters, Romania in the early 1960s began to embrace foreign and domestic policies that were at times sharply at odds with the Soviet Union's own policies. Although Romania had never been a crucial member of the Warsaw Pact, Nicolae Ceauşescu's growing recalcitrance on military affairs and foreign policy posed obvious complications for the cohesion of the alliance.

Developments outside the bloc also contributed to the loosening of Soviet control in Eastern Europe. The perceived threat of German aggression, which for so long had unified the Warsaw Pact governments, had gradually diminished. In the mid-1960s West Germany had launched its *Ostpolitik* campaign to increase economic and political contacts in Eastern Europe, a campaign whose potentially disruptive impact on the Soviet bloc was well recognized in Moscow. Soviet policy in Eastern Europe was also increasingly constrained by the incipient US–Soviet detente, with its promise of strategic nuclear arms accords and increased economic ties. This new relationship gave the Soviet leadership an incentive to proceed cautiously in Eastern Europe before taking actions that could undermine the detente.

Against this backdrop, the events of 1968 unfolded in Czechoslovakia. Sweeping internal reforms during the 'Prague Spring' brought a comprehensive revival of political, economic, and cultural life in Czechoslovakia, but it also provoked anxiety in Moscow about the potential ramifications. Both the internal and the external repercussions of the liberalization in Czechoslovakia were regarded by Soviet leaders as fundamental threats to their sphere of influence in Eastern Europe. The Prague Spring raised doubts about the cohesion of the Warsaw Pact, and those doubts were bound to multiply if the developments in Czechoslovakia proved 'contagious'. Soviet efforts to compel the Czechoslovak leader, Alexander Dubček, to change course were of little efficacy, as all manner of troop movements, thinly veiled threats, and political and economic coercion failed to bring an end to the Prague Spring. Dubček in fact seemed to benefit domestically the stronger the pressure from his Warsaw Pact allies became.

On 17 August 1968, after a spirited, three-day session of the CPSU Politburo, a consensus was finally reached in Moscow in favour of an invasion.[7] The following day, the top Soviet leader, Leonid Brezhnev, informed his East German, Polish, Bulgarian, and Hungarian counterparts of the decision at a hastily convened meeting in Moscow. Unlike in 1956, when Soviet troops intervened in Hungary unilaterally, Brezhnev was determined to give the invasion in 1968 a multilateral appearance. As a result, some 80,000 soldiers from Poland, East Germany, Bulgaria, and Hungary ended up taking part. In reality, though, Operation Danube (the code-name of the invasion) could hardly be regarded as a 'joint' undertaking. Soviet paratroopers and special operations forces spearheaded the invasion, and a total of more than 400,000 Soviet troops eventually moved into Czechoslovakia, roughly five times the number of East European forces. Moreover, the invasion was under strict Soviet command at all times, rather than being left under Warsaw Pact command, as originally planned.

The invasion of Czechoslovakia explicitly introduced what became known in the West as the 'Brezhnev Doctrine' into Soviet–East European relations. In effect, the Doctrine linked the fate of each socialist country with the fate of all others, stipulated that every socialist country must abide by the norms of Marxism–Leninism as interpreted in Moscow, and rejected 'abstract sovereignty' in favour of the 'laws of class struggle'. The Brezhnev Doctrine thus laid out even stricter 'rules of the game' for the 'socialist commonwealth' than in the past:

Without question, the peoples of the socialist countries and the Communist parties have and must have freedom to determine their country's path of development. Any decision they make, however, must not be inimical either to socialism in their own country or to the fundamental interests of other socialist countries . . . A socialist state that is in a system of other states composing the socialist commonwealth cannot be free of the common interests of that commonwealth. The sovereignty of individual socialist countries cannot be set against the interests of world socialism and the world revolutionary movement. . . . The weakening of any of the links in the world system of socialism directly affects all the socialist countries, and they cannot look indifferently upon this.[8]

The enunciation of the Brezhnev Doctrine codified Soviet attitudes toward Eastern Europe as they had developed over the previous two decades. The doctrine owed as much to Stalin and Khrushchev as to Brezhnev, since the policies of these earlier leaders were merely reaffirmed in the Brezhnev era. The promulgation of the Doctrine was none the less significant, both in restoring a firmer tone to Soviet–East European relations and in defining the limits of permissible deviations from the Soviet model of Communism.

For twelve years after the 1968 crisis, the Soviet bloc seemed relatively stable, despite crises in Poland in 1970 and 1976. The facade of stability came to an abrupt end, however, when a severe and prolonged crisis erupted in Poland in mid-1980. The crisis started out modestly enough, as a wave of protests against higher meat prices announced in July; but it soon posed graver complications for Soviet policy than any event had since the late 1940s. The formation of Solidarity, an independent and popularly based trade union which soon rivalled the Communist Party for political power and which represented the interests of the very same working class in whose name the party had always purported to rule, posed a fundamental challenge to Poland's Communist system. Once the magnitude of that challenge had become apparent to Soviet officials, they reacted

with unremitting hostility towards Solidarity. Soviet leaders were equally dis-
mayed by the growing political influence of Poland's Catholic church, which
they regarded as 'one of the most dangerous forces in Polish society' and a fount
of 'anti-socialist' and 'hostile' elements.[9]

Because of Poland's location in the heart of Europe, its communications and
logistical links with the Group of Soviet Forces in Germany, its contributions to
the 'first strategic echelon' of the Warsaw Pact, and its numerous storage sites for
Soviet tactical nuclear warheads, the prospect of having a non-Communist
government come to power in Warsaw or of a drastic change in Polish foreign
policy was cause for alarm in Moscow. Soviet foreign minister Andrei Gromyko
spoke for all his colleagues when he declared at a CPSU Politburo meeting in
October 1980 that 'we simply cannot and must not lose Poland' under any
circumstances.[10] Although Khrushchev had been willing in 1956 to reach a modus
vivendi with the Polish leader Władysław Gomułka, the situation in 1980–81
was totally different. Gomułka, despite all his heterodoxies, was a devoted
Communist, and Khrushchev could be confident that socialism in Poland and
the Polish–Soviet 'fraternal relationship' would continue and even thrive under
Gomułka's leadership. Brezhnev and his colleagues had no such assurances about
Poland in 1980–81.

By stirring Soviet anxieties about the potential loss of a key member of the
Warsaw Pact and about the spread of political instability throughout Eastern
Europe, the Polish crisis demonstrated, as the events of 1953, 1956, and 1968
had previously, the degree of change that was 'acceptable' in the Soviet bloc. The
crisis in Poland was more prolonged than those earlier upheavals, but the leeway
for genuine change was, if anything, narrower than before. Plans for the
imposition of martial law began to be formulated almost from the very first day
of the crisis.[11] Although the plans were drafted by the Polish general staff, the
whole process was supervised and moved along by the Soviet Union. The constant
pressure that Soviet political and military leaders exerted on Polish officials
thwarted any hope that Stanisław Kania, the Communist Party first secretary
until October 1981, might have had of reaching a genuine compromise with
Solidarity and the Catholic church. From the Soviet Politburo's perspective, any
such compromise would have been at best a useless diversion or at worst a form
of outright capitulation to 'hostile' forces. The only thing Soviet leaders truly
wanted during the crisis was to get the Polish authorities to implement 'decisive
measures' as soon as possible against the 'anti-socialist and counter-revolutionary
opposition'.

The Soviet leadership's pursuit of an 'internal solution' to the Polish crisis was
by no means a departure from its responses to previous crises in Eastern Europe.
In Hungary and Poland in 1956 and in Czechoslovakia in 1968, the Soviet
Union applied pressures short of direct intervention and sought to work out an

internal solution that would preclude the need for an invasion. In each case, Soviet officials viewed military action as a last-ditch option, to be used only after all other measures had failed. In Poland in 1956 an internal solution that left Gomułka in power did prove feasible, whereas in Hungary and later in Czechoslovakia all attempts to reassert Soviet control from within proved futile, leading in the end to direct Soviet military intervention. During the 1980–1 Polish crisis, Soviet officials drew up plans for a full-scale invasion, but these plans were to be implemented only if the Polish authorities failed to restore order on their own. Preparations for the imposition of martial law began long before Soviet military officials started laying the groundwork for an invasion, and the internal option was deemed throughout to be vastly preferable to direct 'fraternal assistance' from outside. Only in a worst-case scenario, in which the martial law operation collapsed and full-scale civil war erupted in Poland, does it seem at all likely that the Soviet Union would have shifted towards the 'external' option.

If Operation X (the code-name of the martial law operation) had indeed collapsed amid widespread violence in December 1981 and the Soviet Politburo had been forced to decide whether to send in troops, the consequences of such a choice would have been immense. The difficulty of carrying out an invasion of Poland and of coping with its aftermath would have been so extremely great that it would have changed the course of Soviet policy in Eastern Europe for many years to come. As it was, the success of Wojciech Jaruzelski's internal solution precluded any test of Moscow's restraint and restored conformity to the Soviet bloc at relatively low cost. The surprisingly smooth imposition of martial law (*stan wojenny*) in Poland also helped prevent any further disruption in Soviet–East European relations during the last year of Brezhnev's rule and the next two and a half years under Yuri Andropov and Konstantin Chernenko.

The lack of any major political turmoil in Eastern Europe between 1982 and 1985 seems especially surprising at first glance, for this was a period of great uncertainty, not only because of the post-Brezhnev succession in Moscow but also because of the impending successions in most of the other Warsaw Pact countries. The last time the Soviet Union had experienced a prolonged leadership transition, between 1953 and 1956, numerous crises had arisen in the Eastern bloc: in Plzeň and East Germany in June 1953, in Poznan in June 1956, and in Poland and Hungary in October–November 1956. Moreover, during the period 1953–6, all the East European countries underwent changes in their Communist Party leadership, just as the Soviet Union did. By contrast, no such upheavals or leadership changes occurred between 1982 and 1985. This unusual placidity cannot be attributed to any single factor, but the martial law crackdown of December 1981 and the invasions of 1956 and 1968 probably constitute a large part of the explanation. After Stalin's death in 1953, the limits of what could be changed in Eastern Europe were still unknown, but by the early 1980s the Soviet Union had evinced its willingness and ability to use extreme measures, whenever necessary, to prevent or reverse 'deviations from socialism'. Thus, by the time Mikhail Gorbachev became General Secretary of the CPSU in March 1985, the internal political complexion of Eastern Europe seemed destined to remain within the narrow bounds of orthodox Communism as interpreted in Moscow.

5.3. The Dynamics of Soviet Hegemony in Eastern Europe

Soviet hegemony in Eastern Europe after 1945 had three key dimensions: military, political, and economic. The different forms of Soviet power tended to reinforce one another, in so far as military and economic influence could be translated into political control. Warsaw Pact manœuvres, for example, were often held to achieve political ends, and economic pressure and incentives could be used to bring wayward states into line. This section will examine the three aspects of Soviet power, focusing on only one side of the Soviet–East European power relationship. The other side of the relationship—that is, the East European states' leverage *vis-à-vis* the Soviet Union—was by no means unimportant, but the chief concern here is with the dynamics of Soviet hegemony. The extent to which the East European states were able to constrain and inhibit Soviet power will be discussed in section 5.4.

Military Aspects

The most conspicuous element of Soviet power in Eastern Europe was the deployment of formidable military strength. Hundreds of thousands of Soviet troops were stationed in Poland (1945–93), Romania (1945–58), Czechoslovakia (1968–91), Hungary (1945–91), and the former East Germany (1945–94), and hundreds of thousands more were based in the western military districts of the Soviet Union. Large quantities of Soviet weapons, including tanks, armoured combat vehicles, artillery, fighter aircraft, bombers, and nuclear and conventional missiles, were deployed on East European soil. The Soviet Union maintained exclusive control over Warsaw Pact communications networks, joint air defence systems, and logistical supply lines. In addition, the extensive links between Soviet and East European party and military leaders, the influence of the Soviet and allied security organs, and the dependence of Eastern Europe on the Soviet Union for weapons and spare parts enabled Soviet commanders to wield a good deal of formal and informal control over the non-Soviet Warsaw Pact armed forces. Soviet control was especially pervasive over the East German Nationale Volksarmee (NVA), which even in peacetime was wholly subordinated to the Soviet-dominated Joint Command of the Warsaw Pact. In wartime, the NVA and all the other Warsaw Pact armies (other than the Romanian) would have been placed under the direct control of the Soviet high command, in accordance with secret bilateral agreements concluded in the late 1970s and early 1980s.

Nor was Soviet military power in Eastern Europe maintained merely for appearance's sake. In the first fifteen years after Stalin's death, Soviet troops intervened on three occasions—in East Germany in 1953, Hungary in 1956, and Czechoslovakia in 1968—to counter perceived threats to Soviet interests in the region. The Soviet Union's demonstrated willingness to use force in these instances was at least as important as the presence of Soviet troops on East European territory in precluding violent challenges to the local Communist regimes. By the same token, when specific challenges did arise in Eastern Europe, the record of previous Soviet interventions lent greater credibility to Moscow's warnings and threats, and thus helped forestall the need for direct intervention. During a political crisis, conspicuous Soviet and Warsaw Pact troop manœuvres were often enough to bring overwhelming pressure to bear on both the government and the population.

Soviet military power in Eastern Europe was reinforced by the military strategy of the Warsaw Pact, which in effect preserved a Soviet capability to intervene in other member states. The Pact's strategy was virtually identical to Soviet strategy for Europe in its emphasis on a 'blitzkrieg'—style assault by combined Soviet and East European forces against Western Europe. To support this strategy, the military establishments in Eastern Europe (other than Romania) geared most of their training, tactics, and military planning towards offensive operations, and devoted little time to defensive arrangements that might have been used to resist Soviet intervention in their own countries. Even the unique system of National Territorial Defense (*obrona terytorium kraju*) in Poland, though defensive in nature, was designed entirely to protect against nuclear air attacks from the West. By compelling the East European states to concentrate exclusively on perceived threats from the West and not on more plausible threats from the East, the Warsaw Pact's strategy prevented those states from developing an adequate defensive capacity against 'fraternal' invasions.

In other ways, too, the Warsaw Pact bolstered Soviet military control over Eastern Europe. The formation of the Pact in 1955 served to legitimize the continued deployment of Soviet troops in Hungary and Romania after the signing of the Austrian State Treaty had eliminated the ostensible justification for their presence. The status-of-forces agreements concluded with Poland (1956), Hungary (1957), East Germany (1957), and Czechoslovakia (1968) enabled the Soviet Union to safeguard the 'temporary' presence of its forces in the region while passing off a large share of the stationing costs to the host countries. The Warsaw Pact also became a leading organ for the defence of 'socialist internationalism' and 'socialist gains'—that is, for joint interventions against wayward allies, as in Czechoslovakia in 1968. To that end, the joint military exercises that began in October 1961, in addition to serving as a form of coercive diplomacy during crises, were valuable in providing coordinated training and preparations for the Warsaw Pact armies in case direct intervention proved necessary.

The Soviet Union's global military power also played a vital role in maintaining hegemony over Eastern Europe. The threat of Soviet nuclear or conventional retaliation helped deter the Western allies from coming to the defence of East European countries when the Soviet Union intervened. Similarly, the NATO governments recognized that even if they did respond with military force they would have little chance of success, given the Soviet Union's local force preponderance and logistical advantages. Past Soviet interventions in Eastern Europe thus helped consolidate Moscow's claim to a sphere of influence in the region—a sphere that was further buttressed by the emergence of strategic nuclear parity between the superpowers in the 1960s and early 1970s. US Secretary of State Dean Rusk acknowledged as much in 1964 when he declared that 'our capacity to influence events and trends within the Communist world is very limited. But it is our policy to do what we can.'[12]

Political and Ideological Aspects

Compared to most other highly unequal inter-state relationships, the Soviet relationship with Eastern Europe was marked by a far greater number of intrusive political controls. Some of these controls were overt and widely discussed; others were surreptitious and never mentioned openly. One of the standard ways in which Soviet officials gained broad influence was by cultivating close personal and political ties with East European Communist Party leaders, both in their initial selection and during their subsequent careers. During the Stalin era, Soviet control over East European leaders was pervasive and conspicuous. The situation changed after Stalin's death, with the dissolution of the Cominform in April 1956 and the gradual removal of the most blatant forms of Soviet interference in East European domestic affairs in the 1950s and early 1960s. Nevertheless, Moscow still retained at least some say in most leadership changes in the Eastern bloc. The long-time Communist Party leader in Hungary, János Kádár, was installed after a Soviet invasion of his country. Many other East European Communist leaders—Gustáv Husák and Miloš Jakeš in Czechoslovakia; Edward Gierek, Stanisław Kania, and Wojciech Jaruzelski in Poland; and Erich Honecker in East Germany—came to power under Soviet auspices after their predecessors had incurred Moscow's displeasure. Similarly, Todor Zhivkov's emergence as a compromise leader in Bulgaria in 1954 was effected by means of Soviet support. The pivotal role that the Soviet Union played in the selection of these and other East European leaders usually enabled Soviet authorities to exert far-reaching influence on the policies of the new leaders. The close relationships fostered by high-level Soviet officials with their East European counterparts also helped ensure that party leaders in Eastern Europe would not attempt, at a later stage, to assert too great a degree of autonomy.

Besides exerting influence over leadership selection, the Soviet Union sought to strengthen its ties and to coordinate policies with Eastern bloc officials through regular bilateral and multilateral meetings. Because bilateral meetings were more effective in allowing Moscow to communicate and enforce its views, Soviet leaders traditionally preferred this sort of consultation with their allies. That was especially the case under Stalin and Khrushchev, and it continued during the Brezhnev era, when bilateral summits were held annually at summer resorts in the Crimea. Top-level bilateral meetings also occurred regularly under Brezhnev's successors. Further bilateral contacts took place via the Soviet liaison officers and embassy representatives stationed in each of the bloc countries, as well as through meetings between the Soviet Central Committee secretary responsible for intra-bloc relations and his East European counterparts. Starting in the early 1970s, Soviet leaders also showed greater interest in multilateral fora, such as the Council for Mutual Economic Assistance (CMEA), the Warsaw Pact joint committees, and various cultural and scientific exchanges. New multilateral organs were formed within the Warsaw Pact, including the Council of Defence Ministers in 1969 and the Council of Foreign Ministers in 1976. These and other multilateral bodies proved to be useful instruments for coordinating policies and for strengthening the 'organic' links between the Soviet and East European military, economic, and scientific bureaucracies. Those links, in turn, facilitated greater Soviet control over the region's Communist Party leaders.

As a further means of retaining political and ideological sway in Eastern Europe, the Soviet Union was able to rely on the monitoring and clandestine activities of the Soviet security and intelligence services. When the Communist regimes were first established in Eastern Europe, Soviet officials were instrumental in creating local secret police forces analogous to those operating in the Soviet Union itself. For many years, and particularly during the Stalin era, the East European security organs were mere appendages of the Soviet security apparatus. The situation was aptly described by one of Stalin's top aides and eventual successor, Nikita Khrushchev, in his memoirs: 'The security organs [in Eastern Europe] worked under the direct supervision of "advisers" who had been sent from the Soviet state security apparatus, rather than under the supervision of the East European governments themselves. . . . Our "advisers" were in all the [East European] countries, and their role was very shameful.'[13] Later on, the East

European secret police forces were not quite as pervasively controlled by the Soviet Union as they had been in Stalin's time, but they remained the most steadfastly pro-Moscow element in the East European states, consistently placing Soviet interests ahead of their own national interests. Furthermore, even in the 1970s and 1980s the Soviet security forces, in particular the KGB, kept a tight rein on the Eastern bloc intelligence agencies and continued to use those agencies to promote Soviet political and military objectives. What is more, the KGB's activities extended well beyond its dealings with the allied secret police forces to include the recruitment of Soviet agents and their installation in key positions throughout the political and military command structures of the East European countries. In other ways as well, such as providing information to Soviet political leaders about social trends in the East European countries, the Soviet security and intelligence services played a crucial role in the maintenance of the Soviet sphere of influence in Eastern Europe.

These various methods of political control were reinforced by the commonality of interests that usually existed between Soviet and East European élites. These common interests stemmed from more than the fact that the East European élites were ultimately beholden to the Soviet armed forces for their security and continued tenure. Even if they had had less of a stake in maintaining good relations with Moscow, most East European leaders would have been willing to adhere to Soviet methods of 'socialist development', since by doing so they could bolster their own political positions and solidify the dominant role of their domestic Communist Parties. In this sense, the measures that were desired by Soviet leaders for the countries of Eastern Europe—the maintenance of supreme authority by the Communist Party, the retention of a highly centralized party structure, and state control over the press and all publishing outlets—were also likely to be the measures preferred by the leaders of those countries themselves. This natural overlapping of interests between Soviet and East European élites greatly enhanced the efficacy of Soviet political power in the region.

Economic Aspects

The Soviet Union also wielded far-reaching economic power over the East European states, of which five—Poland, Czechoslovakia, Hungary, Bulgaria, and Romania—were founding members of the CMEA in 1949. (East Germany was admitted the following year.) In the 1940s and 1950s Soviet economic power in the region was augmented by the transfer of German industrial plants to Soviet territory, by the extraction of war reparations from East Germany, Hungary, Romania, and Bulgaria, by the establishment of Soviet-dominated joint enterprises, and by trading arrangements slanted in favour of the Soviet Union. The net outflow of resources from Eastern Europe to the Soviet Union was approximately $15 billion to $20 billion in the first decade after the Second World War, an amount roughly equal to the total aid provided by the United States to Western Europe under the Marshall Plan.[14] Moreover, during Stalin's time Soviet leaders directly controlled the economic policies of the bloc governments as they steered the East European countries—all of which, except Czechoslovakia, had been predominantly rural in the pre-war era—along the path of crash industrialization.

In later years, Soviet economic power stemmed from the sheer size of the Soviet economy compared to the East European economies, as well as from the Soviet Union's abundant natural resources and certain structural features of CMEA. The Soviet GNP was three to four times the size of the combined GNPs of all the other members of CMEA, and the Soviet Union possessed vast supplies of oil and raw materials, producing 97.7 per cent of CMEA's crude oil, 90.4 per cent of its natural gas, 97.4 per cent of its iron ore, 72.7 per cent of its steel, 98.2 per cent of its manganese, and similar percentages of other resources in any given year.[15] The East European states, by contrast, were largely devoid of natural resources and were unable to purchase oil and other commodities in sufficient quantity on the world market because of their lack of hard currency. Furthermore, from the mid-1970s on the East European states found the relative prices for trade with the Soviet Union to be far more advantageous than the prices for comparable trade with non-CMEA countries. Hence, for economic as well as political reasons, the Soviet Union was the dominant supplier and market for the East European countries (except Romania after the 1960s). In the early 1980s, roughly 40–50 per cent of total East European foreign trade (including that of Romania) was conducted with the Soviet Union.

The extent of Soviet economic preponderance was even greater than this percentage may imply, for it does not take into account the nature of the bilateral trade relationship between the Soviet Union and each of its East European partners. In return for exports of oil and raw materials, which could easily have been sold for greater returns in the West, the Soviet Union imported machinery, electronic equipment, and consumer and agricultural products from Eastern Europe, most of which were of inferior quality by Western (though not Soviet) standards and therefore would have been unmarketable, or saleable only at highly disadvantageous prices, outside the Soviet bloc. This trading pattern reinforced East European economic dependence on the Soviet Union in two respects.

First, the potentially autarkic Soviet economy, unlike the East European economies, depended relatively little on foreign trade, including trade with Eastern Europe. Trading activities represented only 6–8 per cent of the Soviet GNP compared to 45–50 per cent of the East European GNPs, and most of the products the Soviet Union imported, especially those from Eastern Europe, could have been replaced fairly easily. In contrast, the energy supplies and other raw materials purchased by the East European countries from the Soviet Union, especially those imported by East Germany, Hungary, Poland, and Bulgaria, were so vital to their economic development that cutting off these supplies would have resulted in economic chaos almost immediately.

Secondly, the capacity of the Soviet economy to absorb goods that would have been unacceptable on the world market allowed the East European regimes to continue production of low-quality items without due regard for international competitiveness. This situation ultimately retarded economic progress in the East European states and forced them to rely to an even greater degree on the Soviet market. The importance of the Soviet market, in turn, encouraged East European planners to concentrate on products whose sole customer was the Soviet Union, thus further distorting sectoral development in the East European economies and further attenuating the range of market options outside the Soviet Union. In all these ways the Soviet Union avoided becoming economically vulnerable in its trade with other CMEA members, while the East European states found, by contrast, that 'all aspects of [their] trade with the USSR—the level, the composition, the terms, and the balance and how it [was] financed—[were] critical for [their] economic development.'[16]

The Soviet Union's economic power over Eastern Europe was further strengthened by CMEA's non-convertible currency system. The individual East European currencies were 'commodity non-convertible', meaning that currency from one East European country could not be converted for commodities in another country unless detailed arrangements based on national five-year plans were worked out in advance by the respective foreign trade ministries. To simplify these transactions, the CMEA countries used an accounting unit known as the 'transferable rouble' which, despite its name, was not transferable at all even within the bloc, much less outside CMEA. Although limited multilateral clearing facilities for intra-CMEA trade did exist (at least after the early 1970s), in very few cases could one country's trade surpluses with another CMEA member actually be transferred to help balance trade deficits with a third. Instead, virtually all trade had to be conducted bilaterally, a pattern that, because of the dominant Soviet economic position within the bloc, slanted intra-CMEA trade even further towards the Soviet Union.

The CMEA currencies were also externally non-convertible—that is, they were financially non-convertible outside the bloc. Hence the East European states could not ordinarily obtain hard currency on foreign exchange markets and had to make do with what they could get from exports, Western loans, and the limited reserves of CMEA's two banks. Added to this were the protectionist pressures, inefficiency, and constraints on innovation generated by the centralized foreign trading system in each East European country. These financial and systemic pressures inhibited the East European governments from conducting a greater portion of their trade with non-CMEA countries, leaving them with no real alternative but to conduct most of their trade bilaterally with other CMEA members, particularly the Soviet Union. The maintenance of a separate financial bloc among CMEA countries thereby reinforced Soviet economic preponderance.

In turn, the Soviet Union was able to use its economic leverage to promote 'socialist integration' within CMEA. In accord with Soviet preferences, 'socialist integration' was pursued through greater intra-bloc coordination of centralized planning and control, especially in areas of advanced science and technology. Although this policy ensured that economic integration would not cause undue reliance on market mechanisms, the inefficiencies of centralized planning deprived most integrationist programmes of even minimal flexibility, an obstacle compounded by the objections of some East European countries (most notably Romania) to plans for a precise 'division of labour' among CMEA countries. Consequently, most attempts to develop formal mechanisms of economic integration, particularly supranational institutions, never came to fruition. Only a very modest degree of integration actually took place. Still, Soviet leaders were able to use informal pressure to help make up for the dearth of formal supranational institutions. Moreover, some of CMEA's multilateral and bilateral joint ventures, including joint energy production and refining, were successful. The CMEA countries also managed to form two multilateral banks—the International Bank for Economic Cooperation in 1964 and the International Investment Bank in 1971—and to establish a Comprehensive Programme of Integration in 1971 and a Comprehensive Programme on Science and Technology in December 1985. These programmes encouraged more coherent long-range planning and capital ventures within CMEA and a certain degree of specialization, and they also facilitated the implementation of reforms which, though market-orientated, were largely compatible with the exigencies of centralized planning. In the end, however, intra-CMEA integration produced few tangible benefits for the Soviet Union.

5.4. The Limits of Soviet Power in Eastern Europe

In the first forty years after the Second World War, the Soviet Union at times fell short in its ability to control political trends in Eastern Europe. This was due, in part, to the limited utility of Soviet military power. The Soviet Union's armed presence in Eastern Europe was indeed formidable, but not so formidable as to deter and overcome all threats to Soviet hegemony. Soviet military forces did not forestall challenges in Yugoslavia in 1948, East Germany in 1953, Poland and Hungary in 1956, Albania in 1961, and in other countries on other occasions. Nor did they prevent certain of these challenges—in Yugoslavia and Albania and to a lesser extent in Romania—from succeeding. In addition, there were further constraints on the most obvious manifestation of Soviet military power, namely, the use of armed force. Invasions and the direct use of military force occurred only in the East European countries that were of critical geostrategic importance to the Soviet Union (i.e. the northern tier states and Hungary). Moreover, the prospect of incurring heavy casualties and of being compelled to undertake a bloody occupation of a 'fraternal' East European country induced Soviet leaders to forgo the use of force when it seemed likely that invading troops would encounter large-scale resistance among the indigenous armed forces and population. Such was the case, for example, with Yugoslavia, Romania, and Poland. Although this consideration did not figure as prominently when the decision was made to invade Afghanistan in 1979, the subsequent embroilment of Soviet troops there underscored the dangers of military intervention. During the Soviet Politburo's deliberations about Poland in 1980–81, top officials repeatedly emphasized that they did not want to become bogged down in a 'second Afghanistan'.[17]

Furthermore, even in cases when the Soviet Union did resort to the use of force, there were limits on what military power alone could accomplish. This was especially apparent in Czechoslovakia after the August 1968 invasion, and it would have been even more true of Poland if Soviet troops had intervened massively in 1981. The use and the threat of armed force, though crucial for precluding unfavourable developments and safeguarding perceived Soviet interests in Eastern Europe, were insufficient to assure long-term control in the region. To be sure, military power—whether in the form of Soviet troop deployments, the deterrent effect of past invasions, coercive pressure brought on by troop manœuvres, 'internal solutions' such as occurred in Poland in 1981, or direct military intervention—was the underpinning of Soviet influence in Eastern Europe during the whole period from 1945 to 1985; but the extent of Moscow's success in preserving a sphere of influence could not be determined by its military strength alone.

Much as there were limits on the efficacy of Soviet military power, so too there were limits on Soviet political leverage. Despite the extensive network of formal and informal controls wielded by Soviet leaders, and despite the commonality of interests that often existed between Soviet and East European élites, several East European governments attempted to deviate sharply from Soviet policy and even to seek outright autonomy. Such was the case in Yugoslavia and Albania (and to a lesser extent Romania), where Tito and Hoxha (and Ceauşescu) took the precautionary step of eliminating the pro-Moscow factions in their Communist Parties while staking out positions independent of the Soviet Union. A similar situation might have arisen in Czechoslovakia had Soviet tanks not moved in shortly before the Extraordinary 14th Congress of the Czechoslovak Communist Party was due to convene. Equally important, Soviet political controls were not able to forestall occasional revolts 'from below', especially those originating from economic turmoil, as in East Germany in 1953, Hungary in 1956, and even more dramatically in Poland in 1980–81.

Soviet political leverage in Eastern Europe was also limited—in a more subtle but no less important way—by domestic political constraints within the Soviet Union itself. The legacy of Stalin's tight grip on the East European countries in the 1940s and early 1950s meant that any appreciable loosening of Soviet control over the region would encounter staunch opposition in the CPSU Politburo, as Khrushchev discovered in 1956–7. Later on, when Brezhnev made a commitment to preserve the 'socialist commonwealth' at all costs, the stakes involved in maintaining or losing that commitment were bound to rise over time. Hence Soviet leaders became increasingly unwilling to take steps that could endanger the short-term cohesion of the socialist commonwealth. Proposals that might have engendered a looser but, in the long run, more viable Soviet–East European relationship—akin to the Soviet Union's relationship with Finland—were almost certainly rejected at an early stage, if they were broached at all. This constraint in turn circumscribed the flexibility of almost every aspect of Soviet policy in the region.

Perhaps the greatest limits on Soviet power in Eastern Europe were on the economic side. On most of the occasions when the Soviet Union attempted to use its regional economic preponderance for coercive purposes—as against Yugoslavia in 1948, Albania in 1961, and Romania in 1964–5—the sanctions and pressure achieved little and indeed in many respects were counterproductive.[18] Yugoslavia and Romania escaped any lasting economic damage when they turned to the West for trade and assistance, and Albania relied on China to make up for the loss of Soviet aid (though the Albanian economy was more seriously hurt by the sanctions than either the Yugoslav or the Romanian). Thus, in each of these cases, the main effect of the sanctions was to widen the split between the East European state and the Soviet Union. In other cases where the *potential* for economic coercion would have been much greater, the actual *use* of coercion would have made no sense. During the crisis in 1980–81, for example, a cut-off of Soviet oil shipments to Poland would have quickly brought the Polish economy to a halt. Such a step, however, would have served no purpose other than to create even greater turmoil. Hence Soviet oil and natural gas exports and economic aid to Poland flowed without interruption during the entire crisis and, indeed, substantially increased. In private, Soviet officials bitterly complained about the economic burden that these extra shipments were imposing on the USSR, but they realized that they had little choice.[19] The actual leverage that the Soviet Union could bring to bear in this case, as in numerous others, was much less than the country's economic potential alone would have suggested.

ic power were also apparent in the perennial
to alleviate the economic woes of the East
-1950s on, Soviet officials were well aware
Europe could easily translate into political
promote better economic conditions
a lack of concerted attention to the pro-
s on the Soviet Union's own economic
system that Stalin created was of some
wn, but the system's pervasive inefficiencies,
, and other shortcomings baulked efforts in the 1960s and
shift to an 'intensive' growth strategy based on greater productivity and
rapid technological progress. Fundamental reform seemed the only way to rectify
these deficiencies, but neither Brezhnev nor his two immediate successors were
willing to venture far down this path, in part because of worries that sweeping
economic reform might eventually require major political concessions as well.
As a result, the Soviet Union in the early to mid-1980s was confronted by deepening stagnation at home and was still unable to assume more than a negligible
role in the world economy. *Vis-à-vis* Eastern Europe, Soviet economic power
was of far greater importance, but even there the range of options was constrained by the Soviet economy's inherent weaknesses.

5.5. The Transformation of Soviet Policy in Eastern Europe, 1985–1991

When Mikhail Gorbachev came to power, the Soviet–East European relationship initially changed very little. By the spring of 1988, however, Soviet policy
towards Eastern Europe started to loosen, heralding a fundamental shift in
Gorbachev's approach. As the pace of perestroika and glasnost accelerated in the
Soviet Union, the 'winds of change' gradually filtered throughout the Eastern
bloc, bringing long-submerged grievances and social discontent to the surface.
Under growing popular pressure, the regimes in Hungary and Poland embarked
in 1988–9 on much more ambitious paths of reform than even Gorbachev
himself had yet adopted. As ferment in those two countries and elsewhere in the
region continued to increase, the tone of Gorbachev's public comments about
Eastern Europe grew bolder. By early to mid-1989 it had become clear that the
Soviet Union was willing to permit far-reaching internal changes in Eastern
Europe that previously would have been ruled out and forcibly suppressed under
the Brezhnev Doctrine.

Significant though the first wave of reforms in Hungary and Poland had been,

the full magnitude of the forces that Gorbachev's policy un[...]
Europe became apparent only during the last few months of[...]
events occurred that would have been unthinkable even a year [...]
peaceful revolutions from below in East Germany and Czechosl[...]
dismantling of the Berlin Wall; popular ferment and the downfall [...]
Zhivkov in Bulgaria; and violent upheaval and the execution of Nicol[...]
Elena Ceauşescu in Romania. As one orthodox Communist regime after [...]
other collapsed, the Soviet Union expressed approval and lent strong support [...]
the reformist governments that emerged. Soviet leaders also joined their East
European counterparts in condemning previous instances of Soviet interference
in Eastern Europe, particularly the 1968 invasion of Czechoslovakia.[20] Unlike in
the past, when the Soviet Union had done all it could to stifle and deter political
liberalization in Eastern Europe, there was no doubt by the end of 1989 that the
East European countries would have full scope to pursue drastic economic,
political, and social reforms, including the option of abandoning Communism
altogether.

In every respect, Gorbachev's approach to Soviet–East European relations
from mid-1988 on was radically different from that of his predecessors. Previous
Soviet leaders had sought to maintain Communism in Eastern Europe, if
necessary through the use of armed force. Gorbachev, by contrast, wanted to
avoid military intervention in Eastern Europe at all costs. Hence his paramount
objective was to defuse the pressures in the region that might eventually have
led to violent anti-Soviet uprisings. This objective in turn required him to go
much further than he initially anticipated. In effect, the Soviet Union ended up
promoting internal crises in Eastern Europe while there was still some chance of
benefiting from them, rather than risk being confronted later on by widespread
violence that would virtually compel Gorbachev to send in troops. The hope
was that by supporting sweeping but peaceful change in the region in the near
term, the Soviet Union would never again have to contend with large-scale out-
breaks of anti-Soviet violence, as Khrushchev had had to do in 1956. This basic
strategy, of encouraging and managing intra-Pact crises in order to prevent much
more severe crises in the future, achieved its immediate aim, but in the process
it both necessitated and ensured the demise of East European Communism.

By effectively doing away with the Communist bloc, Gorbachev vastly improved the climate for East–West relations (including East–West trade) and
eliminated the burden that Eastern Europe had long imposed on Soviet economic
and military resources. He also removed a major impediment to his domestic
reform programme. Whereas previous Soviet leaders had invoked the concepts
of 'socialist internationalism' and a 'socialist commonwealth' to confer 'legitimacy'
on the traditional Marxist–Leninist model, Gorbachev and his aides could point
to the developments in Eastern Europe as evidence of the model's bankruptcy.

The turmoil that Gorbachev allowed and even encouraged in the Eastern bloc countries thereby negated a key external prop on which his opponents in Moscow might have relied. In all these respects, the dissolution of Soviet hegemony over Eastern Europe was highly beneficial for the Soviet leader.

At the same time Gorbachev's policy, for all its positive aspects, was fraught with serious costs. By late 1990 the Soviet Union was unable to salvage what little remained of its leverage in Eastern Europe. Even before the Warsaw Pact was formally abolished in July 1991, the limited effectiveness of the alliance had disappeared. All the internal political changes in Eastern Europe that the Warsaw Pact was supposed to prevent occurred in 1989 and 1990, most notably in the GDR. The elaborate command-and-control infrastructure that Soviet leaders worked so long to develop for the Pact disintegrated, and pressures rapidly mounted for the withdrawal of all Soviet troops and weapons from the region. All Soviet forces were gone from Hungary and Czechoslovakia by mid-1991 and from Poland by September 1993. The final pull-out of troops from eastern Germany in September 1994 brought to an end the presence of the former Soviet army in Eastern Europe, thus completing the demise of the Warsaw Pact.

The fate of CMEA was no better. Although most of the East European states after 1989 still relied heavily on the Soviet Union for trade and energy supplies, the inexorable trend in the region was towards much greater economic contact with the West. The new East European governments regarded CMEA as a cumbersome, antiquated organization that should be abolished, and they drafted formal proposals to that effect. Soviet leaders, too, soon acknowledged that the organization had never come close to living up to its stated aims, and that its functions had been overtaken by events. Even if drastic reforms could have been implemented in CMEA (which they were not), the organization was doomed by the upheavals of 1989–90. Hence, like the Warsaw Pact, it was formally disbanded in mid-1991.

In all these ways, events moved so far and so fast in Eastern Europe, and the Soviet Union's influence in the region declined so precipitously, that the fate of the whole continent eluded Soviet control. The very notion of a 'socialist commonwealth' lost its meaning once Gorbachev not only permitted, but actually facilitated, the collapse of Communist rule in Eastern Europe. Despite the benefits Gorbachev gained from the disintegration of the bloc, his political fortunes suffered once the lingering remnants of the socialist commonwealth were formally dissolved. Domestic recriminations and controversy over the 'loss' of Eastern Europe contributed to the resurgence of harder-line forces in Moscow between the autumn of 1990 and the summer of 1991. Not until after the aborted coup attempt of August 1991, and the dissolution of the Soviet Union as a whole four months later, was it clear that Soviet hegemony in Eastern Europe was gone for good. Any hopes that orthodox Communist elements in

Moscow might have had of some day resurrecting the 'socialist bloc' were shattered once the Soviet state itself followed the Warsaw Pact and CMEA into oblivion.

5.6. Conclusion

Until the late 1980s the Soviet Union's determination to preserve a Communist sphere of influence in Eastern Europe was not in doubt. Despite important changes in Soviet policy and the growing complexity of the East European societies, the main Soviet objective in the region—the maintenance of a political–ideological bloc and a military buffer zone—remained unchanged. The gradual transition from 'dominance' to 'hegemony' after Stalin's death was never followed by a transition to 'primacy' or anything close to it. Until Gorbachev came to power the 'rules of the game' within the Communist bloc, as codified by Soviet military interventions in East Germany in 1953, Hungary in 1956, and Czechoslovakia in 1968, as well as by the threats against Poland in 1980–81, still prohibited 'deviations' from the basic principles of Marxism–Leninism. Any threat to the security of an East European Communist regime, whether internal or external, was regarded as a threat to Soviet security as well. The Soviet Union's failure to relax its hegemony over Eastern Europe and move towards a relationship of genuine primacy is what ultimately ensured the collapse of Soviet power in the region. The maintenance of a hegemonic relationship depended on the Soviet Union's willingness to resort, in extreme cases, to military force. Once the military option was no longer deemed viable in either Moscow or the East European countries, the whole edifice crumbled and there was nothing to take its place.

This is not to imply, however, that the collapse of the Soviet sphere of influence was inevitable. In retrospect everything seems inevitable, but the reality is always more complex. If Gorbachev had been determined to uphold Communist rule in Eastern Europe, as his predecessors were, he undoubtedly could have succeeded. The Soviet Union in the late 1980s still had more than enough military strength to enforce the Brezhnev Doctrine, provided that officials in Moscow had been willing to shed blood. Gorbachev's acceptance and even encouragement of the peaceful disintegration of the bloc thus stemmed from a conscious choice on his part, a choice bound up with his domestic priorities and his desire to do away with the legacies of the Stalin era that had blighted the Soviet economy. Any Soviet leader who was truly intent on overcoming Stalinism at home had to be willing to implement drastic changes in policy *vis-à-vis* Eastern Europe. Far-reaching liberalization and greater openness within the Soviet Union were incompatible with, and eventually would have been undermined by, a policy requiring military intervention on behalf of orthodox Communist regimes in Eastern Europe. The fundamental reorientation of Soviet domestic goals under Gorbachev therefore necessitated the relinquishment of Soviet hegemony over Eastern Europe, and that in turn swiftly led to the outright collapse of Soviet power in the region.

Chronology

	Domestic	*Regional*	*International*
Feb. 1948	Communists seize power in Czechoslovakia		
June 1948		Soviet–Yugoslav rift emerges in public	
Jan. 1949		Council for Mutual Economic Assistance founded	
Mar. 1953	Josef Stalin dies		
June 1953		Uprising in East Germany suppressed by Soviet troops	
May 1955		Warsaw Treaty Organization created	
Feb. 1956	Nikita Khrushchev delivers his 'secret speech' at the 20th Soviet Party Congress		
June 1956	Riots in Poznan violently suppressed by Polish security forces		
Oct. 1956		Crisis in Soviet–Polish relations defused peacefully	
Nov. 1956		Revolution in Hungary crushed by Soviet invasion	
Spring 1960			Sino-Soviet dispute flares into the open, creating a split in world Communism

	Domestic	Regional	International
Feb. 1961		Rift emerges between Soviet Union and Albania	
Spring 1964		Romania begins to pursue a more autonomous course	
Oct. 1964	Khrushchev is replaced by Leonid Brezhnev		
Jan. 1968	'Prague Spring' begins in Czechoslovakia		
Aug. 1968		Soviet-led forces invade Czechoslovakia	
Dec. 1970	Crisis in Poland leads to Władysław Gomułka's downfall		
May 1971	Walter Ulbricht removed from power in the GDR		
Aug. 1975			CSCE Final Act signed in Helsinki
June 1976	Widespread unrest re-emerges in Poland		
Summer 1980	'Solidarity' emerges spontaneously in Poland		
Dec. 1981	Martial law imposed in Poland		
Nov. 1982	Leonid Brezhnev dies		
Mar. 1985	Mikhail Gorbachev comes to power in Moscow		
Mar. 1988		Gorbachev's visit to Yugoslavia signals shift in policy	
Dec. 1988		Gorbachev pledges to reduce Soviet forces in Eastern Europe unilaterally	
June 1989	Parliamentary elections held in Poland, giving Solidarity an overwhelming victory		
Sept. 1989	Solidarity-led government comes to power in Poland		
Oct. 1989	Erich Honecker ousted in East Germany		

	Domestic	Regional	International
Nov. 1989	Berlin Wall opened		
Nov. 1989	Todor Zhivkov ousted in Bulgaria		
Dec. 1989	Violence engulfs Romania		
July 1990		Gorbachev agrees to accept reunified Germany within NATO	
Oct. 1990		Germany reunified	
Mar. 1991		Military organs of Warsaw Pact abolished	
June 1991		Last Soviet troops pulled out of Czechoslovakia and Hungary	
July 1991		CMEA and remaining components of the Warsaw Pact are dissolved	
Aug. 1991	Attempted hardline coup in Moscow rebuffed		
Dec. 1991		Soviet regime collapses	

Notes

1. The term 'Eastern Europe' is used in this chapter to refer primarily to the six countries other than the Soviet Union that were members of the Warsaw Pact until 1991: Bulgaria, Czechoslovakia, East Germany, Hungary, Poland, and Romania. A few references will also be made to Albania and Yugoslavia.
2. For an overview and critiques of dependency theory see S. J. Rosen and J. R. Kurth (eds.), *Theories of Economic Imperialism* (Lexington, Mass., 1978).
3. See esp. W. Zimmerman, 'Dependency Theory and the Soviet–East European Hierarchical Regional System: Initial Tests', *Slavic Review*, 37 (Dec. 1978), 604–23; C. Clark and D. Bahry, 'Dependent Development: A Socialist Variant', *International Studies Quarterly*, 27 (Sept. 1983), 271–93; J. L. Ray, 'Dependence, Political Compliance, and Economic Performance: Latin America and Eastern Europe', in C. W. Kegley, Jr., and P. McGowan (eds.), *The Political Economy of Foreign Policy Behavior* (Beverly Hills, Calif., 1981), 111–36.
4. See e.g. H. Bull, *The Anarchical Society: A Study of Order in World Politics* (New York, 1977), 213–25; P. Keal, *Unspoken Rules and Superpower Dominance* (London, 1983);

E. Kaufman, *The Superpowers and their Spheres of Influence: The United States and the Soviet Union in Eastern Europe and Latin America* (London, 1976); J. F. Triska (ed.), *Dominant Powers and Subordinate States: The United States in Latin America and the Soviet Union in Eastern Europe* (Durham, NC, 1986).

5. This way of categorizing unequal power relationships is similar, though not identical, to the discussion in Bull, *The Anarchical Society*, 213–19.

6. The notion of a trade-off between 'viability' and 'cohesion' is well presented in J. F. Brown, *Relations Between the Soviet Union and Its East European Allies: A Survey* (Santa Monica, Calif., 1975).

7. 'K voprosu o polozhenii v Chekhoslovakii: Vypiska iz protokola No. 95 zasedaniya Politbyuro TsK ot 17 avgusta 1968 g.', no. P95/1 (Top Secret), 17 Aug. 1968, in Arkhiv Prezidenta Rossiiskoi Federatsii (Moscow), prot. no. 38.

8. S. Kovalev, 'Suverenitet i internatsional'nye obyazannosti sotsialisticheskikh stran', *Pravda* (Moscow), 26 Sept. 1968, 4.

9. 'Vneshnyaya politika PNR na nyneshnem etape (Politpis'mo)', 9 July 1981, cable no. 595 (Top Secret) from B. I. Aristov, Soviet ambassador in Poland, in Tsentr Khraneniya Sovremennoi Dokumentatsii (TsKhSD), Fond (F.) 5, Opis' (Op.) 84, Delo (D.) 596, Listy (L.) 21–34.

10. 'Zasedanie Politbyuro TsK KPSS 29 oktyabrya 1980 goda: Materialy k druzhestvennomu rabochemu vizitu v SSSR pol'skikh rukovoditelei', 29 Oct. 1980 (Top Secret), in TsKhSD, F. 89, Op. 42, D. 31, L. 3.

11. Interview with Colonel Ryszard Kukliński in 'Wojna z narodem widziana od środka', *Kultura* (Paris), 4 (April 1987), 6–7, 17–19. Kukliński, as the top aide to General Wojciech Jaruzelski in 1980–81, was one of five officers on the Polish general staff responsible for devising the plans for martial law. He also was a spy for the US Central Intelligence Agency. He had to flee to the West in November 1981.

12. 'Why We Treat Communist Countries Differently', *Department of State Bulletin*, 51 (April 1964), 13.

13. N. S. Khrushchev, 'Vospominaniya', typescript (Moscow, 1969), vol. 4, pt. d, p. 10.

14. For estimates on the resource outflow see P. Marer, 'The Political Economy of Soviet Relations with Eastern Europe', in Rosen and Kurth (eds.), *Theories of Economic Imperialism*, 231–60.

15. US Central Intelligence Agency, *Handbook of Economic Statistics, 1987*, CPAS-870002 (Sept. 1987), 103–4.

16. M. Bornstein, 'Soviet–East European Economic Relations', in M. Bornstein et al. (eds.), *East–West Relations and the Future of Eastern Europe* (London, 1981), 105–6.

17. 'Ściśle tajne: KPZR o Polsce 1980–81', *Gazeta wyborcza* (Warsaw), 12–13 Dec. 1992, 11. See also 'Dostęp do wszystkiego', *Polityka* (Warsaw), 8 (20 Feb. 1993), 15.

18. R. O. Freedman, *Economic Warfare in the Communist Bloc: A Study of Soviet Economic Pressure against Yugoslavia, Albania, and Communist China* (New York, 1970).

19. 'Dokumenty "Komisji Susłowa"', *Rzeczpospolita* (Warsaw), 26 Aug. 1993, 20 (esp. docs. nos. 6 and 8). This same point was made in 'Polozhenie v PORP posle IX S'ezda', report no. 857 (Top Secret), 4 Nov. 1981, from V. F. Mal'tsev to Konstantin Rusakov, in TsKSD, F. 5, Op. 84, D. 596, L1. 35–53, esp. 53.

20. 'Zayavlenie rukovoditelei Bolgarii, Vengrii, GDR, Pol'shi, i Sovetskogo Soyuza' and 'Zayavlenie Sovetskogo pravitel'stva', *Izvestiya* (Moscow), 5 Dec. 1989, p. 2.

Further Reading

BRZEZINSKI, Z. K., *The Soviet Bloc: Unity and Conflict*, rev. and expanded edn. (Cambridge, Mass., 1967). A standard work covering the period from the 1940s through to the early 1960s.

HUTCHINGS, R. L., *Soviet–East European Relations: Consolidation and Conflict, 1968– 1980* (Madison, 1983). A useful complement to Brzezinski's book, covering the period from just after the invasion of Czechoslovakia through to the rise of Solidarity.

KRAMER, M. N., *Crisis in Czechoslovakia, 1968: The Prague Spring and the Soviet Invasion* (New York, 1996). Covers at length the Soviet–Czechoslovak crisis of 1968.

—— *From Dominance to Hegemony to Collapse: Soviet Policy in Eastern Europe, 1945– 1991* (Pittsburgh, Pa., 1996). A broader reassessment of Soviet policy in Eastern Europe between 1945 and 1991, drawing extensively on declassified archival materials and new memoirs.

MURRELL, P., *The Nature of Socialist Economies: Lessons from Eastern European Foreign Trade* (Princeton, 1990). Both this and Smith are among many useful works on Soviet– East European economic relations.

SMITH, A. H., *The Planned Economies of Eastern Europe* (London, 1983).

CHAPTER SIX

THE UNITED STATES AND WESTERN EUROPE: THE THEORY OF HEGEMONIC STABILITY

Andrew Wyatt-Walter

The theory of hegemonic stability probably remains the most popular and in-fluential theory in the subject of international political economy today. The basic proposition of the theory, that an open or 'liberal' international economic order requires the existence of a hegemonic or dominant power, retains wide support in the field and beyond. Although it has been the subject of consider-able criticism and modification since its elaboration in the 1970s, it has re-mained central to teaching and research in the field, and in international relations more generally. This popularity is not simply due to the apparent parsimony of the theory, nor only because of its obvious appeal to contemporary American scholars concerned about the consequences of US decline. The theory remains central to the discipline at least in part because it provides a powerful and intuitively attractive account of the rise and decline of international economic order over the past century. Even for its critics, which include the present au-thor, the theory provides a stepping-stone towards a deeper understanding of the dynamics of the international political economy. For these reasons alone, one cannot but take it seriously.

This chapter asks what light the theory of hegemonic stability can throw upon US–West European economic relations from 1945 to 1973. Space limitations do not allow a full 'test' of the theory here. However, if the theory is to justify its place within the discipline it must account for the evolution of US–European relations after 1945. The argument given here is that the theory (albeit with some important limitations) is somewhat useful in accounting for the establishment of the post-war international economic system, and particularly the crucial role of US leadership. However, it is considerably less successful in accounting for change in the system over the period considered. Specifically, it suffers from two main defects. First, and predictably, as a 'structural' theory of world economic order, it pays insufficient attention to important 'unit-level' (i.e. state and societal) factors in accounting for change. Secondly, and perhaps more surprisingly, even at the structural level of analysis the theory has shortcomings. Most importantly, its proponents have taken insufficient account of the relationship between economic and security relations among the major countries in the post-1945 period. The chapter argues that the course of post-war international trade and monetary relations was fundamentally shaped by the North Atlantic alliance. This was true both for the establishment of the post-war international economic order, and for its gradual erosion over the course of the 1960s and early 1970s. This suggests that other theories of international economic order are needed to reach an understanding of the dynamics of systemic change, even if they cannot entirely replace the theory of hegemonic stability.

The first section below provides a brief survey of the theory of hegemonic stability and outlines two main competing theories of post-war international economic cooperation, 'embedded liberalism' and 'alliance leadership'. In section 6.2 I then examine the establishment of the post-war economic system in the light of these three theories. A third section considers the role of hegemony in US–Western European monetary and trade relations during the Cold War period until 1973, focusing upon the conundrum of the breakdown of the Bretton Woods system and the relative resilience of the GATT. In the final section, I return to the general theoretical debate and to the question of the overall impact of the security structure upon US–European economic relations.

6.1. Explaining International Economic Openness: The Theory of Hegemonic Stability

The theory of hegemonic stability was a theoretical refinement of a common observation in post-war international relations: US dominance or 'hegemony' was the linchpin of the successful world capitalist economy after 1945. In the late 1940s, not only did the United States possess unrivalled power and prestige, it also had purpose. After intervening in two destructive wars in three decades, the United States wished to remodel fundamentally the structure of international political and economic relations in a manner consistent with its liberal ideals and particular interests. The main legacy of the post-war power and purpose of the United States was the Bretton Woods international monetary system and the GATT-based multilateral trade regime.

In the early 1970s, however, these monetary and trade regimes appeared to be threatened by growing economic conflict among the major industrial countries and associated relative US economic decline. Comparisons with Britain's precipitous decline as the leading power of the nineteenth century and the apparently disastrous consequences for the world economic system in the inter-war period were rife in the literature. This led to renewed attention to the idea that an open and stable world economy was causally related to the existence of hegemony, defined as a relative preponderance of power. As one of the authors of the theory, Charles Kindleberger, put it: 'for the world economy to be stabilized, there has to be a stabilizer, one stabilizer.'[1]

At the risk of oversimplification, two main versions of the theory exist, 'neoliberal' and 'neorealist'. Of the two, the more popular version currently is the neoliberal, in which the idea of international public goods plays a central role.[2] In an international system in which power is well dispersed among states, the provision of international collective goods such as financial assistance in a crisis or well-established rules on international trade is difficult. Individual states have an incentive to free-ride rather than to bear the costs of public goods provision alone. Without international government, only a hegemonic state can provide collective goods. The hegemon will provide such goods because its size ensures that the associated costs of provision are less than the economic benefits that accrue to it.

There is some disagreement over the dependent variable in the neoliberal version of the theory. For Kindleberger, examining international monetary history in the inter-war period, the focus was upon the stability of the world economy. For most international relations theorists, the dependent variable has been systemic openness. Kindleberger was concerned with who, in a potentially unstable system, would provide management functions, particularly a long-term flow of international liquidity and short-term emergency liquidity in a major international financial crisis. He argued that the problem was associated less with the establishment of the system than with its continuing management, and hence was pessimistic about the consequences of hegemonic decline, particularly in a crisis.

Most international relations scholars, following Kindleberger's lead, saw the provision of liberal rules (or 'regimes') fostering openness as the core hegemonic task. The emphasis upon rules rather than crisis management led them to be more optimistic than Kindleberger concerning the possibility of post-hegemonic systemic openness. Collective action problems were more acute in the establishment phase than they were once international regimes were up and running. Keohane argued that hegemony was more important for the establishment of regimes than for their maintenance, allowing the possibility of regime-based cooperation 'after hegemony'.[3]

The neorealist version of the theory of hegemonic stability is less dependent upon the idea of international public goods, though some realists employ similar language. Neorealists hold that states have different policy preferences that depend upon their relative positions in the world economy. A hegemonic state is most likely to favour an open world economy, in contrast to the preferences of medium-sized states. This makes free trade most likely when a hegemon is able to provide carrots and sticks to other states to persuade them to adopt liberal trade policies.[4] In the neorealist version of the theory of hegemonic stability there is an element of exploitation in the system. The hegemon structures the system for its own benefit, although significant benefits for others may result. The hegemon uses its power to enforce other states' compliance with the prevailing rules. Accordingly, realists tend to be pessimistic about the prospects for post-hegemonic cooperation. Hegemonic decline brings with it a declining ability to enforce compliance by others, and a declining hegemonic interest in a system operating more to the benefit of others. Hence, after hegemony, world economic closure is likely, as in the inter-war period.

Common to both versions of the theory of hegemonic stability is a structural focus. The outcome, the openness and stability of the international economic system, results from the distribution of power among states. States are assumed to be rational actors, and domestic policy the product of systemic factors. Perhaps surprisingly, security factors rarely played an important role in the analysis. Realists such as Robert Gilpin did not see the Cold War security structure as significantly affecting economic relations *within* the Western alliance.[5] So, too, neoliberals ignored security. To quote Keohane: 'it is justifiable to focus principally on the political economy of the advanced industrialized countries without continually taking into account the politics of international security.'[6]

Theorists ignored security factors for a number of reasons. First, the introduction of security factors would have greatly diluted the theory's parsimony. Secondly, the growing economic conflict between the major industrial countries in the 1960s and 1970s occurred without the significant erosion of bipolar security structure, suggesting that Keohane's judgement was correct. Thirdly, US attempts to gain leverage in bargaining on monetary and trade matters by linking them to security relations were difficult or counter-productive in a world of 'complex interdependence'.[7] Finally, if the theory was to be grounded upon more than the post-1945 American case and the comparison with Britain in the nineteenth century to be effective, it was best to ignore the large differences between the security structures of the late nineteenth century and the post-1945 era.

An alternative interpretation of post-war Western economic relations accords a central role to security factors. For the want of a better title and with some theoretical licence, I term this the 'alliance leadership' theory. In this interpretation, free trade might only be possible within security alliances, since an open international economy will produce differential gains and hence negative 'security externalities' for some states.[8] Within an alliance, common security interests reduce concerns about relative gains from open trade among allies. The hegemon as alliance leader may even conclude that actively promoting relative gains by allies may be in its security interest, at least if such allies are unlikely to defect. In short, security concerns shape the hegemon's economic relations with its allies, and provide all members of an alliance with an incentive to liberalize trade among themselves rather than with others.

A final interpretation of post-war Western economic relations focuses upon the normative rather than the material foundations of international economic order. The theory of 'ideational consensus' centres upon the role played by a transnational intellectual consensus over the appropriate shape of the international economic system in fostering regime establishment and cooperation. Its most prominent proponent is John Ruggie, with his theory of 'embedded liberalism' in the post-war economic order.[9] This theory does overlap with the theory of hegemonic stability (and alliance leadership), particularly if one stresses the role of the hegemon's culture and domestic ideology in forging such an international intellectual consensus.[10] However, there is a strong sense in Ruggie's theory that inter-state élite agreement over normative principles is only robust if these principles are consistent with the deeper alignment of social forces within the major countries.

Table 6.1 summarizes the main claims of the four theories outlined above. Before proceeding further, it is useful to clarify how each theory understands the relationship between power and interests in the international political economy. The neorealist version of hegemonic stability theory sees interests as deriving from the position of individual states in the world economic structure. Countries with small open economies prefer free trade, as does the hegemon because of its comparative advantage in leading industries, while middle-sized and developing states tend to prefer protection. There is also a dynamic element in neorealist theory, since the erosion of the hegemon's economic preponderance reduces its 'structural' interest in an open world economy. In contrast, the neoliberal version has a more static conception of state interest. Neoliberals presume that all states have a long-run self-interest in an open world economy, but that it may be in the short-run interest of an individual state to protect (i.e. free-ride). Hegemonic power, through the provision of regimes, allows a more enlightened self-interest to surface and cooperation to become sustainable. There is no necessary reason why the long-run interest of states will change over time. The possible exception is the hegemon which, as it declines, finds that its ability to provide new public goods and to maintain existing ones diminishes. While its long-run interest in openness may not alter, the hegemon too may be tempted to free-ride, and the short-run interests of other states may shift in turn.

Table 6.1. Hegemonic stability theory and two alternative explanations: a summary analysis

Phases	Hegemonic stability theory		Alternative explanations	
	Neorealism	Neoliberalism	Alliance leadership	Ideational consensus
Crisis phase	Great power struggle for preponderance	Collapse of previous international regimes	Breakdown of old balance of power	Breakdown of previous transnational societal norms
Regime creation	Hegemonic power imposes order	Hegemonic leadership overcomes collective action problems	Solidification of new alliance structures produces intra-alliance regimes	Based upon the achievement of a new set of norms to govern international and domestic policy
Regime compliance and cooperation	Power-based (hegemon enforces compliance with carrots and sticks)	Regimes enhance transparency and reduce costs of cooperation (existence of common interests), plus hegemonic 'crisis management'	External security threat and alliance leadership by hegemon	Mutual acceptance of normative principles reduces conflict
Hegemonic decline	Regime erosion and collapse as hegemon reacts to consequences of relative decline (but 'lags' may occur)	Some regime erosion is likely as hegemon adjusts to reduced power, but collapse is difficult to predict	Hegemonic decline may result in intra-alliance burden-sharing disputes, disrupting economic relations between allies	Relative hegemonic decline may produce some normative conflict and regime erosion
Multipolarity	'Oligopolistic competition' produces closure of world economy (even if small states prefer openness, collective action problems exist)	Regimes may be self-perpetuating due to common interests (but absence of hegemony may be fatal in a crisis)	Multipolarity produces enhanced relative gains concerns and probably the fragmentation of the world economy	If normative principles are robust and social divisions limited, regime-based cooperation may persist

Alliance leadership theory considers a state's economic interest to be a function of its national security posture. A state will have an interest in economic cooperation with alliance partners, and this interest could change over time should the military alliance erode or should the security options of a country shift. Finally, in the theory of ideational consensus, the definition and elaboration of state interest is dependent upon the formation of a domestic social consensus concerning the relationship of domestic to international economic policy. State interest may evolve over time, but is likely to result from deeper changes at the societal level rather than from the shifting balance of economic power at the international level.

I now turn to consider how the theory of hegemonic stability performs as an explanation of the construction of the major post-war regimes relevant to US–West European economic relations after 1945.

6.2. The US, Europe, and the Establishment of the Post-war Economic System

How and why were the Bretton Woods international monetary system and the GATT international trade system established in the 1940s? Both neorealist and neoliberal versions of the theory are correct in stressing the importance of US hegemonic leadership in establishing Bretton Woods and the GATT in the 1940s. Nevertheless, this section argues that there are two main difficulties with the interpretation offered by the theory of hegemonic stability. First, as Ruggie argued, a normative consensus within and between the major countries facilitated agreement on the basic principles. Secondly, even if one downplays this as a factor, the regimes were largely a product of US–British negotiations in which the United States made major concessions to British demands.

The intellectual consensus at the heart of the post-war economic regimes was real and important, and countries other than the United States—particularly Britain, but also other West European countries—were instrumental in its achievement. For all industrial countries in both Western Europe and North America, the inter-war and wartime experience had made a full restoration of *laissez-faire* capitalism and the gold standard politically unacceptable. It also made some degree of state intervention in the economy necessary. Even so, most countries, particularly Britain and the United States, had a considerable interest in the restoration of a stable and prosperous world economy, and in preventing a relapse into the disastrous 'beggar-thy-neighbour' policies of the 1930s. The only viable compromise was some balance between state interventionism at home and liberalization of international trade and payments abroad. This compromise was necessary within both British and US societies, as well as between their governing élites: weakening support for the New Deal in America meant that Britain tended to be the more staunch supporter of state intervention in the economy. The international institutions that emerged reflected this compromise.

The International Monetary Negotiations

Negotiations on the shape of the post-war international monetary system began between the British and US governments in the depth of the war. The history of these negotiations leading up to the Bretton Woods agreement of 1944 provides only qualified support for the theory of hegemonic stability. US hegemonic leadership was a crucial ingredient in the process, but the need for consensus between the US and British governments gave Britain more influence over the outcome than its economic position alone would have permitted. However, nor is an amalgam of the theory of hegemonic stability and embedded liberalism fully convincing as an explanation of the shape of the post-war monetary order. As we shall see, the international monetary arrangements agreed at Bretton Woods proved completely inadequate by 1947. They were replaced by a set of ad hoc arrangements that owed much to US alliance leadership.

Early British proposals on international monetary arrangements dating from 1941 took shape by 1942 in the so-called 'Keynes plan' for an international clearing union. This was a radical conception, aiming at the collective management of international money by a world central bank. This, Keynes felt, could guarantee plentiful international liquidity for current account deficit countries like Britain, while preventing countries in surplus, like the United States, from pursuing policies that could result in a global liquidity shortage. However, the US government understood that the potential US liability under such a system would be unacceptable to Congress, and it rejected the Keynes plan as too radical and potentially inflationary. The US Treasury's 'White Plan', named after Secretary Morgenthau's deputy in charge of the negotiations, became the basis of the negotiations. The White plan envisaged an International Monetary Fund (IMF) made up of members' contributions of gold and foreign exchange. Countries would be able to borrow very limited amounts from the Fund on a conditional basis to finance temporary balance-of-payments deficits. Nevertheless, the IMF was still a radical departure from what had gone before.

Compelled to accept the White Plan and its relatively tight liquidity constraint, the British government demanded and gained a series of concessions from the US side reflected in the agreement at Bretton Woods. First, the United States offered the famous 'scarce currency clause', allowing the rationing, through the IMF, of any currency that was in scarce supply. Secondly, while discriminatory trade and exchange restrictions should be avoided in principle, they would be allowed in an unspecified 'transition period' after the end of the war. Even after this transition period, countries would be expected to adopt currency convertibility for current account transactions, but not on capital account. Both US and British negotiators accepted restrictions on short-term capital movements (against their domestic financial interests) as a necessary prerequisite for domestic monetary control in a system of pegged exchange rates.

Thirdly, Britain successfully insisted upon a greater degree of national sovereignty over the exchange rate than was initially envisaged by either side. The mutual concern to avoid a repetition of the competitive devaluations of the interwar period had at first led negotiators to propose considerable supranational control over exchange rate policies. The British argued that par values should be fixed but adjustable. In the event of a 'fundamental disequilibrium' in the balance of payments, only par value changes greater than 10 per cent should require Fund approval. Furthermore, the notion of fundamental disequilibrium (implying long-term unsustainability) was highly ambiguous, and limited the Fund's ability to disapprove in practice.

Hence overwhelming US power did not enable the government of the United States simply to 'set the rules' of the international monetary system.[11] Moreover, soon after the rules were laid out in the Bretton Woods agreement, they were found to be completely inappropriate to post-war international circumstances. Reconstruction and development were to be the tasks of the IMF's sister institution, the International Bank for Reconstruction and Development (World Bank), but the Bank had even fewer resources than the Fund. By 1947 the Bretton Woods system had effectively collapsed, as the resources it provided for reconstruction in Western Europe were inadequate.

Despite this fatal inadequacy, the US government pursued Bretton Woods as a policy long after post-war circumstances had rendered it unviable. Understanding that British acceptance of Bretton Woods rules was vital, the United States granted Britain a balance-of-payments loan of $3.75 billion in December 1945, the equivalent of over 40 per cent of total planned IMF resources. This was a doomed strategy. The US Treasury insisted as a condition of the loan that Britain reintroduce sterling convertibility within eighteen months. When it reluctantly did so in July 1947, a run on sterling began which rapidly depleted British reserves. The British government revoked convertibility only seven weeks later.

The failure of Bretton Woods considerably weakened the influence of the Treasury on the US government's European strategy. In the meantime, political events in the form of the beginning of the Cold War conspired to provide the State Department with the means to set out a new and more viable strategy. This had already begun with the announcement of the Marshall Plan in June 1947, and now led to the wholesale abandonment of the Bretton Woods regime and associated policies. Security considerations produced a new kind of US hegemonic leadership that might not otherwise have been forthcoming. Economics had now become the servant of US grand strategy, rather than the reverse.

The geostrategic argument was that the United States had to prevent Western Europe from 'falling like a rotten apple' into Stalin's lap, by providing the finance for Europe's structural payments deficits that the Bretton Woods institutions could not. With Marshall Aid, the US bypassed the IMF and World Bank, and promoted European integration and discrimination against the dollar and US exports. To hard-nosed critics within the US government such as the Federal Reserve and Treasury, the State Department argued that the Marshall Plan represented at most the postponement and not the abandonment of Bretton Woods principles. Marshall planners in the State Department and in the Economic Cooperation Administration, set up to administer Marshall Aid, supported regional integration in Europe. They did so on the grounds that only through a single, integrated European economy and even political system could Europe hope to become 'viable', and hence a strong and stable partner for the United States.[12] While this argument was useful for convincing domestic sceptics of the need for a policy reversal, the clinching argument was that Marshall Aid was in the US security interest. After all, if European 'viability' could only be achieved through full integration, why did the US government not wish to promote regional integration elsewhere?

The International Trading System Negotiations

The United States and Britain, not to mention other countries, were further away from agreement on the basic principles of international trade than they were on monetary issues. During wartime negotiations, the United States attempted to use Britain's financial weakness to obtain a British commitment to the elimination of the system of trade preferences known as imperial preference. This was central to the US State Department goal of eliminating discriminatory trading blocs, seen as the main cause of depression and war. Yet within a few years US policy had shifted entirely towards the promotion of discriminatory European trade integration, and had effectively dropped opposition to imperial preference. As on the monetary side, although the theories of hegemonic stability and embedded liberalism help to explain US leadership and the shape of the agreements reached on international trade, they do not adequately explain this shift in US policy. For this, security factors are again central.

Ever since the US Congress legislated the Reciprocal Trade Agreements Act (RTAA) of 1934, America had been negotiating tariff reductions with its major trading partners. The British feared (correctly) that US Secretary of State Cordell Hull's main goal in the wartime negotiations was to eliminate imperial preference, established at Ottawa in 1932. American political and financial leverage gave

Hull the chance to see his dream realized. Britain reluctantly agreed in principle to the dismantling of imperial preference in the Atlantic Charter of 1941, in the Lend–Lease agreements during the war, and as a condition of the 1945 US balance-of-payments loan.

At the same time, Britain had a considerable interest in the reduction of trade barriers, if not in the elimination of preferences. As with its monetary proposals, the initial British proposal on trade in 1942 called for a supranational inter-national commercial union to establish more harmonious trade relations, and for tariff reductions to be made on a multilateral across-the-board basis. This proposal was aimed at the still high level of US tariffs, and at the US government's preference for a selective item-by-item approach to tariff reduction, which would allow it to continue protection for specific sectors. Britain refused to contem-plate the elimination of preferences unless the United States was willing to accept the principle of large cuts in its tariffs, but protectionist sentiment in the US Congress prevented any such deal.[13] The US government was unable to accept the more radical British approach to tariff-cutting (as it refused to accept Keynes's clearing union), and successfully linked a British commitment to the elimination of preferences to the December 1945 loan.[14] This particular piece of linkage is perhaps the best example of the exercise of hegemonic power in the early post-war period. The problem for the theory of hegemonic stability is that the linkage failed, just as linkage had failed on the monetary side. By late summer 1947, US policy had shifted towards a much more constructive stance.

Before then, the US government persisted in its attempts to eliminate preferences. In late 1946 UN negotiations began in London and continued in Geneva in 1947, aimed at obtaining the agreement of other countries to the Anglo-American agreement of mid-1945 to establish an international trade organization (ITO). As late as July 1947, American trade negotiators such as Francis Wilcox still hoped to use Marshall Aid as an additional source of leverage over Britain on the question of preferences. However, General Marshall himself signalled the reversal in US policy by telegraphing the US delegation in Geneva on 2 August 1947 to accept 'in the circumstances' the British desire to continue imperial preference.[15] As an interim measure before the establishment of the ITO, the twenty-three countries gathered at Geneva signed the General Agreement on Tariffs and Trade (GATT) on 30 October 1947. The GATT was a statement of general trading principles that would underpin the ITO. Article 1 established the principle of unconditional most favoured nation (MFN) treatment, but allowed for the continuation of imperial preference (though tariff negotiations would erode the latter over time).

The shift in US policy was hardly due to a meeting of minds on the specifics of embedded liberalism: the US government continued to anathematize prefer-ences. Rather, as on the monetary side, British cooperation was simply too important for the emerging US strategy of containment of the Soviet Union. The extent of the shift in the US position is also clear from the agreement on Article 24 of the GATT, which allowed the formation of customs unions and free trade areas, further compromising the principle of non-discrimination. Article 24, like the Marshall Plan, was consistent with the new US foreign policy goal of promoting European integration in the interests of Atlantic security. For Britain and for other West European countries, the Cold War helped to shift American policy in a direction more consistent with European interests.[16]

Indeed, over 1947–8 the Cold War led the Truman administration towards an imaginative solution to the post-war European predicament, and to a more flexible interpretation of what the compromise of embedded liberalism would mean in practice. The Soviet threat not only prompted the United States to extend the post-war transition period more or less indefinitely, but also fostered a greater tolerance of serious departures from the US model of capitalism in Western Europe. Of course, US domestic politics had always ruled out global free trade as a serious policy goal, but the promotion of American exports had been such a goal. With the failure of the US Senate to ratify the ITO charter in 1950, the virtual irrelevance of the major international institutions envisaged by the wartime planners was complete. Although the GATT would serve as the platform for multilateral trade liberalization in the 1950s and beyond, it was riddled with so many exceptions to its core principles that it was difficult at the time to be convinced of its potential effectiveness.

6.3. US–West European Monetary and Trade Relations up to 1973

Looking back, it is easy to view the 1950s and 1960s as a golden age of the post-war boom as well as of US–West European economic relations. It is equally tempting to attribute this to the stabilizing influence of US hegemony, particularly given what was to come later once the relative decline of the United States became apparent. The breakdown of the system of fixed exchange rates by early 1973, the first oil crisis, the 1974–5 recession and subsequent macroeconomic and trade policy wrangling between the major countries suggested to many that the United States was no longer sufficiently strong to impose order upon the world economy and on Euro-American economic relations.[17] We have seen that a modified theory of hegemonic stability is useful if not entirely satisfactory as an explanation of the US role in the establishment of the post-war economic regimes. Arguably, however, the real test of the theory must lie in its ability to account for the change in the structure of US–West European economic relations from the late 1940s to the early 1970s. This section argues that the theory of hegemonic stability is least satisfactory as an explanation of these changes, particularly because of its failure adequately to take into account the way in which security factors impinged upon economic relations between the major industrial countries.

The Rise and Fall of the Gold–Dollar Standard

In 1949 the US government proposed the creation of a European Payments Union (EPU) to facilitate the reconstruction of European trade. While it was presented to US critics as a means to the eventual re-establishment of currency convertibility in Europe, in the medium term it meant the continuation of policies that would discriminate against US exports in favour of intra-European trade. This was consistent with the new policy favouring European integration and moving away from Bretton Woods, and with the view that Western security required asymmetric economic arrangements between the United States and Europe. The EPU, in combination with the large devaluations of all major European currencies during 1948–9, resulted in a rapid improvement of the European payments position after 1950. By mid-1952 continental Western Europe was in balance on private-sector trade with the United States. Continuing large flows of US civil and military aid to Europe led to a steady increase in their dollar reserves. Over 1950–57, the Organization for European Economic Cooperation (OEEC) countries' reserves increased by $6.5 billion, of which $5 billion accrued to West Germany alone. This increase in European reserves consisted in almost equal parts of increases in gold and foreign exchange, with new dollar reserves accounting for almost all of the latter. Accordingly, the 1950s saw the rise of the gold–dollar standard, which rested upon a presumption that the dollar would continue to be fully convertible into gold at $35 per ounce.[18]

From 1950, the United States was effectively acting as banker to the Western alliance. Large US current account surpluses were financed by even larger capital outflows and official transfers, leading to the voluntary accumulation of dollar reserves by European countries. The contrast with the inter-war period could not have been greater. Growing confidence in Europe due to rapid growth in incomes and trade eventually enabled the major countries to return to effective current account convertibility at the end of 1958.

However, the gold–dollar standard was in trouble as soon as the transition period for Western Europe had effectively ended. Within a decade, it had collapsed. The trouble began in 1958–9, when the US Treasury lost $3.4 billion in gold reserves, compared to just $1.7 billion over the previous eight years (see Table 6.2). The erosion of the real price of gold due to wartime and post-war inflation had led to a steady reduction in the flow of new gold on to the London

Table 6.2. Selected comparisons of major industrial countries, 1950–1975

Variable	Country	1950	1955	1960	1965	1970	1975
Ratio to	US	1.00		1.00			1.00
US GDP[a]	Germany	0.14		0.22			0.23
	Japan	0.10		0.16			0.33
	UK	0.22		0.21			0.19
	France	0.14		0.15			0.19
Share of	US	17	18	17	16	15	13
world	Germany	3	7	10	11	12	11
exports (%)	Japan	1	2	3	5	7	7
	UK	11	10	9	9	7	5
	France	5	6	6	6	6	6
Share of	US	68	62	47	34	30	27
world gold	Germany	—	3	8	11	11	12
reserves (%)	Japan	—	—	1	1	1	2
	UK	9	6	7	5	4	2
	France	2	3	4	11	10	10

[a] GDP is calculated in constant (1984) $US.
Source: Andrew Walter, *World Power and World Money: The Role of Hegemony and International Monetary Order* (Hemel Hempstead/New York, 1993), 153.

gold market. This developing shortage led European central banks to present dollar balances for conversion into gold at the US Treasury's 'gold window'. In contrast to the previous decade, over 1958–67 increases in foreign exchange reserves (mostly dollars) accounted for 72 per cent of the total increase in global reserves, with new gold reserves adding only 9 per cent and new IMF and BIS (Bank for International Settlements) reserve positions contributing 19 per cent. In other words, the drying up of gold production meant that European countries had only two options: to move towards an effective 'dollar standard' by allowing the gold composition of their reserves to fall steadily, or to try to maintain the gold–dollar standard by asking the United States to convert some dollar reserves into gold.

Robert Triffin was the first to signal that this caught the United States and the world on the horns of a dilemma.[19] If the world continued to rely upon dollar deficits to provide international liquidity, eventually the convertibility of the dollar into gold must be undermined; if the United States took action to reduce or eliminate its deficits to maintain gold–dollar convertibility, the world would be plunged into a liquidity crisis with potentially disastrous consequences. For Triffin and many others, the gold–dollar standard was inherently unstable and required to be replaced by a more rational system akin to that envisaged by

Keynes during the war (this was to become the proposal to create 'special draw-ing rights' within the IMF). Others disagreed, arguing that the gold–dollar stan-dard could be saved by a substantial increase in the real gold price, increasing the supply of new gold, and revaluing US reserves.[20]

An increase in the gold price was politically unacceptable to the US government during the 1960s. It would favour the French, who had openly called for such an increase, and the Russian and South African producers. The United States attempted to persuade other countries to reduce their demand for gold, organ-izing the gold pool (made up of the central banks of the major industrial coun-tries) in 1961 in response to growing pressure in the private gold market. However, continuing large US overall deficits ensured that by the end of 1967 US gold reserves had fallen to $12 billion while short-term liabilities to foreigners amounted to $30 billion. The long-resisted devaluation of sterling in November 1967 unleashed a rush from dollars into gold. This forced the abandonment of the gold pool and the separation of the private and official gold markets in the two-tier arrangement of March 1968. From this time, even the official gold convertibility of the dollar at $35 per ounce was at risk. Everyone realized that any attempt at large-scale conversion of dollars by central banks would force the complete closure of the US Treasury's gold window. It was but a short step to Nixon's decision formally to take the dollar off the gold standard in August 1971.

Hence, the real question was not whether the gold–dollar standard could be saved by an increase in the gold price or by replacing it with a Keynes-style world central bank. It was whether Western Europe, and above all West Germany, would accept a dollar standard. After all, there was never any serious prospect that the United States would significantly reduce the aid, military, and investment outflows producing the overall deficits. These were the very basis of US hegemony within the West, and they continued unabated. Nor, despite their growing cri-ticism of US monetary policy in the 1960s, could West European (or East Asian) countries have seriously desired the economic and political consequences of any such reductions in the US role. There was a series of ad hoc measures designed to limit US capital outflows and to reduce the balance-of-payments costs of foreign troop deployment in the 1960s, but these had limited impact. The pol-itics of the Western alliance were consistent with the dominant role of the dollar within the international monetary system.

The French government understood this linkage, but mistakenly believed that it might be broken. In a famous press conference in 1965, President de Gaulle called openly for the restoration of the gold standard. A barrage of French criticism of US policy followed, suggesting that, through its inflationary payments deficits, the United States was paying for the Vietnam War, Johnson's 'great society', and the acquisition of European assets 'on credit'. The claim that the

United States enjoyed an 'exorbitant privilege' within the alliance and the international monetary system touched a raw nerve in Washington, as did France's policy of demanding gold for French dollar reserves and its withdrawal from NATO's integrated military command. The quest for French monetary autonomy was directly linked to its desire for symbolic military autonomy, resting upon its ability to free-ride upon America's willingness to defend West Germany.

As suggested above, however, this source of apparent French strength constituted the main source of US hegemony within the Western alliance. France could not overcome the effective leverage that the United States enjoyed over Britain, Japan, and West Germany due to their dependence upon US military protection. Although many European leaders outside France agreed with de Gaulle's economic analysis, the United States' most important allies had a basic security interest in the creation of the dollar standard. West Germany was the linchpin of the American strategy. The German government agreed to offset the costs of US troop deployment and prevailed upon the Bundesbank to agree not to convert its dollar balances into gold. The Bundesbank gave a pledge to this effect in the celebrated Blessing letter of March 1967.[21] The United States reached similar agreements with other major holders of dollars, all of which were important and relatively loyal US allies. France's inability to persuade West Germany to accept French military protection in place of that of the United States underlined the basic weakness of de Gaulle's strategy.

Thus between 1967 and 1971 the United States unilaterally changed the basic structure of the international monetary system. It could do so because of its position as leader of the Western alliance. A dollar standard was formally and relatively quietly instituted in the Smithsonian Agreement in December 1971, which revalued other major currencies against the dollar and left the latter inconvertible into gold. However, security leverage could not ensure the stability of the dollar standard. The increasing pre-eminence of domestic economic objectives in American policy thinking, as indicated by growing support within the Nixon administration for a floating exchange rate system, rendered the new system unstable.[22] Furthermore, increasing short-term capital mobility made greater policy coordination between the major countries necessary at the same time as basic policy objectives were diverging. In 1970–1, the US Federal Reserve was reducing interest rates to stimulate a sluggish domestic economy, while the Bundesbank was increasing interest rates to reduce what it saw as largely imported inflation. This led to a massive flow of funds into the Deutschmark (DM) which undermined German monetary policy. When this happened again in early 1973, the Bundesbank convinced the German government that enough was enough, and the DM floated off its dollar peg. The dollar standard lasted for an even shorter period than the Bretton Woods system.

The central problem with the theory of hegemonic stability as an explanation of the evolution of the international monetary system until 1973 is that it ignores the degree of choice available to the US hegemon. The US decision to oppose European calls for a revaluation of gold ensured that the gold–dollar standard was beyond saving. America's ability to foster the emergence of the unstable dollar standard rested upon its security leverage as alliance leader. To concentrate, as does the theory of hegemonic stability, upon the consequences of the economic decline of the hegemon risks missing the point. That said, the neorealist version of the theory usefully links the economic decline of the hegemon with eroding interests in systemic openness. Certainly, there is little doubt that the shift in US policy that did occur reflected a general feeling in the Nixon administration that perceived US relative economic decline made the existing system additionally intolerable. However, the theory is unable to explain why the hegemon was successful in forging a new international monetary system that, although it was more consistent with perceived US interests, was not obviously a step away from systemic 'openness'.

Finally, similar problems afflict the theory of embedded liberalism. The change in regime was hardly the result of a new transnational consensus. Dissatisfaction with US monetary policy was running so high in West Germany and elsewhere from the late 1960s that it is doubtful whether, without German security dependence upon America, the dollar standard (at least in the form in which the United States was offering it) would have been acceptable. Within only a few years, the combination of destabilizing US macroeconomic policy and the rise of detente led to a German decision to abandon the dollar standard altogether.

US–European Trade Relations until the Tokyo Round

By the end of the 1960s Atlantic trade relations had become only slightly less conflictual than monetary relations. This reflected very similar forces: the more rapid economic growth of US allies, the growing penetration of US markets in certain sectors, and the associated deterioration of the US current account position from the mid-1960s. As the neorealist version of the theory of hegemonic stability suggests, relative US decline brought with it a declining interest in the existing system. To this extent, the theory is useful as a broad explanation. However, it is unable to account for the chronology of trade liberalization between the United States and its major allies in Western Europe. The 1960s witnessed more substantial liberalization than the 1950s, when US economic preponderance was much greater.

As early as the mid-1950s, when the European boom was well under way, Congress became increasingly dissatisfied with the apparently slow pace of European trade liberalization *vis-à-vis* the United States. However, in three GATT rounds from 1950, culminating in the Dillon Round of 1960–61, average US tariffs were cut by less than 10 per cent. This was partly because the easier reductions had been made in the 1940s, but also because the item-by-item approach to tariff reduction had run out of steam. Democrats in Congress shifted towards a more protectionist stance over the 1950s. This constrained the Eisenhower administration's authority on tariff cuts (usually to the order of 5 per cent per year), and imposed various 'peril-point' and escape clause conditions.[23]

The passage of the Kennedy administration's Trade Expansion Act of 1962 signalled the reversal of this protectionist trend within Congress. The result was the successful Kennedy Round of 1963–7, when average US industrial tariffs were cut by 35 per cent. In the 1962 Act, Congress handed the new President 50 per cent tariff-reducing authority over five years, allowed the utilization of an across-the board method rather than item-by-item bargaining, limited peril-point and escape clause protection, and authorized negotiations on non-tariff barriers (NTBs). While the immediate reason for the greater success of the GATT in the 1960s lay in the shifting ground of domestic US politics, we must ask what caused this shift.

One explanation is that the Kennedy administration managed the domestic politics of trade policy much better than the outgoing Eisenhower administration. Kennedy undercut forces for protection within Congress by providing adjustment assistance for displaced workers and firms, and bought off politically important sectors like textiles with specific protection.[24] He took charge of the marketing of the proposed legislation, selling the benefits of freer trade to Congress more effectively than Eisenhower.

However, the vigour of the Kennedy administration in pushing for trade liberalization was itself in part the product of two other factors: the perceived need for a renewal of the Western alliance and the rise of the EEC as a trade power of considerable weight in the world economy. Both played central and interconnected roles in Kennedy's speech to Congress of 25 January 1962: 'The growth of the European Common Market—an economy which may soon nearly equal our own . . . [has] laid the groundwork for a radical alteration of the economics of the Atlantic Alliance.'[25] The rise of the EEC and the potential trade- and investment-diversionary impact of the EEC's Common External Tariff (CET) and Common Agricultural Policy (CAP) upon the United States was central, particularly given concern about the deterioration of the US payments position. American trade negotiators understood that the diversity of the EEC would make it impossible for them to negotiate on the old item-by-item basis, requiring the shift to an across-the-board approach.

The economic threat posed by the EEC to the United States was most important in producing the shift in domestic politics. After all, nothing in the bipolar structure of security relations had changed since the 1950s, when intra-Western trade negotiations were less successful. However, the politics of alliance trade had become inseparable from the politics of alliance security. Although one could trace the origins of the Atlantic 'burden-sharing' debate almost to the very beginnings of NATO,[26] the Kennedy administration was signalling publicly in its call for a 'two-pillared' alliance that a much stronger Europe needed to play a greater role within NATO. It is doubtful how serious the United States was in its expressed wish to accord Europe equal status within the alliance. Many European governments, not only the French, saw Kennedy's policy as an attempt to get them to pay more without removing their subordinate status. The US request for a restructuring of the alliance was largely ignored by Western Europe until the Nixon administration's much blunter insistence on a full dialogue in 1971. In the meantime, individual countries such as West Germany quietly made concessions on US troop costs and on trade.

The neoliberal version of the theory of hegemonic stability does help to explain the shift in US economic priorities towards demanding that other countries contribute more to the provision of 'international public goods'. However, this shift constitutes a major difficulty for the neorealist version of the theory. This version holds that the economic decline of the hegemon brings with it a declining interest in systemic openness. Yet the US perception of its relative economic decline produced more active US leadership within the GATT and ultimately much greater trade liberalization than in the 1950s. Thus the direction of causation appears to be the opposite to that predicted by the theory.

The Kennedy Round was in large part a US–European dialogue. Table 6.3 indicates the trade power of the EEC. What the EEC lacked in cohesion on trade policy it made up for in sheer weight in the international trading system.[27] As the CET gradually replaced individual countries' tariffs over 1959–68, the US government understood the implications of this growing weight and shifted its trade policy in response. The United States also assumed that the EEC would eventually expand to take in Britain and other smaller West European countries, although France's 1963 veto of Britain's first application was a major blow to this assumption. The willingness of the EEC (and particularly France) to use this bargaining power to resist US calls for the liberalization of the Community's agricultural trade was indicative of the shift from hegemony towards bipolarity in international trade. The failure to liberalize agricultural trade was one of the major shortcomings of the round; the liberalization of manufacturing trade, through US–EEC bilateral bargains, was its central success.

As suggested above, the neoliberal version of the theory of hegemonic stability does help to explain why eroding US trade hegemony could be consistent with greater trade liberalization. However, the neoliberal version is misleading in its focus on the GATT as an international public good. It ignores the fact that the US–EEC dialogue in the Kennedy Round was a bilateral relationship nested within a military alliance. GATT trade liberalization in the 1960s was

Table 6.3. Percentage shares of world exports (excluding intra-EC exports), 1960–1985

	1960	1970	1975	1985
US	17.2	15.9	15.1	13.8
EC	27.4	26.5	20.4	18.7
US + EC	44.6	42.4	35.5	32.5

Source: Calculated from UNCTAD, *Handbook of International Trade and Development Statistics* (New York, 1992), tables 1.1 and 1.12.

overwhelmingly in products of interest to the major industrial countries, which were members of a US-centred alliance. The GATT system was less a world free trade system than a trade system established by an alliance leader. The 'success' of the Kennedy Round must be qualified accordingly. It was considerably less important for the developing countries, let alone the Soviet bloc countries, which remained outside the GATT. Mutual security interdependence provided the United States and Western Europe with incentives to liberalize trade among themselves. This was partly due to the habit of cooperation and partly because their mutual enrichment would enhance rather than diminish their common security *vis-à-vis* the Soviet Union. However, this was more true of the US–German or US–British relationship than of that between the US and France. As in monetary affairs, so within the GATT France remained the great antagonist for the United States. However, West Germany's inclination to side with the United States rather than France on issues of trade liberalization pushed the Community's trade policy in a more liberal direction.

Comparing Trade and Monetary Evolution

In the post-war economic system GATT survived, but Bretton Woods collapsed. This poses a particular problem for the neoliberal version of the theory of hegemonic stability, which has placed emphasis upon the ability of regimes to outlive hegemonic decline. If both were international public goods, why should one survive and not the other?

The neorealist version of the theory of hegemonic stability is more plausible in the monetary sphere, since it could be argued that US power remained sufficient to engineer a 'breakdown' of Bretton Woods to foster a more liberal international financial system. However, *some* decline was presumably necessary to produce a shift in US interests within the international monetary system; but how much is unclear. The great imprecision of the independent variable of hegemony makes arguments over whether the US has declined 'enough' a bottomless pit. All we are able to say is that from the late 1940s to the early 1970s there was a clear shift in the balance of economic power away from the United States towards other countries in the system, including Western Europe. This places the neorealist version of the theory in considerable difficulty, since it predicts systemic closure as a result of hegemonic decline, yet the GATT was more successful in the 1960s than the 1950s.

Thus, both versions of the theory of hegemonic stability can only be at most half right. The United States had lost interest in the Bretton Woods system by the time of the Nixon administration, and was able to engineer its destruction. The new international monetary system that rose up in its place was a product more of a combination of Anglo-American cooperation and competition in the deregulation of finance than of hegemonic regime creation.[28] However, the GATT, despite some difficulties, continued to be in the interests of the United States and all the other major industrial countries, and this largely explains its resilience. This provides a little respite for the neoliberal version and for embedded liberalism.

Many feared in the early 1970s that the international trading system would go the way of the Bretton Woods system, particularly given the 'new protectionist' response in the West to exports from Japan and newly industrializing countries (NICs). However, much of the so-called new protectionism was quite old, a manifestation of the embedded liberal compromise rather than its breakdown. It was thrust into the light of day by the very success of intra-alliance tariff-cutting in the Kennedy Round. When it was new, it usually represented a common response to a new set of problems that affected both the United States and Western Europe simultaneously. From the late 1960s, rising import penetration in certain manufacturing sectors of the US and European economies produced a protectionist response. In 1968, in response to pressure from the steel industry, the US administration negotiated voluntary export restraints (VERs) on Japanese and European steel exports to the United States. In their wake, VERs on products such as footwear, automobiles, and consumer electronics followed. The basic cause was not simply the overvaluation of the dollar, but a long-term shift of comparative advantage in labour-intensive industries towards Japan and the low-wage newly industrializing countries of East Asia.

The competitiveness of Japan and the East Asian NICs in these sectors was difficult to deal with because it broke the trend of 'intra-industry' trade that had characterized Atlantic trade in the 1950s and 1960s. Intra-industry trade growth and the embedded liberal compromise had been mutually self-reinforcing, since all countries could liberalize trade but maintain similar industrial structures. New protectionism resulted from the gradual opening up of an international trading system that had hitherto been restricted to the North Atlantic area (see Table 6.3). In the Tokyo Round of the GATT, lasting from 1973 to 1979, the US and Western Europe attempted to deal with NTB issues in less buoyant economic conditions. However, they increasingly protected important sectors from growing extra-Atlantic area imports.

Yet even if trade policy-making had become much more difficult, there was certainly no wholesale collapse of the transatlantic trading system, as some had predicted in the early 1970s. The structure of the GATT did not prevent the United States (or Europe) from seeking new solutions in trade policy, as the Bretton Woods system had on the monetary side. It has enabled both to pursue NTB protection to sectors suffering from international competition. It also permitted Europe and, later, the United States to pursue regional arrangements with preferred partners, and to use bilateral mechanisms to place additional pressure on countries like Japan to liberalize. Bretton Woods, by contrast, simply ceased to be in the interests of the major countries, above all the United States and West Germany.

6.4. Conclusions: Security, Society, and Hegemony

Despite its shortcomings, the theory of hegemonic stability will remain central to the study of post-war international relations. As most of its critics accept, the theory usefully points to a direct relationship between the dramatic success of post-1945 international economic regimes, compared to the inter-war experience, and the assertion of leadership by the United States after 1945. It helps to explain why a large state such as the United States should have perceived an *economic* interest in such leadership. More generally, the theory is suggestive as a starting-point for understanding the relationship between the structure of the international political system and the stability and openness of the world economy. For all of these reasons, the theory of hegemonic stability has been highly influential both in academic literature and in more popular accounts of world economic order.

To say that students must study the theory of hegemonic stability, however, is not to argue that it provides an adequate account of post-war international economic relations. As we have seen, two other competing theories, alliance leadership and ideational consensus, suggest that two other important sources of stability existed in post-war economic relations between the United States and Western Europe. Deciding which of these three factors is pre-eminent is probably impossible. This will not satisfy those who prefer parsimonious theories, but some kind of theoretical amalgam seems unavoidable.

We have seen that the two most popular kinds of theory, the two versions of the theory of hegemonic stability and the theory of embedded liberalism, cannot stand by themselves as satisfactory explanations of the construction and evolution of the post-war world economic order. Theorists have ignored the way in which the security structure impinged upon them and modified them in crucial ways. The security structure initially helped to push US hegemonic leadership in a more constructive direction in European terms, away from implementing Bretton Woods-style rules, towards promoting regional integration. By the 1960s, however, the stabilizing impact of the security structure for US–European economic relations had become more ambiguous. In trade, growing US fear of the economic threat posed by the emergence of the EEC led to the success of the Kennedy Round. On the monetary side, however, the security leverage enjoyed by the United States over West Germany and others enabled the United States to marginalize support for alternatives to the unstable dollar standard. Unfortunately, this outcome contributed considerably to the partial erosion of the trade regime in the 1970s.

Michael Webb and Stephen Krasner have argued that there are two possible reformulations of the theory of hegemonic stability in response to the argument that it is often inconsistent with the evidence.[29] The first alternative is that the United States might have declined but still possesses sufficient hegemonic power and interest in maintaining openness in the world economy. The second is to argue that the United States has declined 'enough', but that there is some form of lag between hegemonic decline and the closure of the world economy. The first is unconvincing, not simply because of the problem of adequately defining when hegemony does and does not exist, but also because we have seen that it provides a misleading account of the construction and evolution of the major post-war economic regimes. The second not only suffers from this difficulty, but implies that the theory requires major modification, as Webb and Krasner themselves suggest.

This chapter has argued that alliance politics was crucial to understanding the post-war international economic system. In the late 1940s, US hegemonic leadership of a constructive kind stemmed from security rather than economic motives, and the theory of hegemonic stability diverts our attention from this fact. In addition, the North Atlantic alliance helped to solidify the embedded liberal compromise within and between the United States and Europe. The Soviet threat weakened the influence of forces within US society which might have picked apart embedded liberalism after the New Deal had waned. It also strengthened the hand of those (mainly within the foreign policy élite) who took a more tolerant view of allied economic policy; and it nudged important European countries such as the United Kingdom and West Germany towards the more market-orientated end of the embedded liberalism spectrum.

However, the stabilizing impact of the alliance upon domestic political economy in the major industrial countries had its cost. This was particularly so in the case of the US–Japan relationship, where a consistent US policy of turning a blind eye to Japanese protectionism contributed to the sudden and destabilizing outbreak of popular resentment in the United States in the 1980s. The point can be made more generally. Growing US trade deficits and the difficulties experienced by high-profile US industries in international competition from the 1970s resulted in an increasingly widespread perception in the United States that its provision of 'international collective goods' had imposed net costs upon the US economy. There is little doubt that this perception is an exaggeration, to say the least. The long-term economic and political benefits to the United States of prosperity and stability in Western Europe and Japan, and of a resoundingly successful NATO alliance, have been very large if inherently incalculable. However, the popular demand to shift US foreign economic policy firmly in the direction of national economic interest and away from the goal of alliance solidarity is understandable. The problem is that it goes against the grain of the growing integration of the United States into the world economy.

Thus, although the Western alliance is central to an understanding of both US hegemony and post-war US–European economic relations, a theory of international economic openness or stability that relies entirely upon security structures is also unsatisfactory. Alliances alone are unlikely to be sufficient to produce cooperative behaviour, particularly if (as with the United States at present) there is a strong feeling of exploitation by alliance partners. The relative stability of the post-war regimes was precisely to do with the fact that most of the parties involved perceived them to be legitimate. While there were major senses of grievance, particularly on the part of the French, de Gaulle was unable to convince his European partners that these grievances justified the wholesale rejection of US-led regimes. Although this was partly because of Germany's greater security dependence upon the United States, it was also because the German, British, and other governments often felt French criticisms to be illegitimate. US hegemony worked best when it worked within the transnational norms of the Western countries and while the important countries did not dispute the distribution of alliance burdens. Important work remains to be done on the impact of the shifting security structure upon international economic relations since the early 1970s.

Chronology: US–West European Economic Relations, 1940–1973

Date	Event	Significance
1941–4	US–UK wartime negotiations on a new international monetary and trading system	Technocratic élites in both countries negotiate in circumstances relatively free of normal domestic political pressure

Date	Event	Significance
July 1944	Bretton Woods conference	Creation of the 'Bretton Woods twins', the IMF and World Bank
Dec. 1945	US loan to Britain agreed	US attempt to force Britain to accept the Bretton Woods rules
June 1947	US Secretary of State Marshall announces 'Marshall Aid'	A large step away from Bretton Woods towards direct US aid and promoting regionalism in Europe
July–Aug. 1947	British pound returns to convertibility, but this is revoked as reserves are rapidly drained	Final failure of Hull's vision of forcing Britain to accept Bretton Woods
30 Oct. 1947	GATT signed in Geneva	Interim agreement on trade principles, and draft agreement on the establishment of the ITO by 23 countries
Mar. 1948	Havana World Conference on Trade and Employment	Agreement on the charter of the ITO by over 60 countries
June 1950	Creation of European Payments Union	Facilitated the reconstruction of European trade and payments on a regional basis, rather than on the basis of Bretton Woods
Apr. 1951	Signing of the Treaty of Paris	Created the European Coal and Steel Community
Mar. 1957	Signing of the Treaty of Rome	Created the EEC and Euratom, the former leading to the creation of a large trading bloc, changing the nature of GATT bargaining
Dec. 1958	European currencies become convertible; EPU dissolved	Bretton Woods system rises from the dead, but US gold position begins to deteriorate rapidly
Jan. 1959– July 1968	Progressive internal tariff reductions within EEC	Leads to a customs union within Western Europe and the creation of the Common External Tariff
1960–1	GATT Dillon Round	Meagre results show growing limits of item-by-item bargaining and need for a new US approach
1961–2	Short-term and Long-term Agreements on Trade in Cotton Textiles	Treatment of textiles as a separate category within the GATT, leading to creation of a complex set of bilateral quota arrangements. Facilitates passing of the US Trade Expansion Act
1962	US Congress passes Trade Expansion Act	Essential pre-condition for the success of the Kennedy Round of the GATT

Date	Event	Significance
Feb. 1965	President de Gaulle calls for the restoration of the gold standard	Hardens US opposition to an increase in the price of gold and thus indirectly leads to the gradual emergence of a de facto dollar standard
June 1967	Conclusion of GATT Kennedy Round	Most successful GATT round, but lack of progress on non-tariff barriers leaves problems for the future
Mar. 1968	Two-Tier Arrangement	The effective end of the gold–dollar standard, with the private market price of gold allowed to float above official price of $35 per oz.
1968	US VER agreements on steel exports with EC and Japan	First steps towards the 'new' protectionism
Aug. 1971	'Nixon shock'	President Nixon ends de jure dollar convertibility into gold and imposes a 10% surcharge on imports, forcing allies to negotiate under threat
Dec. 1971	Smithsonian monetary agreement	USA succeeds in having other countries revalue their currencies against the dollar, while maintaining the dollar's gold inconvertibility
Jan. 1973	Britain, Denmark, and Ireland join EC	Further expansion of European Community and growing weight in international trading system
Mar. 1973	Deutschmark floated permanently	End of dollar standard and shift towards system of floating exchange rates and liberalized capital flows
Oct.–Nov. 1973	First OPEC oil shock	Severe deflationary shock to world economy, first major post-war recession, and beginning of petrodollar 'recycling'

Notes

1. Charles P. Kindleberger, *The World in Depression, 1929–39* (Berkeley, 1973), 292.
2. See Charles P. Kindleberger, 'International Public Goods without International Government', *American Economic Review*, 76 (1986), 1–13; Robert O. Keohane, *After Hegemony: Cooperation and Discord in the World Political Economy* (Princeton, 1984); Duncan Snidal, 'The Limits of Hegemonic Stability Theory', *International Organization*, 39 (1985), 579–614; Joanne Gowa, 'Rational Hegemons, Excludable Goods,

and Small Groups: An Epitaph for Hegemonic Stability Theory?', *World Politics*, 41 (1989), 307–24.

3. The regime school paid little attention to Kindleberger's argument that rules would be insufficient in a crisis, when hegemonic power resources would be required for stabilization.

4. Stephen Krasner, 'State Power and the Structure of International Trade', *World Politics*, 28 (1976), 317–43; David A. Lake, *Power, Protection, and International Trade: The International Sources of American Commercial Strategy, 1887–1939* (Ithaca, NY, 1988).

5. Robert Gilpin, *US Power and the Multinational Corporation* (New York, 1975), 104–6.

6. Keohane, *After Hegemony*, 137.

7. Robert O. Keohane and Joseph S. Nye, *Power and Interdependence: World Politics in Transition* (Boston, 1977), 30–1. See also Krasner, 'State Power', 322–3.

8. See Joanne Gowa, 'Bipolarity, Multipolarity, and Free Trade', *American Political Science Review*, 83 (1989), 1245–56; Joseph M. Grieco, 'Anarchy and the Limits of Cooperation: A Realist Critique of the Newest Liberal Institutionalism', *International Organization*, 42 (1988), 485–507.

9. John Gerard Ruggie, 'International Regimes, Transactions and Change: Embedded Liberalism in the Post-war Economic Order', in Stephen D. Krasner (ed.), *International Regimes* (Ithaca, NY, 1983), 195–231.

10. See G. John Ikenberry, 'A World Economy Restored: Expert Consensus and the Anglo-American Post-war Settlement', *International Organization*, 46 (1992), 289–321. The combination of 'hard' and 'soft' hegemonic power has received increased attention in recent years, particularly from the 'Gramscian' school: see Stephen Gill (ed.), *Gramsci, Historical Materialism, and International Relations* (Cambridge, 1993).

11. Joseph S. Nye, *Bound to Lead* (New York, 1990), 39–40. In an otherwise sceptical account of the hegemony thesis as applied to the nineteenth and twentieth centuries, Nye is curiously willing to accept with little argument its applicability to trade and money after 1945. For a more persuasive account see Henry R. Nau, *The Myth of America's Decline* (New York, 1990), pt. II.

12. Andrew Walter, *World Power and World Money: The Role of Hegemony and International Monetary Order* (Hemel Hempstead and New York, 1993), 159–61.

13. Note that the depth of protectionist sentiment in the post-war Congress well into the 1950s is difficult to reconcile with the neorealist view that the hegemon should be more free-trade orientated than medium-sized countries.

14. Interestingly, however, in the 1962 Trade Expansion Act, Congress gave the Kennedy administration the across-the-board tariff-cutting authority for which the British had asked during the war.

15. See Alan Bullock, *Ernest Bevin: Foreign Secretary* (Oxford, 1985), 451–2.

16. Of course, it created a new conflict between British and US policy over the question of Britain's participation in the project of European integration, a conflict on which America also eventually gave way.

17. Wolfram Hanreider, *Germany, America, Europe* (New Haven, 1989), 323–4.

18. See Walter, *World Power*, 163–4.

19. Robert Triffin, *Gold and the Dollar Crisis* (New Haven, 1960).

20. Milton Gilbert, *Quest for World Monetary Order* (New York, 1980).
21. See Gregory F. Treverton, *The 'Dollar Drain' and American Forces in Germany* (Athens, Oh., 1978).
22. Joanne Gowa, *Closing the Gold Window: Domestic Politics and the End of Bretton Woods* (Ithaca, NY, 1983).
23. Robert E. Baldwin, *T. le Policy in a Changing World Economy* (Hemel Hempstead, 1989), 52–6.
24. The Long-term Agreement on Trade in Cotton Textiles of 1962 provided for an international system of bilateral quota arrangements, later extended into the Multi-fibre Arrangement in 1974.
25. Reprinted in Ernest H. Preeg, *Traders and Diplomats* (Washington, 1970), 282–90 (at 282).
26. During the 1950s one of the difficult issues of alliance burden-sharing was the US attempt to get Europe to bear more of the burden of integrating Japan into the world economy. European countries initially refused to provide Japan with full MFN treatment, even after it joined the GATT in 1955. See Gardner Patterson, *Discrimination in International Trade* (Princeton, 1966), ch. 6.
27. World import shares would be a better measure of US and EEC bargaining power within the GATT, but figures on intra-EEC imports were unavailable.
28. On this see Eric Helleiner, 'States and the Future of Global Finance', *Review of International Studies*, 18 (1992), 31–49.
29. Michael C. Webb and Stephen D. Krasner, 'Hegemonic Stability Theory: An Empirical Assessment', *Review of International Studies*, 15 (1989), 183–98 (at 195).

Further Reading

BALDWIN, ROBERT E., *Trade Policy in a Changing World Economy* (Hemel Hempstead, 1989). A readable and informed account which integrates domestic and international political economy approaches to the study of US trade policy.

GOWA, JOANNE, 'Bipolarity, Multipolarity, and Free Trade', *American Political Science Review*, 83 (1989), 1245–56. Explains why alliances might promote open trade.

KEOHANE, ROBERT O., *After Hegemony: Cooperation and Discord in the World Political Economy* (Princeton, 1984). The most influential neoliberal critique of the theory of hegemonic stability.

KRASNER, STEPHEN, 'State Power and the Structure of International Trade', *World Politics*, 28 (1976), 317–43. An influential and nuanced realist account of hegemonic stability theory.

RUGGIE, JOHN GERARD, 'International Regimes, Transactions and Change: Embedded Liberalism in the Post-war Economic Order', in Stephen D. Krasner (ed.), *International Regimes* (Ithaca, NY, 1983), 195–231. The most influential article on the importance of ideas in the post-war order.

WALTER, ANDREW, *World Power and World Money: The Role of Hegemony and International Monetary Order* (Hemel Hempstead and New York, 1993). Argues that in practice, hegemonic roles in the international monetary system since 1870 were often very different from those supposed in the theory.

CHAPTER SEVEN

THE UNITED STATES AND LATIN AMERICA: NEOREALISM RE-EXAMINED

Andrew Hurrell

This chapter will show how theories of international relations can help make sense of US–Latin American relations in the post-war period. Theory is not some kind of magic key that can explain everything or removes the need for detailed historical work. But it is central to the creation of the definitions, concepts, and categories around which the analysis of US–Latin American relations is necessarily conducted; it brings to the surface assumptions that remain explicit and unquestioned in purely descriptive or historical work; it can sharpen our understanding of the main explanatory variables and causal mechanisms; and it provides a coherent framework for systematic comparison across space and time. The focus will be on the role of theory in mapping the landscape and opening up contending explanatory frameworks. The chapter is divided into two sections. The first outlines the four main phases in the evolution of US–Latin American relations in the period from 1945 to 1994 and identifies the most important characteristics of each phase. The second explores the way in which three central theoretical perspectives in international relations—neorealism, dependency theory, and liberalism—each interpret and explain the evolution of this relationship.

7.1. The Evolution of US–Latin American Relations

The Closed Hemisphere, 1945–1965

The central feature of the early post-war period was the 'closing of the hemisphere' and the establishment of a hegemonic system in the region built around

US pre-eminence as the major supplier of trading opportunities, foreign invest-ment, aid, and military equipment and around US-dominated regional insti-tutions.[1] Within that sphere of influence Washington was able to maintain its position as the principal political and economic link between the countries of Latin America and the rest of the world and to set down and enforce definite, though variable, limits on what was permissible in terms of Latin American foreign policies.

US influence within Latin America had of course preceded the Second World War. The Monroe Doctrine, which sought to exclude European powers from the American continent, was first enunciated by President James Monroe in 1823. It was developed in the No Transfer Principle of 1811 and in the Polk and Roosevelt Corollaries to the Doctrine of 1845 and 1904. These formal claims to regional predominance began to gather real force as the United States replaced Britain as the region's pre-eminent economic power, and as Washington became more and more prepared to use its power in pursuit of its Manifest Destiny. Yet despite the steady growth of US influence in the first half of the century, it was the Second World War and then the Cold War that consolidated US hegemony over the region. The outcome of the war left the United States as the world's dominant military and economic power, while the Cold War provided the in-centive to secure and institutionalize its predominance in the region.

The ability of the United States to achieve this degree of control rested on four pillars.[2] First, there was the ability and willingness of the United States to intervene coercively in the internal affairs of Latin American states, as in the cases of Guatemala in 1954, Cuba in 1960–61, or the Dominican Republic in 1965. Secondly, Latin America was closely integrated into a Western security system. The Inter-American Military System rested partly on the formalization of multilateral security relations through the 1947 Inter-American Treaty of Reciprocal Assistance (the Rio Treaty) and the 1948 Charter of the Organization of American States (OAS), partly on a web of bilateral military assistance agree-ments, and partly on the United States' near-monopoly in the supply of arms and military training to the region. Thirdly, the economic dominance of the United States in the aftermath of the Second World War enabled it to consolidate its position as the region's most important trading partner and its major source of foreign investment and foreign aid. This economic dominance both tied the region firmly into the Western economic system and provided Washington with additional sources of power and leverage. Finally, there were no external chal-lengers to US regional power. The influence of Germany and Italy (which had played an important role in the 1930s) had been removed; Britain came (albeit somewhat grudgingly) to accept the region as an American sphere of influence; and in the 1940s and 1950s the Soviet Union was in no sense a global power and had few capabilities with which to promote its influence in Latin America.

Of course, even at the height of US dominance, Latin America's pro-Western alignment was never complete. There was frequent friction with the United States over economic issues and widespread disappointment in the 1940s and 1950s with Washington's refusal to provide precisely the kind of economic benefits to which many Latin Americans felt their diplomatic support entitled them. Moreover, Perón's advocacy of a *tercer via* ('third way'), Mexico's repeated opposition to Washington's Cold War policies, Castro's victory in Cuba, and the independent foreign policies of the Quadros and Goulart years in Brazil in the early 1960s all provide evidence of a powerful nationalist counter-tradition. Nevertheless, if one considers the period from 1945 to the mid-1960s, the extent of US dominance, buttressed by the pro-Western and anti-Communist sentiments of Latin American élites, provide strong grounds for viewing the region as a Western-dominated sphere of influence. On the one hand, Washington could generally count on Latin American support over such major international issues as Palestine, the exclusion of China from the United Nations, the Korean War, and the Cuban Missile Crisis. On the other, Latin America remained distant from both the Afro-Asian and Non-Aligned Movements. Although the region generally voted in favour of decolonization, there was little identification with the driving forces behind the Third World movement of the time: decolonization, non-alignment, and the struggle for racial equality.[3]

Latin America's Emergence and the Challenge to US Hegemony, 1965–1982

The pattern of Latin America's international relations changed significantly between 1965 and 1982 with a decline in Washington's capacity and willingness to maintain its hegemonic role on the one hand, and the emergence of new options and opportunities on the other.[4] The pillars of US hegemony were eroding. First, Washington's ability to intervene coercively was weakened by the traumas of Vietnam, by congressional and public opposition, and by the widespread belief that old-style interventionism was no longer a viable option in Latin America. Secondly, the years after the US intervention of 1965 in the Dominican Republic saw a significant unravelling of the Inter-American Military System, with the rise of Western Europe as the region's major arms supplier and the abrogation of military assistance agreements with the United States by Guatemala and Brazil and the interruption of military cooperation with Chile, Uruguay, Argentina, Nicaragua, and El Salvador. Finally, in the crucial economic area, the role of the United States was changing and disillusion with the promises of the Alliance for Progress and increased economic friction fuelled the perception among Latin Americans that its special relationship with the West was not serving its most immediate and pressing needs.

US policy veered inconsistently during this period, but, in general, its willing-ness to uphold its hegemonic position declined. The military and economic activism and interventionism of the early 1960s were followed by a period of relative disengagement. Under Johnson this was the result of preoccupation with Vietnam. Under Nixon and Ford it followed from the priority given to relations with China and the pursuit of superpower detente. Carter's attempt to move away from the 'inordinate fear of Communism' and to define a new activist agenda in relations with Latin America failed partly because of the mismatch between US and Latin American preferences and priorities, but also because of the return, by 1978–9 of old Cold War fears and preoccupations.

The overall economic salience of the United States declined as Latin America expanded its economic relations with Western Europe, Japan, the Soviet Union, and (particularly in the case of Brazil) Africa and the Middle East. For example, the US share of Latin American exports fell from over 40 per cent in 1960 to 34 per cent in 1970. It was also against this background of increased international assertiveness and as part of a broader process of diversification that Latin America moved from the late 1960s towards a closer alignment with the Third World. This closer alignment could be seen in many areas: in the central role played by Latin American states in the consolidation of the Group of 77 in the late 1960s; in the expansion of Latin American involvement in the Non-Aligned Movement from the presence of just Cuba and three ex-Commonwealth Caribbean observers at Belgrade in 1961 to the participation of fifteen Latin American and Caribbean states and eight observers at New Delhi in 1983; in the activities of Venezuela and Ecuador within OPEC and in Latin American involvement in commodity groups in cocoa, copper, coffee, and sugar; and finally in the central role played by Latin America in the negotiations on a new Law of the Sea and the demands in the 1970s for a New International Economic Order, with Mexico and Peru play-ing a central role in the formulation and promotion of the Charter of Economic Rights and Duties of States in 1974.

Debt and Democratization, 1982–1989

If the 1970s saw both significant economic development and a drive for greater autonomy and independence in foreign policy, these trends were halted with the onset of the debt crisis in 1982. The policy of diversification reached its limits in the late 1970s and was reversed through the 1980s.[5] As the counterpoint to this development, the 1980s witnessed the renewed centrality of United States. Its position as the region's major trading partner was firmly re-established (although still with very substantial differences between Mexico at one extreme and the countries of the Southern Cone, whose trade remains geographically diversified, at the other). Critical decisions on the management of the foreign debt lay in the United States, either with the administration itself or with US-based multilateral agencies or US-chaired committees of private banks. Indeed, the mutual recognition of regional 'spheres of influence' (of the United States in Latin America, Japan in Asia, West Germany in Eastern Europe) was one of the most notable features of the politics of the 1980s debt crisis.

The Reagan administration that came into office in January 1981 placed great stress on recovering its power and authority in the region after what it saw as the weakness and vacillation of the Carter years. Much of the Reagan's administration's 'reassertion of hegemony' was concentrated in Central America and the Caribbean. The civil war in El Salvador and the continued existence of the Sandinista government in Nicaragua were viewed as critical challenges in the global struggle against the Soviet Union. In response, the so-called Reagan Doctrine stressed the need for activist support for anti-Communist 'freedom fighters' (such as the Contras in Nicaragua) and a renewed willingness to intervene coercively—whether directly, as in Grenada in 1983, or indirectly (but on a large scale), as against the Sandinista government in Nicaragua and in support of the government of El Salvador. Further south 'reassertionism' was manifested in the steadfast refusal of the administration to accept inter-state management of the debt crisis, insisting instead on a dominant role for the international financial institutions (the World Bank and the IMF), and on case-by-case negotiations with individual debtors (partly as a way of preventing the formation of a united debtors' cartel). In addition, the US administration sought to press Latin American states towards the liberalization of their trade and investment regimes and to curb their ambitions in the fields of arms production and nuclear development.

For Latin America the 1980s witnessed the worst economic crisis since the 1930s (the so-called 'lost decade'), with the region's per capita GDP falling by 7 per cent between 1980 and 1988 and high levels of financial instability. Only in the political field were significant gains recorded with the steady advance of democratization, so that by the end of the decade only Cuba and Haiti were ruled by clearly undemocratic governments. But for most of the 1980s weak and vulnerable Latin American governments, preoccupied with the daunting twin challenges of democratic transition on the one hand and economic adjustment on the other, faced an international environment with markedly fewer opportunities and dominated by a United States anxious once more to police its own backyard and determined to press its own economic agenda.

Convergence and Cooperation, 1989–1995

The period from the late 1980s witnessed a deep and widespread shift in traditional patterns of inter-American relations, with improved relations and increased cooperation between the United States and its southern neighbours across a range of issues. From support for US action against Iraq, through policies on arms production and nuclear proliferation, to the promotion of democracy, Latin American and US policies moved far more closely into line. Even countries such as Mexico and Argentina, previously known for their strongly nationalist and frequently anti-US foreign policies, moved dramatically towards improved relations with Washington.

In addition, this period saw a notable revival of formal and institutionalized cooperation between North and South America. In the economic field, the most important example was the successful incorporation of Mexico into a North American Free Trade Area (NAFTA). Moreover, President Bush's Enterprise for the Americas Initiative (EAI) of June 1990, together with speeches by senior US administration figures, placed the question of a southward expansion of NAFTA firmly on the political agenda. At the Miami Summit of the Americas in December 1994, a target date of 2005 for the conclusion of a hemispheric free trade area was agreed. Secondly, political regionalism has been revived, most notably in the forum of the Organization of American States. The prospects for the OAS in the late 1970s and early 1980s had appeared exceedingly dim. The organization was paralysed by the deep divisions that existed between the United States and Latin America over the crisis in Central America, and the Falklands/Malvinas War of 1982 represented, for many commentators, the last nail in the coffin of the Inter-American Military System.

Yet the salience of the OAS has increased dramatically in the early 1990s. Although its role in the field of traditional security remains somewhat limited, it has adopted a much more forceful position with regard to the support of democracy. In June 1991 OAS foreign ministers approved the so-called Santiago Commitment, which promised firm support for democracy and resolved that any 'sudden or irregular interruption of the democratic political institutional process' of any one of them would result in the calling of an emergency meeting of foreign ministers. Subsequently the OAS sought to develop a coordinated response to anti-democratic challenges, including the Haitian coup in September 1991 and subsequent attempts to restore Aristide, the so-called *autogolpe* or 'palace coup' by Fujimori in Peru in April 1992, and the Guatemalan coup in September 1993. In addition, participation in elections and political activity has become a more central element of Latin American international human rights law and the international monitoring of elections has become more widespread and accepted.

Finally, changes in the pattern of international relations within the hemisphere have been closely bound up with shifts in development strategy. Thus the period since the late 1980s saw a significant degree of unanimity concerning the need to move away from the kinds of inwardly orientated development policies (based on import substitution, high tariffs, and a large role for the state) that characterized so much earlier Third World thinking. In this period almost all Latin American governments came to embrace some version of economic liberalism, placing greater reliance on market mechanisms, seeking to restructure and reduce the role of the state, and laying greater emphasis on integration in world markets.

7.2. Three Theoretical Perspectives

Neorealism

Writings that have sought to develop an explicitly neorealist account of US–Latin American relations have been relatively rare. Nevertheless, there are three important reasons for starting with realism. First, realism/neorealism has dominated the academic study of international relations, especially in the United States.[6] Secondly, a great deal of historical writing on US policy towards the region has reflected neorealist assumptions. And thirdly, neorealist analyses have important strengths. They are good at unravelling the ways in which external constraints and the structure of the international system shape the foreign policy options of all states, but especially of relatively weak states. They are also good at explaining the logic of strategic interaction when the identity of the actors and the nature of their interests are known and well understood.

A neorealist analysis of US–Latin American relations highlights the following three important features.

Concentration on US policy and the dominance of security concerns Neorealism takes changes in patterns of inter-state relations as the natural object of explanation; concentrates on the evolution of the policies of the most powerful state (in this case the United States); and pays particular attention to the importance of security as the dominant motivation for US policy. Why? Because, to the neorealist, foreign policy will always be heavily influenced, if not determined, by the necessity of seeking security in an anarchic international system. Foreign policy is explained by looking from the outside in and tracking the ways in which states are 'pushed and shoved' by the international system to act in particular ways. Thus US policy towards Latin America will be largely determined by its broader international position and by patterns of conflict and cooperation with other major powers (in this period, with the Soviet Union). Similarly, the international options and opportunities available to Latin America will be largely set by the hegemonic role of the United States.

Neorealism, then, highlights the central and fundamental importance of security as the dominant motivation for US policy. Reflecting such a view, Pope Atkins argues that 'US purposes often have been couched in terms of moral rhetoric but almost always calculated in terms of security.'[7] These security concerns have been of two kinds.

First, there are direct security interests, which have included strategic denial (preventing a hostile external power from gaining influence in the region and the penetration of hostile ideologies); safeguarding the sea lanes of communication (protecting the Panama Canal and the network of military and security facilities in the Caribbean and western Atlantic); and securing the region as a source of strategic raw materials (this was especially important in the Second World War and the Korean War, but even in the 1990s 30 per cent of US oil imports still come from the region).

Second, there are indirect security challenges resulting from political, social, or economic instability in Latin America. US policy-makers have long feared that such instability would bring to power radical nationalist anti-US governments or would create conflicts and crises that could be exploited by Washington's enemies. Fear of political or revolutionary instability pre-dated the Cold War, but the ideological and power political struggle with Moscow heightened the salience of such threats. As the Cold War became an increasingly global conflict after the Korean War, and as competition and conflict shifted increasingly from Europe to the developing world, so the perceived importance of such conflicts for the global balance of power grew and the logic of 'falling dominoes' and alliance credibility became increasingly prevalent: if the US did not respond to challenges even in areas that were intrinsically or objectively 'unimportant', then this would reflect badly on more central alliance relations and would lead the other side to step up the pressure. Thus the logic of rivalry magnified many intrinsically minor conflicts, increased the threat from political instability, and made the Third World 'matter' in new ways that were hard both to define and to limit.[8]

On a neorealist reading the creation of US hegemony owed far more to security imperatives than to either economic imperialism or the urge to promote liberal values. After the relative laxity and openness of the 1930s (the period of so-called 'good neighbour' diplomacy), the security preoccupations that had given rise to the Monroe Doctrine were forcefully revived by the political and ideological concerns of first the Second World War and subsequently the Cold War. Equally, neorealists would underline the extent to which the dominant lines of US actions in Latin America have reflected the evolution of its broader Cold War policy. This was true in periods of relative passivity or neglect, such as during the Eisenhower years or the so-called 'low profile' policies of the Nixon/Ford administrations. In both these cases direct involvement was prompted only by threats that were seen as impinging directly on East–West relations (Guatemala under Eisenhower; Cuba and Chile under Nixon). But the same pattern holds true for periods characterized by greater US activism and involvement, such as under Kennedy and Johnson in the 1960s and Reagan in the 1980s. Thus the launching in 1961 of the Alliance for Progress, with its far-reaching goals of economic development and 'nation-building', was a direct response to the Cuban Revolution and to the perceived need to win the hearts and minds of the developing world; while the large-scale covert intervention against the Sandinista government in Nicaragua in the 1980s formed part of a much broader policy of confrontation with the Soviet Union.

Neorealists, then, claim that their approach captures the dominant motivation behind US policy and that it accurately predicts the overwhelming geographical concentration of US interventionism in Central America and the Caribbean—areas of extremely low economic significance. They would also predict that, when security interests clash with other goals, security would win out. For example, when the more 'progressive' elements of the Alliance for Progress (democrat-ization and land reform) clashed with the perceived need for military action to defeat 'subversion' and to secure the diplomatic support of authoritarian govern-ments, liberal ambitions were sacrificed to the more immediate Cold War imper-atives; or in 1978–9 the more liberal agenda of the Carter administration was displaced by the need to respond to the growing Soviet challenge in the Third World (including in Central America in the period leading up to the fall of Somoza in 1979).

Latin American objectives   Although concentrating on US policy, neorealism claims to capture the essence of Latin American foreign policy goals, above all the attempt to try and constrain and restrict the overwhelming power of the United States. It also claims that it exposes and explores the two major strategic options by which these goals have been pursued: balancing on the one hand and 'bandwagoning' on the other.[9]

Whenever opportunities existed, neorealists would expect to see a policy of seeking to balance the power of the United States through an active policy of diversification. They argue that such a policy has indeed historically formed a central feature of Latin American foreign policies, especially in the period from the Cuban revolution to the onset of the debt crisis in 1982. In this period, major Latin American states tended towards a policy of *constrained balancing*: active efforts to diversify but falling short of close and direct alignment with major antagonists of the United States (both because of the high direct and indirect costs of such a move and because of the absence of a domestic constituency—except under conditions of social and nationalist radicalization). For countries like Brazil, it became the central principle of foreign policy. Diversification in-volved the expansion of ties with Western Europe and Japan; but it also involved the expansion of bilateral ties with other parts of the Third World (especially for Brazil) and the emergence of a distinctly *tercermundisto* (or 'third-worldist') slant to foreign policy, with the involvement of Mexico, Peru, Brazil, and Cuba in calls for a New International Economic Order in the 1970s and increasingly active participation in the Third World coalition. Only in rare cases, out of necessity and/or as a consequence of revolutionary nationalist upheaval, would Latin American countries run the risk of courting direct political or military support from the Soviet Union.

The alternative option is for weaker states entrapped in a great power's sphere of influence to seek accommodation with the local hegemon either in the hope of receiving special rewards ('bandwagoning', in the realist jargon) or in an attempt to restrict the free exercise of hegemonic power through the creation of regional institutions. Realist theory predicts that this kind of behaviour is most likely when power differentials are very great, when there are few external alternatives to accommodation with the hegemon, and when the small state finds itself in close geographic proximity to the hegemon. Such thinking could be seen, for example, in the attitudes of several Latin American states towards the Korean War. In a situation where opposition to Washington involved high risks and costs, why not offer political and diplomatic support in the hope of receiving future economic benefits and rewards?

The nature of economic interests and economic conflict   The third neorealist claim is to expose the 'structural economic conflict' that has existed between the United States and Latin America, and, more generally, between North and South. For neorealists it is axiomatic that development policy will be concerned with both economic development and political autonomy. The constraints of the international system, combined with their chronic domestic vulnerability, mean that Latin American states have sought power and control as much as wealth; have followed development strategies that promoted national control (for example in the fields of nuclear or computer technology); and have worked internationally to achieve these goals by reforming or creating international regimes based on what Stephen Krasner has termed authoritative rather than market-orientated modes of allocation.[10] This has led to persistent conflict with the United States over questions of trade, investment, debt, and environmental management.

There are, however, three sets of weaknesses in this seductive, but often deeply misleading, neorealist picture, as follows.

The contested nature of security   The first criticism exposes neorealism's weakness on what should be its strongest ground, namely the nature and importance of security. It builds on a well-established critique, namely that realists and neorealists take their crucial categories of 'power' and 'interest', or 'security' as self-evident. These are assumed a priori and the neorealist framework provides no basis for understanding the specific content of state policies and the ways in which these change over time. Thus it is indeed the case, as Lars Schoultz puts it, that 'if one wants to understand the core of United States policy toward Latin America, one studies security.'[11] But the meaning of even such an apparently powerful imperative as national security has been deeply contested and is by no means straightforward.

As has been suggested, most security fears during the Cold War focused on fear of instability and the ways in which social upheaval (caused either by poverty or by rapid and destabilizing economic development) might threaten US security. Yet there were very great divisions among policy-makers and public opinion about how this instability might come to constitute a security threat. 'Specifically, there is no agreement on what might cause threatening instability in Latin America, nor is there agreement on what the actual consequences of instability might be.'[12] At one end of the political spectrum conservatives argued that, even if not actually caused by Communism, instability was stirred up by local Communists, aided and abetted by the Soviet Union and its allies. The appropriate response was therefore military intervention to crush 'subversion' and to discourage Soviet interventionism. Liberals argued that only by tackling the underlying social causes of instability could US long-term security be guaranteed. The answer therefore lay in economic development, promoting democracy, and engaging in nation-building.

Partly, then, because of sheer complexity of understanding the nature and significance of instability, partly because of the vagueness of Cold War arguments about credibility, and partly because of the broader loss of consensus that followed the Vietnam War, the evolution of US security interests in Latin America has to be explained by reference to processes internal to the United States. This leads the analyst towards various domestic approaches: (1) cognitive approaches and the exploration of the belief systems of policy-makers (as in Schoultz's work); (2) bureaucratic politics (consistently important, but with the Latin American policies of the Reagan administration providing a particularly good example); or (3) domestic politics explanations (for example, the role that anti-Communism played in the growth of conservatism in the 1970s and the critical importance of Carter's failure to secure firm domestic political support for his alternative foreign policy agenda).[13] Thus, neorealism is correct to highlight the importance of security imperatives, but it is wrong to exclude domestic processes by which the preferences and interests of states are created and evolve.[14]

Domestic developments and evolving interests   For the critics of neorealism, the sources and nature of US–Latin American relations cannot be understood solely, or even predominantly, in terms of power and bargaining because of the degree to which they are shaped by internal politics within Latin America and by the specific histories and identities of Latin American states. This is especially true of the factors which might help explain the shift from one phase in US–Latin Americans to another. Just as it is necessary to look within the United States in order to understand the nature of its security concerns, so too is it important to understand the evolution of Latin American interests and preferences. Thus, for example, the creation of a US sphere of influence was not simply the result of US power and of hegemonic imposition. US hegemony was always based on both coercion and consensus. Alongside Washington's ability to coerce Latin America there was the willingness of Latin American governments to align themselves with the United States and to see themselves as part of the West. This willingness obviously varied from government to government and derived from a variety of factors. In part it rested on strong Western cultural and historical ties; in part it can also be linked to the legacy of panamericanism and the feeling that North and South America shared a common destiny separate from, and superior to, the problems and disputes of the Old World. But much more importantly, it rested on the deeply felt anti-Communism of many Latin American élites. The source of this anti-Communism was only very rarely related to fear of the Soviet Union. Rather, it was closely tied to domestic politics and to the perception that a serious threat of Communist subversion existed within the hemisphere itself. The most extreme examples of this view are to be found in the doctrines of national security that flourished within the military establishments of the Southern Cone and which were used to justify both alignment with the United States abroad and military rule and repression at home.

Equally, the move towards a more assertionist foreign policy and a greater willingness to challenge Washington reflected domestic political change. Domestic social and economic change helped to created a climate for the emergence of more nationalist and assertive governments in Latin America. Political change also made economic growth an ever more important means of bolstering political legitimacy. This led to the declining salience of security issues and to a reassessment of the nature of Latin American economic development. In many, although by no means all, cases this reassessment involved greater economic nationalism and increasing criticism both of the United States and of the international economic system. It led to a greater emphasis on foreign policy independence and on an expansion of relations with Europe, Japan, and (in economic relations) the Soviet Union, as well as closer alignment with the Third World. The dramatic economic changes which Latin America was undergoing in the 1960s and 1970s therefore both underpinned the need and provided the opportunity for more complex and broadly based foreign policies. In both Mexico and Venezuela it was the expansion of oil revenues that provided the economic base for increased international activism. In Brazil it was the vital need to expand exports and guarantee energy supplies that played a major role in pushing a basically pro-Western military government away from its previously close relationship with Washington.

The changing economic context and the shaping of foreign policy   A third area of neorealist neglect concerns the ways in which the international economy constrains Latin American development options and influences the viability of foreign policy goals and strategies. The adoption of development models has consistently been strongly influenced by external shocks and by developments in the international economy. Thus the adoption of import-substitution industrialization (ISI) was in large part a response to the Great Depression and to the Second World War, and it was the growing constraints of the ISI model that pressed Latin America towards a more independent foreign policy. Even more tellingly, it was the onset of the debt crisis and the economic dislocations of the 1980s that undercut the hopes for greater autonomy and independence from the United States. Finally, the shift towards market liberal policies and a more cooperative policy *vis-à-vis* the United States in the 1990s is closely bound up with evolving Latin American perceptions of what constitutes a viable economic model in an increasingly integrated global economy. On this view, neorealism neglects the ways in which developments in the international economy (in technology, communications, and the operation of global markets) have led to profound changes in the ways in which Latin American states define the goals of foreign policy—military security, economic prosperity, and political autonomy— and the range of acceptable trade-offs between them.

Dependency Theory

Dependency theory dominated much Latin American social science (including the analysis of the region's international role) in the 1960s and 1970s. Although drawing on strands within the Marxist tradition, it grew up as a specifically Latin American approach to the analysis of development and is thus of particular relevance to this chapter. Its popularity was increased by the vociferous criticism in both North and South America of US interventionist policies (with the Vietnam War and the US role in deposing Salvador Allende's government in Chile achieving particular resonance).

Dependency theory arose as a critique of liberal and Western ideas of economic development ('modernization theory') which argued that the less developed parts of the world could and would achieve the same growth pattern and path as the industrialized world; and that participation in the international economy was fundamentally positive.[15] 'Dependency theory' is more properly seen as a broad approach or perspective encompassing a variety of writers from many different backgrounds and with many different concerns.[16] Early theorists (such as André Gunder Frank) tended to view dependency theory in terms of a rigid law of underdevelopment and argued that participation in the international economy served only to perpetuate inequality and underdevelopment. In the 1970s, by contrast, theorists such as Fernando Henrique Cardoso and Peter Evans developed a more case-specific 'historical structural' approach which accepted the fact of economic development but which none the less argued that the character of that development would remain indelibly marked (and distorted) by the dependent status of the region.[17] The focus therefore shifted from the notion of the 'development of underdevelopment' to the analysis of 'dependent development'.

In terms of US–Latin American relations, three features should be stressed. First, as with neorealism, dependency theory is systemic. It seeks to account for the behaviour of the units on the basis of the attributes of the system as a whole. But the nature and dynamic of the structure are completely different. Instead of a logic based on power competition in an anarchic state system, the focus of dependency theory is on the dynamics of the world capitalist system and on the economic needs and pressures of the major capitalist state. Moreover, in addition to states, great weight is given to the role of economic non-state actors such as transnational companies, international banks, and international economic institutions, and also to the complex relationship between states and classes. From this perspective, then, the most important motivations of the United States in its policies towards Latin America have been economic in character. Interventionism has been designed to thwart those (radical or nationalist) regimes that have challenged, or threatened to challenge, the economic interests of the United States and its companies in their search for raw materials or markets (as late as the 1950s 40 per cent of all US foreign investment was in Latin America and the Caribbean, concentrated on extractive industries such as oil, iron, copper, tin, and tropical fruits). US imperialism in Latin America is therefore driven by the needs of world capitalism, rather than by geopolitical or security concerns.

Secondly, the power on which US hegemony rested should not be considered solely in terms of inter-state or relational power. Thus, while many of the formal structures of dependency—the reliance of the region on the United States for trade, investment, aid, technology—can be readily incorporated into a neorealist picture of unequal power, what is distinctive about dependency theory is the argument that US power has been maintained and manipulated by transnational class alliances. Internal and external forces are therefore closely related and a central task for the analyst is to trace the coincidence of interests between dominant classes within Latin American societies and those in the core capitalist economies.[18]

It is within the framework of this class-based system that the formal structures of dependency have been able to ensure the continued global pattern of dominance and dependence and the continued external control by the core capitalist states of the destinies of the periphery.

Dependency is a structural condition in which capitalist accumulation does not complete its cycle domestically but relies instead on external factors for its completion. This reliance is of course the central external component of dependency in a literal sense, namely the sense in which a country depends on another for the performance of a basic need. As the local economy opens itself up to the international system, these external factors operate in conjunction with internal (domestic) forces to produce distortions in the domestic system. These distortions (e.g. internal inequality, either across economic sectors, between urban and rural areas, and across classes; authoritarian forms of government) are clearly not the product of either external or internal factors, but of both types of factors working together.[19]

Thirdly, the evolution of Latin American foreign policies needs to be understood in terms of the shifting constraints of the international economy on the one hand, and the shifting sets of state–society relations within Latin American countries on the other. From this perspective, for example, the increased international assertion of the region in the 1970s looks very different. Countries such as Brazil or Mexico had indeed developed strong state structures capable of promoting economic development and of bargaining reasonably effectively with foreign capital. In Brazil this had even involved defining 'an international policy that keeps its distance from American foreign policy on some important points'.[20] Yet, to the dependency theorist, the rhetoric of international assertion failed to recognize: (1) that this bargaining was constrained within an overall 'triple alliance' of state technocrats, multinational companies, and local capital; (2) the continuing powerful external constraints on the region and the degree to which effective control lay with the industrialized states; and (3) the need to examine the distribution of winners and losers within and not just between states—in other words, analysing which classes and groups were gaining from the development that was taking place.[21]

The onset of the Latin American debt crisis in 1982 was viewed by dependency theorists as powerful evidence of the continuing vulnerability and structural dependence of the region. Not only were the hopes of greater autonomy shattered, but the United States was able to exploit the crisis and to use international financial institutions such as the World Bank and IMF, and a new transnational network of US-trained economic technocrats, to impose its own market liberal economic prescriptions on the region. Petras and Morley highlight the continuity of US economic imperialism:

The spectacle of the world's bankers dictating economic policy to the most 'advanced' Third World countries such as Mexico, Brazil and Argentina—specifying trade, investment, budgetary, wage and exchange policies—is reminiscent of the 'custodial' control exercised over the Central American republics in an earlier era by United Fruit and other American corporations.[22]

On this view, then, the so-called 'triumph of liberal economics' appears partly as the result of external imposition and partly as the recognition by Latin American states that, after the demise of the Soviet Union and in an era of capitalist global-ization, there is no other alternative.

Dependency theory arose principally as an attempt by Latin American scholars to understand the nature of the region's political and economic under-development. It became of increasing interest to international relations scholars because of the critical influence that the international system was believed to have on development, and because the approach implied a permanent pattern of dominance and dependence between core industrialized states and the under-developed periphery. Yet one of the difficulties of evaluating dependency ap-proaches (and indeed one of the major criticisms of them) is that a theory of underdevelopment is not the same as a theory of foreign policy or international relations.

As a theory of underdevelopment, dependency theory has been subjected to a barrage of criticisms:[23] that it underestimated the growth potential of peripheral capitalism (as evidenced by the emergence of East Asian economies); that it over-estimated the importance of external factors and ignored the fact that many of the most powerful obstacles to development lay in the domestic system and in the histories of individual states and societies; that it placed too much emphasis on the role of foreign direct investment, downplaying the importance of the international trading and financial system; and that there is no necessary link (or even 'elective affinity') between dependence in the international economy and non-democratic or authoritarian political systems.

As a theory of international relations, two criticisms of dependency theory stand out. First, its economistic bias blinded dependency theorists to the powerful logic of inter-state competition. Thus the constraints facing weak states in Central America resulted far more directly and powerfully from the Cold War-driven imperatives for the United States to police its sphere of influence than from the dynamics of global capitalism. Interventionism was about geopolitics and security, not capitalism and exploitation. Secondly, viewing the preferences of Latin Amer-ican élites solely in terms of transnational class solidarity with capitalists in the core countries grossly underplayed their genuine nationalism and desire for independence and autonomy. For example, Latin American militaries have in many places ceased to be the 'natural allies' of the United States, becoming instead deeply suspicious of the loss of sovereignty involved in close economic liberalization and integration.

While the force of these criticisms should be accepted, there are none the less a number of important arguments that have emerged out of the debates over dependency theory that are very often neglected by other theories, and that are likely to remain central to the analysis of US–Latin American relations. In the first place, it is important to construct a nuanced understanding of US hegemony in which the role of shared values and ideology and the influence of transnational élite coalitions are taken seriously. Perhaps drawing on neo-Gramscian concerns and perspectives, analysts need to examine the ways in which regional hegemons may seek to cement their power through the conscious cultivation of common values designed to legitimize authority.

This leads to the second point, namely the importance of examining politics within the state and the evolving character of state–society relations within Latin American countries—in contrast to neorealism, which denies the need for a theory of the state, and to liberalism, which has often viewed the state simply as a neutral arena of contending social forces. Thus we need to look more closely at the domestic political processes by which those groups espousing the values of the hegemon either are able to achieve predominance or else fail to do so. External pressures and inducements are of course likely to be important; but so too are the ways in which these external 'signals' are received and interpreted within the subordinate state. For example, the realignment with the United States in the period since 1989 has involved changes in social and economic power within Latin American societies and has been effected by new sets of political coalitions built up in support of the project of 'conservative economic modernization' and neoliberal reform.

Finally, the foreign policies of Latin American states remain very heavily influenced by the nature of domestic economic policy and by dominant ideas of economic development. Equally, their vulnerability to the international economy remains a fundamental constraint on their freedom of manœuvre (as evidenced by the renewed instability in Mexico in early 1995 after the bullish optimism of the previous five years). Thus, for all its flaws, dependency theory is substantially correct in arguing that both the interests and the identities of states need to be understood within the context of the 'transnational whole' within which they are embedded.

Liberalism

Liberalism has long formed a central part of the rhetoric of inter-American relations and of the idea of hemispheric solidarity based around republican values, international law, and regional institutions. But for much of the post-war period liberal commentators were on the defensive against the dominance of dependency theory in the 1970s and (after the brief liberal resurgence during the Carter years) against Reaganite cold warriors in the early 1980s. However, since the mid-1980s liberal interpretations of inter-American relations have been gaining ground, claiming to provide a more accurate account of the changes that have taken place in US–Latin American relations in these years. Reflecting core assumptions of liberal theories of international relations more generally, the following two sets of factors are emphasized.[24]

Complex interdependence   For liberals, US–Latin American relations have been transformed by the interdependencies that have grown up on such issues as drugs, migration, and the environment. Thus, for example, 26 million people of Hispanic American origin live in the United States. (accounting for around 10 per cent of the population), while around 10 per cent of the population of the Caribbean islands have moved to the United States since 1945; Latin America produces and trans-ships almost all of the cocaine and marijuana entering the United States; and the United States is increasingly affected by the environmental degradation taking place in Latin America (by direct transborder pollution, as on the US–Mexican frontier, but also by broader problems such as the loss of biodiversity caused by the destruction of the Amazon rainforest).

Liberals predict three effects. First, a reformulation of interests is required. For liberals, the need to deal with these problems has led to progressive changes in the nature of US interests in the region. The earlier focus on military threats and on military responses was often excessively ideological and has been rendered obsolete with the end of the Cold War. Old-style security threats have gone and security needs to be redefined around precisely these kinds of problems. Secondly, growing interdependence creates problems that can only be effectively managed by multilateral cooperation. And thirdly, growing interdependence involves an increasingly dense and important 'transnational civil society' in which non-state actors play an increasingly important political role. Thus liberals point to the dramatic proliferation of organizations and interest groups seeking to influence US policy in the region, such as international banking groups (important in the politics of debt management in the 1980s); church and religious groups (which played important roles on both the liberal and conservative sides of the divisive debates over Central American policy in the 1980s); human rights groups such as Amnesty International and Human Rights Watch; and environmental pressure groups (important, for example, in mobilizing opposition to the North American Free Trade Area).

The changing character of states   Whereas for neorealists it is axiomatic that foreign policies are driven by external pressures, liberals assume that the domestic character of states plays a fundamental role in shaping their international behaviour. On this view, for example, the specifically liberal character of the United States has been of central importance in understanding its objectives and policies in the region. Thus even when the broad goal is security, the way in which that goal is understood and the means by which it is pursued have been consistently influenced by a powerful liberal impulse, stressing the importance of promoting democracy and free markets. Equally, the widespread trend towards democratic governance and market-orientated economic reforms explains a good deal of the improved state of US–Latin American relations since 1989. As will be apparent from earlier sections of this chapter, such arguments are likely to remain unconvincing to both neorealists and neodependency theorists, who would be far more inclined to stress the changing structure of material incentives on which this liberal convergence has come to rest; the changing character of US hegemony; the limits to US interests in democratization; and the geographical unevenness of patterns of complex interdependence.

7.3. Conclusions

This chapter has concentrated on the first two uses of theory developed in the introduction: defining categories and concepts; and opening up contending perspectives as a way of mapping the landscape and sharpening different sets of explanations. It has taken neorealism as its theoretical point of departure, arguing that neorealist theory does have very important things to say about US–Latin America relations, in terms of the constraints of the international system, the importance of security issues, the range of options and strategies available to Latin America, and the relationship between political and economic goals. The chapter then examined the ways in which both dependency theory and liberalism expose the weaknesses and limitations of neorealism by suggesting different kinds of questions, by focusing on different actors, and by shifting the analysis to different levels of analysis.

One point in particular is worth emphasizing. Although neorealism claims to be interested in the 'big picture' and to explain only a small number of big and important things, it is often more useful in analysing power relationships within a particular context.[25] Thus within each of the phases identified in the first part of this chapter, neorealism can provide a powerful and parsimonious account of the range of strategic options and bargaining strategies and the ways in which power balances will shape the range of likely outcomes. Yet because it neglects both domestic social and political forces and the external economic environment (stressed by both liberals and dependency theorists, albeit in very different ways), it does not possess the intellectual resources to answer the broader 'puzzle' and to explain the way in which the relationship has evolved and changed through the period as a whole.

In addition to mapping the landscape, it is also important to note the ways in which each of these three contending theoretical perspectives can be used to structure and carry forward more specific research agendas. First, the simplifying assumptions embodied in neorealism lend themselves to attempts to develop formal models, for example of specific sets of bargaining or negotiation between Washington and Latin America on issues of trade, investment, or the foreign debt. Secondly, theories can help shape more detailed examination of major developments (involving either single cases within the region or, more usefully from a social science perspective, a range of cases compared across time or place). And thirdly, even mistaken theories can have considerable heuristic value, stimulating productive avenues of research. Thus dependency theory spawned a wealth of case studies examining the bargaining relationship between Latin American states and multinational companies, and this led in turn to greater theoretical attention being paid to the nature of the state and questions of state capacity and state autonomy.

Finally, the case of US–Latin American relations underlines the importance of thinking critically about 'who theory is for'. As suggested earlier, 'theory' has played an important part in the politics of US–Latin American relations. The three theoretical perspectives discussed in this chapter have shaped and moulded the identities and the interests of the most important political actors in both the United States and Latin America, and in all three description and prescription are closely, and often confusingly, related. Thus the ritualistic invocation of 'security' and the appeal to the timeless realist truths of the 'national interest' have been consistently used to underpin a particular view of how Washington's Latin American policy ought to be conducted and of the values that should be promoted. Equally, the power of dependency theory has come not from its explanatory capabilities, but from the extent to which it provided the ideological cement for many of the most influential political platforms both in Latin America in particular and in the Third World more generally.

Chronology

Sept. 1947	Inter-American Treaty of Reciprocal Assistance (Rio Treaty)
1947	Brazil and Chile break off diplomatic relations with USSR
Mar. 1948	Charter of Organization of American States (OAS)
June 1950	Start of Korean War
Mar. 1952	Brazil–US Military Assistance Agreement. Between 1952 and 1955 agreements signed with Chile, Colombia, Cuba, Dominican Republic, Ecuador, Guatemala, Haiti, Honduras, Nicaragua, Peru, and Uruguay
Mar. 1954	Tenth Inter-American Conference in Caracas declares that 'domination or control of the political institution of any American State by the international communist movement' constitutes 'a threat to the sovereignty and political independence of the American states' and thus a threat to international peace

Spring 1954	US covert intervention and sponsorship to overthrow Jacobo Arbenz Guzmán's government in Guatemala
Jan. 1959	Cuban Revolution
Mar. 1961	Kennedy announces Alliance for Progress
Apr. 1961	US-supported Bay of Pigs intervention against Castro
1961–3	Seven civilian governments overthrown in military coups
Jan. 1962	Suspension of Castro's government from the OAS
22–27 Oct. 1962	Cuban Missile Crisis
Mar. 1964	Military coup in Brazil (with covert US plans to intervene in support of military rebels which were, in the event, not needed)
Apr. 1965	US military intervention in the Dominican Republic to prevent a 'second Cuba'
1968	Peru expropriates International Petroleum Company (subsidiary of Standard Oil)
1970	US accuses Cuba and USSR of building harbour at Cienfuegos; Salvador Allende elected President of Chile
1971	Chilean Congress approves expropriation of US copper firms Anaconda and Kennecott
May 1972	Signature of SALT I arms control agreement between US and USSR High point of superpower detente
1973	US-supported military coup overthrows Allende
1975	Cuba deploys troops in Angolan civil war (and subsequently in Ethiopia)
Sept. 1977	Carter administration signs the Canal Treaties with Panama
1977–8	Carter administration terminates military assistance to Argentina, Brazil, Chile, Uruguay, Guatemala, and El Salvador because of human rights concerns
July 1978	Civilian rule re-established in Ecuador. Subsequent 'democratic wave' of 1980s includes Peru (May 1980); Bolivia (Oct. 1982); Argentina (Oct. 1983); Uruguay (Nov. 1984); Brazil (March 1985); Paraguay (May 1989); Chile (Dec. 1989)
1979	US 'discovers' Soviet brigade in Cuba
July 1979	Fall of Somoza government in Nicaragua; Sandinista revolution
Dec. 1979	Soviet invasion of Afghanistan
Dec. 1981	Reagan authorizes US support for anti-Sandinista 'Contra' forces
Apr. 1982	Falkands/Malvinas War between Britain and Argentina
Aug. 1982	Onset of Mexican debt crisis
Oct. 1983	US military intervention in Grenada
Oct. 1984	US Congress cuts off aid to Contras
Mar. 1985	Gorbachev becomes leader of CPSU
Sept. 1985	Baker Plan on Latin American debt
1986	Mexico joins the GATT as part of move towards trade liberalization
Aug. 1987	Regional peace initiative in Central America (Esquipulas agreement) sponsored by Costa Rica

Jan. 1989	Cuban troops begin withdrawal from Angola
July 1989	Brady Plan to facilitate rescheduling of Latin American debt
Dec. 1989	US invasion of Panama to remove Manuel Noriega
Feb. 1990	Defeat of Sandinistas in Nicaraguan elections
June 1990	Bush's Enterprise Initiative for the Americas
June 1991	OAS reasserts its role in supporting democracy ('Santiago Commitment')
Aug. 1992	North American Free Trade Agreement agreed between Mexico, US, and Canada
Dec. 1994	Summit of the Americas, Miami

Notes

1. For an overview of US–Latin American relations see G. Pope Atkins, *Latin America in the International Political System*, 2nd edn. (Boulder, Colo., 1989), esp. ch. 5.
2. For a comparative analysis of the concept of a regional sphere of influence and the meaning of hegemony see Jan F. Triska (ed.), *Dominant Powers and Subordinate States: The United States in Latin America and the Soviet Union in Eastern Europe* (Durham, NC, 1986).
3. For a detailed diplomatic history of this period see Stephen G. Rabe, *Eisenhower and Latin America: The Foreign Policy of Anticommunism* (Chapel Hill, NC, 1988).
4. The period of the 1970s and early 1980s is best covered in Kevin J. Middlebrook and Carlos Rico (eds.), *The United States and Latin America in the 1980s: Contending Perspectives on a Decade of Crisis* (Pittsburgh, Pa., 1986).
5. On US–Latin American relations in the 1980s and early 1990s see Abraham Lowenthal and Gregory Treverton (eds.), *Latin America in a New World* (Boulder, Colo., 1994); Jonathan Hartlyn, Lars Schoultz, and Augusto Varas (eds.), *The United States and Latin America in the 1990s* (Chapel Hill, NC, 1992).
6. The differences between realism and neorealism are discussed in Robert O. Keohane (ed.), *Neorealism and its Critics* (New York, 1986).
7. Pope Atkins, *Latin America in the International Political System*, 108.
8. The logic of US involvement in the Third World is usefully explored in Stephen van Evera, 'Why Europe Matters, Why the Third World Doesn't: American Grand Strategy after the Cold War', *Journal of Strategic Studies*, 13/2 (June 1990), 1–49. Realists such as George Kennan or Henry Kissinger have been deeply dismissive of the idea that the region is of any great intrinsic or direct importance to the US, as in the latter's reported remarks to the Chilean foreign minister in 1969: 'You come here speaking of Latin America, but it is not important. Nothing important can come from the South . . . The axis of history starts in Moscow, goes to Bonn, crosses over to Washington, and then goes to Tokyo': quoted in Seymour Hersh, *The Price of Power* (London, 1983).

9. For a clear restatement of this position see Stephen M. Walt, *The Origin of Alliances* (Ithaca, NY, 1987).

10. Stephen D. Krasner, *Structural Conflict: The Third World against Global Liberalism* (Berkeley and Los Angeles, 1985).

11. Lars Schoultz, *National Security and United States Policy toward Latin America* (Princeton, 1987), p. xi.

12. Ibid.

13. It should be noted that some realists accept the importance of goals other than security. Precisely because of the relative absence of major direct security challenges in Latin America and because the US has been so powerful, US foreign policy has often been driven by domestic factors, by interest groups, or by ideology. But the *prescriptive* side of neorealism is sharply critical of these tendencies: foreign policy should be insulated from the vagaries of domestic politics; the 'national interest' should not be understood in terms of competing domestic ideologies or interests. Thus, ideological crusading—whether of a liberal Wilsonian or of a conservative Reaganite variety—is to be abjured, unless it directly serves power-political interests. 'Analytically, realism is sceptical of the ability of states to influence domestic developments in other polities. Such efforts are likely to require considerable resources and wisdom, both of which are usually in short supply. Prescriptively, a basic admonition of realism is that states must guard their own resources; the world is a potentially dangerous place. Interventions, even for the most admirable of purposes, are likely to be costly': Stephen Krasner, 'Realism, Imperialism, and Democracy: A Response to Gilbert', *Political Theory*, 20/1 (Feb. 1992), 49.

14. For an account that stresses the importance of domestically engendered perceptions of foreign affairs see Tony Smith, *America's Mission: The United States and the Worldwide Struggle for Democracy in the Twentieth Century* (Princeton, 1994), esp. ch. 1.

15. On this point see Chapter 9 in this volume by John Darwin.

16. For a review see Gabriel Palma, 'Dependency: A Formal Theory of Underdevelopment or a Methodology for Analyzing Concrete Situations of Underdevelopment?', *World Development*, 6 (Nov. 1978), 881–924; Peter B. Evans and John D. Stephens, 'Development and the World Economy', in Neil J. Smelser (ed.), *Handbook of Sociology* (London, 1988), 739–73.

17. Among the most important works are Fernando Henrique Cardoso and Enzo Faletto, *Dependency and Development in Latin America* (Beverly Hills, 1979); Peter Evans, *Dependent Development: The Alliance of Multinational, State and Local Capital in Brazil* (Princeton, 1981).

18. See Cardoso and Faletto, *Dependency and Development*, p. xvi.

19. James Caporaso and Behrouz Zare, 'An Interpretation and Evaluation of Dependency Theory', in Heraldo Muñoz (ed.), *From Dependency to Development* (Boulder, Colo., 1981), 46.

20. Cardoso and Faletto, *Dependency and Development*, 197.

21. For a clear statement of this see ibid. 212; or Evans, *Dependent Development*, 165.

22. James Petras and Morris Morley, *US Hegemony under Siege: Class, Politics and Development in Latin America* (London, 1990), 38.

23. For a balanced discussion see Stephan Haggard, *Pathways from the Periphery: The Politics of Growth in the Newly Industrializing Countries* (Ithaca, NY, 1990).
24. For a generally liberal interpretation see Abraham F. Lowenthal, *Partners in Conflict: The United States and Latin America* (Baltimore, 1987). On the recent dominance of liberal perspectives see Mark Peceny, 'The Inter-American System as a Liberal "Pacific Union"?', *Latin American Research Review*, 29/3 (1994), 188–201.
25. See Kenneth Waltz, 'A Response to my Critics', in Keohane (ed.), *Neorealism and its Critics*, 329.

Further Reading

ATKINS, G. POPE, *Latin America in the International Political System*, 2nd edn. (Boulder, Colo., 1989). Provides the best overview of Latin American international relations. US–Latin American relations are covered in ch. 5 and inter-American institutions in ch. 8.

EVANS, PETER, *Dependent Development: The Alliance of Multinational, State and Local Capital in Brazil* (Princeton, 1981). An excellent exposition of a sophisticated dependency theory approach applied to the case of Brazil.

LOWENTHAL, ABRAHAM, and TREVERTON, GREGORY (eds.), *Latin America in a New World* (Boulder, Colo., 1994). Analyses US–Latin American relations in the 1980s and 1990s and includes both US and Latin American perspectives.

MIDDLEBOOK, KEVIN J., and RICO, CARLOS (eds.), *The United States and Latin America in the 1980s: Contending Perspectives on a Decade of Crisis* (Pittsburgh, Pa., 1986). A wide range of contributions cover both economic and security issues in the period of the 1970s and early 1980s.

SCHOULTZ, LARS, *National Security and United States Policy toward Latin America* (Princeton, 1987). Provides by far the best critical analysis of US security policy towards the region.

TRISKA, JAN F. (ed.), *Dominant Powers and Subordinate States: The United States in Latin America and the Soviet Union in Eastern Europe* (Durham, NC, 1986). Analyses the concept of sphere of influence and the nature of regional hegemony.

CHAPTER EIGHT

THE UNITED STATES AND EAST ASIA: CHALLENGES TO THE BALANCE OF POWER

Yuen Foong Khong

International relations analysts of the structural persuasion are prone to view post-war US actions in East Asia as a function of the bipolar competition between the United States and the Soviet Union. The leading US role in fighting two major land wars in Asia—in Korea (1950–3) and Vietnam (1965–75)—is seen as an expression of power-balancing behaviour engendered by a bipolar international system. As the leading proponent of the structural perspective, Kenneth Waltz, put it: 'In a bipolar world there are no peripheries. With only two powers capable of acting on a world scale, anything that happens anywhere is potentially of concern to both of them.'[1]

The international systemic pressures acting on US President Harry Truman at the time of North Korea's invasion of South Korea are eloquently summarized by Waltz: 'President Truman . . . could not very well echo Neville Chamberlain's words in the Czechoslovakian crisis by claiming that the Koreans were a people far away in the East of Asia of whom Americans knew nothing. We had to know about them or quickly find out.'[2] Similarly, the historian George Herring sees the United States' involvement in Vietnam as the 'logical, if not inevitable, out-growth of a world view and policy, the policy of containment, which Americans in and out of government accepted without serious question for more than two decades'.[3] From the structural perspective, this twenty-year consensus on, and pursuit of, containment is but the most obvious policy manifestation of the US–Soviet rivalry in a bipolar world.

How robust is this correlation between system structure and the US proclivity for military action in East Asia? If one merely looks for the 'military effects' of 'structural causes' the cases of Korea and Vietnam would seem to offer impressive circumstantial evidence for the importance of international structure.[4] If, however for the same period (i.e. holding system structure constant), one also finds instances where US inaction led to substantial power accretion, whether material or psychological, by the Soviet bloc, the correlation between structure and military action would seem less impressive and perhaps even spurious.

It is possible to think of two major episodes in East Asia in which the United States stood by while the power of its rival, the Soviet bloc, was significantly augmented: the victory of Communism in China in 1949 and the victory of Vietnamese Communism at Dien Bien Phu in 1954. In both cases, the United States contemplated stopping or reversing Communist gains, but in both cases policy-makers refrained from military action. If bipolarity is associated with cases of 'drawing lines' against the extension of Communist power (in Korea in 1950 and in Vietnam in 1965) as well as its opposite, standing aside (in China in 1949 and in Vietnam in 1954), the notion of structure is probably too indeterminate to help us understand the sources of America's East Asia policies.

A second approach to thinking about the US response to East Asian conflicts is to temper the emphasis on international systemic pressures without ignoring them. One might focus instead on the historical context and its impact on the calculations of policy-makers responsible for those decisions. Part of the historical context is of course the bipolar world in which the United States found itself. Thus events in remote areas will concern both superpowers, especially if they have implications for the psychological or material balance of power.[5] But super-power 'concern' need not always translate into action. It is a constant and it hovers in the background. Other aspects of the historical context come into play: the relevant cast of characters or decision-makers, the domestic political scene, and contingent factors or events (such as the explosion of a Soviet nuclear device). Often, it is how these aspects blend together that gives shape and content to foreign policy decisions. In effect, this is the approach taken by most historical monographs on American foreign policy.

This chapter offers a third approach to understanding the different US responses to the four East Asian conflicts noted above. It explores the degree to which US responses to these conflicts are connected to one another and suggests the following argument: whether and how the United States responds to an earlier crisis acts as an important constraint on its response to the next crisis. Applied to the four East Asian conflicts, the argument runs as follows. 'Losing China' in 1949 decreased the likelihood that the United States would stand by in 1950 when North Korea attempted to incorporate the South by force: for after failing to draw the line against Communism in 1949, it was increasingly likely that the United States would do so in the following year, when Communism seemed to be on the march in the same geographic area. Yet when success prompted the United States/United Nations to cross the thirty-eighth parallel to 'liberate' North Korea, the line was 'overdrawn': China felt its security was threatened and entered the war, fighting the United States to a standstill. The experience of overdrawing the line in Korea injected such a strong dose of caution in the United States that when the next Communist challenge in East Asia came with the impending fall of North Vietnam, the United States refrained from any more line-drawing—despite urgent pleas from the French for American intervention and despite President Eisenhower's likening the failure to stop Communism in Vietnam to a repeat of 1930s appeasement. The line in Vietnam, however, was eventually drawn in the mid-1960s with the US decision to fight another Asian land war so as to prevent South Vietnam from becoming Communist.

In other words, there exists a pattern in the US response to Communist challenges in East Asia: whether and how it drew a line in one case would have an important bearing on whether and how it would draw a line in a subsequent challenge. This argument is akin to the second approach described above in its emphasis on the historical context. However, the notion of historical context adopted here is narrower, or more precise, depending on one's point of view: it singles out the 'legacies of previous decisions' for analysis and it explores how these legacies affect the domestic political discourse and the drawing of lessons. In the parlance of international relations theory, a 'path-dependent' approach is being adopted here.[6] The argument presented here also differs from the international systemic argument in that it looks to constraints imposed by previous choices, rather than to the static international system, in its pursuit of an understanding of current choices.

We begin by discussing the US response to the impending victory of Mao Zedong's Chinese Communist Party, the strategic consequences of that response, its impact on subsequent domestic political discourse and 'learning', and how these 'legacies' in turn affected the US response to the next crisis, Korea. It is important to stress at the outset what is not being argued here. It is not being argued that US actions during the earlier crisis were the sole or decisive factor behind US actions in the later crisis: such monocausal explanations are rarely adequate in understanding international politics. Other historically contingent factors or factors unrelated to the previous decision (or 'non-legacies') are obviously important and will be brought into the analysis as appropriate; but the aim is to weave together the strands of the 'legacies' thesis, to see what the tapestry is like. Perhaps the simplest way to summarize the thesis of this chapter is to say that the decisions formulated by the United States with respect to these four East Asian challenges were not independent of each other.

8.1. The Chinese Civil War

The victory of Communism in China and the North Korean invasion of South Korea were nine months apart. If the structural perspective that 'in a bipolar world there are no peripheries' is applicable in understanding why the United States intervened with military force in the latter case, it should also help us in understanding the former. China is arguably the first and most significant East Asian test case of the importance of this bipolar logic.

US officials were indeed concerned about the outcome of the Chinese civil war. In December 1945 President Truman sent George Marshall to mediate between Mao Zedong's Chinese Communist Party (CCP) and Chiang Kai-shek's Nationalists (the KMT), in the hope of averting a civil war. Marshall had little success and a full-scale civil war for the control of China broke out in 1947. US aims between 1946 and 1949 were hardly impartial. It sought a coalition government, but on terms favourable to the KMT; it continued supplying military and economic aid to the KMT; it wanted to deny Manchuria to the Soviet Union; and, most of all, it wanted to forestall a Communist victory. Melvyn Leffler best summarizes US consciousness about the balance-of-power implications of a Communist China: 'The great fear of the Truman administration was that the Russians would ensconce themselves in Manchuria, northern China, and Korea, integrate the resources of this region with the Soviet Far East, and establish a power complex in East Asia that resembled the one that the Japanese had in the 1930s.'[7] John Carter Vincent, who was Secretary of State Dean Acheson's main adviser on China, also saw the primary aim of US policy as preventing 'China's absorption into a Russian orbit'.[8]

If these balance-of-power concerns were as central as the structuralist perspective assumes, then it must be paradoxical that they did not translate into a firm policy posture, or the dispatch of US troops from Korea or Japan to help the KMT, when the latter was losing, but that an alternative view, emphasizing the strategic insignificance of China and downplaying the power implications of a Communist China, prevailed and became the basis for a policy of disengagement. The dispositions of the chief policy-makers and the permissive domestic political context within which they operated explain why this view prevailed. 'Atlanticists' like Marshall, Acheson, and Kennan were preoccupied with Europe; they considered China as part of the periphery. Pressures from the 'Asia-firsters' in Congress were troublesome, but they did not have a major impact on policy before the Korean War. China, historians like to point out, was number thirteen on the joint chiefs of staff's list of sixteen countries considered vital to the national security of the United States.[9]

In part because of these factors, the United States could see clearly (in ways it could not in Vietnam in the 1960s) the weaknesses of its East Asian client, and, more importantly, could factor those assessments into its policy-making. Chiang and the KMT were deemed incompetent and corrupt. US economic and military aid had been poorly used or squandered and the State Department China specialists all concurred that Chiang would lose the civil war. By early 1949, therefore, a decision was made to distance the United States from Chiang, and the prospective consequences of 'losing China' were deemed 'deplorable' but 'not catastrophic'.[10] Policy-makers emphasized the nationalist, not socialist, credentials of Mao, and deduced that a China under Communist rule would soon develop divergent interests from those of the Soviet Union. Tito's carving of an independent path for Yugoslavia against Soviet wishes was seen as a model for China. Acheson was especially enamoured of the view of Mao as an Asian Tito. The role of the United States was to drive a wedge between China and the Soviet Union.

With the CCP as competent as the KMT was incompetent, with the negative consequences of a CCP-ruled China watered down, and with America's resources committed elsewhere by Atlanticists who saw China as peripheral, it does not come as a surprise that the United States stood by as China fell under Communist control in late 1949. As the State Department's White Paper explaining the fall of China put it, 'nothing this country [the United States] did or could have done within the reasonable limits of its capabilities could have changed that result; nothing that was left undone by this country has contributed to it.'[11]

There is no doubt that Truman and Acheson were wise to recognize the limits of American power, given the situation in China. What is puzzling from the structural perspective is that the balance-of-power implications of a Communist China were not given more weight or the strategic implications taken more seriously. Instead of seeing Communist China as adding to the power of the Soviet bloc in the short to medium term, Acheson and his advisers preferred to focus on the long-term tendencies of Chinese nationalism. The latter would cause China to pursue its own national interests, which were likely to diverge from those of the Soviet Union. History proved that their prognostications were correct—in the long run: what they missed was the twenty-year interregnum, in which, despite strains, the Soviet–Chinese alliance (formalized in February 1950) bore down heavily on the United States. Dean Rusk, Acheson's Assistant Secretary of State for Far Eastern affairs, appreciated that in May 1950, when he pointed out that 'the loss of China to Communists marked a shift in the balance of power in favor of Soviet Russia and to the disfavor of the United States.'[12] Structuralists would expect such shifts to be resisted with more vigour than was demonstrated by the Truman administration in the late 1940s.

Thus, bipolarity notwithstanding, the United States acted as if China were in the periphery. The price of that strategy was that for the next twenty years the United States saw itself as being confronted by a Communist monolith, consisting of the Soviet Union and China, who were seen as intent on extending their influence by supporting wars of national liberation in the Third World. The policy implications of Rusk's comment about the shift in the balance of power were well grasped by Waldo Heinrichs when he wrote that the establishment of the People's

Republic of China in October 1949 was a 'catalytic event'. Henceforth, 'policy makers were determined to allow no more lost Chinas; the line must be drawn.'[13]

8.2. The Korean War

If China ranked number thirteen in 1947 in terms of its strategic value to US national security, Korea ranked fifteenth on a list of sixteen countries.[14] As the ranking suggests, China mattered more than Korea in the global balance of power. Yet it was in Korea, not China, that the United States intervened with air, naval, and ground forces to save the southern part from Communism. How is one to account for that?

The fact that North Korea resorted to military invasion to attempt to unify the country helps explain why US policy-makers thought a military response was necessary. So does the perception that the North's military action was inspired and supported by the Soviet Union. Another important consideration, anticipated by the passage from Heinrichs quoted above, was the US failure to do more to prevent or postpone the fall of China and its consequences. Since the significance of this factor has not been emphasized in the literature, it will be given more attention here.

Coming so soon after the fall of China, the explosion of a Soviet nuclear device, and the signing of the Soviet–Chinese friendship treaty, the North Korean attack could not be allowed to succeed because such a success would be a tremendous psychological and material boon to the Communist side. US military planners had warned against allowing the Soviet Union to forge 'the largest industrial potential . . . in the Far East' by combining resources from Manchuria, China, and Korea.[15] With Manchuria, China, and North Korea already leaning towards the Soviet Union, only South Korea remained to be brought into the orbit.

Yet more important than preventing the augmentation of Soviet power was the issue of US prestige and credibility. At the first Blair House meeting on 25 June, Truman agreed with General Omar Bradley that Korea was as good as any place to draw a line against Communist expansionism. Truman believed that 'if we let Korea down, the Soviet [sic] will keep right on going and swallow up one piece of Asia after another.'[16] Truman's metaphor was no doubt informed by the lessons of the 1930s, but a more recent event was probably also salient: the United States had stood by when the first piece of Asia—China—fell into Soviet mouths. Acheson echoed Truman's fears when he opined that 'the Kremlin was calculating that, after the loss of China, it could win another easy victory in South Korea and undermine the US position in Japan.'[17] John Lewis Gaddis summarizes these psychological factors eloquently when he writes: 'To a nation still recoiling from the "loss" of China, still brooding over the "lessons" of Munich, Korea quickly became a symbol of resolve regardless of its military–strategic significance.'[18]

The US response to China also affected the US response to Korea because of the domestic reverberations of the former. Losing China gave fuel to Senator Joseph McCarthy's charges that the State Department was infiltrated by Communists; it also empowered the 'Asia-firsters' in Congress. In fact, the fall of China had undermined the domestic credibility of the Truman administration. Seeking to point out the domestic sources of Truman's decision to fight in Korea, Richard Whelan has argued that 'criticism of the Truman administration's repudiation of Chiang had become so intense that the president's failure to oppose Communist aggression, *wherever* it might have occurred, could well have led to his impeachment and would almost certainly have led to Acheson's.'[19]

One need not accept the supposed link between not opposing Communist aggression and impeachment to appreciate the domestic constraints operating on Truman; nor need one accept Whelan's assumption of 'wherever', for it mattered greatly that the 'wherever' in this case was Korea, a geographical area contiguous with China and the second case of possible Communist victory in two years. Warren Cohen's assessment of the China factor in the administration's decision-making is more measured and to the point: 'Unspoken was another grave concern—for the political future of Harry Truman, for his ability to govern . . . His administration had been accused of betraying China, of allowing the Soviet Union to expand its influence into Asia. Acheson's relative indifference to Asia was notorious . . . Failure to respond in Korea could be politically catastrophic.'[20]

Not many analysts dissent from the judgement that the United States was correct to oppose the violent incorporation of the South by North Korea. Most, however, question the wisdom of the US/UN forces moving north to liberate North Korea and thereby do in reverse what North Korea had failed to do by invading the South. The decision to go north was made by the United States and was dictated in part by the momentum of victory in South Korea, in part by the personality of General MacArthur (who also wished to reopen the Chinese civil war), as well as by the consensus prevailing in the Truman administration. In its hurry and perhaps hubris in marching north, however, the United States neglected Chinese warnings that such an advance would be considered a threat to China's security. When the United States ignored the warnings and proceeded, China entered the war. China's intervention made the war bloody and costly: it suffered over 1.5 million casualties; the US losses numbered 140,000; and close to 4 million Koreans lost their lives. The war also set back US–Chinese relations for twenty years. An armistice was eventually signed in July 1953, with the thirty-eighth parallel reinstated as the demarcation line between North and South Korea.

8.3. Vietnam, I: 1954

Less than a year after the signing of the Korean armistice, the United States was faced with another Communist challenge in East Asia, this time in Vietnam. Although Ho Chi Minh had declared Vietnam independent from France in 1945, the French quickly made their way back. However, the Vietminh or Vietnamese Communists under Ho resisted French attempts to reinstate their rule and, despite negotiations and temporary truces, serious fighting erupted in 1946. Eight years of war followed, with the French gradually losing ground despite massive financial aid from the United States. By the spring of 1954, both sides were gearing up for the final battle. French troops had staked out a position and planned to draw the Vietminh out and defeat them on the plains of Dien Bien Phu.

The Vietminh, under the command of General Vo Nguyen Giap, chose not to meet their opponents head-on. Instead, they laid siege to the French garrison by taking up positions in the surrounding hills, using artillery they had taken apart, carried up the hills, and reassembled, to bombard the French position. The position of the French garrison became extremely precarious and it was at this point that Paris requested the use of American air power to 'relieve' the surrounded garrison. Paris presented the confrontation at Dien Bien Phu as an attempt by world Communism—acting through its Vietnamese proxies—to chalk up another victory, and this interpretation fell on receptive ears in Washington.

To be sure, the United States had sided with France right from the beginning. Its affinity for self-government in the Third World notwithstanding, it had, by the start of the French–Vietminh war, determined that it needed France on its side to counter the Soviet Union in Europe. Ho Chi Minh, the leader of the Vietminh, was seen more as a Communist loyal to the Soviet Union than as a nationalist fighting for Vietnamese self-rule. As Dean Acheson put it in 1949, 'Question whether Ho as much nationalist as Commie is irrelevant . . . all Stalinists in colonial areas are nationalists. With achievement natl aims (i.e. independence) their objective necessarily becomes subordination state to Commie purposes.'[21]

The fall of China had made US policy-makers extremely sensitive about further losses, especially in East Asia. In April 1950 the National Security Council warned that additional 'extension of the area under the domination of the Kremlin would raise the possibility that no coalition adequate to confront the Kremlin with greater strength could be assembled'.[22] As pointed out above, US concern about additional real estate gains by the Soviets in Korea, so soon after the fall of China, was a major factor behind the Truman administration's decision to intervene militarily to save South Korea. The Korean War in turn reinforced US fears about the inexorable advance of Communism. Although Vietnam was not about to be 'lost' in 1950, the United States began to provide financial support to the French in their war against the Vietminh, such that by 1954 it was underwriting 80 per cent of France's war costs.

Given the structural context and US worries about the power and psychological implications of losing Vietnam, it would stand to reason that, when the crux came, the United States would do what was necessary to save it. The crux came during Eisenhower's watch, and despite strong pressures from the French and some of his own advisers, Eisenhower decided against military intervention, in full realization that US inaction would result in the loss, at the very least, of the northern part of Vietnam. This decision must seem puzzling to those who emphasize the importance of international structural constraints on US actions. For here is an instance, at the height of the bipolar contest, in which the chief protector of US security interests decided to let go of Vietnam in spite of its avowed strategic significance.

Examining the historical context of 1954 offers a way out of this puzzle. The recent experience of the Korean War, its impact on the domestic political discourse, and the lessons drawn from it all militated against drawing another line in 1954. In 1954, US credibility was less of an issue than it had been in 1950 because the United States was not as directly involved in Vietnam as it had been in South Korea. Eisenhower's worry was that once he committed US military power, US prestige would be at stake. Proponents of military intervention, such as Admiral Radford, argued that US prestige was already at stake in Vietnam, and they had a point. What gave Eisenhower's argument weight, however, was the recent experience of Korea. Here the United States had intervened, at substantial cost to itself, to save a friend (not an ally); and, while its more ambitious goal of liberating North Korea was not accomplished, it did help restore the status quo ante. US military intervention in Korea, in other words, had shored up US prestige and credibility to the extent that they would not be easily undermined by a failure to respond to the challenge in Vietnam.

However, although Eisenhower's statements seemed to suggest that US credibility was not at stake, his actions were more ambiguous. He and his Secretary of State, John Foster Dulles, gave serious consideration to using air power to bombard the hills around Dien Bien Phu in which the Vietminh were ensconced. They talked about camouflaging US planes, about denying US involvement if discovered, and about the political conditions for success. Eisenhower showed sufficient interest to allow Dulles to seek congressional authorization for the President to use force to save the French. Others in the administration, including Admiral Radford, Vice President Richard Nixon, and, in all likelihood, Dulles himself, were also urging military action.

Some analysts have argued that Eisenhower very cleverly used the consultation with congressional leaders to deflect pressures in favour of intervention. But part of the reason for consulting Congress was to avoid Truman's mistake of committing US forces to Korea without asking Congress—when the Korean War turned nasty, the administration shouldered most of the blame. In 1954 it was deemed wiser to test the congressional waters first. When Dulles invoked the domino theory to alert congressional leaders to the stakes in Dien Bien Phu, their reaction was quite different from that which Dean Acheson received during the Greek crisis of 1947. Instead of asking the administration to take the case to the American public, the congressional leaders responded: '*We want no more Koreas with the US furnishing 90% of the manpower.*'[23]

The meaning and significance of that congressional retort have not been fully appreciated by historians and political scientists. Three assumptions informed the congressional response. First, although Dulles had mentioned the use only of air and naval power, the congressional leaders believed that 'once the flag was committed the use of land forces would inevitably follow.'[24] Secondly, the congressional leaders were not opposed to military intervention per se; what they opposed was a military situation (as in Korea) where the United States supplied 90 per cent of the manpower (and thereby suffered the bulk of the casualties). Hence their counter-proposal to Dulles: get US allies, especially the British, on board, and congressional authorization will be forthcoming. Thirdly, unilateral intervention was unappealing because of the prospect of the United States fighting China essentially alone, as in Korea, if intervention in Dien Bien Phu brought China into the war. After all, the United States did not complain about furnishing most of the manpower before China intervened in the Korean War.

Interestingly, Eisenhower did try to interest British Prime Minister Winston Churchill in joining the United States to save the French at Dien Bien Phu. In a letter to Churchill, Eisenhower invoked the lessons of the 1930s to emphasize the stakes involved in Vietnam. Churchill and his Foreign Secretary, Anthony Eden, demurred, thinking that the United States was trying to get Britain involved in an intractable situation where the chances of Chinese intervention and therefore military escalation were high. With the British unwilling to join in, Eisenhower decided against drawing the line at Dien Bien Phu.

The above account of Eisenhower's response to the Dien Bien Phu crisis has focused on how the recent experience of 'Korea' shaped (1) the administration's assessment of whether US prestige was at stake, (2) the constraints congressional leaders placed on the executive, and (3) the all-round desire not to fight China again and alone. All three factors helped nudge Eisenhower in the direction of non-intervention. It is in this sense that the 1954 decision is connected to the previous US response to Communist challenges in East Asia.

8.4. Vietnam, II: 1965

The Vietminh timed their victory well. One day after the French surrender, the Indochina phase of the Geneva conference began. The Geneva agreements of 1954 divided Vietnam into two zones of regroupment. The Vietminh and their supporters were to regroup north of the seventeenth parallel, with French forces regrouping in the south. The agreement stipulated that the seventeenth parallel was not a political or territorial boundary, for the eventual fate of Vietnam was to be decided by national reunification elections in 1956.

'The [Eisenhower] administration', according to George Herring, 'regarded the loss of northern Vietnam—"the keystone to the arch of Southeast Asia"—with concern.'[25] Not drawing the line in 1954 increased the administration's sense of responsibility for ensuring that what remained of Vietnam was not lost. Between 1954 and 1960 it put in place a series of structures and personalities that would constrain the options of subsequent administrations. Institutionally, the creation of the South-east Asian Treaty Organization (SEATO) soon after the fall of Dien Bien Phu lent expression to Eisenhower's and Dulles' emphasis on multilateral efforts to deter Communist advances. With SEATO in place, the United States would have the wherewithal to cajole, and to require, the military support of third countries in future encounters with Communist expansionism in South-east Asia. Psychologically, in the aftermath of Dien Bien Phu, there was the perception that the United States had a moral, if not legal, commitment to help South Vietnam fend off future Communist encroachment.

With the departure of the French, it also fell to the United States to help to set up, and subsequently nurture, a non-Communist government under Ngo Dinh Diem in the South. Despite doubts about Diem's leadership, the United States continued to provide substantial economic and military aid to South Vietnam, in the hope that this would enable the Diem government to 'build a nation'. When Diem decided against holding the unification elections of 1956— as stipulated in the Geneva agreements—the United States acquiesced in his decision. As Eisenhower himself realized, Ho Chi Minh was likely to receive 80 per cent of the vote in such an election.

For reasons that have been discussed elsewhere, Diem did not use his time or US support effectively.[26] Diem's inability to forge a national consensus and deprive the Communists of support, despite massive US aid, is reminiscent of Chiang Kai-shek's ineptitude in China. In the early 1960s Hanoi approved the formation of the National Liberation Front (NLF) for South Vietnam and the campaign to take the South by military force began. The Kennedy administration was determined to prevent South Vietnam from losing the ensuing struggle, and in November 1961 the US President approved the dispatch of additional military advisers to South Vietnam. With this action the United States crossed a psychological barrier: it would no longer be abiding by the Geneva agreements' ceiling of 750 advisers. By the end of 1962 there were over 12,000 US military personnel in South Vietnam. In short, the Kennedy administration deepened the US commitment to the survival of South Vietnam.

Despite the influx of US resources, Diem was not winning the fight against the NLF. US frustrations with the Diem government reached a climax when the latter reacted most insensitively to Buddhist monks who had immolated themselves to protest against the regime's suppression of religious and civil liberties. These unpopular events gave Diem's generals an excuse to stage a US-approved coup to depose Diem and his brother, Ngo Dinh Nhu. Unfortunately, the coup led to the killing of the Diem brothers, which was not sanctioned by the United States. Three weeks later Kennedy was shot in Texas.

In the year between Kennedy's assassination and Lyndon Johnson's landslide electoral victory, South Vietnam witnessed seven coups and counter-coups. By the time of Johnson's inauguration, his administration was already close to a decision to bomb North Vietnam. The war in the South was heating up. North Vietnam's infiltration of men via the Ho Chi Minh Trail into South Vietnam was seen as the root of the problem, and a major purpose of the bombing would be to convince Hanoi that the United States was serious in its opposition and that Hanoi should cease sending troops down to subvert the South. The bombing campaign—Operation Rolling Thunder—was given the green light in late February 1965. It failed to deter the North Vietnamese, who continued to send men into the South and to win important battles.

In the summer of 1965 the Johnson administration was faced with the prospect of introducing ground troops in South Vietnam to fight the NLF guerrillas and North Vietnamese regulars. Without US military intervention, there was a strong possibility that South Vietnam would fall under North Vietnam's control within a year. In July, President Johnson approved the sending of 100,000 US combat troops to South Vietnam to do battle against North Vietnam and the NLF.

Thus, by the early 1960s the United States was already considering the seventeenth parallel as a political boundary of sorts, again contrary to the Geneva understandings. A major purpose of SEATO was to see to it that the line was not crossed; if it was, in the fashion of North Korea's crossing the thirty-eighth parallel into South Korea, united action by SEATO signatories would come to the aid of South Vietnam. Yet because North Vietnam's strategy in the 1960s was not based on outright invasion, the conditions under which SEATO would operate became blurred. America's SEATO allies could not agree that it was a case of outright aggression. Many—including some US officials—saw the conflict in Vietnam as a civil war. Thus the united action deemed so desirable by the Eisenhower administration was difficult to obtain in Vietnam; the United States continued to bear the brunt of the effort in preventing South Vietnam from falling.

When the moment of decision—should the United States fight another Asian land war to keep South Vietnam in non-Communist hands?—arrived in July 1965 the legacies of previous decisions weighed heavily on US policy-makers' minds. But this did not mean that the decision to fight a ground war was predetermined. It would have been difficult to back away from US commitments built through the years, but it was not impossible. The record suggests that a few of Johnson's influential advisers, including George Ball and Clark Clifford, spoke strongly against committing ground troops, while others—Dean Rusk, McGeorge Bundy, William Bundy, Robert McNamara—advocated military intervention. Arrayed against this latter group, the 'doves' would clearly seem to have little chance— were it not for the fact that Johnson himself was far from eager to engage in another Asian land war.

In a crucial decision-making meeting on 21 July 1965, George Ball made the case against sending combat troops on the grounds that Vietnam was a bad place to make a stand. Ball suggested drawing the line in Thailand. 'Thailand has proven a good ally so far . . . If we wanted to make a stand in Thailand, we might be able to make it.' The President expressed anxiety about the consequences of not drawing the line in South Vietnam: 'Won't these countries [allies in East Asia and elsewhere] say that Uncle Sam was a paper tiger, wouldn't we lose credibility breaking the word of three Presidents, if we did as you have proposed?' While Johnson worried about allies, Rusk worried about adversaries: 'If the Communist world finds out we will not pursue our commitments to the end, I don't know where they will stay their hand.'[27]

Although the international considerations were paramount, domestic politics was also important in nudging the Johnson administration in the direction of intervention. Johnson worried that if South Vietnam fell, it would result in the kind of domestic backlash that resulted from the loss of China in 1949–50. As he told Doris Kearns in his own vivid way: 'I knew that Harry Truman and Dean Acheson had lost their effectiveness from the day that the communists took over China. I believed that the loss of China played a large role in the rise of Joe McCarthy. And I knew that all these problems, taken together, were chickenshit compared with what might happen if we lost Vietnam.'[28] What Johnson meant was that the domestic backlash would be even more divisive, and could under- mine his domestic credibility in ways much more serious than in the case of Truman.

Related to this domestic backlash argument is a legislative argument, advanced most systematically by Larry Berman. According to Berman, 'the overriding con- cern of domestic politics in July 1965 was Lyndon Johnson's intent that the Great Society reach legislative fulfillment.'[29] Losing Vietnam in the summer of 1965 would incur the kind of domestic and congressional backlash that would derail his 'great society' programmes.

In the summer of 1965, therefore, the combined weight and impact of previous responses and non-responses to the three earlier East Asian conflicts were keenly felt by the Johnson administration. The gradual deepening of the US commitment to South Vietnam, beginning with Eisenhower and continuing under Kennedy and Johnson, followed directly from the 1954 decision to tolerate the loss of North Vietnam. Johnson also anticipated that the domestic consequences of inaction in Vietnam would be analogous to that of inaction in China. There would be a McCarthyite anti-Communist backlash, and his enemies would use the fall of Vietnam as a means to destroy the progressive social legislation he wanted Congress to pass.

The Korean experience was also highly relevant to the Johnson administration's decision-making. Korea was widely known as the 'forgotten war' in the early 1950s. The public then saw it at best as a stalemate and at worst as a failure. By the late 1950s, however, opinion polls showed that the public had begun to consider the war as a qualified success.[30] As I have argued elsewhere, many of the 'dos' and 'don'ts' of Vietnam were seen through the lens of the US experience in Korea. The 'lessons of Korea' informed the Johnson administration's assessment of the nature of the Vietnamese conflict (aggression), the stakes involved (high), the ethical soundness of military intervention (good), the prospects of victory (realistic), and the dangers (provoking Chinese intervention).[31] The weight of these lessons predisposed the Johnson administration towards military intervention, although an all-out bombing attack or ground invasion of North Vietnam was ruled out. These 'restraints' were imposed by a President acutely conscious of needing to avoid the mistake made by Truman and MacArthur during the Korean War, namely that of provoking Chinese intervention.

In short, by the time we come to the last major East Asian challenge, the US response was not influenced merely by its immediately previous response (Vietnam in 1954). To be sure, US failure to draw a line in 1954 did set in motion a chain of events that narrowed the range of US options in 1965; but the US responses to earlier East Asian challenges in China and Korea also figured prominently in the decision-making of the mid-1960s. Aspects of these earlier episodes, their domestic consequences, and lessons derived from them all helped to shape the form as well as the fact of the US intervention.

8.5. Conclusion

The purpose of this chapter has been to suggest a line of analysis that sees an explanatory connection linking US responses to the four most important

Communist challenges to the balance of power in East Asia. How and whether the United States responded to an earlier challenge, it has been argued, exercised a profound impact on the US response to a later challenge. Thus failure to respond to the fall of China contributed to a perception of international strategic and domestic political vulnerability that made it difficult for the United States not to intervene in Korea. The US intervention in Korea, the abortive attempt to 'liberate' North Korea, and the consequences of these actions in turn made the Eisenhower administration extremely cautious in deciding whether to respond militarily to the Vietminh's siege of the French garrison at Dien Bien Phu. The decision not to intervene in 1954 to 'save' the northern part of Vietnam, however, set the United States on a path and mode of thought that increased the likelihood that it would intervene in Vietnam in 1965.

This line of analysis, with its emphasis on the legacies of previous decisions, cannot, and does not, pretend to offer a complete explanation for the US decisions examined here. Other factors peculiar to the historical moments at which each of the decisions was taken—such as the personalities of the chief policy-makers and domestic political considerations unrelated to previous decisions—need to be factored in in order to arrive at a full explanation. If the analysis has succeeded in bringing to the fore a hitherto neglected but important constraint—the legacies of previous decisions—on US decision-making with respect to challenges to the balance of power in East Asia, and if it has been able to account for variation in US responses in ways unaccounted for by international systemic approaches, it will have served its purpose.

Chronology

Sept. 1945	Ho Chi Minh proclaims independence of Vietnam from France
Nov. 1946	French–Vietminh War begins
Mar. 1947	Truman Doctrine announced
Apr. 1947	Joint Chiefs of Staff rank China number 13 and Korea number 15 on a list of 16 countries whose defence is vital to US national security
Oct. 1949	Mao Zedong's Chinese Communist Party wins control of China; establishes People's Republic of China
9 Feb. 1950	Senator Joseph McCarthy claims State Department infiltrated by Communists: 'red scare' begins
15 Feb. 1950	China and Soviet Union announce the formation of a 30-year alliance. Russia will provide $300 million in credits to China
Mar. 1950	Soviet Union announces it has atomic bomb

June 1950	North Korea invades South Korea. President Truman commits US forces, under UN auspices, to repel the invasion
Nov. 1950	US troops march into North Korea to 'liberate' it. China enters Korean War
July 1953	Korean Armistice signed
Mar. 1954	Siege of Dien Bien Phu begins
Apr. 1954	France asks for US air strikes to relieve siege; President Eisenhower, after giving serious consideration to the request, decides against military intervention
May 1954	French garrison in Dien Bien Phu surrenders. Ends French rule in Indochina
June–July 1954	Geneva conference. Vietnam provisionally 'divided' into north and south along 17th parallel, pending settlement via reunification elections in 1956
Sept. 1954	South-East Asian Treaty Organisation is created. Members are the US, Britain, France, Australia, New Zealand, the Philippines, Thailand, and Pakistan
Nov. 1961–June 1962	Number of US military advisers in South Vietnam increased from 700 to 12,000 by Kennedy administration
Nov. 1963	South Vietnamese President Ngo Dinh Diem deposed and assassinated in coup. President Kennedy assassinated three weeks later
Feb. 1965	President Johnson approves Operation Rolling Thunder, the systematic bombardment of North Vietnam
July 1965	Johnson sends 100,000 combat troops to South Vietnam to fight Vietnamese Communists
Jan. 1968	Tet offensive. Vietcong guerrillas and North Vietnamese regulars attack major South Vietnamese cities, indicating to US that Vietnam War far from won. US has half a million troops in Vietnam
Mar. 1968	Johnson announces partial bombing halt and tells American public he will not run for re-election

Notes

1. Kenneth Waltz, *The Theory of International Politics* (Reading, Mass., 1979), 171.
2. Ibid. 170.
3. George Herring, *America's Longest War: The United States and Vietnam 1950–1975*, 2nd edn. (New York, 1986), p. xii.
4. Waltz, *Theory*, ch. 8. The US intervention in Vietnam is viewed as a case of 'overreaction', which in turn is a characteristic of bipolar systems.
5. Material power is based on military, industrial, and economic resources; see views cited in notes 7, 15, and 22 below. Psychological power is based on perceptions of

one's credibility and ability to keep promises; see views cited in notes 16, 17, and 27 below. American policy-makers, as these notes indicate, were equally concerned about both kinds of power—for itself and its adversaries—in the post-war era.

6. As Stephen Krasner puts it: 'Historical developments are path dependent; once certain choices are made, they constrain future possibilities.' See his 'Sovereignty: An Institutional Perspective', *Comparative Political Studies*, 21 (1988), 67.

7. Melvyn P. Leffler, *A Preponderance of Power: National Security, the Truman Administration, and the Cold War* (Stanford, Calif., 1992), 127.

8. Ibid. 129.

9. John Lewis Gaddis, *The Long Peace: Inquiries into the History of the Cold War* (Oxford, 1987), 78.

10. Warren Cohen, 'Acheson, His Advisers, and China, 1949–1950', in Dorothy Borg and Waldo Heinrichs (eds.), *Uncertain Years: Chinese–American Relations, 1947–1950* (New York, 1980), 15.

11. Cited in Gaddis, *Long Peace*, 75.

12. Cited in Rosemary Foot, *The Wrong War: American Policy and the Dimensions of the Korean Conflict, 1950–1953* (Ithaca, NY, 1985), 52.

13. Waldo Heinrichs, 'American China Policy and the Cold War in Asia: A New Look', in Borg and Heinrichs (eds.), *Uncertain Years*, 289.

14. See John Lewis Gaddis, 'Korea in American Politics, Strategy, and Diplomacy, 1945–50', in Yonosuke Nagai and Akira Iriye (eds.), *The Origins of the Cold War in Asia* (Tokyo, 1977), 281.

15. Leffler, *Preponderance*, 247.

16. Ibid. 366.

17. Ibid. 367. Adam Ulam appeared to confirm Dean Acheson's view when he argued that US inaction in China suggested to Stalin that the US might have written off the Asian continent. See Ulam, *Expansion and Coexistence: The History of Soviet Foreign Policy, 1917–67* (New York, 1968), 519.

18. John Lewis Gaddis, *Strategies of Containment: A Critical Appraisal of Postwar American National Security Policy* (Oxford, 1982), 110.

19. Richard Whelan, *Drawing the Line* (Boston, 1990), 119.

20. Warren Cohen, *The Cambridge History of American Foreign Relations, IV: America in the Age of Soviet Power, 1945–1991* (Cambridge, 1993), 67–8.

21. Cited in Gaddis, *Long Peace*, 90.

22. Herring, *America's Longest War*, 11–12.

23. Cited in Yuen Foong Khong, *Analogies at War: Korea, Munich, Dien Bien Phu and the Vietnam Decisions of 1965* (Princeton, 1992), 76 (emphasis italics added). Among the congressional leaders who felt this way were Richard Russell and Lyndon Johnson.

24. Ibid. 77.

25. Herring, *America's Longest War*, 41.

26. For a superb account of Diem's regime and its excesses see Stanley Karnow, *Vietnam: A History* (New York, 1983), ch. 6. For the impact of Diem's policies on the countryside, see also Jeffrey Race, *War Comes to Long An* (Berkeley, 1972).

27. Khong, *Analogies at War*, 127–8.

28. Quoted in Doris Kearns, *Lyndon Johnson and the American Dream* (New York, 1976), 252–3.

29. Larry Berman, 'Waiting for Smoking Guns: Presidential Decision-making and the Vietnam War, 1965–67', in Peter Braestrup (ed.), *Vietnam as History: Ten Years after the Paris Peace Accords* (Washington, 1984), 16. See also Berman's *Planning a Tragedy: The Americanization of the War in Vietnam* (New York, 1982), ch. 5.

30. See Khong, *Analogies at War*, 114–15.

31. Ibid., ch. 2.

Further Reading

BORG, DOROTHY, and HEINRICHS, WALDO (eds.), *Uncertain Years: Chinese–American Relations, 1947–1950* (New York, 1980). High-quality essays, with comments, on the factors influencing America's China policy.

CUMINGS, BRUCE, *The Origins of the Korean War, II: The Roaring of the Cataract* (Princeton, 1990). A magisterial analysis of the factors leading the two Koreas and the United States towards war.

FOOT, ROSEMARY, *The Wrong War: American Policy and the Dimensions of the Korean Conflict, 1950–1953* (Ithaca, NY, 1985). Emphasizes the strategic interaction between the US and China and its influence on decision-making.

KAHIN, GEORGE McT., *Intervention: How America Became Involved in Vietnam* (New York, 1986). Perhaps the seminal work on the making of America's Vietnam policy, 1945–65.

KHONG, YUEN FOONG, *Analogies at War: Korea, Munich, Dien Bien Phu, and the Vietnam Decisions of 1965* (Princeton, 1992). Includes an analysis of the impact of the lessons of history on US Vietnam decision-making in 1954 and 1965.

LEFFLER, MELVYN, *A Preponderance of Power: National Security, the Truman Administration, and the Cold War* (Stanford, 1992). Emphasizes the military–security considerations underlying US policy.

II *Other Regions and States*

CHAPTER NINE

AFRICA AND WORLD POLITICS SINCE 1945: THEORIES OF DECOLONIZATION

John Darwin

Neglect of the relationship between the industrial, more or less developed countries of the 'North' (including the former Soviet Union and Japan) and the less developed countries of the 'South' is one of the most striking features of modern international relations theory. This neglect is all the more remarkable since for much the largest part of the world's population, the most important change in international politics since 1945 has been the transformation of North–South relations through the demolition of the colonial empires and the various semi-colonial regimes (for example, the unequal treaty system in China) through which Northern dominance was mediated. By contrast, the main schools of international relations theory have been preoccupied with issues of primarily intra-Northern or even intra-Western significance. Thus, while it can be adapted to understanding the contemporary issue of international action against ecological degradation, 'regime theory' was originally concerned with explaining the politico-commercial relations of the developed world. Theoretical models of 'complex interdependence' and 'transnationalism' sought to show how older notions of the 'national interest' as the diplomatic objective of states had been outmoded by new imperatives of international cooperation and by the new institutions associated with the growth of multinational economic enterprise. Models of hegemonic stability and instability, and their influential progeny, the theory of great power 'overstretch', sought to explain (with little success) the shifts of predominance within the developed great power world of the North. A notable feature of their flimsy characterizations of imperial power was the lack of any insight into the varied means by which imperial states asserted control over their spheres of formal rule and informal influence; and of any analysis of how imperial weakness at the periphery affected great power competition.

Thus, in different ways, the most fashionable theories of the last twenty-five years all betray their origins in an US or Eurocentric obsession with superpower rivalry and the changing balance of strength within the West. They have little to offer the study of North–South relations, let alone the explanation of the seismic change in world politics brought about by decolonization (in its broader meaning of the collapse of the colonial and semi-colonial system). At best they hint at some of the calculations which may have affected the willingness of the imperial powers to give up formal colonial rule. But we look to them in vain for a wider perspective on the shifts in the political, economic, strategic, cultural, and demographic patterns which made up the substance of North–South relations in colonial and post-colonial times.

Two academic consequences have followed. First, to a large extent the study of North–South relations has become the preserve of area studies—specialized scholarly ghettos where the unique character of the 'area' and the premium value of specialized regional knowledge are fiercely defended at the expense of cross-regional comparison, let alone wider generalization. Secondly, in so far as any general theory has survived this academic balkanization, it has been in the various forms of dependency theory—perhaps because only dependency theory has enjoyed a degree of political sponsorship (though from different sources) comparable to that bestowed on fashionable West-centred theories of international politics.

The wider results of this state of affairs have been triply unfortunate. First, lacking any real sense of the dynamics of North–South relations, we have been tempted to treat the symptoms of international instability in Africa and Asia or in Latin America as regional sideshows, mere fall-out of superpower rivalry, or as parochial affairs of no general significance. Secondly, the inadequacy—or doctrinal rigidity—of dependency theory (discussed below) has left a void all too easily filled by the bland universalism of market theories with their naïve indifference to historical experience and cultural diversity. Thirdly, in the aftermath of Soviet decolonization and with the prospect of a dramatic shift in the global economy as the Asia–Pacific Rim and other former Third World economies grow rapidly, we are poorly placed to understand the significance of the first post-war era (1945–90) in world politics, or to measure the changes that may be in store.

The purpose of this chapter is to consider what kinds of theoretical explanation can contribute to our understanding of North–South relations in the particular case of Africa since 1945. This will entail a review of the main groups of theories which claim to throw light on decolonization and its aftermath: theories of dependency, of nationalism, and of modernization as well as 'historical theories'—

Table 9.1. Decolonization: theories and problems

Theory	Problem		
	Late colonial initiatives	Timing of independence	Post-colonial politics
Dependency	Intensified exploitative relationship	Recruiting new comprador élites	Continued economic exploitation
Modernization	Acceleration of economic modernizing project	Semi-modern élites contest for power	Modernizing project continued
Nationalism	Appeasing of nationalist pressures	Elite and popular mobilization achieved	Nation-building continued
Peripheral	Seeking new collaborators	No more collaborators on old terms	Informal empire and new metropolises
Disimperialism	Last brief phase of colonial engagement	Mutual disengagement	—
Instability	Weakened metropolises seek new colonial resources	Breakdown of control over political change	Failure of informal empire in bipolar conditions

the generalizations thrown up by historians looking comparatively at the decay of colonial systems in different parts of the world (see Table 9.1). But the first task is to establish the main outlines of Africa's international history since the Second World War and to take a closer look at the events and processes which any useful theorizing should help to illuminate.

9.1. Africa's International History since 1945

It is tempting to suppose that Africa's relations with the industrial and post-industrial world of the North since 1945 have been comparatively uncomplicated. A continent almost completely under European rule (or effective domination) in 1945 emerged in the 1960s to enjoy post-colonial freedom and assert black equality in a world increasingly sensitive to the legacies of racial oppression. But after a 'start in freedom' the African states rapidly belied the early promise of political and economic progress, gradually relapsing into military dictatorship, one-party rule, and economic mismanagement. After forty years of independence, Africa came to appear increasingly peripheral in world affairs. Having ceased with the end of the Cold War to be a platform for the proxy conflicts of the superpowers, it reverted instead to being a casualty ward of broken-backed states, a dead-end region from which the withdrawal of the colonial powers appeared in retrospect the one rational act of their rule. Africa's career in world politics since 1945, we might conclude from this glance, had been marginal, brutish, and short.

If we examine African history more closely this facile picture rapidly dissolves. What emerges instead is a much more complex interaction with the North and international politics than that suggested by the simple tale of liberation and disillusionment. Furthermore, theoretical approaches that take proper account of Africa's experience of decolonization and its aftermath might allow us to draw fruitful comparisons between the reciprocal effects of the continent's participation in world politics and those of other 'ex-colonial' regions including the Arab Middle East and South, South-east, and even East Asia.

It might have been expected that the course and outcome of the Second World War would have led to the rapid termination of the European colonial empires in Africa as elsewhere. After all, France, the second greatest European colonial power, had been crushingly defeated in 1940 in a devastating blow to the prestige usually thought an indispensable ingredient of colonial authority. Its economy had been badly damaged by German occupation and by the effects of its use as a battleground in the struggle for Europe. Moreover, requiring liberation at the hands of the Anglo-Americans, France could have little realistic claim to great power status and its colonial empire appeared at the mercy of its great power allies, the more powerful of which was deeply hostile to French imperial pretensions.[1] Britain's situation was much less unfavourable but far from strong. Dependent upon US economic aid in wartime, with a huge burden of post-war economic reconstruction in store, the British had also suffered humilating imperial defeats, notably in the east. Their rule in India had been rocked by a major rebellion in 1942 and by 1945 was teetering on the edge of breakdown. Like France, Britain faced great European uncertainties. With the likelihood that the United States might withdraw once more into isolation, the two West European powers confronted the dual burden of occupying, administering, and feeding much of Germany and of resisting the aggrandizement of the Soviet Union. As if these external commitments were not enough, the domestic legacy of wartime, especially in Britain, was a widespread demand for costly and far-reaching social renewal: a welfare state to replace the warfare state.

In these circumstances, with such urgent European and domestic priorities and with their colonial authority under heavy strain, a drastic reappraisal of the costs and benefits of colonial empire, especially in tropical Africa where economic benefits before 1939 had been minuscule, would not have been surprising. In fact, the response of the colonial powers at this conjuncture in world politics was to reinforce their colonial project in tropical Africa and deepen colonialism. This deepening took a number of forms. The French approach was, at the political and constitutional level, to insist upon the closer integration of the mother country and its African colonies: under the 1946 constitution they were to form part of the French Union and to be represented in the French parliament. France's African subjects could aspire to be citizens of France Overseas but not of independent African nations.[2] Economically, closer integration was to be achieved by the creation of FIDES, a fund for economic development whose real purpose was to bind the African colonies more closely to the metropolis and to develop their potential as markets and suppliers. Portugal, the third largest colonial power in Africa, also tightened its grip on its possessions through closer economic and political controls and through the encouragement of Portuguese settlement. Between 1950 and 1973 the number of white settlers in Angola and Mozambique quadrupled to some 550,000. The same overall pattern can also be seen in British colonial Africa. Here too the post-war years saw the intensification of state-directed economic development in an effort to increase colonial production. Swarms of agricultural experts descended upon the African territories. Agricultural improvement led to an elaborate web of rules and regulations for countering soil erosion and livestock disease. European settlement in East and Central Africa was vigorously promoted. London tried to build up stronger and more viable colonial states in order better to secure its economic objectives—a plan which led to the creation of the Central African Federation (now Zimbabwe, Zambia, and Malawi) under effective white settler control in 1953. Far away in the 'white' South, the post-war years saw the accession to power of an Afrikaner nationalist government in 1948, determined to entrench white supremacy through an apartheid state, with the rigid separation and subordination of non-white social, economic, and political aspirations.

The relative weakness and insecurity of the European powers in the post-war world thus brought paradoxical consequences in colonial Africa, chiefly because Africa's political, economic, and even strategic importance had been unexpectedly enhanced by the war and its unpredicted outcome. For a decade it seemed that the 'second colonial occupation',[3] softened in places by political concessions to the small African educated élite, would ensure a continuing close European–African partnership, even if the price of closer economic integration turned out to be the gradual concession of greater African self-government—a price the British were willing to pay in settler-free West Africa.

In reality this remarkable late-imperial initiative proved to be the last gasp of European colonialism on the continent. Helped by a pre-war legacy of political organization, chiefly rooted in the narrow circle of the urban educated class, there was widespread if loosely coordinated African resistance to the post-war advance of the colonial state. In West Africa Kwame Nkrumah exploited socio-economic grievances to forge a mass following for his Convention People's Party and embark on a programme of 'positive action' (demonstrations and organized political unrest) which yielded the promise of internal self-government by 1951. In Central Africa there was fierce African resistance in Nyasaland (Malawi) to the prospect of a white-ruled federation. In 1952 the Mau Mau uprising opened eight years of emergency rule and counter-insurgency in Kenya and signalled the end of white settler society. In South Africa the 'Defiance campaign' and opposition to the new apartheid order throughout the 1950s culminated in the violent disturbances at Sharpeville in 1960. By that time, insurrection against Portuguese rule in Angola was under way. Perhaps only the rapid political and constitutional concessions introduced by the British and French in West Africa by the later 1950s prevented a similar spiral of anti-colonial disorder there.

Yet it would be wrong to deduce that the transfers of power which occurred in sub-Saharan Africa after 1957 were merely a face-saving response to the breakdown of colonial rule and the failure of the colonial 'project'. In Nigeria and French West Africa the colonial powers offered independence well before organized mass nationalism could challenge their authority. To general aston-ishment, the Belgians threw in their hand and withdrew from the Congo in 1960, leaving behind scarcely any semblance of a successor government. By contrast, in East Africa, the British in 1959 were still talking of delaying self-government for a further fifteen years. There and in Central Africa the move towards full independence on the basis of African majority rule came suddenly and at break-neck speed—though not in Rhodesia (Zimbabwe). South of the Zambezi and in the great southern third of the continent, comprising Angola, Mozambique, Namibia, Zimbabwe, and South Africa, African majority rule was to be delayed for up to a generation after the intense phase of 1957–64. Curiously, it was the smallest and weakest of the European colonial powers—Portugal—that was the last to surrender its colonial domain, leaving the two 'settler states' as the final bastions of white power in Africa.

Decolonization in Africa was not a measured progression from empire to nation-state in which imperial reappraisal was hastened by colonial revolt. More-over, the erratic course of political and constitutional change produced un-intended consequences that were a far cry from the hopes and expectations of colonial policy-makers. The transfers of power had often been accelerated in the hope of installing new successor government of 'moderate' nationalists loyal to the new representative institutions planted by the mother country, sympathetic to the mixed economy of private and state capitalism, enthusiastic for economic development (along approved Western lines), and eager to remain part of the post-imperial associations of influence devised by Paris and London—the French

Community and the British Commonwealth. The early signs had been encouraging. The authority and moderation of post-colonial leaders like Nkrumah, Kenyatta, Nyerere, Kaunda, and Houphouët-Boigny belied the apocalyptic warnings of colonial diehards. But from the ex-imperial, and especially British, point of view this bright prospect soon clouded over. By the mid-1970s despotic or one-party rule, military coups, economic mismanagement, political corruption, flirtation or worse with Marxism and the Soviet bloc, combined with a rhetoric of grievance directed at the former colonial powers, were seen in the West as characteristic of the African post-colonial condition, with the grotesque dictatorships of Idi Amin and the 'emperor' Bokassa as a grim reminder of the extremes of post-independence misgovernment.

In the context of international politics, the 1970s and early 1980s marked sub-Saharan Africa's passage from a sphere of predominantly Western political and economic influence, however limited, into a battleground where East and West contended for primacy, often through sponsorship of revolutionary and counter-revolutionary movements (as in Ethiopia or Angola) or through military or other kinds of authoritarian regime. The instruments of influence were economic aid and, as elsewhere in the world, the supply of military hardware and training—a significant contribution to the militarization of African societies. This pattern of unstable superpower competition was accentuated by the prolonged delay in the liberation of the southern third, where guerrilla and economic warfare spread their effects over much of the subcontinent between 1960 and 1990. Even in those parts of Africa unaffected by this protracted freedom struggle, the 1980s witnessed widespread breakdown in the economic and social structures of the new states. Famine, tidal waves of refugees, internal conflicts frequently rooted in ethnic competition or, as in Somalia, in the factional struggles of rival warlords, and a matching deterioration in economic performance and prospects: by some measures at least, thirty years after its 'year' in 1960, Africa had become once again the 'dark continent'.[4]

In this gloomy setting, the end of the Cold War was a hopeful sign. It promised the end of superpower proxy conflicts and greatly strengthened the demand for democratic government in many African states. It created the international conditions in which a transfer of power in South Africa became easier. It held out the hope that international agencies, especially the United Nations, would be able to intervene more effectively where internal breakdown threatened regional stability. More ambiguously, the drying-up of Soviet aid made conformity with the disciplines and dogmas of the World Bank much harder to resist for many debt-ridden states. The record since 1989 has been mixed. But it would be a mistake to conclude that the symptoms of disorder on the African continent signify a descent into an international anarchy. Far from it. On three counts at least, post-independence Africa has displayed a notable stability. The legitimacy of boundaries inherited from the colonial period, arbitrary as they are by ethnic, cultural, or economic criteria, have been almost universally respected (the contrast with the Middle East is striking). Secondly, with rare and trivial exceptions, the African states have not engaged in inter-state warfare. Thirdly, for all the weaknesses revealed in the administrative apparatus of the post-colonial states, none has yet disintegrated or suffered (with the possible exception of Ethiopia) a significant loss of territory. Here, it might be said, is food for European thought.

9.2. In Search of a Theoretical Framework

How far is it possible to accommodate sub-Saharan Africa's complex and disturbing international history since 1945 within a broad theoretical framework? Is it possible to devise a generalized explanation both for Africa's liberation from colonial rule and for its various post-colonial travails? Could such a theory be useful not only in illuminating the decolonization experience in different regions of Africa but also in allowing some comparisons to be drawn between Africa's place in contemporary world politics and that of other regions in the 'South'?

Largely by default, theories deriving ultimately from the insights of Lenin in *Imperialism: The Highest Stage of Capitalism* (1916) have exerted the greatest influence upon both popular and academic conceptions of North–South relations in general and North–Africa relations in particular. Lenin himself had argued that the survival of capitalism dictated a path of imperial expansion to secure monopoly outlets for the export of surplus capital. Competition between the capitalist imperial powers would produce international conflict, while the colonial masses would eventually revolt against exploitation and immiseration, liquidating the monopoly profits sustaining capitalism at home. In this way, colonial revolution would be the signal for the general downfall of capitalism—a connection that lent enormous significance to the otherwise parochial struggles of far-flung nationalist movements. Even more encouraging to nationalists was Lenin's insistence that the collapse of colonial power was predetermined and unavoidable: time was on their side. To some enthusiastic observers, the inter-war depression revealed the prophetic accuracy of Lenin's theory.[5] Nevertheless, by the late 1940s and 1950s, its inadequacy as a framework for understanding European colonialism in Africa was patent. Capitalism had survived its greatest trial. Surplus capital was hard to find. The colonial masses showed few signs of revolutionary consciousness. It was now hard to believe that a fuse lit on the Gold Coast or in Kenya would explode capitalism in its Western heartlands. After all, the foremost capitalist power after 1945 had been signally indifferent to colonial expansion, at least in the territorial sense so visible in Africa.

Not surprisingly, therefore, those who had drawn inspiration from Lenin were obliged to revise his theory substantially. In the 1950s and 1960s their ideas converged with those of a new school of economic theory which had grown up in Latin America, originally under the leadership of Raul Prebisch. A sophisticated version of this new thinking on 'dependency' was set out by Paul Baran in a highly influential book *The Political Economy of Growth* (1957).[6] Baran stressed the 'violent, destructive and predatory' character of the Western intervention in 'weaker countries'. Economic 'backwardness', he argued, was not the result of a spontaneous failure to modernize, but arose from the deliberate actions of Western capitalism. Because its economic interest lay in exploiting the commodity exports of such 'backward' countries, the West was determined to block or repress any pattern of economic development incompatible with this preference: in particular the emergence of industrial capitalism in non-Western countries.

In terms of international relations theory, the significance of Baran's argument lay in the emphasis he put upon the ability of Western capitalism to recruit allies in 'weaker countries'; his suggestion that Western countries systematically promoted political regimes that would meet their specific economic requirements; and the applicability of his model as much, if not more, to technically independent countries as to colonies. It was the 'comprador administrations' in power in such countries that were the vital instruments of capitalist influence. They represented a fusion of commercial interests bound up with the export of commodities, landowners, and local industrial monopolists (often financially dependent upon the commercial and landed sectors) whose prosperity was tied to the preservation of small protected markets. Western capital and economic and military assistance were deployed to prop up regimes of this kind or the military dictatorships to which they passed control in times of crisis.

Though Baran cited the Middle East regimes as perfect examples of 'comprador administrations', the analysis he offered was taken up with greatest enthusiasm by Latin American writers and those studying the continent. An important theoretical essay by T. Dos Santos elaborated Baran's argument by showing how economic development 'towards the interior'—and concomitant escape from dependence upon commodity exports—were effectively barred by a form of 'Catch 22'.[7] Internal industrialization was bound initially to increase dependence upon imports and thus to trigger currency depreciation (except in the improbable event of a large amount of altruistic foreign economic aid being made available). In the ensuing political and economic crisis, the errant state would be forced back into line by a combination of external pressures and the old local oligarchies. For Dos Santos, therefore, no change of policy within one country to achieve diversification and industrialization could work, unless the international political and economic system was also modified. 'Dependent development' on this view was essentially a function of the international system.

The relevance of all this to an understanding of Africa's place in world politics was obvious.[8] The pursuit of commodity exploitation appeared to fit perfectly with the phase of more intensive colonialism after 1945. The Latin American case showed that for the purposes of Western capitalism it was immaterial whether the desired economic regime was sustained by colonial rule or by a 'comprador administration'. Western economic aid could be readily explained as an attempt to buttress compliant post-colonial governments against internal dissent. The timing of the transfers of power and the appearance of multinational enterprise could be accounted for by the growing internationalization of capitalism. In this new phase of capitalism's career, the maintenance of monopoly zones for the surplus capital of one imperialist state had become obsolete. Moreover, international capital would no longer tolerate the confrontationist tactics of old-style colonialism because of the risk that vital 'comprador' elements might be alienated and driven into socialism. Instead, formal colonial rule should be brought quickly to an end so that new collaborative regimes friendly to multinational capitalism could be safely installed and lent the necessary external support. Sovereign independence merely introduced what Kwame Nkrumah described as 'neocolonialism' (in a book optimistically subtitled *The Last Stage of Imperialism*). The Western powers, faced with the massively rising costs of welfare at home and the arms race abroad, required more than ever a maximum return from the operations of international capital.[9]

In their various forms, some of which stressed the possibility of reform, some of which insisted that only by global revolution could Third World countries be released from the treadmill of commodity production and growing impoverishment, dependency theories thus seemed highly relevant to an understanding of Africa's place in world politics. They offered a plausible explanation of the links between the visible changes within Western capitalism, the break-up of the colonial empires, the post-colonial links between the West and independent African countries, and the continuing, often deepening, poverty of post-independence Africa. But there were also many awkward facts not easily accommodated within the dependency paradigm. First, the great variety of African economies made it hard to believe that a common economic imperative had caused the exceptionally rapid sovereignty transfers of the period 1957–64. Secondly, the evidence that international capitalism, or multinational commercial interests, constituted the decisive influence upon the political and constitutional timetables laid down by the colonial powers in the 1950s and 1960s is tenuous. Thirdly, the results of political independence, however constrained by poverty and weakness, went far beyond the purely instrumental function of smoothing the path for international capital: if that *had* been the intention, it was to be sadly disappointed. At the very least, African states turned out to be far less susceptible to this form of disguised domination than dependency theories implied. Fourthly, dependency theories applied to African decolonization greatly oversimplified the political and economic motives of African politicians, even those most amenable to Western interests. The socio-economic categories carried over from Latin American cases —the landed, commercial, and industrial sectors—made a poor fit with African conditions. Fifthly, a dependency-type analysis ignored the influence of ethnic or tribal factors in the approach to independence and in the post-colonial state and simply wrote out of the script a force which is fundamental to understanding the politics of almost every sub-Saharan African state. Sixthly, the stress upon the importance of the 'comprador administration', the shifting needs of international capital, and the determination of Western capitalism to check the growth of Third World industrialism is extremely difficult to square with the chronology of liberation in the southern third. Here indeed, little seems to conform to the model.

Nevertheless, a theoretical framework based upon the antagonism between the interests of a group of powerful industrialized states—the 'West'—and poor, weak countries in Africa, is not easily demolished by specific objections of this sort. Immanuel Wallerstein's 'capitalist world-system' theory, set out with greatest elegance and economy in his *Historic Capitalism* (1983), displays remarkable virtuosity in finding a place for ethnic and racial factors and even in explaining the role of the Soviet Union in a world system divided between a capitalist 'core', an exploited 'periphery', and a 'semi-periphery' which embodied elements of both and which usually functioned as an adjunct of the core's domination. (The Soviet Union was defined as a semi-peripheral state.)[10] Wallerstein's thesis has generated a debate extending far beyond contemporary Africa and its place in world politics. It is, however, vulnerable in the vacuousness of some of its key concepts (what constitutes the semi-periphery?); in its insistence that absolute immiseration was the invariable fate of the periphery; in its exaggeration of the power and importance of 'anti-systemic' (i.e. anti-capitalist world system) movements; and in its apparent reduction of all political life in the periphery to forms of response to the core.[11] For all its seductive comprehensiveness, Wallerstein's vision of modern world history still leaves a good deal of Africa's recent international history unexplained.

Two other 'global' theories have competed with dependency theories to explain Africa's post-war international development, though their international content is far less explicit than that of dependency theories. 'Modernization' theory was influential in the 1950s and 1960s but then underwent an intellectual collapse from which it may yet recover. Perhaps the most powerful statement of the modernization hypothesis was W. W. Rostow's *The Stages of Economic Growth* (1960), significantly subtitled *A Non-Communist Manifesto*. The work of David Apter on Ghana represented an earlier and more specifically African version of a similar approach.[12] For Rostow (who was not primarily concerned with the colonial

world), colonialism formed a necessary transitional stage to allow capitalist countries to insert the infrastructure required to achieve economic modernity (defined as the situation where 'growth' becomes the 'normal condition' and social,
cultural, and political blockages are removed). Rostow believed that the effect of
colonial rule was to move a colonial society 'along the path towards take-off',
partly because 'modernization of a sort' was one object of colonial policy. Colonial rule broke down when coalitions of local politicians emerged in 'semi-
modernized settings' to demand self-rule or seize it by force. Rostow implied
that the termination of colonial rule was a stage in a modernizing project which
led on to the construction of an 'effective centralized national state', itself a necessary condition for 'take-off' into self-sustaining economic growth. Theories
of this sort laid great emphasis upon the political role of a modernizing élite in
colonial societies, deeply impregnated with Western ideas, keenly envious of the
economic and political progress of the West, and equally resentful of their exclusion from power at the hands of an alien and unsympathetic colonial regime.
The revolt of the partially 'modernized' class—like the 'verandah boys' of the
colonial Gold Coast—was thus the key factor in the timing of political independence. Thereafter, a new élite set about building a centralized state to realize its
ambition of economic and social modernity along Western lines.

The flaws in this imaginative account of colonial and post-colonial Africa are
not hard to spot. As a description of the purpose of colonial rule it was at best
fanciful and certainly reductionist. It greatly exaggerated the importance of modernized, or even semi-modernized, élites in the ending of colonial rule (how numerous were they in the Belgian Congo?), partly because it underestimated the
significance of rural politics and failed to notice how far the Western-educated
minority was constrained by the need to collaborate with vernacular rural élites.
Like most versions of dependency theory, it offered no explanation of the role
of ethnic or tribal factors in colonial and post-colonial politics. Most seriously
of all, perhaps, its emphasis upon the building of the centralized, development-
minded state as the main agenda of the new political class came to appear almost
absurdly inapposite as a description of post-colonial African politics. A fair assessment might be: not so much a theory, more a manifesto—as indeed Rostow's
subtitle pronounced it to be.

In certain respects, theories of nationalism might be regarded as a subdivision
of modernization theories. The most sophisticated accounts of the emergence of
nationalism all stress how intellectual or socio-economic change generated a felt
need for ethnic mobilization and the creation of states whose political and cultural
boundaries were congruent.[13] A sense of national identity—even if defined min-
imally as shared hostility towards alien rulers—seemed to be the cement bind-
ing together the disparate movements formed against colonial governments in
the period before the rapid transfers of power. 'Building a nation' seemed to be

the most powerful ideological drive behind anti-colonial movements and in the early phase of independence. Publicly, at least, African leaders eschewed ethnic or tribal loyalties and spoke the language of nations and nationalism. The very survival of the ex-colonial states as political units, it might be argued, constitutes hard evidence that some sense of nationhood had been diffused through the diverse cultural zones the colonial regimes had cellotaped together. More than that, the often stormy relations of African states with the West could readily be explained as the sensitivity of newly awakened national feelings and an insistence upon their being treated respectfully by former masters and overmighty foreigners. Even the tentative experiments in panafricanism, and the appearance of the Organization for African Unity, could be seen as expressing a yearning towards a common African nationhood, rather as Arab nationalism both complemented and competed with loyalty to the Arab states.

Nevertheless, theories of nationalism offer only limited insight into Africa's relations with the West, or North, since 1945. It is hard to detect in the late colonial period the levels of intellectual or socio-economic change that would have been required to disseminate a sense of nationhood—or even of its necessity—widely through most colonial communities in sub-Saharan Africa. The nationalist movements that appeared in the last phases of colonial rule were umbrella organizations that relied upon mobilizing disparate followings for whom loyalty to a putative nation-state was rarely the most urgent priority. The real, as opposed to purely rhetorical, content of such nationalist feeling is very difficult to assess.[14] Nor is the assumption that nationalist mobilization was the decisive factor in ending colonial rule inherently very plausible. Calculations of national interest by the colonial powers were a necessary part of their decision whether or not to contest the claims of nationalist politicians. Through much of sub-Saharan Africa, they scarcely bothered: where they did, in the southern third, the weakness of nationalism was starkly exposed. Finally, since independence, the political history of much of sub-Saharan Africa has been testimony more to the fragility of nationalism than to its importance. Nation-states, characterized by a real congruence between their political and cultural frontiers, or even by a high level of internal solidarity, have been conspicuous by their absence. Cultural nationalism has faced an uphill struggle against the penetration of foreign languages and lifestyles. In many states, if not all, internal politics have often been dominated by issues of ethnic (i.e. tribal) rather than national self-assertion.[15] At the very least, we might conclude, to understand Africa's changing place in world politics as the product of the triumph of nationalism would require an idiosyncratic definition of an elusive phenomenon.

Have 'historical theories', the generalizations propounded by historians, fared any better? They may claim to be more respectful towards the empirical data, and they embody, in part, a rejection of overschematized accounts offered by the dependency, modernization, or nationalist schools. But they are prone to self-imposed limitations, explaining at best a part of Africa's international history since 1945. They are also vulnerable to the same challenge as more 'theoretical' theories when they stray far from their empirical heartland.

Three historical theories are worth attention. The first and perhaps best-known is the 'peripheral' theory of decolonization to be found in the writings of Ronald Robinson, together with J. A. Gallagher the seminal academic influence on the modern study of imperialism and decolonization.[16] Robinson's starting-point is the vital importance of local collaboration to the viability of colonial rule, and the readiness of imperial powers to work through informal empires of influence where these offered economies of effort. The critical factor in the viability of colonial rule was the constantly shifting relationship between rulers and collaborators. To rule, the colonial power had constantly to recruit new collaborators, especially since the tendency of colonial policy and of the socio-economic changes colonialism brought about was to pile up enemies. The significance of constitutional change was to be sought in the veiled attempt to find new allies in colonial society and reward them sufficiently. How, then, was the timing of colonial independence to be explained? Robinson suggested that in the medium term the odds were tilted against the colonial rulers' being able to recruit new allies fast enough: it was easier to form anti-colonial coalitions than collaborative ones. Sooner rather than later, the rulers ran out of collaborators and were compelled to depart. But since they had no prejudice against informal empire, they were willing enough to strike new bargains, trading constitutional independence for future economic, political, or strategic cooperation. Within the West, moreover, a shifting power distribution meant that the old colonial powers transferred their imperial functions to the new Western superpower which took over the portfolio of informal empires around the world.

In Robinson's argument the initiative for change lay with the local collaborators in colonial politics. But this seemed to pay too little attention to the changing attitudes and interests of the colonial powers themselves, whose response, as we have seen, was sometimes to struggle fiercely to maintain their colonial authority, but often to make a rapid settlement and withdraw. To take account of this variable response, R. F. Holland proposed instead a theory of 'disimperialism' which stressed that within all the European colonial powers after 1945 there occurred sooner or later a fundamental reappraisal of national interests.[17] Strategically this meant defence against the Soviet threat in Europe rather than imperial defence; economically it meant recognition that industrial rather than colonial markets offered the best opportunities; socially it meant the priority of welfare expenditure at home over the costly maintenance of imperial prestige. Even the most recalcitrant and backward of colonial powers, Portugal, eventually adopted this new political orientation and threw in the colonial towel in

1974. There was also a colonial dimension to disimperialism, since on the part of African societies and economies as well there was a recognition that whatever benefits colonial rule might once have conferred, they had ceased to outweigh the costs it inflicted. Mutual disenchantment and imperialist disillusion were the key to the comparatively uncontested transfers of power in much of tropical Africa.

Robinson and Holland offered a flexible and undogmatic framework for understanding the end of the colonial order in Africa and the substitution of looser forms of Western influence in its place. It might be objected that Robinson lays too much stress upon the role of the collaborators, as if the colonial power itself lacked the initiative to create new allies. If this were true, it could only be because the willingness to inject resources into colonial politics—the means by which collaborators had originally been recruited—had disappeared. In that case the trail led back from the politics of the periphery to the imperial headquarters and recalculations of national interest there. Holland, on the other hand, arguably overstresses 'cool reappraisal' when in some cases there is evidence to suggest that staying on was the intention almost until the last moment. The end of colonial rule was the result not of planned withdrawal but of the sudden discovery that without the drastic reinforcement of the colonial presence the limited political changes introduced in the post-war years were about to render the colony ungovernable. Moreover, all the colonial powers (with the possible exception of Belgium) hoped to exert a degree of post-colonial influence which in Britain's case turned out to be wildly unrealistic.

One way of drawing together the threads of African decolonization has been by means of an explanation in terms of 'systemic instability'.[18] The argument here is that the relations between the colonial powers and their subjects were indirectly destabilized by the growing relative weakness of the European metropoles triggered by the Second World War. To recoup their strength, they were driven to exploit their colonies more vigorously, but in doing so stimulated new levels of colonial resistance. In earlier periods, a colonial power in such difficulties had recourse to two alternative tactics. It could repress, and thus impose new terms of collaboration; or it could adopt a policy of 'salutary neglect', easing the pressure on its colonial subjects until the anti-colonial movement subsided. After 1945, however, the leading colonial powers found both options unavailable. Increased repression was made difficult (though not impossible) by wider international considerations (in Britain's case, the need to hold together the Commonwealth as a vehicle of influence; concern about American opinion; and, from the mid-1950s, anxiety about Soviet influence in the colonial and ex-colonial world). Repression was also unattractive on grounds of cost. On the other hand, having embarked upon political devolution as the counterpart of accelerated economic development, the colonial powers found it impossible to control the pace of change by other means. By the end of the 1950s it was becoming obvious that 'managing' the transformation of colonial empires into spheres of informal influence would be impossible without the willingness of the metropole to offer much more generous economic and political inducements than the British (though not the French) were prepared to fund. Informal empire under these conditions was likely to prove as expensive as formal. Within a few years of the transfers of power, with the extension of superpower competition into Africa in the wake of the Congo crisis of 1960–63, virtually all traces of the old colonial regime in British Africa had disappeared. Only in francophone and lusophone Africa, in different ways and for different reasons, was continuity more evident.

The attractions of this theory lie mainly in its attempt to show how international, metropole, and colonial politics interlocked at crucial stages to produce a particular chronology of decolonization in Africa. It argues that the catalyst for instability in the colonial system was the international decline of the colonial powers. It suggests that the reason why the southern third was liberated so much later was because there the will and the means to repress, absent for domestic and international reasons elsewhere, were abundantly available until the costs were very much higher. But, as with other historical theories, its plausibility rests ultimately upon documentation: archival evidence of more deliberate reappraisal in the metropoles would damage its credibility. A wider objection, as to the other historical theories, is its limitations as a guide to the post-colonial relations between Africa and the West, or North.

9.3. New Perspectives

It may be that to grasp the wider implications of Africa's changing place in world politics since 1945 we need both a new definition of decolonization and a way of periodising its unfolding. Thus decolonization should be defined not as a constitutional procedure—the transfer of power—but as the break-up of a 'colonial world order' which had exhibited political, diplomatic, economic, cultural, and even demographic characteristics. Once the international conditions which had made this colonial order viable had been destroyed by the accelerating relative decline of its principal guardians, the European colonial powers, the whole rickety system became unstable. But what was critical for the post-colonial aftermath was the fact that African decolonization took place in a bipolar world in conditions of superpower competition and against a background of ideological conflict. Weak post-colonial states thus enjoyed surprisingly strong international bargaining power with which to extract foreign economic and military aid.

State-to-state aid and investment reinforced étatist tendencies in economic management, assisted by the allure of Soviet-style methods of industrialization. The timing of political change in the southern third was governed significantly by the fall-out from this superpower competition, most visible in the Soviet–Cuban intervention in Angola. Looking back from the mid-1990s we can see that the period from 1945 to 1990 is characterized by a certain unity: the crisis and dissolution of the colonial order under conditions of bipolar competition. After 1990, with the end of the Cold War, we enter a new era in which the fragility of the African states may no longer be compensated for by an enhanced international bargaining power, and when the final completion of the liberation process will sharply reduce Africa's salience in international politics.

Historians and theorists of international relations have been curiously reluctant to acknowledge that the great wars of Africa and Asia (the Korean War, the Indo-China and Vietnam Wars, and the Arab-Israeli wars) and lesser conflicts since 1945 were essentially wars of colonial succession, arising directly or indirectly from the break-up of empires and of the old colonial order. Perhaps as a result, they have failed to notice what underlies much of the upheaval and instability in Africa and Asia during the last fifty years: the struggle to build a durable international order in the vast domain of the South (where state structures were weak and nationality ill-defined) in a period when the North itself was riven by ideological conflict and profound internal change.

Like other world regions, sub-Saharan Africa's experience of the post-colonial order has been powerfully shaped by its interaction with this emerging 'new North' of competitive superpowers, displacing the 'old North' of the European colonial powers. Superpower rivalry spread ineluctably into Africa in the 1960s and 1970s on the heels of liberation and created the international environment in which the new states defined their values and interests. There were certain benefits: the 'new North', unlike the old, eschewed direct rule and championed formal state sovereignty. Both superpowers offered inducements which allowed regimes to entrench themselves against internal opponents (a mixed blessing). But the costs in proxy wars, militarization, and ideological 'noise' were high, often intensifying the instabilities that arose from existing ethnic and regional divisions. Here, too, sub-Saharan Africa eventually came to share the sombre experience of other ex-colonial regions where local strife was caught up with global rivalry in the fluid, unstable setting of the post-colonial order. In the new phase of world politics which has just opened, the 'new capitalist North' has as its counterpart a 'new South' with its mixture of tiger economies and poverty zones. Both may break up into regional blocs or form new alignments. In any event, the last remains of the distinctive post-colonial landscape of 1945–90 will gradually disappear. History may not have ended, but we shall need a new international perspective to make sense of a new world.

Chronology

	Africa	International politics
1945	'Second colonial occupation' begins	
1948	Riots in West Africa signal acceleration of political change in colonial Africa; National Party triumph in S. Africa	Berlin Blockade: onset of cold war; First Arab–Israeli War
1949		Creation of NATO
1950–2	Mau Mau insurgency begins	Korean War (1950–3)
1956	Independence of Sudan	Suez crisis
1957	Independence of Ghana as first new state in Black Africa	Treaty of Rome creates EEC
1958	de Gaulle promises independence to francophone Africa	
1960	The 'Year of Africa': 16 new African states enter the UN, 14 of them francophone. Sharpeville massacre in S. Africa	
1960–3	Congo crisis	Berlin crisis (1961)
1962		Cuban Missile Crisis
1965	Rhodesian unilateral independence with white minority rule	Vietnam War intensifies
1966	Nkrumah overthrown by military coup	
1967	Outbreak of Nigerian civil war	Six-Day Arab–Israeli war
1968		British announce withdrawal from East of Suez
1971	Idi Amin coup in Uganda	India–Pakistan war; Sino-American rapprochement begins
1973		End of Vietnam War negotiated; third Arab–Israeli war
1974–6	Collapse of Portuguese rule in Africa; Soviet–Cuban intervention in Angola; Rhodesian guerilla war intensifies; major disturbances in S. Africa; Ethiopian coup installs Soviet-backed Marxist regime	Fall of Saigon to Vietcong (1975); Watergate scandal
1979	End of white rule in Rhodesia	Fall of Shah of Iran; Russian invasion of Afghanistan
1980	Zimbabwe independent under black majority rule	
1985	Soweto insurrection in S. Africa	
1988	Brazzaville Agreement for withdrawal of Cubans from Angola and early independence of Namibia	

Africa	International politics
1989	Collapse of Soviet satellite regimes in Eastern Europe
1990–1 Fall of Marxist regime in Ethiopia	Gulf War; break-up of the Soviet Union
1992 Whites' referendum in S. Africa approves moves to black majority rule	
1994 First multiracial election in S. Africa and installation of Nelson Mandela as President	

Notes

1. For US attitudes towards the colonial empires during the Second World War see W. R. Louis, *Imperialism at Bay* (Oxford, 1977).
2. See D. B. Marshall, *The French Colonial Myth and Constitution-making in the Fourth Republic* (New Haven and London, 1973).
3. For an analysis of the 'second colonial occupation' see D. A. Low and A. Smith (eds.), *History of East Africa*, iii (Oxford, 1976), intr.
4. By the late 1980s sub-Saharan Africa (excluding South Africa), with a population of 450 million, had a GDP the same as Belgium's. Belgium's population was 10 million. Deindustrialization and falling living standards had been key features of the 1980s. See World Bank, *Sub-Saharan Africa: from Crisis to Sustainable Growth* (Washington, 1989).
5. See esp. J. Strachey, *The Coming Struggle for Power* (London, 1932). V. I. Lenin, *Imperialism: The Highest Stage of Capitalism* (Moscow, 1982).
6. P. Baran, *The Political Economy of Growth* (New York, 1957).
7. T. Dos Santos, 'The Crisis of Development Theory and the Problem of Dependence in Latin America', in H. Bernstein (ed.), *Underdevelopment and Development* (Harmondsworth, 1973).
8. See S. Amin, *Neocolonialism in West Africa* (Eng. trans. Harmondsworth, 1973).
9. K. Nkrumah, *Neocolonialism: The Last Stage of Imperialism* (London, 1965).
10. I. Wallerstein, *The Capitalist World-System* (Cambridge, 1979), 31; *Historic Capitalism* (London, 1983); see also his *Politics of the World Economy* (Cambridge, 1984).
11. For a highly effective, though sympathetic, critique see D. A. Washbrook, 'South Asia, the World System and World Capitalism' in S. Bose (ed.), *South Asia and World Capitalism* (Oxford, 1990).
12. W. W. Rostow, *The Stages of Economic Growth: A Non-Communist Manifesto* (Cambridge, 1960); D. Apter, *Ghana in Transition* (New York, 1963; first published as *The Gold Coast in Transition*, Princeton, 1955). Apter later wrote *The Politics of Modernization* (Chicago, 1965).

13. E. Kedourie, *Nationalism*, 4th edn. (Oxford, 1993; first publ. 1966); E. Gellner, *Nations and Nationalism* (Oxford, 1983); B. Anderson, *Imagined Communities: Reflections on the Origin and Spread of Nationalism* (London, 1983; 2nd edn. 1991). Much of Anderson's book recycles the familiar argument that nationalism represented the yearning of excluded local élites for a place in the administrative sun. Its principal insight, the role of print in stimulating distinct vernacular cultures, was anticipated in the writings of the Canadian historian H. A. Innis thirty years before.

14. See e.g. J. Lonsdale and B. Berman, *Unhappy Valley* (London, 1992); J. Iliffe, *A Modern History of Tanganyika* (Cambridge, 1979); T. Ranger, *Peasant Consciousness and Guerilla War in Zimbabwe* (London, 1985).

15. A recent and acerbic analysis is to be found in J.-F. Bayart, *The State in Africa* (Eng. trans. London, 1993). Its French title is indicative: *La Politique du Ventre*.

16. See R. Robinson, 'The Non-European Foundations of European Rule: Sketch for a Theory of Collaboration', in R. Owen and B. Sutcliffe (eds.), *Studies in the Theory of Imperialism* (London, 1972).

17. R. F. Holland, *European Decolonization 1918–1981* (London, 1985).

18. For an analysis along these lines see J. Darwin, *Britain and Decolonization* (London, 1988) and *The End of the British Empire* (Oxford, 1991).

Further Reading

CROWDER, M. (ed.), *Cambridge History of Africa, VIII: 1940–1975* (Cambridge, 1984). The best introduction to regional developments in the continent in the late colonial and post-colonial period: the chapters by J. D. Y. Peel and Crawford Young are especially good.

DARWIN, J., *Britain and Decolonization* (London, 1988). A survey of Britain's retreat from colonial power since 1945, emphasizing the interconnections between international, domestic, and colonial politics.

FIELDHOUSE, D. K., *Black Africa 1945–1980: Economic Decolonization and Arrested Development* (London, 1986). Presents a crisply unsentimental (and anti-dependency) view of African economic shortcomings by one of the most authoritative writers on the history of multinational enterprise in Africa.

HARGREAVES, J. D., *Decolonization in Africa* (London, 1988). Offers a general coverage of the end of colonial rule in Black Africa.

SOMERVILLE, K., *Foreign Military Intervention in Africa* (London, 1990). Provides a useful survey of the first post-colonial period.

CHAPTER TEN

THE MIDDLE EAST: THE ORIGINS OF ARAB–ISRAELI WARS

Avi Shlaim

The Middle East has been one of the most volatile and violent subsystems of the international political system since the end of the Second World War. Post-war history in the Middle East has been punctuated by an unusually high number of full-scale, inter-state wars. The aim of this chapter is to explore the underlying causes of the largest category of Middle Eastern wars, namely, the Arab–Israeli wars. Wars which are not directly related to the Arab–Israeli conflict, like the Yemen war of 1961–4 and the Iran–Iraq war of 1980–88, lie outside the scope of this chapter. Within the scope of this chapter are all seven major Arab–Israeli wars: the 1948 Palestine War, the 1956 Suez War, the June 1967 Six-Day War, the 1969–70 War of Attrition, the October 1973 Yom Kippur War, the 1982 Lebanon War, and the 1991 Gulf War. The origins of these wars will be examined in an attempt to see whether any general patterns emerge.

10.1. The Level-of-analysis Problem

In dealing with the origins of wars, as with any other class of international events, it is important to be clear about the level of analysis. J. David Singer, in a famous article, identified the two most widely employed levels of analysis in international relations: the international system and the national subsystem. The first level of analysis focuses on the international system and its impact on the behaviour of states; the second focuses on domestic influences on states' behaviour *vis-à-vis* other states. The first level of analysis has the advantage of giving generalizable and parsimonious explanations of the external behaviour of states, whereas the second level calls for richer detail, greater depth, and more intensive portrayal of the domestic roots of international events.[1]

Another well-known treatment of the level-of-analysis problem in international relations is Kenneth Waltz's book *Man, the State and War*. This work is more directly relevant to the present inquiry than Singer's article because it deals specifically with the causes of war. Waltz discusses the contribution which classical political theory makes to our understanding of the nature and causes of war. He does so by identifying three principal themes or images of international relations: war as the consequence of the nature and behaviour of man, as the outcome of the internal organization of states, and as the product of international anarchy.[2]

In Waltz's analysis the state is the most important actor in international politics and the principal cause of war in the international system. All three images are concerned with influences that incline the state to go to war: the first image stresses the personality and beliefs of the leader as a cause of war; the second image stresses domestic political forces as the cause of war; while the third image stresses the regional and international power game as the cause of war. Waltz's conclusion is that the first two sets of influences are relatively unimportant, whereas the third set of influences is critical. In other words, states do not resort to war because of the personality of the leader or because of their domestic political structure or ideology but because of pressures emanating from the international environment.

Waltz's three images of international relations constitute a useful analytical framework for thinking about the causes of war. One of the strengths of the framework lies in its universal applicability. The framework can be employed to analyse the causes of a single war or a series of wars in any region at any period in history. The post-1945 Middle East is no exception. If applied to the outbreak of Arab–Israeli wars, this framework would suggest three lines of enquiry: the psychological factors rooted in human nature, the organizational and ideological factors rooted in the domestic environment, and the systemic factors rooted in the international environment. The framework would also suggest that systemic factors are much more important than the other two sets of factors in explaining the outbreak of Arab–Israeli wars.

Yet, precisely because it is so broad and all-encompassing, Waltz's analytical framework is less than ideal for the purposes of this particular chapter. In the first place, there is no justification for assuming a priori that systemic factors connected with the regional and international power game are more important than the other factors in motivating states to go to war. This is an empirical question which can only be answered after reviewing the relevant empirical evidence. Secondly, the relative weight of individual, domestic, and systemic influences is likely to vary from one Arab–Israeli war to another. Thirdly, these three sets of influences cannot always be fitted into neat and separate categories because they intermingle and shade into one another.

A different analytical framework is therefore proposed here, a framework tailored to the particular circumstances of the Middle East. This framework identifies three central factors that contribute to the outbreak of wars in the Middle East: the Arab–Israeli conflict, inter-Arab relations, and the involvement of the great powers in the affairs of the region. Like Waltz's framework, this alternative analytical framework involves a threefold division. But whereas Waltz's three levels are the individual, the state, and the international system, this framework focuses attention on three sets of interactions between states. States are the principal unit of analysis in this framework. The states in question are Israel, its Arab neighbours, and the great powers: Britain, France, the United States, and the Soviet Union. These states dominated the international politics of the Middle East in the aftermath of the Second World War; and it is the policies and actions of these states which are assumed to be the principal cause of war in the region. A word of explanation about the three factors that make up this framework of analysis may therefore be in order.

10.2. Israel, the Arab States, and the Great Powers

The conflict between Israel and the Arabs is one of the most profound and protracted conflicts of the twentieth century and the principal precipitant of wars in the Middle East. There are two major dimensions to this conflict: the Israeli–Palestinian dimension and the Israeli–Arab dimension. The origins of the conflict go back to the end of the nineteenth century when the Zionist movement conceived the idea of building a national home for the Jewish people in Palestine. This project met with bitter opposition on the part of the Arab population of the country. The upshot was a clash between two national movements for possession of Palestine. There were two peoples and one land; hence the conflict.

The neighbouring Arab states became involved in this conflict on the side of the Palestinian Arabs in the 1930s. After the creation of the State of Israel in 1948, the main weight of the conflict shifted from the local or inter-communal level to the inter-state level. In 1967 the conflict was further complicated by Israel's capture of the West Bank from Jordan, the Golan Heights from Syria, and the Sinai Peninsula from Egypt. From this point on, these states had a direct territorial dispute with Israel quite apart from their commitment to the Palestinian cause.

On the root cause of the conflict there are widely divergent views. Most Arabs maintain that the root cause of the conflict is the dispossession and dispersal of the Palestinian Arabs, an original sin which was compounded by Israel's subsequent territorial acquisitions. In their view, Israel is an inherently aggressive and expansionist state and the real source of violence in the region.[3] Most Israelis, on the other hand, maintain that the root cause of the conflict is not territory but the Arab rejection of Israel's very right to exist as a sovereign state in the Middle East. According to this view, the basic Arab objective is the liquidation of the State of Israel, while Israel acts only in self-defence and in response to the Arab challenges.[4] But whatever one's view of the origins and nature of the Arab–Israeli conflict, there can be no doubt that this conflict has been a major cause of wars in the Middle East.

A second source of tension and instability which at least on one occasion, in June 1967, helped to tip the balance in favour of war, is to be found in the relations among the Arab states. In theory all Arab states subscribe to the ideal of Arab unity, but in practice inter-Arab relations are characterized more by conflict than by cooperation. Israel is widely held to be one of the few solid pillars propping up Arab unity, the one issue on which all Arabs, whatever their other differences may be, can agree. Opposition to Israel follows naturally from the belief that the inhabitants of the various Arab states, including the Palestinians, form a single nation and that Israel has grossly violated the sacred rights of this nation.

A distinction needs to be made, however, between the rhetorical and the operational levels of Arab foreign policy. Whereas at the rhetorical level the Arab states have been largely united in their commitment to oppose Israel, at the operational level they remain deeply divided. The conservative states have tended to advocate containment of the Jewish state, while the radical states have tended to advocate confrontation. For this reason, the conventional wisdom on Israel's role in inter-Arab relations is not entirely convincing. As a number of scholars have pointed out, the conflict with Israel has imposed enormous strain on the inter-Arab system.[5] Far from serving as a goad to unity, the question of how to deal with Israel has been a serious source of dissension and discord in inter-Arab politics.

A third source of instability and war in the Middle East is the involvement of the great powers in the affairs of the region. Two features of the Middle East help to account for the interest and rivalry it has evoked among the great powers in the twentieth century: its geostrategic importance and its oil reserves. Great power involvement is not, of course, a feature unique to the Middle East but one that affects, in varying degrees, all regions of the world; what distinguishes the Middle East is the intensity, pervasiveness, and profound impact of this involvement. No other part of the Third World has been so thoroughly and ceaselessly caught up in great power rivalries. No other subsystem of the international political system has been as deeply penetrated as the Middle East.[6]

The dominant great powers in the Middle East have been the Ottoman Empire until its dissolution in 1918, Britain and France until, roughly, the Suez War of 1956, the United States and the Soviet Union from Suez until the dissolution of the Soviet Union in 1991, and the United States on its own since 1991. So much stress has been laid on the role of these external powers that the history of the modern Middle East, in the words of Malcolm Yapp, has often been written as though the local states were 'driftwood in the sea of international affairs, their destinies shaped by the decisions of others'.[7] Yet this is a false picture, popular as it is with Middle Easterners and outsiders alike. From Yapp's detailed historical survey it emerges quite clearly that the dominant feature in the relations between international and regional powers is the manipulation of the former by the latter.[8]

A perceptive survey of the period 1955–67 by Fawaz Gerges reaches the same conclusion: the superpowers were rarely able to impose their will on the smaller states of the Middle East.[9] Although the local states depended on their respective superpower patrons for diplomatic support, economic aid, and the supply of arms, they managed to retain considerable freedom of action. Yet no account of the origins of Arab–Israeli wars would be complete if it ignored the role played by outside powers.

When the role of the great powers is considered alongside the other two factors—the Arab–Israeli conflict and inter-Arab relations—we begin to get some idea as to why the international politics of the Middle East are so complex, endemically unstable, and prone to violence and war. Against this background, what is surprising is not that seven full-scale Arab–Israeli wars have erupted in the post-war period, but that some of the other crises in this volatile region did not end up in war. Our next task is to assess the relative weight of these three factors in the origins of each successive Arab–Israeli war, bearing in mind that these factors often interact in complex and curious ways.

10.3. The Palestine War, 1948

The 1948 Arab–Israeli war was the climax of the conflict between the Jewish and Palestinian national movements which had been three decades in the making. As the mandatory power in Palestine, Britain had repeatedly tried and failed to find a solution that would reconcile the two rival communities in the country. In February 1947, the British Cabinet decided to refer the problem to the United Nations and the struggle for Palestine entered its most critical phase. On 29 November 1947 the United Nations passed its famous resolution which proposed the partition of Palestine into two states, one Jewish and one Arab. The Jews accepted the partition plan; all the Arab states and the Palestinians rejected it vehemently. The Palestinians launched a campaign of violence to frustrate partition and Palestine was engulfed by a civil war in which the Jews eventually gained the upper hand. At midnight on 14 May 1948, upon expiry of the British mandate, the Jews proclaimed the establishment of an independent state which they called Israel. The following day the regular armies of the Arab states intervened in the conflict, turning a civil war into the first full-scale Arab–Israeli war, a war which ended in defeat for the Arabs and disaster for the Palestinians.

Arab solidarity in the struggle for Palestine was more apparent than real. The Arab states, loosely organized in the Arab League, loudly proclaimed their solidarity with the Palestine Arabs and promised to provide money and arms. But behind the rhetoric of solidarity, the reality was one of national selfishness and dynastic rivalries, notably between King Farouk of Egypt and King Abdullah of Jordan. King Abdullah, who had reached a secret agreement with the Jewish Agency to partition Palestine at the expense of the Palestinians, was reluctant to play the part assigned to him in the Arab League's invasion plan. This invasion plan was designed to prevent the creation of a Jewish state, whereas his plan was to let the Jews have their state and annex to his kingdom much of the territory assigned by the UN to the Arab state.[10] Divisions of this kind go a long way to explain the failure of the Arab states to coordinate their diplomatic and military strategies in the battle for Palestine.

Of the great powers, Britain was most directly involved in the lead-up to the Palestine War. Britain's policy during the twilight of the Palestine mandate is a subject of some contention. Pro-Zionist writers have assigned to Britain a large share of the blame for the outbreak of the Palestine War, claiming that Britain armed its Arab allies and encouraged them to wade into Palestine and destroy the Jewish state at birth. There is no evidence, however, to sustain this charge, and considerable evidence to suggest that Britain tried to persuade the Arabs not to resort to war.[11] On the other hand, Britain refused to assume responsibility for implementing the UN partition plan on the grounds that the use of force would be required. So the real charge against Britain is not that it plotted war against the infant Jewish state but that its abdication of responsibility at the critical moment allowed Palestine to slide into chaos, violence, and bloodshed.

The United States played a less central but equally controversial role in the events surrounding the Palestine War. US policy was a series of swings of the pendulum between the pro-Zionist White House and the pro-Arab State Department. In the autumn of 1947, against the advice of the State Department, President Harry Truman decided to support partition. In March 1948, the State Department concluded that partition was impracticable and submitted instead a proposal for a United Nations trusteeship over Palestine. Both Truman and the State Department later urged the Jews to delay their declaration of independence and undertake on-the-spot negotiations in Palestine. But when the Jews proclaimed their state, Truman, without consulting the State Department, accorded it immediate de facto recognition.

If the United States was first to accord de facto recognition to the State of Israel, the Soviet Union was first to accord de jure recognition. The Soviet Union supported partition and the creation of a Jewish state chiefly in order to weaken the British position in the Middle East. In early 1948 the Soviet Union permitted the emigration of East European Jews and sent a shipment of 10,000 rifles and 450 machine-guns. During the summer of 1948, in violation of the UN embargo, the Jews received more substantial shipments of arms from the Eastern bloc which helped to tip the military balance against their opponents.

The critical factor in the outbreak of the Palestine War was thus the dispute between the Jews and the Arabs. The Palestinian attack on the Jews provoked the civil war while the Arab invasion in May 1948 provoked the official war. Inter-Arab rivalries contributed much less to the outbreak of this war than they did to the subsequent military defeat. None of the great powers wanted war in Palestine; but Britain lost control of the situation, while support from Washington and Moscow encouraged the Jews to proceed to statehood by force of arms.

10.4. The Suez War, 1956

If in 1948 the great powers played a lesser role on the Middle East stage than the regional actors, in 1956 the reverse was true. The war which broke out in October 1956 pitted Britain, France, and Israel against Egypt. One of the many paradoxes of this war was that Britain and Israel, despite the bitter legacy of the past, joined arms to attack an Arab state which had long been associated with Britain. Another paradox was that Britain and France, old sparring partners in the Middle East, found themselves on the same side in this war.

The motives which produced this unlikely alliance are not difficult to fathom. Britain was the prime mover. After the Free Officers' revolution of July 1952 Britain came under growing pressure to withdraw its forces from the strategically important Suez Canal base. With Colonel Gamal Abdel Nasser as President, Egypt became the standard-bearer of radical pan-Arab nationalism. Prime Minister Anthony Eden regarded Nasser as the chief enemy of the British presence in Egypt and as the chief threat to the entire British position in the Arab world. Comparing Nasser with Hitler, Eden was convinced that the right response to this challenge was confrontation, not appeasement. For Eden, Nasser's nationalization of the Suez Canal in July 1956 was the last straw. He concluded that Nasser would have to be removed from power if Britain were to maintain its position as a great power in the Middle East. The French also regarded Nasser as an enemy, not least because of his arms supplies to the Algerian rebels, and they too firmly set their face against appeasement. To the Israelis, Nasser was a bitter and dangerous foe and they were particularly troubled by his actions in closing the Gulf of Aqaba to Israeli shipping and in sending *fedayeen* units across the border into Israel. But it was the Czech arms deal of September 1955 which began to tip the balance in the Israeli Cabinet in favour of a pre-emptive strike against Egypt.

Thus the three countries each had their own reasons for wanting to go to war with Egypt. But although their war aims were not identical, they were all united by the determination to knock Nasser off his perch. The French took the lead in mediating between Israel and Britain and in organizing the secret meeting on 22 October 1956 at which the infamous collusion took place. At this meeting a plan of action was agreed and embodied in what became known as the Protocol of Sèvres. The tripartite attack on Egypt a week later proceeded broadly in line with this plan. Collusion led directly to the collision at Suez.

One of the distinguishing characteristics of Suez was that it was the result of a war plot. Indeed, while conspiracy theories are common, especially in the Middle East, Suez is one of the few genuine war plots of modern history. Britain, France, and Israel deliberately, carefully, and secretly planned their joint attack on Egypt. The Arab world was deeply divided in the mid-1950s between the radical states, led by Egypt, and the conservative monarchies, led by Iraq; but this division was not a direct cause of the Suez war. Similarly, the Soviet Union and the United States, though increasingly involved in the affairs of the Middle East, played no direct part in the events that led to war. Once the war broke out, the Soviet Union scored some cheap propaganda points by threatening rocket attacks against the attackers while the real pressure for halting the attack came from Washington. The crucial factor in the origins of the Suez war was the convergence of British, French, and Israeli plans to inflict a military defeat on Egypt and to bring about the downfall of Nasser.

10.5. The Six-Day War, 1967

Whereas the Suez War had been the result of deliberate planning, the Arab–Israeli war of June 1967 was the result of a slide into crisis. President Nasser appeared to challenge Israel to a duel but most observers agree that he neither wanted nor expected a war to take place. What he did was to embark on an exercise in brinkmanship which went over the brink. On 13 May 1967 Nasser received a Soviet intelligence report which claimed that Israel was massing troops on Syria's border. Nasser responded by taking three successive steps which made war virtually inevitable: he deployed his troops in Sinai near Israel's border; he expelled the United Nations Emergency Force from Sinai; and, on 22 May, he closed the Straits of Tiran to Israeli shipping. On 5 June Israel seized the initiative and launched the short, sharp war which ended in a resounding military defeat for Egypt, Syria, and Jordan.

The decisive factor in triggering the crisis that led to the Six-Day War was inter-Arab rivalries. It may sound perverse to suggest that the war owed more to the rivalries between the Arab states than to the dispute between them and Israel, but such a view is supported by the facts. The Arab world was in a state of considerable turmoil arising out of conflict and suspicions between the radical and the conservative regimes. A militant Ba'ath regime rose to power in Syria in February 1966 and started agitating for a war to liberate Palestine. President Nasser came under growing pressure to stop hiding behind the skirts of the United Nations and to come to the rescue of the embattled regime in Damascus. While Nasser suspected his Syrian allies of wanting to drag him into a war with Israel, they suspected that, if push came to shove, he would leave them to face Israel on their own. Nasser's first move, the deployment of the Egyptian army in Sinai, was not intended as a prelude to an attack on Israel but as a political manœuvre designed to deter the Israelis and to shore up his own prestige at home and in the Arab world. This move, however, started a chain reaction which he was unable to control.

In early May 1967 the old quarrel between Israel and the Arabs seemed almost irrelevant. As Malcolm Kerr observed in *The Arab Cold War*, the Arabs were more preoccupied with one another than they were with Israel. Even when the Israelis first appeared on the scene, they were there merely as a football for the Arabs, kicked on to the field first by the Syrian hotheads and then again by Nasser. The Israelis, however, took a different view of themselves. It became a case of the football kicking the players.[12]

The superpowers did very little to prevent the slide towards war. The Soviet Union fed Nasser with a false report about Israeli troop concentrations and supported his deployment of Egyptian troops in Sinai with a view to bolstering the left-wing regime in Damascus and in the hope of deterring Israel from moving against this regime. Its subsequent attempts to restrain Nasser had very little effect. It probably hoped to make some political gains by underlining its own commitment to the Arabs and the pro-Israeli orientation of US foreign policy; but it seriously miscalculated the danger of war and was swept up in a fast-moving crisis which it had helped to unleash.

The United States features very prominently in Arab conspiracy theories purporting to explain the causes and outcome of the June war. Nasser's confidant Mohamed Heikal, for example, claims that Lyndon Johnson was obsessed with

Nasser and that he conspired with Israel to bring him down.[13] Such explanations, however, are transparently self-serving in that they assign all the blame for the war to the United States and Israel and overlook the part played by Arab provocations and miscalculations.

In fact, the US position during the upswing phase of the crisis was hesitant, weak, and ambiguous. President Johnson initially tried to prevent a war by restraining Israel and issuing warnings to Egypt and the Soviet Union. Because these warnings had no visible effect on Nasser's conduct, some of Johnson's advisers toyed with the idea of unleashing Israel against Egypt. Johnson himself was decidedly against giving Israel the green light to attack. His signals to the Israelis amounted to what William Quandt termed 'a yellow light'; but, as for most motorists, the yellow light amounted to a green light.[14]

10.6. The War of Attrition, 1969–1970

The Israeli–Egyptian War of Attrition, which lasted from March 1969 to August 1970, was a direct result of the problems created for the Arab world by the Six-Day War. Israel had not only won a resounding military victory but had ended the war in possession of large tracts of Arab land—the Golan Heights, the West Bank and the Sinai Peninsula. UN Resolution 242 of 22 November 1967 called on Israel to withdraw from these occupied territories in return for peace with the Arabs; but the Israelis and the Arabs interpreted Resolution 242 rather differently and Israel's position progressively hardened. Israel became attached to the new territorial status quo and was confident of its ability to maintain this status quo indefinitely. Its strategy was to sit tight on the new ceasefire lines until the Arabs had no alternative but to accept its terms for a settlement.

For a short period the Arabs closed ranks against the common enemy and the bitter consequences of defeat; but gradually the old divisions reasserted themselves. The main division was between the advocates of a political settlement and those who believed that what was taken by force could only be recovered by force. At the summit conference held in Khartoum in late August 1967, these divisions were papered over by means of a resolution which was dubbed the 'three noes of Khartoum'—no recognition, no negotiations, and no peace with Israel. The conference demonstrated the uselessness of pan-Arabism as a framework for deciding a realistic policy towards Israel. The political option was rejected even at a time when an Arab military option palpably and painfully was not available. While Arab unity was preserved at the declaratory level, at the practical level each Arab state was left to decide for itself how to go about recovering the territory it had lost.

President Nasser adopted a strategy which fell into three phases: the purely defensive phase of re-equipping and reorganizing the Egyptian armed forces, leading to the second phase of active deterrence, which would be followed finally by the liberation of the territory that had been lost. Nasser's central aim after the 1967 defeat was to lift the Middle East dispute from the local level, at which Israel had demonstrated its superiority, to the international level. He therefore set out to involve the Soviet Union as deeply as possible in the Middle East problem. If a satisfactory political settlement could be reached with Soviet help, that would be fine; but if a political solution could not be found, the Soviet Union would be under some obligation to help Egypt develop a military option against Israel.[15]

The Soviet Union stepped up considerably its material and military support to Syria and Egypt after the 1967 defeat and it also became deeply involved in the diplomacy of the Middle East dispute. Although it was opposed to the resumption of all-out war, it supported the Egyptian commando raids across the Suez Canal which developed, by March 1969, into what became known as the War of Attrition.

Nasser decided to begin a war of attrition only after it became clear that diplomacy alone could not dislodge Israel from Sinai and after enlisting Soviet support for limited military action against Israel. The aim of the war was to bring about Israel's withdrawal from Sinai. The strategy adopted was that of a limited but prolonged war which would exact heavy casualties, exhaust Israel psychologically, and impose an intolerable burden on the Israeli economy. Israel's aim during the run-up to the War of Attrition and during the war itself was to preserve the territorial, political, and military status quo created by the Six-Day War. In all other Arab–Israeli wars, the side that started the war did so in order to preserve the status quo. This was true of the Arabs in 1948 and of Israel in 1956 and 1967. In the War of Attrition, the side that started the war, Egypt, was not out to defend but to change the status quo.[16]

10.7. The Yom Kippur War, 1973

The War of Attrition ended in a military draw between Israel and Egypt and was followed by a deadlock on the diplomatic front which remained unbroken until 6 October 1973, when Egypt and Syria launched their well-coordinated surprise attack against Israel. The outbreak of the Yom Kippur War can be traced to three factors: the failure of all international initiatives for the resolution of the Arab–Israeli dispute; the emergence of an Arab coalition which was able and willing to do battle with Israel; and the steady flow of arms from the superpowers to their regional clients.

International initiatives for the resolution of the Arab–Israeli conflict failed largely as a result of Israeli intransigence. After Anwar Sadat succeeded Gamal Abdel Nasser as President in September 1970, there was a distinct shift in Egyptian policy away from military activity towards the quest for a political solution. Sadat's public declaration in February 1971 of his readiness for a peaceful agreement with Israel was a significant turning-point in the generation-old conflict. But the deadlock over the implementation of UN Resolution 242 could not be broken because Israel flatly refused to return to the lines of 4 June 1967. On 4 February 1971 Sadat put forward his own plan for an interim settlement, based on a limited Israeli pull-back from the Suez Canal and the reopening of the canal for international shipping, but this plan, too, was rejected by Israel. Continued Israeli stonewalling persuaded Sadat, by November 1972, that a resort to force was essential in order to break the pattern of standstill diplomacy. From that point he started planning the military offensive which was code-named Operation Spark.

Under the leadership of Golda Meir, Israel kept raising its price for a political settlement just when Egypt became convinced of the need for a historic compromise. Immobilism was the hallmark of Mrs Meir's foreign policy. Holding on to the territories acquired in 1967 gradually replaced the quest for a settlement as Israel's top priority. Mrs Meir continued to proclaim Israel's desire for peace, but this was a pious hope rather than a plan of action. Her actual strategy was to let Sadat sweat it out, with his range of options constantly narrowing, until he was left with no choice but to accept Israel's terms for a settlement. The consequences of this strategy were to miss the opportunities for a peaceful settlement of the dispute and drive Israel's opponents to launch another round of fighting.

Israel's intransigence gave the Arab states a powerful incentive to set aside their differences and formulate a joint strategy for the recovery of their territory. The early 1970s were an era of rapprochement and growing cooperation in inter-Arab politics. Relations between Egypt and Syria developed into an effective strategic partnership, and relations between Egypt and Saudi Arabia also improved after Nasser's death. On the Arab side, Sadat was the main mover and planner on the road to war. His strategy was to mobilize all the resources of the Arab world, including the oil weapon, for the forthcoming confrontation with Israel. It was he who took the lead in forging the alliance with Syria, in setting strictly limited aims for the joint operation, and in provoking the international crisis in which the superpowers, he believed, were bound to intervene in order to secure a settlement.

Soviet policy in the period 1970–3 was inconsistent and contradictory. The Soviet Union's overall policy of detente with the United States led it to behave with great caution in the Middle East. It was Moscow's refusal to give Egypt the weapons it needed to have a viable military option against Israel that prompted Sadat, in July 1972, to expel the Soviet military advisers from his country. By the beginning of 1973, however, the Soviet Union had resumed arms supplies to Egypt in the knowledge that an offensive against Israel was being planned; and it continued to urge its Arab allies to avoid war while supplying them with sufficient arms to enable them to resume hostilities.[17]

The United States contributed to the outbreak of the Yom Kippur War indirectly and inadvertently by supporting the Israeli policy of trying to maintain an untenable status quo. Republican President Richard Nixon and his National Security Adviser, Henry Kissinger, approached the Middle East from a globalist perspective and sought to keep the Soviet Union out of the area. They perceived Israel as a strategic asset and a bastion of regional stability. They embraced the Israeli thesis that a strong Israel was the best deterrent to war in the Middle East. In accordance with this thesis, they provided Israel with economic and military aid on an ever-growing scale while declining to put pressure on it to return to the pre-1967 lines. Even after Sadat expelled the Soviet advisers the United States persisted in this standstill diplomacy, which eventually provoked Egypt and Syria not into accepting Israel's terms for a settlement but into resorting to war.

10.8. The Lebanon War, 1982

The 1982 Lebanon War was the result of the unresolved, or only partially resolved, dispute between Israel and the Arabs. The origins of this war can be traced back to the rise to power in Israel in 1977 of the right-wing Likud Party headed by Menahem Begin. It was Israel's invasion of Lebanon in June 1982 which started the war there and provoked the clash with the PLO and Syrian forces on Lebanon's territory. Officially the war was called Operation Peace for the Galilee to suggest that its purpose was purely defensive, namely, to secure the Galilee against attacks from the PLO forces stationed in southern Lebanon. But the broader aims of the war were to create a new political order in Lebanon, to establish Israeli hegemony in the Levant, and to pave the way to the absorption of the West Bank in line with the Likud's nationalistic ideology of Greater Israel. In this sense, the Israeli invasion of Lebanon was only the culmination of a long process of Israeli intervention in domestic and regional Arab politics.[18]

Internal political divisions in Lebanon and inter-Arab rivalries did not directly cause the war, but they facilitated and encouraged Israeli intervention. Lebanon itself had no territorial dispute with Israel and had only half-heartedly participated in the 1948 Arab–Israeli war. But the weakness of the Lebanese state and the fragmentation of Lebanese politics not only permitted but invited intervention by outside powers, notably Syria and Israel. Palestinian presence in Lebanon greatly added to this internal turmoil which in 1976 erupted into a civil war. Syria intervened in the civil war on the side of the Christian forces against the Lebanese left and the PLO. By maintaining a large military presence in Lebanon, Syria became the de facto arbiter of Lebanese politics, thus accentuating further the geopolitical contest with Israel for mastery in the Levant.[19]

Another major rift in the Arab world opened up when President Sadat signed the Camp David accords with Israel in 1978 and a peace treaty in 1979. Throughout the Arab world Sadat was denounced as a traitor and Egypt was drummed out of the Arab League. Syrian President Hafez al-Asad was one of Sadat's fiercest critics, arguing that the only way to negotiate with Israel was by maintaining a united Arab front. Sadat argued in self-defence that Egypt's peace treaty with Israel was only a first step towards comprehensive peace in the Middle East. The Likud government, however, exploited Egypt's disengagement from the conflict in order to press its strategic advantage against the rest of Israel's Arab opponents and especially against the Palestinians.

The chief architect of Israel's war in Lebanon was defence minister Ariel Sharon. A ruthless and cynical politician, he was also a great believer in using force to solve political problems. Sharon's 'big plan' had a number of objectives. The first objective was to destroy the military infrastructure of the PLO in southern Lebanon and thereby to break the backbone of Palestinian resistance to the imposition of permanent Israeli rule over the West Bank. The second objective was to help Bashir Gemayel, leader of one of the Christian militias, in his bid for power so as to bring about a new political order in Lebanon which was expected to be amenable to a peace agreement with Israel. The third objective was to defeat the Syrian forces in Lebanon and to replace the Syrian protectorate of the country with an Israeli protectorate. In short, the idea was to use Israel's military power in order to accomplish a politico-strategic revolution round Israel's eastern and northern borders. It was not the much-vaunted Israeli aspiration to peaceful coexistence with the Arabs that inspired this war but Sharon's relentless drive to assert Israeli hegemony over the entire region.[20]

Israeli propaganda surrounding the invasion dwelt on the security threat posed by the PLO presence in southern Lebanon. But in July 1981 the United States had negotiated a ceasefire between the two arch-enemies, the PLO and Israel, and over the next year the border between Lebanon and Israel remained quiet. It was not the military power of the PLO but its growing political moderation that provoked anxiety in Jerusalem. The war party was simply waiting for a pretext to invade Lebanon, and on 3 June 1982 a pretext arrived in the form of an assassination attempt against the Israeli ambassador in London. The attempt was ordered not by the PLO but by the renegade terrorist, Abu Nidal; nevertheless, on 6 June six Israeli divisions crossed the border into Lebanon, signalling that a full-scale war was intended rather than a small retaliatory raid.

The United States played only a limited role in the events leading up to the war in Lebanon, while the Soviet role was negligible. Neither superpower was particularly interested in Lebanon, but they became involved in response to promptings by their local allies. Israeli propaganda charged the Soviet Union with aiding and abetting the PLO. But Soviet policy, as usual, was confused and contradictory. It is true that the Soviet Union enabled the PLO to stockpile large quantities of weapons in Lebanon, but at the same time it was urging the PLO to suspend military action and to moderate its position so as to open the way to a political solution. The arms were given reluctantly to placate the PLO and enable it to negotiate from a position of relative strength.

The United States was dragged into the Lebanese quagmire by its importunate Israeli ally. Republican President Ronald Reagan looked at the Middle East through Cold War spectacles and held decidedly pro-Israeli views. To secure American backing, Israeli officials stressed that their plan would weaken the pro-Soviet forces in the Middle East: Syria, the PLO, and the radical factions in Lebanon. At a meeting in Washington in May 1982, Secretary of State Alexander Haig told Ariel Sharon that the United States would understand a military move only in response to an 'internationally recognized provocation'. Sharon chose to interpret Haig's convoluted statement as a 'green light' to invade Lebanon. While the Reagan administration did not positively desire war in Lebanon, it had not done enough to prevent it. On 1 September 1982 President Reagan belatedly announced his plan for a Palestinian homeland in association with Jordan. It was a good plan; but, like so many other plans for the peaceful settlement of the Arab–Israeli dispute, it foundered on the rocks of Israeli intransigence.

10.9. The Gulf War, 1991

Iraq's invasion and annexation of Kuwait on 2 August 1990 provoked a protracted and tense international crisis which culminated in war on 16 January 1991. All the Arab states of the Middle East and the Gulf, Israel, Iran, Turkey, and the great powers were involved, in one way or another, in the Gulf crisis and war. By far the most important factor in precipitating this war, however, was the crisis in inter-Arab relations. The Gulf War surpassed even the Six-Day War as the nadir of pan-Arabism in the post-Second World War era.

The Gulf War had its origins in an intra–Arab conflict which Saddam Hussein, the President of Iraq, tried, with only partial success, to turn into an Arab–Israeli conflict and which ended up as a conflict between the Western powers and Iraq—the first major conflict since the end of the Cold War.

Iraq's invasion of Kuwait was the last chapter in the Iran–Iraq war. During this war, which was started by Iraq in 1980 and lasted eight years, the oil-rich Gulf states and the Western powers helped create a monster in the shape of Saddam Hussein. Nevertheless, they expected this monster to behave reasonably after the war, at least as far as their interests were concerned. But on 2 August 1990, Saddam suddenly turned against his makers by gobbling up Kuwait.

Saddam accused Kuwait of stealing Iraqi oil by extracting more than its share from the Rumaila oil field, which straddles the border between the two countries, and of inflicting massive losses in oil revenue on Iraq by exceeding its OPEC production quota, thereby depressing the price. But Saddam's motives for annexing Kuwait went well beyond this technical dispute over oil quotas and oil prices. Saddam was a gambler playing for big stakes. He annexed Kuwait for both economic and geopolitical reasons. He was strapped for cash, so he went on a big bank raid; but he also wanted to improve Iraq's access to the Persian Gulf and to secure its dominance over the entire region. In 1990, as in 1980, he moved against a neighbouring country as part of the same drive for power, wealth, territorial expansion, and military aggrandizement. The second move, however, was a considerably more serious violation of international law than the first because it was an attempt to snuff out an independent state and a member of the United Nations.

The Arabs were so deeply divided in their response to the Iraqi invasion of Kuwait that not even the fiction of a unified Arab nation could be sustained. Sudan, South Yemen, and the PLO sided with Iraq. Egypt and Jordan wanted to mediate, to work out an Arab solution to the dispute, and to forestall outside intervention. Nearly all the other Arab states denounced the Iraqi invasion and some perceived it is a threat to their own security. The merger of Iraq and Kuwait would have been a formidable combination both in economic and in geopolitical terms. It was widely suspected that Saddam's next target would be the Saudi oilfields just across the border from Kuwait. Syria was another potential target. Syria and Iraq were united by the same Ba'ath ideology but divided by bitter enmity, and there was a danger that Iraq would sooner or later seize the opportunity to settle old scores. Thus some of the most conservative regimes in the Arab world found themselves on the same side as the more radical regimes in opposing the Iraqi invasion of Kuwait.

Israel's position in the Gulf crisis and war was distinctly anomalous. On the one hand, Iraqi aggression against a fellow Arab country seemed to support the often-repeated Israeli claim that much of the violence and instability in the Middle East is unrelated to the Arab–Israeli conflict. On the other hand, by posing as the champion of Palestinian national rights, Saddam managed to mobilize a significant degree of Arab popular opinion, secular as well as Islamic, on his side. On 10 August 1990 Saddam shrewdly proposed a possible Iraqi withdrawal from Kuwait if Israel withdrew from all occupied Arab territory. This proposal, though rejected outright by both Israel and the United States, created some sort of a linkage between the Gulf crisis and the Arab–Israeli crisis. For the remainder of the Gulf crisis, Israel tried to maintain a very low profile. Even Iraqi missile attacks on Israeli population centres, following the outbreak of hostilities, could not elicit military retaliation on Israel's part. This uncharacteristic Israeli forbearance ultimately defeated Saddam's efforts to turn an Arab–Arab conflict into an Arab–Israeli one.

The Soviet Union, in the final stages of disintegration, was unable to play an independent role in dealing with the crisis and the United States was left to make all the running. The Iraqi annexation of Kuwait presented the United States with a series of challenges—to its interests in oil, to its interests in Saudi Arabia, and to its prestige in the Gulf. It also challenged the old territorial order that Britain and France had imposed on the region after the breakup of the Ottoman Empire. Each of these challenges was serious enough; the combination ensured that Iraq's aggression would not go unanswered.

The US government refused to negotiate, and took the lead in sending troops to the Gulf, building up an impressively large coalition, passing all the necessary resolutions in the United Nations, and issuing an ultimatum to Iraq. When Iraq failed to comply, the United States and its allies launched Operation Desert Storm. The two aims of the operation were to eject the Iraqi forces from Kuwait and to restore the Kuwaiti government, and these aims were quickly and easily achieved. The overthrow of Saddam Hussein, the villain of the piece, was not an official war aim but his survival in power certainly took some of the sheen off the allied victory.

10.10. Conclusion

This brief survey of the origins of Middle East wars reveals a bewildering array of political forces operating in the region. The three factors identified at the beginning of this chapter—the Arab–Israeli conflict, inter-Arab relations, and great power involvement—are unquestionably all important in explaining the causes of war. Yet the relative weight of the three factors varies considerably from war to war. Naturally enough, in the majority of Middle East wars the most salient factor was the Arab–Israeli conflict. Inter-Arab relations were a salient factor in the outbreak of the Six-Day War of June 1967 and the 1991 Gulf War. Great power involvement is not as salient a factor as the first two but it did contribute to the outbreak of the Suez War and the Gulf War.

Keeping in mind the three levels of analysis suggested by Kenneth Waltz helps us to make sense of the complex forces that culminated in seven full-scale Arab–Israeli wars. Far from leaving us with the impression of bewildering complexity, this analytical device helps us to pinpoint the chief factors in the making of each of these wars. Our empirical survey, however, illustrates not only the strengths but the limitations of this analytical device. Waltz suggests that level three (systemic factors) is much more important than level two (domestic factors) or level one (personality factors) in explaining why states go to war. Our survey suggests that the three levels of analysis intermingle and shade into one another. While systemic factors are indeed critical in shaping foreign policy, domestic and personality factors also play a part. It is too simplistic therefore to confine an account of the origins of a war to one level of analysis, however significant and revealing it might be. The other two levels of analysis also need to be taken into consideration and, just as importantly, the inter-relationship between the three levels needs to be explored.

Britain's decision to attack Egypt in 1956, for example, cannot be adequately explained in terms of Britain's great power interests in the region; Eden's personal and highly subjective image of Nasser as another Hitler was a crucial ingredient in this decision. Similarly, Nasser's actions during the crisis of May–June 1967 were shaped much more by a desire to bolster his personal prestige at home and in the Arab world than by a desire to challenge Israel to a duel. Finally, Israel's decision to invade Lebanon in 1982 owed much more to the Greater Israel ideology of the Likud and to Ariel Sharon's incorrigibly aggressive instincts than to any external threat.

To sum up, when discussing the origins of each Arab–Israeli war, the aim should not be to single out one factor but to assess the relative weight of various factors. Because there are so many factors at play, and because these factors are so closely related to one another, it is difficult to determine the precise causes of each Arab–Israeli war. But difficulty should not be confused with impossibility.

Chronology

29 Nov. 1947	UN resolution for the partition of Palestine
Dec. 1947–May 1948	Civil war in Palestine
15 May 1948	Proclamation of the State of Israel and outbreak of the Palestine War
Feb.–July 1949	Israel concludes armistice agreements with Egypt, Jordan, Lebanon, and Syria
May 1950	Tripartite Declaration (Britain, France, and United States) on regulating the supply of arms to the Middle East

July 1952	Free Officers' revolution in Egypt
Feb. 1955	Baghdad Pact concluded between Iraq and Turkey
Sept. 1955	Czech arms deal; military pact between Egypt and Syria
July 1956	Egypt nationalizes Suez Canal
29 Oct. 1956	Outbreak of Suez War
Mar. 1957	Israeli withdrawal from Sinai
Feb. 1958	Syria and Egypt merge to form the United Arab Republic (UAR)
July 1958	Revolution in Iraq
Jan. 1964	Palestine Liberation Organization (PLO) founded on the initiative of Arab League to represent the Palestinians
Feb. 1966	Left-wing coup in Syria followed by increased PLO activity against Israel
5–10 June 1967	Six-Day War
1 Sept. 1967	Arab League summit at Khartoum: 'The three noes'
22 Nov. 1967	UN Security Council Resolution 242
Mar. 1969–Aug. 1970	Israeli–Egyptian War of Attrition
Sept. 1970	Jordanian civil war, 'Black September'
28 Sept. 1970	Nasser dies; Anwar el-Sadat succeeds
Feb. 1971	Israel rebuffs Sadat's peace overture
July 1972	Sadat expels Soviet military advisers
6–25 Oct. 1973	Yom Kippur War
22 Oct. 1973	UN Security Council Resolution 338 calls for direct negotiations
21 Dec. 1973	Geneva peace conference
18 Jan. 1974	Israeli–Egyptian disengagement agreement
31 May 1974	Israeli–Syrian disengagement agreement
26–29 Oct. 1974	Arab League summit at Rabat recognizes PLO as 'the sole legitimate representative of the Palestinian people'
4 Sept. 1975	Israeli–Egyptian interim agreement, Sinai II
1975–76	Outbreak of Lebanese civil war
June 1976	Syrian military intervention in Lebanon
May 1977	Likud defeats Labour in Israeli elections
1 Oct. 1977	Joint statement by US and USSR for reconvening the Geneva peace conference
Nov. 1977	Sadat's historic visit to Jerusalem
2–5 Dec. 1977	Arab Front of Steadfastness and Opposition meets in Tripoli
6–18 Sept. 1978	Camp David Accords signed by Israel and Egypt
2–5 Nov. 1978	Arab League summit at Baghdad denounces Camp David Accords
Feb. 1979	Iranian Revolution
Mar. 1979	Treaty of Peace between Egypt and Israel signed in White House
Nov. 1979	Soviet invasion of Afghanistan

Sept. 1980	Outbreak of war between Iraq and Iran
6 Oct. 1981	Sadat is assassinated; Hosni Mubarak succeeds
Apr. 1982	Israeli withdrawal from Sinai completed
6 June 1982	Israel invades Lebanon
1 Sept. 1982	Reagan plan for Middle East peace
July 1985	Israel withdraws from Lebanon, but forms 'security zone' in south
Dec. 1987	Intifada begins
2 Aug. 1990	Iraq invades Kuwait
16 Jan. 1991	Outbreak of Gulf War
Oct. 1991	Madrid peace conference
June 1992	Labour defeats Likud in Israeli elections
13 Sept. 1993	Israel and PLO sign Oslo accord
26 Oct. 1994	Israel and Jordan sign peace treaty

Notes

1. J. David Singer, 'The Level-of-Analysis Problem in International Relations', in Klaus Knorr and Sidney Verba (eds.), *The International System: Theoretical Essays* (Princeton, 1961), 77–92.
2. Kenneth N. Waltz, *Man, the State and War: A Theoretical Analysis* (New York, 1959).
3. See e.g. David Hirst, *The Gun and the Olive Branch: The Roots of Violence in the Middle East* (London, 1977).
4. See e.g. Yehoshafat Harkabi, *Arab Strategies and Israel's Response* (New York, 1977).
5. Malcolm Kerr, *The Arab Cold War: Gamal Abd al-Nasir and his Rivals, 1958–1970* (London, 1971); Michael C. Hudson, *Arab Politics: The Search for Legitimacy* (New Haven, 1977); Fouad Ajami, *The Arab Predicament: Arab Political Thought and Practice since 1967*, updated edn. (Cambridge, 1992); Stephen M. Walt, *The Origins of Alliances* (Ithaca, NY, 1987).
6. L. Carl Brown, *International Politics and the Middle East: Old Rules, Dangerous Game* (Princeton, 1984), 4.
7. M. E. Yapp, *The Near East since the First World War* (London, 1991), 3.
8. Ibid. 438.
9. Fawaz A. Gerges, *The Superpowers and the Middle East: Regional and International Politics, 1955–1967* (Boulder, Colo., 1994).
10. Avi Shlaim, *Collusion across the Jordan: King Abdullah, the Zionist Movement and the Partition of Palestine* (Oxford, 1988).
11. Ilan Pappé, *Britain and the Arab–Israeli Conflict, 1948–51* (London, 1988).
12. Kerr, *The Arab Cold War*, 126.
13. Mohamed Heikal, *1967: Al-Infijar* [1967: The Explosion] (Cairo, 1990), 371–2.

14. William B. Quandt, *Peace Process: American Diplomacy and the Arab–Israeli Conflict since 1967* (Washington, 1993), 48.
15. Mohamed Heikal, *The Road to Ramadan* (London, 1975), 46, 165.
16. Yaacov Bar-Siman-Tov, *The Israeli–Egyptian War of Attrition, 1969–1970* (New York, 1980), 3.
17. Mohamed Heikal, *Sphinx and Commissar: The Rise and Fall of Soviet Influence in the Arab World* (London, 1978), 253–4; Galia Golan, *Soviet Policies in the Middle East: From World War II to Gorbachev* (Cambridge, 1990), 82–5.
18. Kirsten E. Schulze, 'The Politics of Intervention: Israel and the Maronites, 1920–1984', D.Phil. thesis (University of Oxford, 1994).
19. Patrick Seale, *Asad: the Struggle for the Middle East* (London, 1988).
20. For a fuller account see Avi Shlaim, 'Israeli Interference in Internal Arab Politics: The Case of Lebanon', in Giacomo Luciani and Ghassan Salamé (eds.), *The Politics of Arab Integration* (London, 1988), 232–55.

Further Reading

BAILEY, SIDNEY D., *Four Arab–Israeli Wars and the Peace Process* (London, 1982). A detailed account of the 1948, 1956, 1967, and 1973 wars with an emphasis on UN peacekeeping. Includes numerous appendices of UN reports and resolutions.

BROWN, L. CARL, *International Politics and the Middle East: Old Rules, Dangerous Game* (Princeton, 1984). Reflections on international politics in the Middle East by a historian of the region.

DUPUY, TREVOR N., *Elusive Victory: the Arab–Israeli Wars, 1947–1974* (London, 1978). A full and balanced account of the wars written by an American military historian.

GERGES, FAWAZ A., *The Superpowers and the Middle East: Regional and International Politics, 1955–1967* (Boulder, Colo., 1994). A perceptive analysis of the relationship between superpowers and local powers and of the origins of the 1956 and 1967 wars.

GOLAN, GALIA, *Soviet Policies in the Middle East: From World War II to Gorbachev* (Cambridge, 1990). A general account of Soviet policies in the Middle East which includes a chapter on every major war.

HARKABI, YEHOSHAFAT, *Arab Strategies and Israel's Response* (New York, 1977). An analysis of the aims of the two sides in the conflict by one of the leading Israeli students of the Arab–Israeli conflict.

HERZOG, CHAIM, *The Arab–Israeli Wars* (London, 1982). An Israeli view of the Arab–Israeli wars written by a former Director of Military Intelligence and President of the State of Israel.

SHLAIM, AVI, *War and Peace in the Middle East: A Critique of American Policy* (New York, 1994). A brief introduction to the international politics of the Middle East since the end of the First World War.

SPIEGEL, STEVEN, *The Other Arab–Israeli Conflict: Making America's Middle East Policy from Truman to Reagan* (Chicago, 1985). A president-by-president account of America's involvement in the Arab–Israeli conflict.

YAPP, M. E., *The Near East since the First World War* (London, 1991). A comprehensive political history with many insights on the involvement of the Middle East in international politics and a useful annotated bibliography.

CHAPTER ELEVEN

JAPAN: REASSESSING THE RELATIONSHIP BETWEEN POWER AND WEALTH

Takashi Inoguchi

The relationship between power and wealth has been a popular topic for discussion in the study of international relations since ancient times. In this chapter power is defined as military capacity, rather than more broadly as the ability to achieve desired outcomes, while wealth is defined as economic success. The distinction between high politics and low politics, or between security and business concerns, has been the norm in foreign policy debates since the nineteenth century. Although the distinction between the two may have been much sharper in the nineteenth century than it is in the latter half of the twentieth century, the distinction is to a great extent retained not only in foreign policy institutions but also in academic specialization, where a division exists between the study of international security and that of international political economy.[1] Thus the question often arises as to which of the two aspects is more important in driving the state to action and shaping its foreign policy. When power is stressed in relation to wealth, such characterizations as the garrison state, the war state, and the global security state are used. When wealth is stressed in relation to power, the types used are the trading state, the merchant state, and the semi-sovereign state.[2] In other words, certain types of attention to and allocation of power and wealth produce certain types of state.

Underlying the distinction is the premiss that the search for power and wealth involves a kind of trade-off in shaping policy and action, namely a choice between 'guns and butter' in allocating scarce resources for the overall national benefits. In more concrete terms, the war state's propensity to spend money on weapons

I am grateful to Ngaire Woods for most useful suggestions made on an earlier draft of this article.

and war is assumed to have negative effects on the country's economic development, since military expenditures are often regarded as non-productive expenditures. In contrast to the war state, the trading state's propensity to spend money
on market sales and technological innovation is assumed to have positive effects
on the country's economic development.

In the post-1945 context, such a premiss often plays a part in the reasoning of
those who assess the merits and demerits of one country's commitment to global
and regional security tasks. The argument, roughly, goes as follows. When the
United States was able and willing to shoulder such tasks more or less single-
handed, no trade-off between guns and butter was perceived. However, the
United States, now keen to assert its position as a first-rank global power, has
come to see its commitment to global and regional security tasks as a liability.
If the United States had not spent so much on shouldering security burdens, the
argument goes, it would be in much better shape now.

A parallel argument is made in respect of the United States' allies (Japan and
Germany in particular), namely that these allies have enjoyed steady economic
growth because they have not faced large non-productive expenditures. These
countries, it is argued, should now assume security burdens on behalf of the
United States. Because they were constrained from developing their own independent armed forces after defeat in the Second World War, they spent most of
their scarce resources on productive opportunities, developing infrastructure
and industry, expanding market sales, and innovating products. The result is
that, unencumbered by national, regional, and global security tasks, they have
become much richer in terms of per capita income.

On the basis of this argument many policy disputes have taken place between
the United States and its allies, especially Japan and Germany. The argument advanced by the United States is that as long as it and its allies share the same set
of values and goals, such as free trade and the market economy, peace and stability, and human rights and democracy, and as long as there is a trade-off between
power and wealth, reciprocity has to be at the core of the allied relationship—
not only in security areas but also in economic areas. In other words, common
responsibilities should be shared. In principle, the allies of the United States
concur with this argument. The question becomes to what degree and in what
fashion the task of coordination and cooperation can be achieved.[3]

This chapter attempts to see the relationship between power and wealth from
an angle different from the 'trade-off' perspective. This is not to deny that the
trade-off exists; my intention here is rather to examine it by looking more closely
at Japanese development since 1945.

Before tackling this subject itself, it will be useful to examine a brief chronology of events that have taken place since 1945. I shall then introduce the Yoshida
Doctrine, the core doctrine that has guided the post-1945 Japanese nation, and

discuss it in relation to such characterizations of Japan as the trading state, the semi-sovereign state, and the capitalist developmental state. Finally, I will consider the notions of national identity and the memory of the past in my attempt to elucidate Japan's historic oscillations between seeking power in the traditional sense and seeking wealth.[4]

The Chronology given at the end of the chapter lists thirty key events as a brief, if prosaic, summary of Japan's history since 1945. Taking the five periods highlighted on the chronology in turn, I will analyse the relationship between power and wealth in each.

11.1. Occupation by the Allied Powers, 1945–1952

In the period 1945–52 Japan was externally powerless. It was occupied by the allied powers and its armed forces were disbanded. In terms of wealth, Japan was at its nadir. In terms of per capita income, even in 1950 Japan registered close to bottom position in Asia when the Philippines was one of the richest countries in the region.[5]

Japanese leaders learnt several lessons from their defeat. These lessons became incorporated into the Yoshida Doctrine, named after Shigeru Yoshida who was Prime Minister at the critical juncture of making peace with the allied powers; it was he who both concluded the Japan–US Security Treaty and promulgated the new constitution of 1952. The Yoshida Doctrine does not exist as a document but rather is a term used to describe Prime Minister Yoshida's core guidelines concerning Japan's options.

The Yoshida Doctrine is widely interpreted as consisting of the following three key components.[6] First of all, once you are beaten, you had better behave as the vanquished. You do not have to pretend you are strong. Secondly, you should concentrate your efforts on what you are allowed and able to do. If the Japanese are not allowed to have armed forces, their efforts should focus on their activities as engineers and merchants. Thirdly, the major cause of Japan's present predicament was its deviation from alignment with the maritime powers, that is, Britain and the United States, in the 1930s and 1940s. Japan should stay within an alliance with the major maritime power, which in the post-1945 context meant the United States.

These principles were given concrete expression in the form of: the Japan–US Security Treaty; the new constitution, with its famous pacifist preamble and Article 9; and related legal and institutional arrangements that were largely made on the basis of the state-led legacies to overcome depression and mobilize resources for war in the 1930s and 1940s intended this time for economic reconstruction and development.

It is arguable that the Japan–US Security Treaty and its new constitution made Japan a semi-sovereign state largely devoid of its own autonomous capacity to resort to war in cases of international disputes. Japan's imperial army was disbanded and its newly emerging self-defence force was not to be given any authority to wage wars, its mission being defined exclusively in terms of defence. Moreover, Japan's self-defence force was widely regarded as being ineffective even for defending the country without the full involvement of the US armed forces.

The decision by the Supreme Commander of the allied powers to make the best use of the existing governing institutions during the occupation meant that the Japanese state bureaucracy was kept largely intact, although the military bureaucracy was disbanded and the Ministry of Internal Affairs was divided into a number of more specialized agencies, excluding its more repressive aspects. A large state bureaucracy was given much authority during the occupation. The military ceased to exist. Political parties were largely disbanded on charges of their collaboration in the war. Big business was also punished politically for war collaboration and the *zaibatsu* fragmented into a number of business firms to attain economic democratization.

All this meant that economic bureaucracy reigned supreme during the Occupation. The Ministry of International Trade and Industry, the Ministry of Finance, and the Headquarters for Economic Stabilization (later to become the Economic Planning Agency), along with other economic agencies, were able to exercise a lot of influence in shaping Japan's post-war direction, advantaged by the war-devastated economy, beset by shortages, in which economic bureaucracy took precedence over other economic actors. On this basis, the economy started to grow by leaps and bounds after a decade of interruption and subsequent devastation by war.

11.2. Political Stabilization and Economic Take-off, 1952–1960

The period 1952–60 was essentially a period of industrialization in Japan; it was also the period, politically, when the centre-right hegemony was established. Politicians of the centre-right aimed to revise the constitution to make Japan more sovereign and intended to conclude peace treaties with the Soviet Union and subsequently with China in order to counterbalance Japan's overdependence on the United States. In these aims they failed; but they were able to 'normalize' much of what were regarded as the distortions created by the occupation in such areas as anti-monopoly measures, police conduct, and school textbooks.

Although the Japanese leaders who presided over the conclusion of the Security Treaty were pro-American, thereafter a different stream of thought surfaced in Japan. This is often called the 'nationalist school', although there was no such thing as a cohesive set of ideas and sentiments. Prime Ministers Ichiro Hatoyama (1955–7), Tanzan Ishibashi (1957–8), and Nobusuke Kishi (1958–60) can be included in this school, although their respective tasks were very different. Hatoyama concluded diplomatic normalization with the Soviet Union. Ishibashi wanted to achieve the same with China, but his tenure in office lasted only one month. Kishi achieved a partial rectification of the imbalance in reciprocity by revising the terms of the Japan–US Security Treaty.

During this second post-war period Japan's incorporation into international organizations began. In particular, Japan acceded to the General Agreement on Tariffs and Trade in 1953 and became a member of the United Nations in 1955. Membership of these international organizations bestowed on Japan the much-sought-after re-entry into the international community. GATT restored market access and the UN restored self-esteem. Both were essential for a newly industrializing country.

In this second post-war phase the momentum of economic development was utilized fully to build industrial infrastructure such as power stations, roads and ports, and steel mills, and to export commodities of comparative advantage such as textile products and small-scale machines. Although economic growth rates in the second period were high, per capita income remained low. A majority of Japanese were not yet feeling the trickle-down effects of emerging prosperity in any tangible form.

11.3. Stability and Prosperity, 1960–1973

The third period started when, in view of an estimated annual growth rate of over 7 per cent, Prime Minister Hayato Ikeda announced a plan which promised to double incomes in one decade. Having failed to promote projects of a more right-wing persuasion, playing up law and order issues in the latter half of the 1950s, in the 1960s the government pursued a more 'economic'-orientated conservative policy, essentially shirking more confrontational political issues, until the outbreak of the first oil crisis.

During this period Japanese leaders seemed to equate power with wealth. It is no wonder that a power-orientated French President, Charles de Gaulle, somewhat pejoratively called a business-orientated Japanese Prime Minister, Hayato Ikeda, a 'transistor salesman'.

Japan attempted to gain power abroad by expanding its access to markets, both by identifying niches for export commodities and assuring energy and food supplies. As a major source of energy supply, Japan was encouraged to substitute petroleum for coal by the United States in 1960.[7] As Japan became a newly industrializing economy, so too it started to expand the Asian market more consciously than before, using policy instruments such as war reparations, official development assistance, and export-promoting assistance to business firms in the form of, for example, low-interest loans. Along with efforts to assure petroleum supply, the petrochemical industry came to flourish in the 1960s and thereafter.

After joining the Organization for Economic Cooperation and Development, the International Monetary Fund, and a host of other international economic institutions as well as becoming a founding member of the Asian Development Bank in the 1960s, Japan's self-esteem went up considerably, and hosting the Olympic Games in Tokyo in 1964 boosted it further. Increasing self-confidence and pride went hand in hand with the rise of Japan as an economic power.

Japan's basically pro-American policy line did not change during this third period; rather it was used to a full extent. The Vietnam War aroused some anti-American sentiments, but Japan consistently supported the Unites States' war efforts. In so doing the government had to sacrifice some of its pledges, including the three non-nuclear principles (the principles of not manufacturing nuclear weapons, not importing them, and not allowing them to pass through Japanese territory) and the definition of the Far East.

The pragmatic application of Japanese diplomacy, when coupled with its semi-sovereign status and the historical debt of war, aggression, and colonialism Japan owed to the neighbouring countries such as Korea and China, produced a trade relationship with China reminiscent of China's traditional tributary trade. This relationship lasted through the 1960s until diplomatic normalization between Japan and China in 1972. With Korea, over this period, Japan maintained a sense of complex (i.e. very political) deals prior to the conclusion of the Basic Treaty in 1965.

11.4. Overcoming Depression and Emerging as an Economic Superpower, 1973–1985

The fourth period commenced with the eruption of several crises. Japan's habit of taking the United States for granted had become excessive, and in four instances in the early 1970s led to a series of unwelcome surprises. Japan was first taken by surprise when the United States imposed an export ban on beans in response to textile deals with Japan: the US government deemed it imperative to act in defence of its domestic products of textiles and beans. Secondly, the United States terminated the gold–dollar standard without prior notification, let alone consultation. Thirdly, the United States normalized diplomatic relations with China while allowing Japan to act as a US pawn, supporting Taiwan's membership of the United Nations until the last moment. Fourthly, the oil crisis erupted despite the general, if vague, pledge by the United States about petroleum supply when Japan shifted its major energy source from coal to petroleum.

These four events shook Japan. A number of points were made clear. First, Japan should not expect the United States to behave as its patron when it came to certain critical economic issues. Secondly, Japan was not trusted by the United States in matters of high politics. Thirdly, Japan should not rely on one single supplier for energy and food resources, but should indeed accelerate the diversification of suppliers of these resources.

A general lesson was drawn: increasingly, Japan needed to enhance its power and position since its economic interests hinged upon global market access. The United States could not be relied upon to guarantee everything. The pursuit of wealth needed to be accompanied by an associated enlargement of power. It is not coincidental that the notion of comprehensive security was propounded after the first oil crisis. It was intended primarily to alert the population to the increased need to assure energy and food supply. But it went beyond that. It meant that Japan could and should translate its wealth into power so that Japan's economic interests, so large and so scattered around the globe, might be properly protected. Given the generally inward-looking pacifism of the nation, Japan's military force could not be used even for strict defence purposes in securing Japanese interests. Rather, Japan's comparative strength in industrial, financial, and technological areas could be utilized to secure relations with its potential and present adversaries.

Pursuing this strategy of comprehensive security, along with the more general business strategies of saving energy, automating many manufacturing processes, and advancing technological innovation, Japan forged ahead of other Group of Seven (G7) countries in overcoming inflation, minimizing unemployment, and enhancing industrial competitiveness throughout the prolonged oil crisis-induced recessions between 1973 and 1985.[8]

11.5. Challenges of Globalization and Liberalization, 1985–1994

The fifth period of Japan's post-war international relations began with the Plaza accord. In 1985 the G7 countries agreed to accommodate the cheap dollar policy of the United States. The exchange rate of the yen *vis-à-vis* the US dollar rose steadily, in a trend precipitated by US difficulties in achieving government budgetary and trade balances. It was widely believed in the United States that at least the US trade balance, the bulk of which was with Japan, might be rectified by having the yen valued more highly against the dollar. Yet nothing of that sort happened. Rather, Japan's economic boom was accelerated, with its exports rising steadily. To avoid the negative effects of US trade protectionism Japan's direct investment in the United States surged, achieving the number one position towards the end of the 1980s. All of these developments alarmed the US government, which was determined to push the Japanese government into adopting a fixed position on market liberalization and implementing it, given the large US trade deficit and the ever strong temptation of the US Congress to introduce protectionist legislation. Hence successive, intense, and acrimonious trade negotiations ensued between the United States and Japanese governments, especially in the 1990s.

Over the same period world politics was transformed by the end of the Cold War and the disintegration of the Soviet Union. With the end of the Cold War the United States initially hoped that it could utilize its now supreme military dominance to achieve its goal of a new world order; but this hope was soon dashed.

Not only the end of the Cold War but two other endings have unleashed new social forces in every corner of the world. They are the so-called ends of geography and of history. Richard O'Brien and Francis Fukuyama have spread these notions around the globe. The end of geography means the globalization and liberalization of economic and financial activities, making geographical distance somewhat meaningless. The end of history means the disappearance of a contending set of ideas against capitalist democracy when Communism ceased to be an ideology of widespread appeal, making the path of capitalist democracy much more uncertain and hazardous. These three kinds of social forces have made Japan's search for power and wealth very complex.[9]

The Japan–US Security Treaty has had to change fundamentally despite its facade having been maintained. Its anti-Soviet nature has been diluted while its role as a linchpin of regional security has been stressed on both sides of the Pacific. While Japan has not been able to break out of its inward-looking pacifism, it has been pressed both from within and from without to play more of a role in global security and politics. Self-confidence born of economic success and nationalistic identity has strengthened Japan's voice in the world arena, while the United States is pressing Japan to enhance its global roles in harmony with the United States. A somewhat half-hearted compromise solution to these demands is the steady increase in Japan's peace- and security-related activities, especially within the frameworks of UN peacekeeping operations and bilateral military consultations with a number of neighbouring countries.[10]

Japan's emergence as a global economic power has required it to adapt its once very successful economic system to a new global economy. A majority of the developmental-cum-regulatory roles of economic agencies have come to be regarded as more harmful than helpful in this respect, despite having been among the primary factors elevating Japan into the rank of an economic superpower. Economic agencies have been particularly scrutinized in the wake of the deep and prolonged recession that followed the half-hearted financial market liberalization. Japan's former success makes it hard to adapt to a new global environment. Yet it is important that it does so if it is to play a leadership role in market liberalization and regional integration in such arenas as the GATT and the Asia–Pacific Economic Cooperation conference (APEC), in which a free trade area is envisioned by 2020. Without such credibility Japan's wealth will become more difficult to sustain. A global free trade regime is of paramount interest to Japan.

Norms and values are another aspect of the global arena in which Japan has been slow to adapt. In a new environment where global values and common norms are stressed, most Japanese leaders can contemplate shared norms and values only within national borders. The issues concerned range from human rights to environment, from AIDS to abortion. Japan's relative tardiness in taking a leadership role in these areas again makes its pursuit of power relatively less successful.

11.6. Western Views of Japan: Semi-sovereign State, Trading State, and Capitalist Developmental State

So far in this chapter I have briefly outlined the chronology of post-war Japan and looked at the relationship between power and wealth in five phases of Japan's international relations. Before summing up and making a general assessment of the relationship, it is worth examining three notions that have been used, mostly by Americans, in relation to the development of Japan since 1945: the semi-sovereign state, the trading state, and the capitalist developmental state. The authors of these notions are Douglas MacArthur, Richard Rosecrance, and Chalmers Johnson respectively.[11]

General Douglas MacArthur, Supreme Commander of the allied powers in Japan for the period between 1945 and 1952, reportedly said that the Japanese were like 12-year-old children. He might not have used the actual word 'semi-sovereignty' but what he meant was very close to what is normally meant by that term. Like a child dependent on others, Japan does not enjoy the power of using force for the settlement of international disputes; it has to rely on others.

The irony of Japanese development is that defeat in war and the drastic change in the international configuration of power wrought by the victory of the allied powers was conducive to Japan's recovery from ashes and revitalization of economic growth. The Cold War between the United States and the Soviet Union helped Japan to concentrate its efforts on economic recovery and development under the benign aegis of the United States. Thus Japan's defeat in the Second World War was a blessing in disguise. This was the spirit of the Yoshida Doctrine: you must make best use of the circumstances given to you by historical vagaries.

Liberated from the militaristic zero-sum-game perspective which had been ingrained by years of intermittent wars and economic depressions, Japan was able to plot its course primarily in economic terms, with global and national security exigencies largely shouldered by the United States through the Japan–US Security Treaty.

During the first few years after 1945, the United States aimed to ensure that Japan would not be capable of mounting a military challenge to the dominance of the United States in the Pacific, even if this meant slowing down the recovery and reindustrialization of Japan. Subsequently, the intensification of the Cold War led the United States to alter its approach towards Japan in a number of significant ways.

First of all, the United States wanted Japan to recover from defeat rapidly so that it could be one of the key countries that could be used for anti-Communist containment in the Far East. Its military bases should be made as accessible to US use as possible. Japan should be made responsible for its own internal security and industrially capable of sustaining both itself and US military activities. Furthermore, in pursuit of such quick and sustained economic recovery and reconstruction, Japan should be encouraged to expand its overseas markets. All the reformist policy lines of the occupation forces in the previous years came to be steadily played down.

In the early post-war years the United States had encouraged democratization, even with the consequence of helping left-wing electoral expansion, dismantling big business cartels, and supporting trade unions resorting to general strikes. By the late 1940s, however, the United States wanted to see political stabilization under the fledgling centre-right hegemony and economic reconstruction under the planning and guidance of economic bureaucrats.

The central element in the general change in US foreign policy in the late 1940s was the exclusion of the Soviet Union. Germany and Japan were kept docile, and all the allied powers were kept closely inside the Western camp. Germany and Japan too were kept inside, with the United States as the 'cap on the bottle'. With this general policy change, Japan, along with Germany, followed the policy line of delegating its national security to the United States and concentrating on domestic economics and politics. Herein lie the origins of what was to be later called the semi-sovereign state and the trading state.

The notion of the semi-sovereign state is used in the sense that Japan does not enjoy the capability to use military force autonomously for the resolution of international disputes. It abrogated its right to do so in the 1952 constitution, which was essentially drafted by the occupation forces in the immediate post-war years. The Japan–US Security Treaty, also put into effect in 1952, in tandem with Japan's restored independence, has made Japan's defence role subordinate to US definitions of security. As the Cold War between the United States and the Soviet Union intensified between 1945 and 1952, so too the version of the Japanese constitution promulgated in 1946 was superseded by the Security Treaty and new constitution concluded in 1952. Japan's semi-sovereign status has been kept intact until now. Even the revision of the Security Treaty in 1960, which made it obligatory for the United States to undertake consultation with Japan prior to military action on Japan's behalf, has not restrained the scope and method of US action in and outside Japan. Nor, it seems, has the return of the Okinawa islands to Japan in 1970 altered this semi-sovereign status. Rather, it seems that even after 1970 the United States has retained the freedom of action it had enjoyed in the Okinawa islands under its occupation.

Yet despite all these constraints placed on Japan, Japan has not been unhappy about its semi-sovereign status. Japan's unconditional surrender taught the Japanese to efface themselves in the international community. The military path to their search for an honourable position and international prestige was relinquished and replaced by the economic path. If the Japanese aim of catching up with the West could not be fulfilled by military means, then it must be pursued by other routes, i.e. the economic route. This choice was both self-conscious and strongly determined by the circumstances in which Japan was placed. As the Yoshida Doctrine stated, it is best for the vanquished to be docile to the victors and compliant with their wishes. At the same time, Japan's choice was strongly influenced by its circumstances. Unconditional surrender to the allied powers brought about the occupation and reform of Japan along lines largely determined by the United States. As long as the United States gives its security umbrella to Japan, whether for purposes of defence or deterrence, con-tinues to want the pacifist constitution preserved, and wants to act as Japan's guardian under the Japan–US Security Treaty, the Japanese do not see their semi-sovereign status as a problem. Indeed, it is a gift from heaven, a golden oppor-tunity of which best use should be made.

Furthermore, semi-sovereign status was perfectly consonant with the stage of economic development in Japan. It forced Japan to seek economic ways of catching up with the West. In the first place, global market access, especially access to the US market under the largely benign liberal international economic order or 'pax Americana', was crucial to Japan's swift recovery. The international economic environment in the third quarter of the twentieth century, with the world economy on an upward trend, was favourable to Japan's policy line, with market access on the whole easy to acquire. Secondly, in the immediate post-war years of ruin and shortages the Japanese economy found itself about to resume the acceleration of economic growth which had started in the 1930s but which had been interrupted by the war and defeat. As food and energy were supplied, production resumed and the acceleration of the economy followed. Already in the late 1940s there were indications that the Japanese economy was on a path to a remarkable recovery and reconstruction, despite the somewhat gloomy picture often portrayed of Japanese political instability at that time. The wartime destruction of manufacturing facilities turned out to be a blessing in disguise as it facilitated the renewal of facilities, most importantly of manufacturing technologies.

Thirdly, the government's wartime economic mobilization apparatus was kept largely intact. The bureaucratic sector was needed for the allied powers' occupation and thus kept largely undamaged. Those ministries emerging from defeat in positions of greater power were economic ministries. The Japanese economy, best categorized as a late-comer, still only just industrializing, was at the same time a heavily regulated economy where the economic bureaucratic apparatus made a significant difference to its economic growth. This is why Japan was called the capitalist developmental state in the second and third quarters of the twentieth century. Although not as omnipotent as they are often portrayed, these economic apparatuses were far from insignificant.

The combination of the semi-sovereign state and the capitalist developmental state was the best characterization of Japan from the 1950s through to the first oil crisis of 1973. This was the Japan of the Rising Sun, as the *Economist* called it. Yet in the 1970s and 1980s Japan was increasingly seen as a menacing economic giant. Japan came to be portrayed as a free-rider in the international economy and as an economy of excessive heterogeneity. These criticisms often arose in part out of jealousy, ignorance, and enmity. According to this view, Japan was a free-rider in two arenas: security and economy. Japan was a security free-rider because it did not fully shoulder its security costs; and an economic free-rider because it did not make serious efforts to maintain a liberal economic order.

According to this view, Japan is an abnormal state: first, because it does not have the will and capacity to determine its fate by military means; secondly, because it is seemingly equipped with bureaucratic and non-bureaucratic apparatuses which make its economy almost impermeable from outside. The combination of these characterizations makes Japan a trading state. The trading state is a country consciously using its governmental apparatus to promote production and trade while remaining outside international security efforts in order to maximize its commercial benefits and strength.

It is clear that these characterizations stem from the same combination of the semi-sovereign state and the capitalist developmental state. As Japan's economic status has steadily risen, its origins both as a semi-sovereign state and as a capitalist developmental state have tended to be forgotten. It is worth examining how the image of Japan as the trading state evolved from the 1970s through to the 1990s.

As Japan's economic success continued and was further enhanced even after the first oil crisis, efforts to identify the secrets of this success flourished. The United States was plagued by a perceived decline in industrial competitiveness and overseas overcommitments in security. In consequence, it started a witch-hunt against Japan, arguing that Japan was a free rider both in security and economic terms and that Japan's 'abnormalities' required reform. The argument was that Japan flourished both because it shied away from its substantial security burdens and because it made itself deliberately impermeable from outside.

Although these arguments shed light on how Japan has been driven by the single-minded search for further wealth rather than power in international relations since 1945, care has not been taken to back this argument up in comparative historical terms. A number of studies using historical quantitative data demonstrate that the proposition that economic growth is burdened by military expenditure is no more robust than the proposition that economic growth is accelerated by military expenditure.[12] In post-1945 Japan the economy has indeed grown unburdened by large military expenditure. Yet other cases do not bear out a causal link. South Korea and Taiwan, both garrison states at the height of the Cold War, flourished in tandem with large-scale military expenditure. Similarly, the proposition that an economy somewhat unfriendly to foreign trade and investment partners benefits more than an economy friendly to such partners is no more robust than the reverse proposition. In the post-1945 Japanese case the former proposition seems to have been at least partially vindicated. Yet in North Korea, for example, the economy did not flourish despite its basic unfriendliness to trade and investment partners.

Despite the general frailness of these arguments, especially when they are subject to scrutiny by causally constructed statistical models using multiple regression analysis, the Japanese case after 1945 seems to indicate that these propositions are to an extent valid. Nevertheless, the arguments have been exaggerated out of proportion as Western moods have changed. For instance, at one time Japan was portrayed as muddling through the post-war years with very little long-term thinking or planning in its national security policy; at another time as having envisaged a long-term strategic design very early after defeat in the Second World War. In a similar fashion, at one time Japan has been portrayed as mobilizing resources on an ad hoc basis in economic development, and at another time as having had a grand economic development plan, implemented in a highly self-conscious fashion.

Western writing on Japan seem to swing from one extreme view to another in accordance with the prevailing ease or unease about Japan's rise in wealth and power. When Japan seems unthreatening, they can afford to be benign: for instance, they can praise Japan for its consensus orientation and collective sense of purpose. If they find Japan menacing or competitive, they cannot afford such interpretations, and are inclined instead to point out the fissures and fragility in the Japanese system.

11.7. Conclusion

I have so far argued that the relationship between power and wealth in Japan's post-1945 history can be assessed fruitfully using such concepts as the semi-sovereign state, the capitalist developmental state, and the trading state. In other words, much of Japan's post-1945 development and behaviour displays features which conform to the key characteristics of these notions. First, Japan is not equipped with armed forces with an autonomous command and a will and capability to exercise military force for the resolution of international disputes. The constitution has been interpreted as forbidding this. Also, the Security Treaty with the United States gives the latter a primary role in Japan's defence and deterrence. Secondly, Japan has devoted its attention and resources to the advancement of wealth, even making it the business of the state through the conscious and astute use of public policies and institutions to prepare, promote, and propel business. Thirdly, Japan is interested in securing global market access considered indispensable for Japan, as a country not endowed with many natural resources. Japan must purchase most resources, especially energy resources, from abroad by selling whatever it can provide at comparative advantage, whether it is silk, steel, or semiconductors.

However, despite the ease with which Japan's post-1945 success is explained in these terms, the same concerts do not explain what has taken place of late. First the evolution of the semi-sovereign state over fifty years indicates that constraints as interpreted by the Japanese government and as imposed by the international environment can change. The major constraining variables, such as the military predominance of the United States and the inward-looking pacifism of Japan, are not permanent features of the world. In short, in the Japanese equation, power, especially in terms of status and prestige, is increasing its weight *vis-à-vis* wealth. Similarly, Japan stopped being a capitalist developmental state more than two decades ago. Japan's public policies and institutions, originally designed for developmental purposes, now tend to hinder its growth. The state now seems to encourage stabilization and rent-seeking. In short, in the Japanese equation, the disadvantages of the regulatory and rent-seeking functions of the state have expanded very significantly. Finally, Japan also ceased being a trading state more than two decades ago, with the end of the public-sector predominance over the private sector. The days are over when most business firms were eager to receive administrative guidance from the state. In the 'good old days' they could be allocated foreign reserves, subsidies, or insurance in trade and investment by the state. Now, exports and imports, foreign direct investment, and official development assistance have come to play the kind of role the ideal-type trading state would not willingly permit. Power considerations have come to play a much more salient role.

So, what, we might ask, is the most fundamental, underlying drive that led Japan to progress from being an utterly poverty-stricken, vanquished nation to one of the world's richest nations in well under fifty years? Japan evolved from a nation with no armed forces to a nation with a defence budget registering third in the world by the end of the Cold War. The nation which was granted United Nations membership with much difficulty in 1953 is now seeking permanent membership with veto power on the United Nations Security Council.

My answer, albeit admittedly tentative, is that the sense of national identity and the national memory of Japan's modern history propel the Japanese in such a way as to seek honour and prestige, position and status in the community of nations. Having been menaced by foreign powers in the seventh, thirteenth, sixteenth, and nineteenth centuries, the Japanese coped with these threats by enhancing their security and economic position. In the ancient Japanese state, defence lines were consolidated on the southernmost islands. In medieval Japan, land-based interests were united. Later, Japan pursued all-out modernization efforts under the slogan 'rich country, strong army'. When the Japanese state was defeated in the mid-twentieth century, a similar resolve was made. The difference in adaptation is natural to Japan. Adapting to all kinds of change by accepting constraints and working around them to their best advantage is perhaps the best way of summarizing the Japanese relationship between power and wealth. The way in which the Japanese have sought power and wealth depends mostly on the circumstances in which they find themselves. In the last half-century in Japan the stress has happened to fall particularly strongly on wealth.

Chronology

(1) Allied powers' occupation
1945   Japan's unconditional surrender to allied powers
1945–52   Allied powers' occupation of Japan

1950–53   Korean War

1952   Japan regains independence; Japan–US Security Treaty and Japan's new constitution

(2) Political stabilization and economic take-off

1953   Japan's accession to the GATT

1955   Japan's accession to the UN; LDP becomes the ruling party (to 1993)

1956   Japan–USSR diplomatic normalization

1960   Income-doubling plan announced

(3) Stability and prosperity

1964   Bullet train installed; Tokyo Olympic Games held; Japan's accession to OECD

1965   Vietnam War intensifies

1969   Student revolts on campus

1971   US returns Okinawa islands to Japan

(4) Overcoming depression and emerging as an economic superpower

1973   First oil crisis

1976   Western summit begins

1979   Second oil crisis

1981   Reaganite Cold War started

(5) Challenges of globalization and liberalization

1985   Plaza accord by G7; Maekawa report on market liberalization submitted to Prime Minister Nakasone

1989   Fall of Berlin Wall

1991   Gulf War; collapse of USSR

1993   Fall of LDP from power

1994   Socialist Prime Minister takes office; Higuchi report on peace and security policy submitted to Prime Minister Murayama

Notes

1. For the standard conceptualizations of power and wealth see e.g. Klaus Knorr, *Power and Wealth* (New York, 1973); David A. Baldwin, *Paradoxes of Power* (Oxford, 1989). For the academic bifurcation see e.g. the differences between the two US-based journals, *International Security* and *International Organization* in the 1970s and 1980s. More generally see A. J. R. Groom and Margot Light (eds.), *Contemporary International Relations: A Guide to Theory* (London, 1994).

2. See e.g. various writings by Harold Lasswell, I. F. Stone, Gabriel Kolko, Richard Rosecrance, Naohiko Amaya, and Chalmers Johnson; also note 11 below.

3. See e.g. David Denoon, *Real Reciprocity* (New York, 1993).
4. See e.g. Takashi Inoguchi, *Gaiko taiyo no hikaku kenkyu: Chugoju, Eikoku, Nihon* (A Comparative Study of Diplomatic Style: China, Britain, Japan) (Tokyo, 1978).
5. The best standard works on the Japanese economy and politics during the post-1945 period are many books by Takafusa Nakamura and Junnosuke Masumi respectively.
6. See e.g. Masataka Kosaka, *Yoshida Shigeru* (Tokyo, 1961).
7. Frank Gibney, *The Pacific Century* (New York, 1993).
8. See e.g. the trilogy dealing primarily with the features of Japan during this period: Kozo Yamamura and Yasukichi Yasuba (eds.), *The Political Economy of Japan: The Domestic Foundation* (Stanford, Calif., 1987); Takashi Inoguchi and Daniel Okimoto (eds.), *The Political Economy of Japan: The Changing International Context* (Stanford, Calif., 1988); Shumpei Kumon and Henry Rosovsky (eds.), *The Political Economy of Japan: Social and Cultural Dynamics* (Stanford, Calif., 1993).
9. Richard O'Brien, *The End of Geography* (London, 1993); Francis Fukuyama, *The End of History and the Last Man* (New York, 1991). My own analysis of global changes in terms of international security, global economy, and domestic governance is found in Takashi Inoguchi, *Sekai hendo no mikata* (Global Changes: An Analysis) (Tokyo, 1994).
10. My own analyses of Japan's foreign policy during the fourth and fifth periods are found in Takashi Inoguchi, *Japan's International Relations* (London, 1991) and *Japan's Foreign Policy in an Era of Global Change* (London, 1993).
11. Richard Rosecrance, *The Trading State* (New York, 1985); Chalmers Johnson, *MITI and the Japanese Miracle* (Stanford, 1983).
12. See e.g. Michael D. Ward, David R. Davis, and Corey L. Lofdahl, 'A Century of Tradeoffs between Defense and Growth: the Case of Japan and the United States', *International Studies Quarterly*, 39/1 (March 1995), 27–50.

Further Reading

BALDWIN, DAVID, *Paradoxes of Power* (Cambridge, 1989). A thorough re-examination of the concept of power in the broadest sense of the word.

INOGUCHI, TAKASHI, *Japan's International Relations* (London and Boulder, Colo., 1991). A lucid analysis of key aspects of Japan's international relations from the first oil crisis up to the end of the Cold War.

—— *Japan's Foreign Policy in an Era of Global Change* (London, 1993). A work that stresses the inseparability of domestic politics and foreign policy amid major global change.

JOHNSON, CHALMERS, *MITI and the Japanese Miracle* (Stanford, Calif., 1983). A detailed historical study of Japan's Ministry of International Trade and Industry, with a thesis that some government intervention, when pursued with tenacity and agility, makes a difference to economic performance.

KNORR, KLAUS, *Power and Wealth* (New York, 1973). One of the most often cited references concerning the relationship between power and wealth.

ROSECRANCE, RICHARD, *The Trading State* (New York, 1985). A most readable book showing how some states flourish by focusing their activities on international commerce.

CHAPTER TWELVE

THE STUDY OF CHINA'S INTERNATIONAL BEHAVIOUR: INTERNATIONAL RELATIONS APPROACHES

Rosemary Foot

China's international behaviour since 1949 has been described by many as unstable. There has been variation in Beijing's own self-identity, and it has established a number of relationships from which it has eventually retreated.[1] Notwithstanding China's own claims that it has followed a consistent and principled line in its foreign relations and in the objectives that it has pursued, significant and consequential policy shifts have occurred.

Our task as analysts has been to find the best means of explaining these shifts. A central puzzle has been to establish whether factors external to the Chinese state best explain them, or whether we should give primary attention to the domestic realm. Although we are not precluded from combining these factors, choosing one or the other as an entry point, or as the independent or dependent variable, inevitably produces different explanatory outcomes.

Much of the literature that deals with Chinese foreign policy behaviour, although extremely valuable, has tended not to be explicit about the selective processes that have underpinned the argument, or about the theoretical positions that have been taken. By contrast, this chapter attempts to show what happens when we are explicit about the analytical paths chosen, and how international relations approaches can illuminate the study of Chinese foreign policy.[2] Specifically, the chapter uses two of the central paradigms in international relations—realism and liberalism—in order to examine their power as explanatory devices. It separates out realism and liberalism in order particularly to show the strengths and weaknesses of the former—the dominant approach in international relations—in the

Table 12.1. International relations approaches and the study of China's international behaviour

Approach	Actors	Objectives	Focus
Realism	Unitary states (China, Soviet Union, USA)	Search for security against military threat	Anarchical international system
Liberalism	Policy élites within historical–cultural setting	Combination of objectives linking domestic with external	China

specific case of China. This examination of the two approaches will also allow us to contrast and compare the kinds of evidence, the types of actor, and the views of the world each adopts (see Table 12.1).

Four particular episodes from the post-1949 period have been chosen with these objectives in mind: (1) China's decision to 'lean towards the Soviet Union' in 1949 and to sign the Sino-Soviet Treaty of Alliance in February 1950; (2) its decision to break off relations with Moscow and strike out in the role of a self-reliant autonomous international actor in world politics;[3] (3) its decision to effect a rapprochement in its relations with the United States in 1971–2; and, finally, (4) its decision in 1982 to adopt what Beijing described as an 'independent foreign policy' in which China would give greater stress to matters of sovereign independence in the context of a more complex and balanced set of international relationships.[4]

12.1. A Realist Perspective

Briefly stated, the basic tenets of realism, including structural realism, are that states are the most important actors in international relations, the international system is the most important level of analysis, and the dominant concern of states is with power and security.[5] For a realist, a state's foreign policy is heavily determined by its search for security in an anarchical, competitive, self-help international system; thus enhancement of a state's military capabilities is deemed a priority. Additionally, it might be seen as necessary to form a military alliance with another state or states. According to Stephen Walt, for example, such alliances might well be formed to balance against threats that are a function of 'power, geographical proximity, offensive capabilities and perceived intentions'.[6]

Bearing these features in mind, how far will this focus on security, military power, and external threats take us in the attempt to explain the four positions China has taken in the period since 1949? Who are the central actors in the explanation, what are deemed to be the primary objectives, and what kinds of evidence are deemed most significant?

Leaning to One Side

In June 1949 Mao made an important speech in which he announced China's decision to 'lean to one side', that is, towards the Soviet bloc. Six months later, he visited Moscow to formalize that decision through the signature of the Sino-Soviet Treaty of Friendship, Alliance, and Mutual Assistance. In both cases, realists would make the persuasive argument that security interests rather than ideological predilection were at the root of those moves. The PRC government, after all, was established in October 1949, at the height of the Cold War, when the structure of the international system was bipolar. The United States had demonstrated its hostility towards the new leadership in Beijing in various ways. It had continued to provide military assistance to the Chinese Nationalists throughout the civil war. During the final stages of that conflict, the Communists had based their deployment of military forces on the assumption that the United States might intervene in support of the Nationalists. Even as Nationalist forces faced defeat, Washington again demonstrated its basic hostility by imposing conditions that the incoming, victorious government had to satisfy before recognition could be contemplated. More broadly still, the United States seemed set to dominate China's security environment for a long time to come. America's large navy and air force, built up over the course of the Second World War, and its acquisition of bases in the western Pacific, ensured its continuing presence around China's borders.

If we accept Walt's explanation for the formation of alliances—that most are formed to balance against threats—then we have a ready explanation for China's decision to 'lean to one side'. This decision was taken because it provided Beijing with access to military *matériel* and offered the new regime a relationship that would operate to deter any overt US military moves against China. To support this we might note that Chinese leaders began to explore with Stalin in June 1949 the prospect of Soviet supply of Yak fighters and heavy bombers, and the setting-up of a training school for Chinese pilots and technicians.[7] More significantly still, during Chairman Mao Zedong's and Premier Zhou Enlai's visit to Moscow in the winter of 1949–50 the two countries signed the Sino-Soviet Treaty of Alliance, which in its most significant clause read: 'should either of the Contracting Parties be attacked by Japan or by states allied with Japan and thus find itself in a state of war, the other Contracting Party shall immediately extend military and other assistance with all the means at its disposal.'[8]

Subsequent international developments reinforced the argument that Soviet security guarantees were both essential and materially beneficial, especially in the military field. With the outbreak of the Korean War, the Truman administration decided to station the US Seventh Fleet between the Chinese mainland and the island of Taiwan, an action that demonstrated that the United States had upgraded the strategic significance of the island and that it had decided to intervene directly to bolster the Chinese Communists' major political enemies. As Korean hostilities intensified and US-led UN forces moved closer to China's north-eastern border, the security threat to the new Communist authorities increased. The deterrent value of China's treaty of alliance with the Soviet Union seemed overwhelmingly to be vindicated by the fact that the United States refrained from overtly extending the war to Chinese territory. Moreover, during the course of the conflict the material benefits of the alliance were made plain, as the Soviets transferred equipment for more than sixty army divisions and ten air force divisions, plus 80 per cent of the ammunition. Soviet airmen also took part covertly in air combat operations.[9]

Such military assistance continued over the next few years, culminating in the signature in 1957 of a secret agreement, the 'Sino-Soviet New Defence Technical Accord', in which Moscow offered to supply Beijing with a prototype atomic bomb, missiles, and relevant technical information.[10] In fact, such material support went well beyond military aid: between 1950 and 1957 Moscow undertook what has been described as 'one of the largest scale transfers of technology from one country to another in history',[11] with Soviet advisers established in the major ministries and thousands of blueprints for factory development being made available.

Thus far, the realist explanation has led to a focus on the threatening nature of the external environment, and on China's presumed need to augment its capabilities, particularly its military strength. Except in the establishment of relative capabilities, it provides little incentive to examine the domestic realm, either in terms of leadership preferences or in terms of the condition of China as a newly established socialist state. Predominantly, the focus is on Beijing's security needs in a bipolar system divided into two hostile blocs.

The Sino-Soviet Split

Moving to our second major turning-point in Chinese foreign policy, why in the realist view did the alliance begin to founder from approximately 1958 and break down completely by 1963? Realists would argue that over this period it became clear that the Soviet Union was no longer interested in providing security guarantees to its Chinese ally. Focusing on the constraints imposed by the bipolar system and the experience of hot war in Korea, the argument would be that the core relationship—that between the superpowers—began to assume overwhelming importance and to shape the choices of other actors in the global system more directly. The Korean conflict focused attention, inter alia, on the risks of superpower engagement, the constraints on the use of nuclear weapons, and the need to manage and condition the behaviour of alliance partners in ways that would contribute to systemic stability. In other words, events heralding changes in the configuration of power had served to modify the relationship between the superpowers, forcing Beijing and Moscow in turn to re-evaluate their relationship.

The summit conference at Geneva in 1955 could be viewed as an early Soviet–American attempt to explore better ways of managing the East–West balance of power.[12] Technological developments in 1957 also had their impact on the superpower relationship. The Soviet test-firing of a missile in August and the October launch of the first orbiting satellite were considered by Moscow as likely to heighten Washington's security concerns and thus boost the US desire to negotiate. The Soviet Union also believed that they were now in a better position to deter nuclear war. These conclusions underpinned a growing desire in both capitals to attempt to manage the nuclear relationship, including the prevention of the acquisition of such weaponry by other states such as West Germany, Japan, and China. Thus in 1959 Khrushchev cancelled the agreement with China to supply a prototype atomic bomb, arguing that 'if the Western countries learn that the Soviet Union is supplying China with sophisticated technical aid, it is possible that the socialist community's efforts for peace and relaxation will be seriously sabotaged.'[13]

Such deliberations between Washington and Moscow over arms control matters, although lengthy and difficult, finally resulted in the signature of the Partial Test Ban Treaty in 1963. This event was also marked by the opening of direct polemics between China and the Soviet Union.[14] For the Chinese, the Soviet signature of the treaty encapsulated Moscow's loss of determination to protect the interests of its most significant ally, and instead to concentrate on developing the 'superpower condominium' with Washington. As detente evolved between 1958 and 1963, Chinese security interests were directly affected. US hostility towards the PRC remained high, and Washington had further deepened its ties with the Nationalists on Taiwan, deploying on the island nuclear-tipped surface-to-surface missiles and constructing a runway that could accommodate B-52 bombers. Washington's behaviour towards Taiwan during the 1958 Straits crisis stood in stark contrast to the qualified levels of support Beijing received from Moscow. Where the United States 'assembled off the China coast the most powerful armada the world had ever seen: six carriers, with a complement of 96 planes capable of delivering nuclear weapons, three heavy cruisers, forty destroyers, a submarine division, and twenty other support craft',[15] the Soviet Union was advocating caution in Beijing, fearful that war over the offshore islands would baulk progress on the arms control agreement and the more general detente between East and West that it sought. From the Chinese perspective, therefore, it was becoming steadily clearer that the Soviet Union valued its relationship with the United States more highly than its relationship with the PRC, and that the security guarantees inherent in the Treaty of Alliance were becoming worthless. In these circumstances, why continue with the relationship?

Rapprochement with the United States

As the Sino-Soviet dispute unfolded, its military–strategic dimensions began to assume greater prominence. For the realist, it is this aspect of a rift that was increasing dramatically in gravity that best explains the next major change in Chinese behaviour: the Sino-US rapprochement of 1971–2. Reports in 1966 indicated that the Soviet Union was transferring some of its best-trained forces from Eastern Europe to the Sino-Soviet border. Moscow also signed a twenty-year defence pact with the Mongolian People's Republic which soon resulted in the stationing of some 100,000 Soviet troops in that country, supplemented by tank and missile units. Then, in August 1968, Soviet and other Warsaw Pact forces intervened in Czechoslovakia, a move later to be justified by Brezhnev in terms of the concept of 'limited sovereignty'. The argument ran that Czech reforms were destroying the socialist achievements of the people of that country and that other socialist countries thus had a duty to intervene.

Growing Sino-Soviet tension culminated in the 1969 border war between the erstwhile allies, which was accompanied by a Soviet hint that it might launch an attack against Chinese nuclear installations.[16] The Chinese also became aware of Soviet contingency plans to conduct a 'surgical strike' against the country as a prelude to airborne operations and the occupation of parts of China north of the Yangtze.[17] By 1970 there were thirty Soviet divisions stationed along China's northern border; by 1973 the number had risen to forty-five. In the Chinese perception, the Soviet Union had become the most aggressive and expansionist power in the global system, especially when viewed against the US defeat in and withdrawal from Vietnam. In these circumstances, security imperatives led Beijing to search for protection from the one state in the global system which, though weakened, was still best placed to provide something of a check on Soviet ambitions.

The Chinese therefore indicated their interest in repairing the relationship with the United States. They were ready to put the Taiwan issue to one side, and to form a tacit although not formal alignment with the United States. As new understandings between the two countries were reached in the decade after the 1972 Nixon visit, these led to the US provision of intelligence information on the disposition of Soviet forces on the northern border, the establishment of a monitoring station on that border, US support for sales of Western arms to China, and eventually the offering of its own dual-use technology and defensive weapons on a case-by-case basis.[18] The international configuration of power had changed once again, it seemed, and China had found it necessary to adjust relationships in order to guard against the primary threat to its existence over this period, namely the Soviet Union—a state that was bearing down on its northern border. The new relationship with the United States also provided Beijing with the means to enhance its stagnating military capabilities and to increase its ability to deter Soviet military attack.

An Independent Foreign Policy

By the early 1980s, however, Chinese leaders were thinking of adjusting their pattern of alignments once again to a position that was more nearly equidistant between the two superpowers. Again, for the realist, considerations of the balance of power provide a means of understanding this further shift. In the Chinese leadership's view, the US defence build-up under President Reagan had succeeded in raising the United States to the point where it represented a potential hegemonic threat at least equal to, certainly no longer less than, that posed by the Soviet Union. Moreover, the doctrine which carried Reagan's name foreshadowed a more active anti-Communist stance, especially in the developing world. By contrast, with Moscow bogged down in an unpopular and costly war in Afghanistan, its relations with key East European allies in some disarray, and its economic and military support for Vietnam and Cuba increasingly burdensome, the trend of events seemed decidedly to be moving in Washington's favour. There were also some signs that Moscow itself had come to recognize its increasingly unfavourable international position and in response had begun to seek an improvement in relations with Beijing, to include a call for the resumption of negotiations on a range of issues and the re-establishment of political, cultural, and economic ties.[19]

As a result of such reflections on global developments (alongside specific irritations in the bilateral relationship with Washington), China announced at the Twelfth Party Congress in September 1982 its 'independent foreign policy'. Thenceforth, China would manœuvre more freely within the 'strategic triangle'. As the then Party General Secretary, Hu Yaobang, explained it to the Party Congress, it meant that China would never 'attach itself to any big power or group of powers', and would never yield to big power pressure.[20] Relations with Moscow began their steady if cautious improvement, which in turn had beneficial effects on China's security in other areas, most notably with respect to India and Vietnam. Beijing had established a platform from which to launch a more balanced and nuanced set of relationships in the global system.

This review represents a realist case for the understanding of shifts in China's pattern of alignments since 1949. In our focus on these four major shifts, realism has provided us with a plausible and parsimonious explanation. The point of entry into the explanation of the four decisions has been the outcomes themselves, outcomes which are intimately linked to what is perceived as an anarchic international system. China's search for security in such an international system has led it, this approach contends, to eschew ideological preference and to focus instead on balancing against major threats to its existence.

However, while these features of realism render it attractive and compelling, there are certain matters that are left unexplained, and certain major pieces of evidence that are ignored. For example, realism cannot explain why some Chinese leaders did not support the breach in relations with Moscow, or the opening to the United States in 1971. Nor does it give us any insight into how a particular leadership position came to prevail over another, or explain why it took so long for the rapprochement with the United States to occur, given that the preconditions for a tilt in Washington's direction were present from the early 1960s. It also assumes that the concept of security itself is uncontestable and well understood, and applies without much variation in every case, including the Chinese. Thus realism does not deal with the particularities of timing or how the decisions themselves were reached. It assumes that the structure of the international political system directs governments along paths that are obvious, and that there is little room or need for debate over options.

To explain these matters of timing, attitudes towards security, and whether other alternatives were in fact believed to have been available, we need to be receptive to what I term here the liberal perspective: an approach that gives primacy to domestic factors. As such it is a more China-centred way of looking at China's own foreign policy behaviour. It thus highlights the differences rather than the similarities in state behaviour. Another important feature of this perspective is that it demonstrates ways in which the domestic and international can be shown to be linked.

12.2. A Liberal Perspective

Liberalism as it is defined in this chapter offers a more complicated picture than realism. It focuses on other actors besides states, would see the state as a social–historical phenomenon, and would not regard interests as fixed. As suggested above, it recognizes the critical importance of domestic factors, including individuals, interest groups, and bureaucracies operating within a particular political–cultural setting. Thus the idea of national interest is unravelled, and certain features of particular societies are given greater attention and greater explanatory weight. The domestic, in fact, becomes the independent variable.

In the case of China, certain authors have found it valuable in the explanation of that country's behaviour to focus on what has been termed its 'informal ideology' or the world-view of policy élites,[21] both of which have been shaped fundamentally by Chinese history, especially the period termed the 'century of humiliation', 1840–1949. Informal ideology has been defined as the 'complex of cultural values, preferences, prejudices, predispositions, habits, and unstated but widely shared propositions about reality that condition the way in which political actors behave'. It is, therefore, far less systematic than formal ideology, more intuitive, less restricting, and more long-lasting.[22] Authors adopting these approaches implicitly or explicitly reject the notion that states are basically alike, and that difference in state power is the key determinant of behaviour. Instead, they focus attention on a country's historical–cultural experience as interpreted by central decision-makers.

The longevity of the leaders of the Chinese revolution and their monopoly on the formulation of policy has made it profitable to examine what Carol Lee Hamrin has termed their 'generational world-view that combines certain traditional values with an adopted ideology, and is based on a shared historical experience in the decades of war that bridged the dynastic and post-1949 periods'. There are various elements that make up this world-view, but for a number of specialists on China it includes the determination to maintain autonomy and distance in foreign relationships, the fear that foreigners will engage in domestic subversion, and a preoccupation with state sovereignty. It also encompasses a belief in China's greatness as a nation, a greatness which has not been adequately recognized, and a preoccupation with making China powerful and prosperous, and able to hold up its head proudly.[23]

Evidence to support leaders' preoccupations with such concerns is readily available in the context of the four major decisions referred to above. It is widely accepted that Mao dominated the decision-making process until just before his death in 1976. From the end of the decade, Deng Xiaoping became the paramount leader to whom all major decisions were referred. Thus their world-views, in particular, are important in reaching an understanding of the decisions that provide the focus for this chapter.

Leaning to One Side

With the liberal perspective as a starting point, the decision to 'lean to one side' and form an alliance with Moscow appears to have been driven by rather different impulses from those underpinning realist explanations. Mao's voice was undoubtedly the dominant one in the decision, and his approach to the matter betrayed his preoccupation with internal subversion. He was equally concerned with the opportunities external enemies might find to link up with domestic opponents in order to subvert socialism in China as Mao had defined it.[24] In 1949 the Chairman apparently believed that the progress of the domestic revolution—that is, the undermining of those who ranged between doubters of the faith and the 'counter-revolutionaries'—depended on there being a decisive break with the West. Mao wanted to 'open a new stove' and 'sweep the house clean before entertaining guests'; that is, to remove all vestiges of the imperialist past before establishing new sets of diplomatic relationships on the basis of equality.[25] However, sweeping the house clean was made more difficult because of the presence in China of those who had 'illusions about the United States . . . They are easily duped by the honeyed words of the US imperialists, as though these imperialists would deal with People's China on the basis of equality and mutual benefit without a stern, long struggle . . . They are the supporters of what [US Secretary of State] Acheson calls "democratic individualism"' which provided the United States with a 'flimsy social base in China'.[26] Whereas others in China apparently favoured a more independent stance in world politics, Mao deemed 'leaning to one side' imperative in order to break this bond between 'Chinese doubters' and 'US imperialists'. The explicit link with Moscow via the alliance, for its part, symbolized a crucial severance of connections with the imperialists, and gave a guarantee of a new status as socialist ally. It also undermined the position of those within China who remained distrustful of Communist rule.

Additionally, the tie to Moscow was perceived as critical to maintaining the momentum of the revolution. It afforded China access to material assistance and guaranteed diplomatic recognition at a time when the Chinese leadership was convinced that the United States and other Western countries would not move swiftly to offer such recognition.[27] On this point the liberal perspective, like realism, does identify a US threat, but the nature of the threat Washington was seen to pose went beyond a fear of military attack.

The Sino-Soviet Split

The 1950s became known as the 'honeymoon' period in Sino-Soviet relations, when ties seemingly were fully cemented and ostensibly were deemed mutually beneficial. Nevertheless, the new start that the relationship with Moscow had afforded carried within it the seeds of the eventual foundering of the Sino-Soviet alliance and of the decision to set out on the road of a self-reliant autonomous actor in world politics.

From the mid-1950s, with the rise in Beijing's international status, the stabilization of its economy, and the dynamic progress of its revolution, Mao had begun to question the appropriateness of the Soviet developmental model that

China had adopted so wholeheartedly from the early part of the decade. The Soviet presence had become all-pervasive: many advisers were in the central ministries, Soviet blueprints and planning ideas were dominant, and its military and strategic doctrines were embraced. One effect of this presence was to undermine any sense of the value of the Chinese Communists' own past experience. However, Mao's concerns were not simply that agriculture and labour-intensive measures were being neglected in favour of capital-intensive heavy industry, or that aspects of 'people's war' were being denigrated; his fear was that the close links with Moscow were perpetuating a 'dependence mentality' in China and providing opportunities for the Soviet leadership to penetrate the domestic polity. As one author has argued, Mao 'came to believe that close alliance with the Soviet Union carried with it three dangers: psychological dependence, the importation of harmful ideas, and Soviet political influence on the domestic political process within China'.[28] Whereas other Chinese leaders, such as the defence minister, Peng Dehuai, believed the link with Moscow to be beneficial to attempts to make the People's Liberation Army a professional fighting force, Mao was suspicious that such ties provided Moscow with opportunities for penetration. In other words, from this perspective, the growing strain in relations had less to do with Soviet neglect of China's foreign policy interests (although that certainly was a source of irritation and concern), and more to do with the sense that China since 1950 had leant too far towards Moscow, exposing itself to unacceptable levels of interference.

Evidence that Mao had begun to interpret the closeness in relations as verging on Soviet control and interference came swiftly in the period 1958–60. As noted earlier, in 1957 Moscow and Beijing had signed a technical accord in which Khrushchev had agreed to supply vital information to aid the Chinese manufacture of nuclear weapons. By 1958 Moscow was signalling that, rather than China engaging in the expense of obtaining its own independent nuclear capability, it would be far better to rely on the Soviet nuclear umbrella, an argument the Chinese swiftly rejected.[29]

Moscow also received short shrift when it attempted to bind Beijing more tightly to it in the conventional military field. In April 1958 the Soviet defence minister wrote to his Chinese counterpart suggesting joint construction of a long-wave radio transmission centre and a radio receiving centre for long-range communications designed for commanding Soviet submarines in the Pacific. In the Soviet view, Moscow and Beijing would construct this station jointly, but Moscow would bear all the costs and would then allow joint use of the facilities. Three months later, the Soviet Union further suggested building a joint submarine fleet. Instead of seeing both these offers as tangible evidence of the benefits of the Sino-Soviet alliance, China, primarily because of its concerns about threats to its autonomy, chose to interpret them as part of Moscow's attempt to limit

Beijing's independence of action. With respect to the radio station, the Chinese counter-proposed that they would bear the construction costs and be the ones to offer joint use of the facilities. Similarly, development of a Chinese navy was much to be preferred to the idea of a joint submarine fleet. As Mao remarked to the Soviet ambassador: ' "You may label me as a nationalist".' Mao went on: ' "In that case, I will reciprocate by saying that you have extended Russian nationalism to China's coastline [sic]". '[30]

Fear of subversion from within and infection from what came in 1962 to be termed a revisionist Soviet Union became a major preoccupation in Maoist thinking over the next few years. Mao, having institutionalized the relationship with the Soviet Union, particularly between 1953 and 1957, came to see Moscow rather than Washington as the prime subversive force. In 1961 and 1962, whereas other Chinese leaders were calling for the amelioration of relations with Moscow and a concentration internally on recovering from the disastrous effects of Great Leap Forward policies, Mao saw this as further evidence that the Soviet Union had linked up with those in China seeking to subvert his version of socialism.[31] From this perspective, the Great Proletarian Cultural Revolution, which began in earnest in 1966, can be understood primarily as a desire to root out 'Khrushchev-style revisionism' in China. More broadly, it was a movement to purify the revolution from within and to bring forth a generation of revolutionary successors worthy of the Long March leadership. Despite its significance in Chinese social history, and its foreign policy implications, it is ignored in the realist analysis of China's international behaviour. During this period China faced a hostile Soviet presence on its northern border and a hostile US presence in the south as the United States stepped up its involvement in Vietnam. At the same time Beijing withdrew all but one of its ambassadors from abroad, and its behaviour served to alienate a number of its traditional Third World supporters.

Rapprochement with the United States

The Sino-Soviet border war of 1969 represented a new form of Soviet threat and penetration to be added to earlier attempts at political interference. Chinese leaders moved to bring the worst excesses of the Cultural Revolution to a close, and to return its ambassadors to their postings abroad. They also took the revolutionary decision to improve relations with the United States. Yet Beijing's choice of movement towards Washington in order to cope with this new level of threat was still controversial: it was subject to the same type of analysis (especially by Mao's designated successor, Lin Biao, and Mao's wife, Jiang Qing) as that operating against Moscow. For such 'radicals' or 'ultra-leftists' the primary concern was not the Soviet Union as military opponent, but remained domestic subversion and the need to retain 'revolutionary purity', resting on the sustained belief (closely identified in the past with Mao) that domestic enemies would take opportunities to link up with foreign foes. Such beliefs dictated that China should continue to keep all foreign contacts to a minimum. For others within the leadership, however, sometimes referred to as the 'moderates', the primary focus had become the direct military threat that Moscow now posed to a politically and economically weakened China.[32] As a result of US defeats in Vietnam, Washington could now be seen as a secondary enemy, its imperialist presence in East Asia declining. In these circumstances, a temporary alliance with it against a more aggressive Soviet Union seemed prudent.

The divisions between these two groups in the Chinese leadership were temporarily resolved when Mao himself threw his weight behind 'moderates' who argued for the need to seek a rapprochement with the United States. The realists seem vindicated, therefore, when they identify Moscow's military actions and China's security needs as determining the shift towards Washington. However, if we approach this topic from the point of view of the leadership's 'world-view', or its 'informal ideology', then security once again becomes a more complex concept. The Soviet intervention in Czechoslovakia and Brezhnev's enunciation of the doctrine of 'limited sovereignty' followed closely by the Sino-Soviet border conflict, raised the spectre that the Brezhnev Doctrine might itself be used to justify interference in China's domestic affairs. The fighting on the border was one part of a more widespread threat seen as emanating from the Soviet Union.

Moreover, the timing of the Sino-US rapprochement was dictated not so much by the Sino-Soviet border war—although that helped to support the position of the 'moderates'—but crucially by events in China itself (and in the United States). For the Chinese leadership, it was imperative to resolve the internal debate over which of the superpowers represented the primary threat to the Chinese regime. It was valuable for the domestic victors in this struggle to be able to demonstrate that the US administration under President Nixon had come to accept China as a permanent fixture in the global system, and to recognize that the United States could not prevail in Vietnam and that its past policy towards China had been a failure. Various US administration statements between 1969 and 1971 provided China with the evidence to confirm these points. It was also helpful to the further advancement of relations when Nixon in July 1971 described China as potentially one of the five great economic powers in a multipolar world order.[33] The United States had come to accept that it should recognize China on the basis of the five principles of peaceful coexistence—principles that the Indian and Chinese Prime Ministers first elaborated in the mid-1950s—with their emphasis on mutuality, equality, and non-interference. Washington no longer challenged the claim that Taiwan was a part of China, or the argument that the PRC should represent China in the United Nations.[34] At last, China's status as an independent socialist state had been accepted by the leading state in the international system. Once such terms had been clarified, the 1972 Nixon summit with Mao and Zhou could go ahead.

An Independent Foreign Policy

With Mao's death in 1976 and the subsequent overthrow of the radical faction headed by the so-called 'gang of four', the concern about infection from outside forces diminished, but it was never entirely eradicated, as Deng Xiaoping was soon to discover. Deng, often described as more pragmatic than Mao, and having as his primary goal the economic modernization of China, finally consolidated his hold on power in 1978. Immediately he attempted to embark on a new economic programme that would deliver rapid economic growth, loyalty to the post-Mao regime, and protection against the Soviet Union in order to allow concentration on domestic priorities. Deng's opening to the West was startling in its comprehensiveness. It comprised not just the 1979 normalization of relations with the United States, and vastly increased foreign trade and investment, but also in 1980 the related entry into the keystone (and previously reviled) economic institutions such as the IMF and World Bank. Nevertheless, concerns about the political–cultural impact that the spread of foreign ideas and influences were having frequently resurfaced.

In December 1980, for example, a central work conference decided inter alia to adopt measures to curb the spread of foreign ideas and to cancel or reduce the scope of certain major projects that required substantial foreign involvement. The conference also took a much harder line on the issue of arms sales to Taiwan, a matter that involved only Western states, especially the United States. In February 1982 another work conference tried to find a balance between the needs of the reform policy and the 'ideological contamination' that foreign, especially Western, contacts brought in their wake, while maintaining the tough stance on Taiwan.[35]

From this perspective, therefore, the 'independent foreign policy' elaborated by Chinese leaders in the summer and autumn of 1982 comes to be explained less by any shift in the global balance of power in Washington's favour and more as a response to the internal controversies surrounding the economic modernization policy and concern about the 'spiritual pollution' that could come with too close a relationship with the United States. Moreover, whereas Reagan was threatening to undertake a more aggressive and interventionist policy in the Third World, and especially with respect to the remaining Marxist regimes, Leonid Brezhnev, for the first time since the Cultural Revolution, acknowledged that China as a socialist country had no reason to feel threatened by his 'doctrine of limited sovereignty' with its interventionist overtones. Neither did Moscow pose any challenge to Beijing's assertion that Taiwan was a part of China.[36] Thus the 'independent foreign policy' represented for Deng and his supporters an important means of striking a compromise with those in the leadership who had doubts about the wisdom of his reform policy. More broadly, with its emphasis on independence, it helped legitimize Deng's position and the reform effort that remained his central objective. Hence, once again, thoughts about how best to protect regime security and to reduce opportunities for domestic subversion were central elements in the decision-making process. From such concerns flowed the Chinese decision to move towards a more nearly equidistant position between the two superpowers. China began to improve its relationship with the Soviet Union, a clear and realizable goal once Beijing had formally articulated its 'independent foreign policy'.

12.3. Conclusion

It is not unusual to find the realist and liberal approaches to Chinese foreign policy merged into one explanation. Foreign policy analysis models similarly encourage this conflation of external and internal influences as a solution to the multicausal nature of any explanation. However, by exposing each of these approaches in an explicit way we can be more receptive to the causal hierarchies that are at work for particular authors, and which evidence is deemed of primary significance.

For realists, it is the outcomes themselves that provide the starting-point for the explanation—whether that is the outcome of the Sino-Soviet alliance, the Sino-American rapprochement, or some other major development in policy. Thus, realists view developments in the external environment as being of critical importance. Moreover, they have identified the primary interest of the state in question to be the maintenance of national security. The characteristics of that state—its historical development and experiences, and the interpretation of those experiences by policy élites—are regarded as neither especially significant nor perhaps knowable with any degree of accuracy. As Waltz has put it in justification of this approach, structural realism tells us 'a small number of big and important things'.[37]

However, examination of these same events from the liberal perspective suggests that realism might give us parsimony at the expense of accuracy. Perspectives that focus on domestic factors as the primary causal explanation (difficult though domestic influence might be to gauge in evidential terms, especially in the case of a closed society such as China) point us in the direction of a polity that is strongly influenced by its own historical experience, certainly conditioned by the external system of which it is a part but in no sense determined by it. For those who give primacy to domestic factors, outcomes are less central than the policy formulation process and the way in which needs are interpreted by particular decision-makers. Where realism assumes the concept of national interest to be unproblematic, liberalism points to the complex strands that might contribute to the construction of interests. Where realism defines security straightforwardly in terms of external military threats, liberalism suggests the need to construct a definition of security that emerges from a particular historical–cultural setting as mediated by élites. In consequence, such a definition of security might change (albeit slowly) over time. The liberal perspective thus celebrates not similarity but variety, even uniqueness, in the behaviour of states.

Realism has been described as a 'useful first cut', before the need to move on to more detailed explanations,[38] and there will be times when the 'first cut' explanation that realism offers will appear as a relatively unproblematic starting-point. In the case of China, it is clear that a realist perspective has provided a part of the explanation, and that it is possible to weave the realist definition of security into the world-view that has been in operation for Chinese leaders. Nevertheless, the explanation of China's changing alignments that it offers is only a partial one: it has missed the richness of China's own experience, and of its leaders' interpretations of their environment.

Chronology

	Domestic	International
1949		Chinese leaders in Moscow in June and again in December
June 1949	Mao makes 'lean to one side' speech on eve of June visit	
1 Oct. 1949	Formal establishment of PRC	
14 Feb. 1950		Signature of Sino-Soviet Treaty of Alliance
June 1950– July 1953		Korean War
June 1950		US stations Seventh Fleet in Taiwan Straits
Oct. 1950		China enters Korean War
1952	China embarks on first five-year plan	
1954		US signs mutual defence treaty with Taiwan

	Domestic	International
1954–5		First Taiwan Straits crisis
1955		Geneva superpower summit
1957		Signature of Sino-Soviet New Defence Technical Accord
		US deploys Matador missiles on island of Taiwan
	Mao begins to criticize post-Stalin leadership	
		Soviets test-fire missile and launch satellite
1958	China launches Great Leap Forward Economic Programme	
		Second Taiwan Straits crisis
		USSR suggests China rely on its nuclear umbrella, and offers various joint military facilities
1959		Khrushchev reneges on agreement to supply sample atomic bomb; cautions China to be more conciliatory over Taiwan
1959–61	Failure of Great Leap leads to large-scale famine in countryside	
		Sino-Soviet polemics intensify
1962	Mao describes Soviets as revisionists	
		Sino-Indian border war; China views Soviet actions as partial to India
		Cuban Missile Crisis helps accelerate superpower detente
1963		Signature of the Partial Test Ban Treaty between US, UK, and USSR. Sino-Soviet polemics now out in the open
1965		US steps up scale of involvement in Vietnam
1966	Cultural Revolution begins in China	
		Numbers of Soviet troops on Chinese border begin to increase
	China recalls all but one of its ambassadors from abroad	
1968		Soviet and Warsaw Pact forces intervene in Czechoslovakia
	Most violent phase of Cultural Revolution brought to a close	

	Domestic	International
1969		Enunciation of Brezhnev doctrine; Sino-Soviet border war: USSR tests US reaction to possible Soviet strike at Chinese nuclear installations; USA begins to wind down troop presence in Vietnam
1971		Kissinger in China, July and October; China enters UN
	Lin Biao attempts coup and dies in air crash while trying to escape	
1972		Nixon in China and signs Shanghai Communiqué sealing rapprochement
1974	Zhou Enlai comes under indirect attack for his search for 'white friends', 'big friends', 'wealthy friends'	
1976	Death of Zhou and Mao	
1978	Deng consolidates position as paramount leader; promotes economic reform policies more vigorously	
1979		Diplomatic relations established between China and US
1980		China enters IMF and World Bank
	Central work conference tries to scale back foreign presence in China	
1981		Reagan's defence build-up reported in great detail in China
1982	Central work conference held in attempt to control spread of foreign ideas while maintaining reform programme	
		China's independent foreign policy announced; Brezhnev's conciliatory speech at Tashkent

Notes

1. See e.g. Steven I. Levine, 'Perception and Ideology in Chinese Foreign Policy', in Thomas W. Robinson and David Shambaugh (eds.), *Chinese Foreign Policy: Theory and Practice* (Oxford, 1994), 36; Samuel S. Kim, 'China as a Regional Power', *Current*

History, 91/566 (Sept. 1992), 247–8; Harry Harding, 'China's Changing Roles in the Contemporary World', in H. Harding (ed.), *China's Foreign Relations in the 1980s* (New Haven, 1984).

2. A recent attempt to fill the 'longstanding gap between the field of international relations studies and those who, schooled in the area studies tradition, study Chinese foreign policy' is the volume edited by Robinson and Shambaugh, *Chinese Foreign Policy*.

3. The phrase 'self-reliant autonomous international actor' is taken from Michael B. Yahuda, *China's Role in World Affairs* (London, 1978).

4. For one explanation of the 'independent foreign policy' see Carol Lee Hamrin, 'China Reassesses the Superpowers', *Pacific Affairs*, 56/2 (Summer 1983).

5. The central texts are Hans Morgenthau, *Politics among Nations* (New York, 1948), and Kenneth N. Waltz, *Theory of International Politics* (Reading, Mass., 1979).

6. Stephen Walt, *The Origins of Alliances* (Ithaca, NY, 1986), vi.

7. Chen Jian, 'The Sino-Soviet Alliance and China's Entry into the Korean War', Cold War International History Project, working paper no. 1 (Washington, 1992), 14.

8. The published text of the 1950 treaty can be found in a number of places including Raymond L. Garthoff (ed.), *Sino-Soviet Military Relations* (New York, 1966), 203–5 and Xue Mouhong and Pei Jianzhang (eds.), *Diplomacy of Contemporary China* (Hong Kong, 1990), 491–3. The wording quoted here is taken from the latter text. Chinese sources claim that it was at their insistence that the phrase 'all means at its disposal' was inserted. See excerpts from Wu Xiuquan's memoirs in *Beijing Review*, 26/47 (21 Nov. 1983), 18.

9. Details of the equipment transfer are contained in Zhai Zhihai and Hao Yufan, 'China's Decision to Enter the Korean War: History Revisited', *China Quarterly*, 121 (March 1990), 111–12; Russian air activity is detailed in Jon Halliday, 'Air Operations in Korea: The Soviet Side of the Story', in William J. Williams (ed.), *A Revolutionary War: Korea and the Transformation of the Postwar World* (Chicago, 1993).

10. John Wilson Lewis and Xue Litai, *China Builds the Bomb* (Stanford, Calif., 1988), 40–1, 62.

11. Kenneth Lieberthal, 'Domestic Politics and Foreign Policy', in Harding (ed.), *China's Foreign Relations in the 1980s*, 48.

12. J. P. D. Dunbabin, *The Cold War: the Great Powers and their Allies* (London, 1994), 144–9.

13. Lewis and Xue, *China Builds the Bomb*, 64–5; Gordon H. Chang, *Friends and Enemies: The United States, China, and the Soviet Union, 1948–1972* (Stanford, Calif., 1990), esp. chs. 6–8.

14. For a useful compilation of some of the central arguments and documents that make up these polemics see John Gittings, *Survey of the Sino-Soviet Dispute* (Oxford, 1968).

15. Chang, *Friends and Enemies*, 185.

16. Lowell Dittmer, *Sino-Soviet Normalization and its International Implications, 1945–1990* (Seattle, 1992), 188–91.

17. William T. Tow, *Encountering the Dominant Player: US Extended Deterrence Strategy in the Asia-Pacific* (New York, 1991), 213.

18. For a discussion of many of these elements see Banning N. Garrett and Bonnie S. Glaser, 'From Nixon to Reagan: China's Changing Role in American Strategy',

in Kenneth Oye et. al., *Eagle Resurgent? The Reagan Era in American Foreign Policy* (Boston, 1987).

19. Harry Harding, *A Fragile Relationship: The United States and China Since 1972* (Washington, 1992), 121–3.
20. *Beijing Review*, 25/37 (13 Sept. 1982), 29.
21. See e.g. Levine, 'Perception and Ideology in Chinese Foreign Policy', and Carol Lee Hamrin, 'Elite Politics and the Development of China's Foreign Relations' in Robinson and Shambaugh (eds.), *Chinese Foreign Policy*.
22. Levine, 'Perception and Ideology', 34.
23. Ibid. 43–4; Hamrin, 'Elite Politics', 80; David Shambaugh, 'Growing Strong: China's Challenge to Asian Security', *Survival*, 36/2 (Summer 1994).
24. The work of Stuart Schram can usefully be consulted by those interested in coming to grips with the complexities in Mao's thinking.
25. Xu Xin, 'Changing Chinese Security Perceptions', North Pacific Cooperative Security Dialogue, working paper no. 27, April 1993, 3.
26. Mao Zedong, 'Cast Away Illusions, Prepare for Struggle', *Selected Works*, iv (Beijing, 1969), 427.
27. Chen, 'The Sino-Soviet Alliance', 10–11.
28. Goldstein, 'Sino-Soviet Relations', 240–1.
29. Lewis and Xue, *China Builds the Bomb*, esp. ch. 3; Alice Langley Hsieh, 'The Sino-Soviet Nuclear Dialogue: 1963', in Garthoff (ed.), *Sino-Soviet Military Relations*, esp. 160.
30. Xue and Pei (eds.), *Diplomacy of Contemporary China*, 139–42.
31. For a discussion that distinguishes sharply between Mao's concerns about state sovereignty and his greater fear of psychological dependence on the Soviet Union see Steven M. Goldstein, 'Nationalism and Internationalism: Sino-Soviet Relations', in Robinson and Shambaugh (eds.), *Chinese Foreign Policy*. Yahuda in *China's Role*, ch. 6, discusses some leaders' preferences for a modified link with the Soviet Union at a time of vulnerability.
32. See e.g. Thomas Gottlieb, *Chinese Foreign Policy Factionalism and the Origins of the Strategic Triangle* (Santa Monica, Calif., 1977). Such factionalism continued into the 1970s and beyond. For one fascinating analysis of the mid-1970s see Kenneth Lieberthal, 'The Foreign Policy Debate in Peking as Seen through Allegorical Articles, 1973–76', *China Quarterly*, 71 (Sept. 1977).
33. Speech given by President Nixon to mid-western news media executives, 6 July 1971. Excerpts quoted in *China: US Policy Since 1945*, Congressional Quarterly Inc. (Washington, 1980), 322. That this statement was seen as significant by Chinese leaders is suggested in Henry Kissinger's memoirs: *White House Years* (Boston, 1979), 748–9. For discussion of some of the earlier statements see ibid. 179–92.
34. The Shanghai Communiqué can be read in Harding, *A Fragile Relationship*, 373–7. Reference to the five principles of peaceful coexistence is made at 375. Washington did make a doomed attempt to prevent Taiwan's expulsion from the UN and to support membership for both Chinas. See Rosemary Foot, *The Practice of Power: US Relations with China since 1949* (Oxford, 1995), ch. 2.

35. Kenneth Lieberthal, 'Domestic Politics and Foreign Policy', in Harding (ed.), *China's Foreign Relations*, 64–5.
36. Harding, *A Fragile Relationship*, 121.
37. Kenneth N. Waltz, 'Reflections on *Theory of International Politics*: A Response to My Critics', in Robert O. Keohane (ed.), *Neorealism and its Critics* (New York, 1986), 329.
38. G. John Ikenberry, David A. Lake, and Michael Mastanduno, *The State and American Foreign Economic Policy* (Ithaca, NY, 1988), 5. See also F. Zakaria, 'Realism and Domestic Politics: A Review Essay', *International Security*, 17 (Summer 1992).

Further Reading

GARVER, JOHN W., *Foreign Relations of the People's Republic of China* (Englewood Cliffs, NJ, 1993). A comprehensive textbook that synthesizes the latest scholarship and recent primary material on China's foreign relations.

HARDING, HARRY (ed.), *China's Foreign Relations in the 1980s* (New Haven, 1984). An integrated set of high-quality essays that elaborate the wider context in which to understand China's foreign policy.

KIM, SAMUEL S. (ed.), *China and the World: Chinese Foreign Relations in the Post-Cold War Era* (Boulder, Colo., 1994). A useful compilation of essays that, through an analysis of selected issues, focuses on how China relates to the outside world.

ROBINSON, THOMAS W., and SHAMBAUGH, DAVID (eds.), *Chinese Foreign Policy: Theory and Practice* (Oxford, 1994). One of the best collections of essays available, which makes an explicit attempt to assess domestic and external sources of Chinese foreign policy.

YAHUDA, MICHAEL B., *China's Role in World Affairs* (London, 1978). This valuable text approaches the subject from the perspective of the Chinese leadership and its articulation of China's place in the world.

III *International Institutions*

CHAPTER THIRTEEN

THE EUROPEAN UNION IN THE 1990s: REASSESSING THE BASES OF INTEGRATION

Paul Taylor

Theorizing about society implies a claim to understand future patterns of human interaction on the basis of a vision of the present: when we say that we wish to understand the system, and that theorizing helps us to do this, we are really claiming an understanding of what the system will do in the future. One problem of theorizing, however, is that the future has always surprised us. We erect our momentary deductions into claims about a timeless reality, but even the most ambitious theory is paradoxically bound to its own time.

When we look back over the history of the European Community we need, therefore, to deal with three kinds of understanding.[1] First is our understanding of the development of the Community in empirical terms, judged from the current perspective: its history. Second is the various theories about the Community in the various stages of its development: what contemporary students thought the reality to be. And third is a current evaluation of those ways of understanding in the light of its history: we need to evaluate the timelessness of the claims, and inevitably propose new theories.

13.1. Nature of the Reaction against Integration

Prior to 1991 federalists could still find evidence to justify their hope that there would be a complete Union of Europe, while at the other extreme hardline

Parts of this chapter are updated and modified versions of material from the author's *International Organization in the Modern World* (London, 1993).

intergovernmentalists asserted that the Community was a group of states, with relationships like those between any other members of international society. In this chapter it will be shown that there are other possibilities; among these, a particular final form of the Community can be identified for the first time in the 1990s. The Maastricht Treaty of 1991 narrowed the options, and in particular Article 3(b) headed off, for the time being, any further trend to a more centralized form of federalism. Article 3(b) enshrined 'subsidiarity':

In areas which do not fall within its exclusive competence, the Community shall take action, in accordance with the principle of subsidiarity, only if, and in so far as, the objectives of the proposed action cannot be sufficiently achieved by the Member States and can, therefore, by reason of the scale or effects of the proposed action, be better achieved by the Community.

Any action by the Community shall not go beyond what is necessary to achieve the objectives of this Treaty.

Subsidiarity marked the reaching of a new plateau in the Community's evolution in the first years of the 1990s. A new phase of integration, followed by a period of consolidation, had occurred on at least two earlier occasions, and indeed can be said to be a feature of the historical process of regional international integration in Western Europe. In 1965 a period of *lourdeur* followed crisis, and this occurred again in the late 1970s, as in the 1990s, after a period of enthusiasm.[2] The achievement of further integration has been followed by a phase of adjustment to the new circumstances on the part of the state. This also implies that the state and the collectivity can coexist. It further raises the possibility that they may develop a symbiotic relationship with each other, which is discussed below.

What explains the appearance of the hesitations which led to subsidiarity, with its implied challenge to federalist centralization? The Maastricht Treaty is an illustration not so much of spillover as of overspill from the period of integrative momentum which culminated in the Single European Act in 1986 and led on to the completion of the 1992 single market process. But well before this had happened a range of doubts and difficulties appeared. These took a different form and appeared in a different mix in the various member states of the Community.

There was generally a certain ennui, not to mention disillusion, with the political process in member countries, especially in Britain, France, Germany, and, as always, Italy. There was an impatience with national governments which was easily diverted, sometimes deliberately by national authorities, to a European level. This background contributed to the success of the anti-Europeans in stirring up popular interest, which was readily focused on the evidence of inefficiency and waste at the European level. This may be linked with a realization that things had indeed got to the point at which bonds could be forged between the member states which would be hard to break. For a large number of British, for instance, Maastricht brought home that the choice of Europe was not just a tactical move, a living in sin, which could be revoked at will, but more of a marriage with long-term commitments.

The Maastricht Treaty provoked a vision of stark alternatives: state or Europe. Whether it really demanded a choice between the two was beside the point. The Community never prospered when it seemed to be involved in a zero-sum game with the nation-state, if governments pretended that they had to opt for one or the other. Progress was always more likely when it appeared possible, even by resort to some subterfuge, to link the strengthening of the Community with the well-being of the separate states as distinct entities: to present integration as a reinforcement of autonomy. But at a time of recession in the 1990s the alternative routes to recovery—common action through the Community, or competitive unilateralism in individual states—were more widely seen as mutually exclusive and destiny-laden. Clearly neither public nor élite attitudes could support the former without hesitation; there was, therefore, a hankering after competitive unilateralism.

But this was nothing unusual: the same thing had happened in the mid-1970s, when Europe could have solved the problems resulting from the weakness of the dollar by moving quickly to a joint response in the form of monetary union. The governments simply did not have the mutual confidence to make that jump. Nor did they in the early 1990s when it came to dealing with recession: measures for joint recovery could have been planned more energetically at the level of the Community, and the more rational technical option would have been to work together vigorously at that level.

Occasionally there were complaints from national governments about the difficulty of doing something in the face of opposition from Brussels. Frequently in Britain this was linked with the demonizing and externalizing of the Community institutions. There were Brussels directives which did not suit British interests—or the interests of some group or other—newly defined as sacred to 'our culture'.[3] Such judgements were made without regard to the fact that the national authorities had necessarily been involved in making the directives in the first place. Feelings of subjugation by external forces which were beyond their control chimed well with the anger of those who were the victims of the recession: unemployment was running at record levels, and even the principle of public welfare itself was sometimes under attack. And governments liked the implication, as they pulled the strings, that they were also merely puppets in thrall to Brussels.

There were also echoes of what Stanley Hoffman had called in the 1960s the 'logic of diversity'—the idea that the variety of ways in which the member states related to the outside world necessarily imposed limits upon integration among them.[4] The ending of the Cold War and the uniting of Germany sharpened a general awareness of a shadow of the past. Germany appeared in an older suit of clothes as a middle European power, and the Kohl government was seen to be struggling to find ways of reconciling a more active *Ostpolitik* and a continuing active *Westpolitik*. How would special German interests in Central Europe, and a more active engagement there, affect German commitment to the European Union? The British government began to wonder whether the special relationship with the USA was not preferable to involvement in a European foreign policy arrangement that had failed over the former Yugoslavia. Greece was clearly following its own line in the Balkans, and Italy was also pursuing its own interests in new frameworks in south-eastern Europe.

It was not just that the logic of diversity was visible: those who were cautious about Europe were ready to develop that diversity further. In Britain Euro-sceptics wanted to believe that Europe and America were alternatives. But this had never been the case: in April 1994 the US ambassador to the United Kingdom, about to retire from London, felt obliged to point out that 'if Britain's voice is less influential in Paris or Bonn, it is likely to be less influential in Washington.'[5] As President Kennedy had told Harold Macmillan thirty-four years earlier, so Ray Seitz told John Major in 1994: the special relationship with the United States and full participation in the European Union should not be seen as alternatives. The special relationship had a future if Britain was an active partner in Europe.

In the recession of the early 1990s there were frequent demands for separate and competing national efforts with regard to commercial opportunities in the Far East. It was argued that excessive concern with European markets had meant that opportunities outside had been lost. Relaunching integration in the early 1980s had been one response to the challenge from the Far East in high-technology products; but, ten years later, the limits of that collective response were visible. The markets in the Far East were now to be the target of intra-European competition about market shares. This could only be at the expense of the development of higher levels of trade interdependence among member states, which was one of the more powerful motors of integration. Thus economic take-off in the Far East now helped to limit the integration of the Community.

13.2. The Measures of Integration

The preceding discussion describes forces pushing to reverse the integration process in the mid-1990s. But there have also been factors working in favour of integration, which are if anything stronger than in 1957 and 1974. These are, first, aspects of popular attitudes; secondly, features of the workings of the institutions of the Union; thirdly, adjustments in the interests of governments and parties; fourthly, developments in the ways in which the civil servants of the member states engaged with each other and with officials in the Brussels institutions; fifthly, the emergence of an increasing range of common principles, norms, and rules in the economic and social arrangements of the member states—i.e. a Community regime had emerged; and sixthly, an increase in the level of economic interconnectedness and interdependence, not least, of course, in trade. Each of these developments will now be briefly considered.

Changes in attitudes are fundamental to the development of an integrated economic zone. They affect the mobility of labour. They are also crucial in developing the habit of not balancing the books of one participating state or territory with others: short-term outflows from one to the other are not significant when attitudes have moved towards the pattern found in a socio-psychological community. It is clear that this is not yet the case in the European Union in the mid-1990s, but that there has been some movement in that direction. Without a growing sense of community there could be no redistribution, while complaints by those in areas showing a net outflow of resources continue.

But there is indeed evidence that public attitudes support the transferring of competence to perform significant tasks, including the conduct of foreign policy, to the Union.[6] Public opinion on the Union, even in the more cautious states, is much more discriminating than the Euro-sceptics would have us believe. And there is also evidence of the appearance of a security community, as Karl Deutsch called it, among the older core states.[7] In other words, citizens of one country are more discriminating in their judgements of the subgroups forming the population of another; and they are more likely to reject military force as a way of settling differences with them. The Franco-German frontier is not now fortified. Neither are the frontiers separating the other member states.

The institutional arrangements of the European Union in the 1990s have been a considerable achievement. It was unlikely that the Community could have survived had the Treaty of Rome been a clearly federalist document. But it was sufficently adaptable for both integrationists and intergovernmentalists—federalists and statists—each of whom claimed to be its sole legitimate interpreter. By the mid-1990s the view has begun to emerge more forcefully that the sovereignty of states—the development of their sense of distinctive identity and the consolidation of national autonomy—is, paradoxically, capable of reconciliation with the strengthening of the Community. This is a recognition of the emerging duality in the Community's arrangements, which may be captured in the word 'symbiosis'.[8] These points are further discussed below.

The external interests of member states passed through a long period of adjustment and convergence. Governments increasingly agreed about the principles on which foreign policy should be based, and indeed by the mid-1980s there was evidence of the view that pursuing their separate interests, where these diverged, should not be taken to the point of endangering the partnership. This was evident in the wording of Title 3 of the Single European Act, called 'Provisions on European Cooperation in the Sphere of Foreign Policy'. In Article 30, 2(c), the governments agreed to 'ensure that common principles and objectives are gradually developed and defined' and that they would 'endeavour to avoid any action or position which impairs their effectivneess as a cohesive force in international relations or within international organizations'.[9]

Even the more cautious states had moved closer to Europe. In Britain Eurosceptics were afraid that in the elections to the European Parliament in June 1994 a massive swing against the Conservatives would be seen as a vote for Europe. Britain had focused increasingly upon Europe and away from the Commonwealth. Similarly, the Danes had gone through a period of adjustment of their policy of semi-attachment. The French also became less involved with the francophone zone and more with Europe, especially under President Mitterrand. This gradual consolidation of the underlying philosophy of collective action of the Community had taken a long time and involved a progressive adjustment of views about the world and related interests.

In the early 1990s the newly independent states of Eastern Europe could not possibly fully understand this adjustment. As yet these states did not share a similar view of the world, because they had not been in a context in which it had to be learned. The injunctions on behaviour which formed regimes could not be learned overnight. But the philosophy underpinning collective action among the member states was not all-encompassing: it was, as with attitudes, a matter of an increasing unity in diversity. In the mid-1990s, however, the logic of diversity has had to be balanced against a logic of convergence.

The growth of converging economic interests has coincided with changes in the working arrangements of national civil servants and in their attitudes towards transgovernmental cooperation. The evidence is overwhelmingly that there has indeed been a Europeanization of bureaucrats, though arguably this has been at the expense of democracy. Too many decisions have been taken without public scrutiny; despite the stipulations of the Maastricht Treaty, the work of the Council of Ministers has still been conducted largely in secret. This problem has not, however, been confined to the workings of the Community: it is a feature of modernized democracies in general, notwithstanding the delusions of potency among some elected representatives in countries such as Britain. As economic arrangements have become more technical, and more susceptible to international influences, so they have become more detached from the scrutiny of generalist members of elected assemblies. Brussels arrangements need to be more open and accountable, but they are illustrative of a more general problem.

There is also an increasing economic interconnectedness between the member states, shown in such developments as the increasing value of mutual trade and the increasing value of Community, compared with national, budgetary flows. About a quarter of the British budget flowed through the Union in 1993. In 1994 the EC budget amounted to a mere 1.27 per cent of Europe's GDP, but 80 per cent of this was administered through member states.[10] Inevitably, and despite the efforts of the more cautious states, this was matched by a greater weight of regulation at the Community level, and an increasing interpenetration of bureaucracies. The changes in the attitudes and behaviour of bureaucrats and politicians alike, and the increasing level of economic connections and transactions, justifies the conclusion that in terms of both formal rules and informal conventions of behaviour there has emerged by the mid-1990s a Community-wide system of governance. There is a Community regime.

13.3. The Theoretical Setting

In any discussion of the theories relevant to the European Union in the mid-1990s account has to be taken of the different purposes of theorizing. These may be to capture the main elements of the process of integration (What drives it forward?); or they may be concerned with the end-situation (Where is the process to end?). But this is frequently a question of emphasis. The main gradualist process theories have certainly returned to favour since the 1990s: neofunctionalism has again attracted the attention of scholars in North America and in Europe because of the drive to greater integration linked with the attempts to complete the single market after 1985.[11] But neofunctionalism is relatively unspecific about the end of the process. In contrast, federalism and consociationalism, discussed below, focus more on the end-situation, though they do have implications for the process itself. (For a summary of the major relevant theories see Table 13.1.)

Neofunctionalism focuses primarily upon the way in which decisions have been taken to further integration. It argues that figures in key institutional settings, especially senior civil servants, are subject to pressures which lead them to expand the scope of integration. The notion of 'spillover' is central in these pressures: problems in existing areas of cooperation could usually be solved, for technical reasons, by extending cooperation further. This logic is reinforced by the socialization of decision-makers resulting from their working together in common frameworks once the integration process started; from the new expectations of powerful lobbies; and from agenda-setting by charismatic personalities like Jacques Delors or President Mitterrand. Enough has been said to indicate that neofunctionalism is mainly about the process of integration rather than the

Table 13.1. Major theories relevant to international integration in Western Europe, 1945–1995

Theory	Main points
Major process theories	
Neofunctionalism	Focuses on integrative dynamics in decision-making system; is gradualist, i.e. stresses way in which a particular act of integration may have implications for further integration; stresses notion of spillover: that goals of a particular act of integration may only be achievable if there is further integration, because of technical links between areas of economic activity; integration tends to involve increasing numbers of areas, and to lead towards those of greater political sensitivity; stresses socialization of decision-makers: they respond to logic of spillover because of experience in transnational decision-making, i.e. coalitions develop of like-minded bureaucrats in different countries; integration also attracts the support of some interest groups
Functionalism	Gradualist but not greatly concerned with details of decision-making; stresses way in which integration may attract popular support if it is seen as beneficial; working together in common institutions helps to create political community at the popular level; within this community there is a working peace system: war is less likely because of functional cooperation; popular support presses for further integration and more common institutions, which lead to more popular support in the political community, and so on: this is the integrative dynamic; form follows function, i.e. every task should be approached at that level and in that manner which is most appropriate to that particular task
Federalism (see also below)	Stresses need to find a constitutional solution to problems of diversity; frequently puts great stress upon the constituent assembly, i.e. a forum of leading politicians who agree a division of powers between the higher level and the constituent parts in the constitution; integration can be achieved at a stroke: diversity in the constituent regions is not a fundamental problem, though it may pose a challenge to those charged with drawing up the constitution

Theories about the end-situation

Federalism (see also above)	The parts and the union are each sovereign in their allocated realm; the federal government is granted sovereignty: at a minimum it acts for the union in external relations; the normal mode of decision-making at the centre is by majority voting; there are constitutional checks and balances between the parts and the union; modern federations tend to encourage cross-cutting cleavages among the parts; the proportionate representation of the parts in the federal government is limited; there are extensive common arrangements for the provision of general benefits
Consociationalism	The parts have a high degree of autonomy; the autonomy of the parts is protected in the consociation; common arrangements are supported as ways of increasing the welfare of the parts and the collectivity; value is attached to the common arrangements as an independent variable which promotes the general interest; the common government is dominated by a cartel of élites; decisions in the cartel are based upon consensus: there is no majoritarianism; the parts are represented at the centre on a strictly proportionate basis; sovereignty is not transferred to the centre; élites seeek to protect the autonomy of the parts
Intergovernmentalism	In a hard version, the states are seen as maintaining primacy in the system unconditionally, and common arrangements are trivial; in a softer version, the states retain primacy and the common arrangements are seen as necessary in the modern world as instruments of state adaptation and survival; the common arrangements are very much a dependent variable, i.e. they exist to serve the state

outcome. However, at various stages in the process a particular outcome may emerge more clearly.

Different outcomes suggest different relationships between the state and the Community. At least five different kinds of such relationship are conceivable. The first is the traditional hard inter-governmental one, which sees the common arrangements as incidental by-products of the relations among states, carrying no threat to their continuing primacy. A second, softer intergovernmentalism sees the Community as involving a set of values which it might be prudent to acknowledge, and, indeed, for political convenience, to genuflect towards, as developments in the Community could conceivably threaten the states; this was arguably the case by the mid-1970s, as illustrated by the summit meeting at Paris in December 1974. At Paris the governments felt able to make concessions towards Europe—direct elections, European passports, etc.—because they felt sufficiently secure to do so, and, indeed, sought to strengthen their defences by setting up the European Council and strengthening the presidency.

In a third view, the developments in the Community are seen as essential to the survival of the state: they help the state to adjust to new circumstances in the modern world. This view, a modern version of the Grotian image of international society, is embodied in Alan Milward's claim that the European Union was merely another mechanism for rescuing the nation-state.[12] A fourth view is that the state and the Community have each acquired legitimacy: the arrangements and politics of the two levels have a degree of autonomy, and the two enjoy a symbiotic relationship with each other. Each has become essential to the survival of the other. In this arrangement states retain sovereignty. Finally, the federalist position sees the Community as being potentially the primary actor, and interprets developments at both levels in the light of this goal. Only in this case is sovereignty transferred to the new centre.

The task facing the student of integration in Europe is therefore to identify the changes in balance, both among the states and between them and the Community; and to focus exclusively on the nation-states is to miss the fundamental changes in the European balance. Although each period produced judgements at the time about likely outcomes of the integration process, there is a stronger sense in the mid-1990s that the form of the end-situation is more clearly visible. Previously that had not been the case, and whatever stage was reached it had always seemed, to enthusiasts and antagonists alike, that progress towards closer union could continue indefinitely. Indeed, the onus usually seemed to be on the sceptics to oppose rather than on the enthusiasts to promote.

Any version of an outcome must contain two elements: a view about the relationship between the states and the collectivity, and a view about the relationship among the states. Each of these views has to be compatible with the other. The former is concerned with vertical links, and the latter with horizontal ones. It seems to the present writer that the most appropriate image of the European Union in the mid-1990s, and one which best portrays its likely end-situation, combines the notions of symbiosis, concerning vertical links, and consociation, concerning primarily horizontal ones.

Consociationalism has been described by Lijphart as having four features, each of which, it is argued, is reflected in the European Union of the mid-1990s.[13] First there must be a number of groups which are in some sense insulated from each other, in that their interests and associations are more inwardly directed than overlapping with those of members of other groups in the same state. In other words, there are relatively few cross-cutting cleavages, and authority within that state is segmented in relation to interest groups. Secondly, the state is domin-ated by what Dahrendorf called a 'cartel of élites':[14] the political élites of the various segments are each involved in some way on a continuous basis in the process of decision-making, and decisions are the product of agreements and coalitions among the members of the cartel. No member of the cartel is placed in the ranks of the opposition in decision-making, as, for instance, in the event of defeat in an election, which would be the case with a majority system. Fur-ther, the cartel need not necessarily require that all actors be positively involved in the same way on all occasions.

The third feature of consociationalism is a logical extension of the cartel principle: it is that all the political élites have the right of veto over decisions. In other words, decisions require a consensus, at least within the segments, or, on some issues which are contentious, among the members of the cartel. Finally, there must be a law of proportionality, which means that the various segments of the population must have proportionate representation in the major institu-tions of the state, the bureaucracy, legal systems, and so on.

The features of consociationalism ensure that the rights and interests of the subordinate sections of society, as interpreted by or filtered through the members of the cartel of élites, are safeguarded. Indeed, political arrangements are so contrived that each minority is protected from the dictatorship of the whole. As will be seen, each of these features is observable in some form in the institutions and procedures of the European Union.

A central problem of consociation is the maintenance of stability. Indeed, the problem implies an irony which is more characteristic of international relations than of stable democracies: the need to generate enthusiasm for stability precisely because of the continuing threat of fragmentation. As Lijphart put it, 'The leaders of the rival subcultures may engage in competitive behaviour and thus further aggravate mutual tensions and political instability, but they may also make de-liberate efforts to counteract the immobilizing and unstabilizing effects of cultural fragmentation.'[15] The immanence of mutual tensions is revealed in the determin-ation of the segments' leaders to defend the separate interests of the groups in the common forum. Leaders of cartels are faced continuously with the dilemma of acting to preserve the general system while at the same time seeking to pro-tect and further the interests of the groups which they represent: again, as in the EU.

With regard to their own groups, élites must be able to rely on a high degree of homogeneity, and be capable of backing this up on occasion with techniques for the maintenance of internal discipline. The stability of the whole may require the discipline of the segments, even in ways which move towards the limit of what is acceptable—controls upon the press, limitations upon freedom of asso-ciation, fixing public appointments, and the like.

Consociationalism reinforces the search for the lowest common denominator, be it a limited consensus among élites or a common interest of segments. The theory underlines the potential for divergence between the interests of élites and the interests of publics. In contrast, the assumption behind federalism in its mainstream form is that the system will, over time, gradually strengthen the perception of the common interest at both the general and the élite level.

In the consociational model the leaders will be activist and politicized in their pursuit of interests in the cartel of élites. Politics will be a serious business as the stakes are high: there is no tendency towards depoliticization. In the federalist process of integration, however, there is an expectation of depoliticization as interests and politics become more homogeneous.

13.4. Consociationalism as a Way of Understanding the European Union

Consociationalism is useful in that it presents a conceivable outcome of the integration process which differs from those indicated by other theories. It highlights the point that integration in the sense of the strengthening of the regional functional systems may be perfectly compatible with continuing cleavages in the existing society of nations.

One reason for this is seen to be that members of the cartel of élites are likely to be faced with a dilemma: they will have an interest in increasing the size of the pie, and the share obtained by their own segment, while at the same time wishing to protect the distinctiveness of their segments in comparison with others, since those segments serve as each member's individual constituency and power base. The process of increasing the size of the total pie encourages the development of inter-segmental social and cultural links alongside the economic ones, which may eventually reduce each segment's viability. Integration may, therefore —apart from committing them to enlarging the pie—also generate in the élites an increasing anxiety about the implications of the strengthening of the horizontal links between the segments since that tends to weaken their constituencies. The status and authority of the members of the cartel are dependent upon their capacity to identify segmental interests and to present themselves as leaders and agents of a distinct, clearly defined community.

Consociationalism, therefore, highlights the politics of the relationship between leaders and led. The interests of leaders may well depart from those of the led during the process. British politics in the mid-1990s is all too redolent of this situation. Prime Minister John Major, because of the major divisions in his party, has attempted to steer a tortuous course between pursuing interests in Europe and power at home.

The theory suggests two ways in which the special interest of the élites may be pursued in the integration process. In the first, members of the cartel of élites make agreements together for their own purposes, even when these conflict with those of the segments which they nominally serve. This was the danger that was advertised by the left wing of the political spectrum in Britain and elsewhere: that European integration was essentially a bourgeois conspiracy of élites and big business, in alliance with governments, against the interests of the mass of the people.[16] In the second a particular élite seeks to use the context of the common arrangements to promote changes which suit the interests of its key supporters in its particular segment, so that its power within the segment is consolidated. In the 1990s the British government opposed the Commission's proposal to introduce a Social Charter into the EC to protect the interests of workers, some would say in order to make the Community a happy hunting ground for capital.[17] The British government opposed any hindrance to capital's exploiting differences in the cost of labour and the level of welfare provision in the various parts of the EC, even though this also meant keeping social security provisions for British workers at a lower level.

Two subthemes could be detected in the British government's position, both of which could be related to its anxiety about preserving its status in its own segment. First, a European Social Charter would enhance the cohesion of labour at the Community level, and therefore had to be resisted; secondly, reducing the level of social provision would enhance its authority in relation to a key group, namely business and industrial leaders. Consociationalism highlights the possible double effects of integration: it strengthens perceptions of the benefits of collective action, but also creates special incentives for élites to resist the development of cross-cutting cleavages.

The theory is also suggestive, however, about existing élites' attitudes towards minorities in the integrating system and the attitudes of the leaders of those minorities. The appearance of regional arrangements provides the leaders of dissenting minorities with a forum within which to push for increased specific returns and separate representation. The traditional theories of integration, functionalism and neofunctionalism, have no way of coping with this observable political fact.[18] Scots, Welsh, Basque, Irish, and even Catalan nationalists have all seen the Community as an opportunity for furthering their cause. Minorities have sought to consolidate direct contacts with the EU, whereas the existing élite cartel members have sought to limit such contacts. The British government, for example, has tended to oppose direct contacts between minorities and the EU, and this has certainly had implications for the perceptions of people in the non-English areas in Britain of themselves as forming distinct communities. The British government has also been reluctant to allow regions to choose their own delegates to the Assembly of Regions proposed in the Maastricht Treaty. Segmental autonomy must be preserved.

Consociationalism provides yet a further part of the explanation of the observed pattern of behaviour of the minorities in the European Community. The universal habit was for them to see the Community as the context in which they could obtain a greater level of independence and at the same time increase the level of specific returns to their groups. One might then expect successful integration to sharpen divisions between minorities and the dominant segments. In the mid-1990s the assertion of the principle of subsidiarity has contained a fundamental flaw from the point of view of those who want to use it to resist a further flow of competences to the Community from the national level. The principle seems to justify a flow of competences down to the local communities within the state. In Britain subsidiarity is not only a tool with which to restrain the power of Brussels, but has also offered support of the claims for autonomy made by the Scots, the Welsh, and the Northern Irish.

The process of decision-making at the centre of the system is also illuminated by the theory of consociationalism. The theory suggests that members of the élite cartel will insist on their right to veto and resist decision-taking on the basis of majorities. Decision-making would become more difficult because of the veto. At first sight the Single European Act and the Maastricht Treaty seem to be evidence of a trend towards majority voting, but in fact the states reserved the right, either explicitly in the Act or in terms of stated intentions, to veto anything which affected their vital interests. The Luxembourg Accord of 1966 which allowed the veto could still be invoked by a government that believes its vital interests are still at risk.[19]

Of course there is evidence to suggest that majority voting has been more frequently used after the amendments and that the Council's work has consequently been speeded up, but the underlying circumstances remain the same: states can veto what they do not like. The success of the French in insisting on the approval of the GATT agreement by consensus in the Council of Ministers at the end of the Uruguay Round of trade negotiations shows that a member state can still evade the formal arrangement of majority voting.

The members of the Council of Ministers and of the European Council do indeed behave like the members of an élite cartel in a consociational multiparty government, with enormously complex consensus-building and a marked tendency to express profound doubts about each other's intentions. Disagreements about policies tend to lead to the disparagement of others' motives at a very early stage: it is very usual for the complaint to be made that other states are not acting honourably in the Community, or are cheating in some way that would not happen at home. In the 1990s an example of this concerned the scandal of 'mad cow disease' in Britain. Protests by the French, the Germans, the Italians, and the Luxembourgeois were immediately treated in Britain as illustrations of the tendency of foreigners to cheat.[20]

The building of consensus in the Community tends to be dominated as much by a fear of being left out as by an enthusiasm for new benefits. As the consociational model suggests, the condition for retaining the common decision-making system is that the fear of fragmentation is greater than the fear of weakening segmental authority. Traditional functionalism or even neofunctionalism indicate the prospect of greater accord as integration proceeds; in contrast, consociationalism puts forward a more complicated arrangement which might be better described as one of confined dissent.

The implications of this for the central bureaucracy—the Commission—are also worth considering. Consociational theory sees the state apparatus as an umpire in the serious game of politics among the élites rather than as a promoter of any specific national ideology. Within an existing consociational state the bureaucracy is an umpire in that it must avoid attaching itself to the ideology of a particular segment. This was also true of the Commission of the European Communities, and this of course is not a particularly original point. But there is a more interesting development of this idea which is suggested by consociationalism. It is that integration pushes the central institution to adopt more frequently, and at an earlier stage of the decision-making process, the role of umpire, unless it has entered into an informal alliance with one or more member states. The task of presenting initiatives which reflect the general community interest is by no means eliminated, but the grand designs are more frequently suspected of being part of a conspiracy to promote the interests of one or more segments at the expense of the others. Initiatives tend to be compromised out of recognition. Members of the pro-European lobby held that this was the consequence of the close involvement of government representatives in decision-making at a very early stage in the formulation of policy by the Commission, as in the Committee of Permanent Representatives.[21] It is hard to see how this could be avoided in the light of the way the decision-making process has evolved over the years.

Consociationalism suggests, first, that pressures to enlarge the role of the Commission as umpire are increased rather than diminished as integration proceeds; and, secondly, that any escape from this dilemma is likely to be at the risk of appearing to favour some segments over others. As the stakes rise, so the members of the élite cartel become more careful to protect their interests and insist that the condition of movement is consensus.

A further insight from consociationalism concerns the staffing of the Commission. Whereas integration theory predicts an increasing preparedness to accept appointments to the central bureaucracy on the basis of ability, regardless of geographical or social distribution, the theory of consociationalism suggests an increasing determination to insist upon proportionality in the central institutions, and indeed an increasing tendency for particular élites to identify their nationals in those institutions as their representatives. In the late 1980s and 1990s the

British government took to making a careful count of the number of its nationals in the Commission and complaining if it judged that it was underrepresented.

Although formally the Commission is a supranational body, responsible for defining and promoting the interests of the collectivity, this is only half the truth. The other half is that the Commission is informally representative, in that its members are chosen by governments to promote positions of which they approve, and governments are likely to turn against Commissioners who fail to do this, as the British government did in the case of Lord Cockfield. Commissioners know that a careful line has be steered between watching out for the interests of the government of the home state and promoting the interests of the Community. Beneath the level of the Commissioners themselves, there are frequently glimpses of coalitions of nationals devoted to protecting interests sought in their home states. Consociationalism provides a useful explanation of why the collegiate principle in the Commission has weakened—dissenting members are now much more frequently identified than formerly—and state governments act as if Commissioners from their states were their representatives.

Conversely, the presidency is superficially an embodiment of the principle of intergovernmentalism: each member state, as a separate state, is placed in charge of the affairs of the Community once every six years (seven and a half years after the admission of Finland, Sweden, and Austria in January 1995). Yet states which have occupied the presidency have generally recognized that they cannot simply use this opportunity to pursue national interests: they also need to promote the interest of the collectivity. They become defenders of the Community and upholders of the interests of their own state, a duality of purpose which is partly the result of socialization—the consolidation of the regime's injunctions on behaviour—and partly the result of the rational calculation that to pursue national interests too blatantly would be counter-productive.

Such a duality is, however, a valuable—indeed, essential—aspect of the working of the Community's institutions in the 1990s. It represents a stable relationship between two necessary imperatives which serve the member states well. There is at one and the same time both integration and state-building, a twin-track process which is particularly evident in the new democracies of southern Europe but is in fact the case for all member states. This is a great achievement for the Community's institutions, and one which could be too easily thrown away with over-rapid expansion from the existing core.

13.5. Consociation and the Regional System

Traditional international relations theory suggests that one way to view Europe is simply as a segment of international society. In this perspective, Europe is seen as a regional grouping of states, each checking the other through a balance of power, and driven by the larger balances in international society, especially that which existed between the superpowers. However, we have seen in the preceding discussion that there is an alternative and more powerful theory with which to understand the dynamics of inter-state relations in Europe in the mid-1990s. This sees the European system of states as having a dual structure. States are held within a consociation, which is one element in the dual structure; this primarily stresses horizontal links between states. The other element in the dual structure is primarily concerned with vertical links, that is, between each state separately and the collectivity. The states are also held in a relationship which is characterized by symbiosis, with states/governments seeing an interest in promoting the Community, and the Community promoting the states. The latter dynamic clearly helps to underpin the autonomy of the segments in the consociation.

But symbiosis also implies a puzzle from the point of view of consociationalism: are the Community institutions about umpiring inter-state disputes, as is the case in consociation, or are they about promoting the interests of the collectivity, as is implied in symbiosis and, of course, gradualist theories of integration like neofunctionalism? The answer is very clear from the preceding discussion: the institutions of the Community, and the history of their development, are themselves likely to be characterized by two paradoxical characteristics. Integration continuously needs to be reconciled with autonomy; further steps towards integration help the state; the state continuously finds ways of protecting sovereignty as the circumstances in which sovereignty is exercised change; the Commission is both an umpire among states, and a promoter of integrative causes. So the Community is not a form of traditional international society, and it is argued here that it is a consociation.

Consociational theory has important implications for the development of international organization at the regional level because it points to the way in which the regional system could develop as a framework for cooperative activity without the implication that the governments' concern to protect their sovereignty, the equivalent of segmental autonomy within states, would be lessened. This is the theme of symbiosis between the participating segments and the collectivity, which is implicit in consociationalism. A concern with sovereignty is very evident in the European Community in the mid-1990s: there is paradoxically an assertion of separateness at the same time as a determined adhesion to the collectivity.

It is not difficult to find equivalents at the regional level of the calculations of the segments within the consociational states. There is the need to promote the common system in order to increase security in the face of both economic and military threats. This need underpins the drive to a single market, as well as the concern to strengthen a common defence, as revealed in the Maastricht

Treaty. There is also the realization that essential utilitarian/economic returns can only be gained within the common system. This is a point of great importance with regard to the emerging regional superpower, Germany: after unification in 1989 Germany's continuing dependence on the regional system was still evident. And within the system the traditional gradualist integration processes are visible. The neofunctionalist dynamics had certainly re-emerged in the drive towards the establishment of the single market by 1992, and later in the continuing pressures towards monetary union; but this has not in any way weakened the consociational image of the Community.

The political element of integration is probably more important than the economic one: once its scope reaches a certain level, states are pushed to accept some constraints in their struggle to promote their own interests by the fear of being marginalized in the common system. The possibility that a coalition could emerge within the cartel of élites whose members would pursue stronger arrangements among themselves to the exclusion of the reluctant partners is a powerful incentive to stay in the game. Hence although Mrs Thatcher may have behaved badly in the cartel of élites, she was determined to remain a member. This circumstance encouraged the French in their use of a particular diplomatic weapon against the British, which again reveals the character of the Community as a consociation. President Mitterrand was quite prepared to remind the British of the possibilities of setting up a two-tier Europe, with the British demoted to the lower tier, should they prove too unreasonable in the context, for instance, of the proposal for economic and monetary union.[22] This behaviour on both sides was as evident in the diplomacy concerning Mastricht in 1989–91 as it had been in that leading up to the Single European Act. On both occasions it was apparent that senior members of the British government, such as Hurd, Howe, Major, and Lawson, were fearful of being marginalized.[23] Both Lawson and Howe resigned at least in part over this issue.

This is not to deny that in a number of member countries there are groups which continue to use the language of federalism: this should not, however, be interpreted as meaning the subjugation of the nation-state to an overarching federal structure in which sovereignty would be transferred to a new centre. In September 1994 the dominant party in the ruling coalition in Germany, the CDU–CSU, proposed in a widely discussed policy paper that the next constitutional confererence on the Community's institutions in 1996 should 'strengthen the EU's capacity to act and make its structures and procedures more democratic and federal'. Indeed, it stated: 'This document must be oriented to the model of a "federal state" and to the principle of subsidiarity. This applies not only to the division of powers but also to the question of whether public authorities . . . should perform certain functions or should leave them to groups in society.'[24] A first reading might suggest that this was the same old theme: an advocacy of more powers for the centre. But it should be noted that subsidiarity was stressed, and that the words 'federal state' are in quotation marks. The claim is often made that subsidiarity is a German contribution, and that it reflects German national interest as well as coinciding with the interests of the German Länder in protecting their position *vis-à-vis* the federal government on EU matters. Elsewhere in the German document, with regard to the voting arrangements in the Council of Ministers, the dual character of the Union is recognized: 'Democratization means striking a better balance between the basic equality of all member states and the ratio of population size to number of Council votes.' The implication of this claim seems to be quite different from that understood by the Eurosceptics in Britain: here is a claim for more power for Germany as a state in the EU, not a recipe for a centralized federal Europe.

Nevertheless, the CDU–CSU document did explicitly repudiate the loose intergovernmental model which the British government advocated under the heading of 'Europe *à la carte*'. What was preferred was a Europe which was generally committed to the setting in place of a stronger structure for the joint management of common policies, always subject to the rule of subsidiarity, and now with the implication that there could be a final settlement on the range of such policies. If this were to be achieved, some states could temporarily move ahead of others—there could be a two-tier or even three-tier Europe, the latter becoming more appropriate as the membership was expanded beyond seventeen to include the states of Eastern Europe. These arrangements should be 'sanctioned and institutionalized in the union treaty or the new quasi-constitutional document' and any trend towards a Europe *à la carte* should be resisted.

The essential difference between the German model of a two- or three-speed Community and the British model was presented by John Major in a speech at Leiden University on 7 September 1994. The British view excluded the assumption of a general ambition to move to a coherent system of collective management subject to agreed reservations in respect of the principle of subsidiarity. Indeed, the irony in the diplomatic stance of the British was that in recommending Europe *à la carte*, and thereby encouraging the uncertainty of the ebb and flow of participation, according to governments' whims of the moment, they increased the risk that the Germans and the French would go ahead to initiate the setting-up of a core of more united states. If the British had taken the initiative in working for a permanent settlement regarding powers, procedures, and policies in 1996, which is now apparently on offer, they could more easily ensure both their own full participation and a package which would be acceptable and which could include a formal guarantee of sovereignty.

British diplomacy in the 1980s gave way to threats from France and Germany to move ahead: the British feared marginalization. In the 1990s they are impaled on the other horn of the same dilemma: in positively asserting the right to marginalization on all policies for all states, they have encouraged the more pro-Union among them actively to promote the creation of a core. This is the underlying flaw in British diplomacy regarding Europe in the mid-1990s.

Risks of federalist outcomes are often exaggerated.[25] Such fears arise from a misunderstanding of the nature of the legal and constitutional arrangements of the European Community. Some developments have indeed substantially affected the procedures of administration and legislation; furthermore, the need to agree rules in common with partners certainly places limitations upon the individual countries' ability to go it alone. But the practice of sovereignty has always involved a compromise with the level of interdependence which prevails at a particular time, or in a particular area. The fact is that all modern states are required to arrange their economic systems in cooperation with other states. In a wide range of areas, ranging from decisions about the safety of medicines to the acceptability of standards of civil liberties, states are subject to pressures from outside the state, and quite frequently these are strong enough to constrain the choice of national governments. The European Community may be seen as a special case of such constraints: what is changed is the wish of national legislatures and governments to do certain things rather than their legal or constitutional right or capacity to do them.

13.6. Conclusions

Modified intergovernmentalism, in the special form of consociationalism, is the most persuasive image of the European Union in the mid-1990s: it is a tightly managed community of states, among which the conventional conditions of sovereignty have been altered. National autonomy has become a means of participating in the common decision-making process, and much less an expression of separateness in the performance of specific tasks. But this also involves a paradox: the Community does not challenge the identity of the member states, but rather enhances that identity. The states become stronger through strengthening the collectivity. This perception has become inherent in the idea of the European Union by the mid-1990s, and is one of the Union's strengths.

It is remarkable that in Western Europe in the mid-1990s some of the oldest fundamental conditions of sovereignty have been weakened without this being seen as challenging sovereignty. In earlier centuries complete independence in the conduct of foreign policy and defence was regarded as fundamental to the idea of sovereignty. There is now an obligation to attempt to coordinate foreign policies at the Community level, and the first steps towards a common defence structure and policy have also been taken. It is striking that even in one of the more cautious states—Britain—55 per cent of the population have supported the proposition that the European Union should be responsible for foreign policy.[26] But these changes have taken place precisely at the point in the development of the European Union at which the member states' leaders and publics have been brought to place more explicit limits upon integration.

The obvious conclusion is that the limits of integration are a consequence of having gone too far with the federal project. More likely, however, reflecting the themes of this chapter, the post-Maastricht crisis is yet another example of the dialectic of the integration process: there is a symbiotic relationship between the growth of the Community and that of the nation-state. Any assertion of the Community is likely to be accompanied by a countervailing development of the nation-state.

Chronology: Development of the EC

Mar. 1947	Belgium, Luxembourg and the Netherlands agree to establish a customs union. Subsequently an economic union is established in October 1947 and a common customs tariff is introduced in January 1948
June 1947	George Marshall offers American aid for the economic recovery of Europe; 16 nations join the European Recovery Programme
Apr. 1948	Founding of OEEC by 16 states
Apr. 1949	Treaty establishing NATO signed in Washington by twelve states
May 1949	Statute of Council of Europe signed in Strasbourg by 10 states
Apr. 1951	European Coal and Steel Community (ECSC) Treaty signed in Paris by 6 states: Belgium, France, Germany, Italy, Luxembourg, the Netherlands
May 1952	European Defence Community (EDC) Treaty signed in Paris by the 6 ECSC states
Aug. 1954	French National Assembly rejects EDC Treaty
Oct. 1954	Western European Union (WEU) Treaty signed by the 6 ECSC states plus the UK
June 1955	Messina conference of the foreign ministers of the 6 ECSC states to discuss further European integration. Spaak Committee established to study ways in which a fresh advance towards the building of Europe could be achieved
Mar. 1957	The Treaties of Rome signed establishing the European Economic Community (EEC) and the European Atomic Energy Community (Euratom)

The author is grateful to Dr Howard Machin, Director of the European Institute at LSE, for permission to use this chronology.

Jan. 1958	EEC and Euratom come into operation
Jan. 1960	European Free Trade Association (EFTA) Convention signed at Stockholm by Austria, Denmark, Norway, Portugal, Sweden, Switzerland, UK. EFTA comes into force in May 1960
Dec. 1960	OECD Treaty signed in Paris. OECD replaces OEEC and includes Canada and USA
July/Aug. 1961	Ireland, Denmark, UK request negotiations with the Community
Jan. 1962	Basic features of Common Agricultural Policy (CAP) agreed
Jan. 1963	General de Gaulle announces his veto on UK membership; signing of Franco-German Treaty of Friendship and Cooperation
May 1964	GATT Kennedy Round of international tariff negotiations opens in Geneva; the Community states participate as a single delegation
Apr. 1965	Signing of Treaty establishing a Single Council and a Single Commission of the European Communities (the Merger Treaty)
July 1965	France begins boycott of Community institutions to register its opposition to various proposed supranational developments
Jan. 1966	Foreign Ministers agree to Luxembourg Compromise; normal processes resumed
May 1967	Denmark, Ireland, UK reapply for Community membership
July 1968	Customs Union completed; all internal customs duties and quotas removed and Common External Tariff established
July 1969	President Pompidou (who succeeds de Gaulle after his resignation in April) announces he does not oppose UK membership in principle
Dec. 1969	Hague summit agrees on a number of important matters: strengthening the Community institutions; enlargement; establishing an 'economic and monetary union by 1980; developing political cooperation (i.e. foreign policy)
June 1970	Community opens membership negotiations with Denmark, Ireland, Norway, UK
Jan. 1972	Negotiations between Community and four applicant countries concluded; signing of treaties of accession; majority in favour of enlargement in French referendum
Sept. 1972	Majority vote against Community accession in referendum in Norway
Jan. 1973	Accession of Denmark, Ireland, UK to the Community
Dec. 1974	Paris summit agrees to the principle of direct elections to the European Parliament and to the details of a European Regional Development Fund (the establishment of which had been agreed at the 1972 Paris and 1973 Copenhagen summits). In addition it is agreed to institutionalize summit meetings as the European Council. Agreement also to give the General Council major responsibility for coordinating the business of the Community
Feb. 1975	Signing of the first Lomé Convention between the Community and 46 underdeveloped countries in Africa, the Caribbean, and the Pacific (the ACP states). The Convention replaces and extends the Yaoundé Convention
June 1975	Majority vote in favour of continued Community membership in UK referendum; Greece applies for Community membership

July 1976	Opening of negotiations on Greek accession to the Community
Mar. 1977	Portugal applies for Community membership
July 1977	Spain applies for Community membership
Feb. 1979	Community opens accession negotiations with Spain
Mar. 1979	European Monetary System (the subject of high-level negotiations for over a year) comes into operation
May 1979	Signing of accession treaty between Community and Greece
June 1979	First direct elections to the European Parliament
Oct. 1979	Signing of the second Lomé Convention between the Community and 58 ACP states
Dec. 1979	For the first time the EP does not approve the Community budget; as a result the Community has to operate on the basis of 'one-twelfths' from 1 January 1980
Jan. 1981	Accession of Greece to Community
Oct. 1981	Community foreign ministers reach agreement on the 'London Report' which strengthens and extends European political cooperation
Jan. 1983	A Common Fisheries Policy is agreed
June 1983	The Stuttgart European Council meeting approves a 'Solemn Declaration on European Union'
Jan. 1984	Free trade area between Community and EFTA established
Feb. 1984	The European Parliament approves Draft Treaty establishing the European Union
June 1984	Second direct elections to the EP
June 1985	Signing of accession treaties between the Community and Spain and Portugal
Dec. 1985	Luxembourg European Council meeting agrees the principles of the Single European Act. The Act incorporates Treaty revisions, gives European political cooperation legal status, and establishes the completion of the internal market by 1992 as a top priority
Jan. 1986	Accession of Spain and Portugal to Community
July 1987	After month's delay caused by ratification problems in Ireland, the SEA comes into force
June 1989	Third direct elections to the European Parliament
Oct. 1990	UK joins ERM
Dec. 1991	The Maastricht Treaty is agreed
Jun. 1992	Danish referendum on Maastricht Treaty: 51% no
20 Sept. 1992	French referendum on Maastricht Treaty: 51% yes
Dec. 1992	New terms agreed for the Danes at the Edinburgh European Council meeting; increases in the EU budget also agreed
May 1993	Danes approve Maastricht, as modified in Edinburgh, in a referendum: 56.8% yes
June 1993	British parliament approves Maastricht Treaty. Copenhagen summit: heads of state and government agree to admit East European countries to the EU, subject to a range of conditions, especially a

	satisfactory performance with regard to economic questions and human rights and democracy
Aug.–Sept. 1993	EU currency crisis, leading to widening of parity margins to 15% for members
Oct. 1993	German Constitutional Court rules Maastricht Treaty compatible with the German constitution
Nov. 1993	Maastricht Treaty enters into force
1 Jan. 1994	European Economic Area begins operation
Mar. 1994	Disagreement about weighted voting arrangements to apply after enlargement. UK vetos proposals to increase blocking minority in the Council of Ministers from two large states plus one small state to two large plus two small
May 1994	European Parliament approves accession of Finland, Sweden, Austria, and Norway; EU agrees Pact for Stability in Europe, regarding protecting borders and respecting minority rights among the prospective member states in Eastern Europe
June 1994	Elections to the European Parliament; federalist candidate for Presidency of the Commission vetoed by UK; Jacques Santer appointed in July
June–Oct. 1994	Referenda in Sweden, Finland, Norway, and Austria; accesion approved in all except Norway
1 Jan. 1995	Sweden, Finland, and Austria accede to EU

Notes

1. For simplicity's sake, the term 'European Community' is used in those parts of the discussion which range backwards and forwards over the point where the EC became the EU.
2. See Paul Taylor, *The Limits of European Integration* (London and New York, 1983); Paul Taylor, *International Organization in the Modern World* (London and New York, 1993), ch. 3.
3. Melanie Philipps, *The Observer*, 14 March 1994; Bernard Levin, *The Times*, 4 March 1994.
4. Stanley Hoffman, 'Obstinate or Obsolete? The Fate of the Nation State and the Case of Western Europe', *Daedalus*, 95 (1966), 862–915.
5. *The Times*, 20 April 1994.
6. See figures in Commission of the European Union, *Eurobarometre*, July 1994, A13, table 3.
7. K. Deutsch et al., *Political Community and the North Atlantic Area* (Princeton, 1957).
8. See Taylor, *International Organization*, ch. 4.
9. Commission of the European Communities, *Bulletin of the European Communities, Supplement 2/86*, Single European Act (Brussels, 1986), 18.
10. *Guardian*, 21 Nov. 1994.

11. For an excellent reconsideration, and critique, of neofunctionalism see Andrew Mor-
    avcsik, 'Preferences and Power in the European Community: A Liberal Intergovern-
    mentalist Approach', *Journal of Common Market Studies*, 31/4 (Dec. 1993).
12. A. S. Milward, *The European Rescue of the Nation State* (London, 1992).
13. Arend Lijphart, 'Consociation and Federation: Conceptual and Empirical Links',
    Canadian Journal of Political Science, 22/3 (1979), 499–515.
14. R. Dahrendorf, *Society and Democracy in Germany* (Garden City, NY, 1967), 276.
15. Lijphart, 'Consociation and Federation', 211–12.
16. See Stuart Holland, *UnCommon Market* (London, 1980).
17. Peter Kellner, *Independent*, 22 March 1989.
18. For accounts of these various theories see A. J. R. Groom and Paul Taylor (eds.),
    Frameworks for International Cooperation (London and New York, 1991).
19. Paul Taylor, 'The New Dynamics of EC integration in the 1980s', in Juliet Lodge (ed.),
    The European Community and the Challenge of the Future (London, 1989), 3–25.
20. 'Mad cow disease'—bovine spongiform encephalopathy or BSE—was a disease found
    in cattle in Britain in the 1980s which affected the nervous system and which it was
    feared could be transferred to humans. Some EC governments banned imports of
    beef from Britain until they were convinced that controls on the slaughter and
    transfer of meat had been sufficiently tightened, so that infected meat could not be
    imported. A number of politicians and 'popular' newspapers in Britain described
    this sensible and legal precaution as blatant, unscrupulous opportunism to improve
    national beef sales at the expense of the British farmer.
21. See Fiona Hayes-Renshaw, 'The Role of the Committee of Permanent Representa-
    tives in the Decision-making Process of the European Community', unpublished
    Ph.D. thesis (University of London, 1990).
22. As on 25 October 1989. This was the lead front-page story in the *Guardian*, 26 Oct.
    1989.
23. See the *Guardian*'s lead story, 'Cabinet rallies to Howe's EMS Flag', 2 Nov. 1989.
24. As reported in the *Guardian*, 7 Sept. 1994, 6.
25. This tendency is exemplified in Mrs Thatcher's keynote speech at the College of
    Europe in Bruges, 30 Sept. 1988.
26. *Eurobarometre*, July 1994, A13, table 3.

Further Reading

BULMER, SIMON, and SCOTT, ANDREW, *Economic and Political Integration in Europe: Inter-
    nal Dynamics and the Global Context* (Oxford, 1994). A comprehensive compendium
    of more advanced theoretical and empirical studies of internal and external aspects of
    the European Union.
DINAN, DESMOND, *Ever Closer Union? An Introduction to the European Community* (Lon-
    don, 1994). A good introduction to the history, institutions, and main policy areas of
    the European Union.

LODGE, JULIET (ed.), *The European Community and the Challenge of the Future*, 2nd edn. (London, 1993). A very useful collection of accessible writings on the major policy areas of the European Community/Union.

STORY, JONATHAN (ed.), *The New Europe: Politics, Government and Economy since 1945* (Oxford, 1994). Contains some useful materials on the European Union's relationships with Eastern Europe in the 1990s as well as a range of helpful contributions on internal questions.

TAYLOR, PAUL, *International Organization in the Modern World: The Regional and the Global Process* (London, 1993; pb 1995). Contains a theoretical overview of the European Union as a regional international organization.

CHAPTER FOURTEEN

THE UNITED NATIONS: VARIANTS OF COLLECTIVE SECURITY

Adam Roberts

The United Nations was from its establishment in 1945 supposed to have at its core what amounted to a system of collective security. While failing to establish such a system, the UN has assisted the emergence of three significant variations on the theme of collective security: (1) the tendency towards regional alliances and multilateral military interventions; (2) UN authorizations of military enforcement activities by states; and (3) peacekeeping operations, mainly under UN auspices.

Created on the basis of blueprints drawn up by the United States, the Soviet Union, the United Kingdom, and their wartime allies, the United Nations had as one of its central purposes the maintenance of international peace and security. A global organization of general competence, in its first half-century it achieved virtually universal membership—something that had always eluded its predecessor, the League of Nations; and it developed roles in a wide variety of fields, including international law, technical cooperation, decolonization, human rights, and economic development. As regards international security, its role has been sometimes marginal, always problematic, but frequently innovative. The central questions addressed here are why the UN has failed to construct the system for maintaining international peace that seemed such a key part of the UN Charter; and how to characterize the UN's role in the complex pattern of arrangements and activities which has in fact emerged.

Some parts of this chapter draw, with much revision, on material published elsewhere: 'The UN and International Security', *Survival*, 35/2 (1993), 3–30; 'The Crisis in UN Peacekeeping', *Survival*, 36/3 (1994), 93–120; and in the introduction (written jointly) to Adam Roberts and Benedict Kingsbury (eds.), *United Nations, Divided World: The UN's Roles in International Relations*, 2nd edn. (Oxford, 1993).

The UN age has also been the nuclear age. The first atomic bomb test took place in July 1945, just one month after the adoption of the UN Charter. The Soviet Union's acquisition of a nuclear weapons capability from 1949 onwards, coupled with the advent of long-range missiles in the late 1950s, confirmed that the world was entering a new security environment, with complex implications for ideas of collective security. The system that emerged was more one of nuclear deterrence by rival powers and alliances than a UN-based security system. The fact that all states were now potentially vulnerable to nuclear attack strengthened the desire of many of them to seek alliance with a nuclear power. It also made nuclear powers nervous about giving general security guarantees indiscriminately to all other states, as the theory of collective security might seem to require.

This chapter adopts a basically historical but not slavishly chronological approach. Like the idea of collective security itself, it draws on both 'realist' and 'idealist' frameworks of thought. It looks briefly at the idea of collective security, and the types of problems encountered in attempts to implement it; pre-1945 efforts at collective security; the UN Charter provisions in the field, which themselves contain some departures from pure ideas of collective security; the UN's achievement in attracting near-universal membership, combined with the substantial failure of attempts to establish a general scheme of collective security; the complex effects of the veto on the UN's security roles; the limits of international economic sanctions as an instrument of collective security; and the fate of early discussions about making military forces available to the Security Council. Then it examines the three particular variations on the theme of collective security: alliances, UN authorizations of force, and peacekeeping. Finally it discusses the UN's overall roles in the security field, and the evolution of the idea of collective security.

14.1. Collective Security

The term 'collective security' normally refers to a system, regional or global, in which each participating state accepts that the security of one is the concern of all, and agrees to join in a collective response to aggression. In this sense it is distinct from, and more ambitions than, systems of alliance security, in which groups of states ally with each other, principally against possible external threats.

The idea of collective security, which was aired at the negotiations which led to the 1648 Peace of Westphalia, has a history almost as long as systems of states.[1] No general system of collective security has ever been created. However, over the centuries the idea has been periodically revived. In addition, many uses of force have had, as part of their public rationale, the claim (not always implausible) that they reflected the collective purpose of the international community, not just the interests of an individual country.

Attractive in theory, ideas of collective security have in practice involved many awkward problems.[2] They depend upon a view of the world as consisting of states all of which have uncontested boundaries and congenial regimes, willing to entrust their security largely to the community as a whole, and to rely on the will and capacity of the major powers to agree on a course of action and follow it. The reality is harsher. States not directly involved do not necessarily see every crisis in terms of aggression versus defence, nor do they rush to take action: they often tend towards neutrality regarding other people's conflicts. If they favour action, different states may favour different ends, and different means. Even if they do agree on the particular course to be taken, states may still disagree over command structures and over burden-sharing—whether of money, military resources, or the risk to their own soldiers' lives. Further, to the extent that groups of states develop a capacity for collective military action, pressures inevitably develop to use it not just for defence but also for other purposes, including interventions within states to stop gross human rights violations or to restore democratic regimes. Finally, there is a conundrum at the heart of collective security thinking: whether it is best organized on a global level, with attendant risks that the system will be overloaded with commitments to numerous states worldwide, in effect globalizing every conflict, or on a regional level, which involves problems of defining the regions in question, warding off dangers of regional hegemony, and avoiding possible disputes about which particular organization should handle a particular crisis. None of these problems has significantly diminished in the course of the twentieth century.

14.2. The First World War and the League of Nations

The First World War led to the growth of ideas about international organization in general and collective security in particular. The way in which the war broke out, and its subsequent course, did much to discredit the idea of the 'balance of power'. A balance between rival states might sometimes keep the peace, but its failure in 1914 had been catastrophic: indeed, it was made worse by the fact that there was a rough balance between the two sides engaged in all-out war. An alternative basis for international security had to be found.

The Covenant of the League of Nations, concluded in 1919 and entering into force in 1920, contained a number of provisions which reflected collective security ideas. Article 10 was typical:

The Members of the League undertake to respect and preserve as against external aggression the territorial integrity and existing political independence of all Members of the League. In case of any such aggression or in case of any threat or danger of such aggression, the Council shall advise upon the means by which this obligation shall be fulfilled.

The weakness of the last sentence of Article 10 was a reflection of deep reluctance among most of the major powers to commit themselves firmly to a military response to an attack on any League member. Some, including the United States, stayed out of the League altogether, for fear of military entanglement. The powers that did join the League hoped that a variety of approaches—including territorial revisions, arms reductions, and a system of international arbitration—would render collective military action unnecessary. In fact, collective security only emerged as a serious plank in the League platform in the early 1930s. Even then, it proved hard to get the major member states to agree on what particular act constituted so clear a case of aggression that there should be a collective military response to it.

The failure of the League of Nations to prevent the outbreak of the Second World War had many causes, but among them was its unconvincing attempt, already evident in the League Covenant, largely to replace the independent military power of sovereign states with a new scheme involving both disarmament and collective security. The League, established in 1920, failed in its security functions, and was formally wound up in April 1946.[3]

14.3. The United Nations Charter

The UN emerged from a wartime military alliance, called the 'United Nations', which saw itself as expressing the collective will of states to resist aggression. The UN Charter, signed on 26 June 1945 by the representatives of fifty states in San Francisco, and entering into force on 24 October 1945, was intended by its framers to provide a more complex and realistic framework regarding the possession and use of force than that of the League Covenant.

The Charter's overall approach is to stress that force may be used only for fundamentally defensive purposes, and preferably on a collective basis. In Chapter VII (on Action with Respect to Threats to the Peace, Articles 39–51) it seeks to establish a general system of collective security, but this is qualified by Article 51, which preserves 'the inherent right of states to individual or collective self-defence', at least until the Security Council has taken necessary measures. In Chapter VIII (on Regional Arrangements, Articles 52–4), emphasis is placed on the role of regional arrangements or agencies in maintaining peace, so by no means all collective security eggs were in the UN basket.

The Charter's acceptance of the role of individual states and their armed forces is further indicated by the fact that it says less about disarmament than had the League Covenant. Articles 11 and 26 refer to disarmament and the regulation of armaments, but in cautious terms. The framers of the Charter were anxious not to commit the UN to unrealizable goals in this sphere. As in some other matters, the UN Charter went with, rather than against, the grain of the anarchic society of states.

The key body for organizing collective international enforcement action is the UN Security Council. This consisted originally of five permanent members (China, France, the Soviet Union, the United Kingdom, and the United States) plus six others elected for two-year terms by the General Assembly, which contains all the member states of the UN. In 1965 the number of non-permanent members was increased to ten, bringing the Security Council's total membership to fifteen. It has a clearer structure for reaching key decisions than the League Council had. For a substantive resolution to pass it requires nine affirmative votes from the Council's fifteen members, and it can be vetoed (see below) by any one of the five permanent members.

The Charter conferred on the Security Council a considerable degree of authority over other UN members. It was given responsibility for determining the existence of threats to the peace, on the basis of a less legalistic definition of the circumstances in which it could act than that in the League Covenant. Under Chapter VII it had the power to decide what military or other measures should be taken 'to maintain or restore international peace and security' (Article 39). It was supposed to have military forces at its disposal, and to get advice and assistance from the Military Staff Committee, consisting of the chiefs of staff of the five permanent members (Articles 43–8). However, the wording of even these provisions is cautious, and leaves many key questions to be determined. Thus Article 47(3) says of forces placed at the disposal of the Security Council: 'Questions relating to the command of such forces shall be worked out subsequently.'

Apart from the Security Council, some of the other 'principal organs' established by the UN Charter, especially the General Assembly and the office of the Secretary-General, have had a significant role in security matters. The General Assembly as the plenary body is responsible for much of the work of the UN: it controls finance, and adopts resolutions on a huge range of issues. On a few occasions when the Security Council was not able to act, the General Assembly also played a key part in initiating or providing guidance for peacekeeping operations. It has frequently debated and passed resolutions on a wide range of issues relating to the use of force.

The role of the Secretary-General has developed very significantly since 1945, and has come to involve a wide range of functions, including fact-finding; mediating in disputes between states; and responding to rapidly moving crises in which other UN bodies, because of disagreement among members or the sheer pace of events, have only limited possibilities of doing anything. In particular, the Secretary-General has had a major part in proposing and supervising the deployment of peacekeeping operations.

14.4. The Attainment of Near-universal Membership

The UN, along with its specialized agencies, has achieved virtually universal membership. This is partly because, from the start, it has risen above the League, and ridden with the spirit of the times, in its formal acceptance of the twin ideas of the equality of states and of peoples. Throughout its history the UN has had as members the great majority of existing states. Their number has grown, owing to successive waves of decolonization and to the disintegration of large federal states, including the Soviet Union and Yugoslavia in 1991–2. In 1945 the UN had 51 original members; by 1961, 100; by the end of 1984, 159; and by January 1995, 185. By a perverse paradox, the UN, identified in so many minds with internationalism, presided over the global triumph of the idea of the sovereign state.

The most conspicuous case of non-membership of the UN was the People's Republic of China from the revolution in 1949 until 1971. During that time China was represented at the UN by the regime in Taiwan. Since 1971 the UN's claims to near-universalism have had real substance. Non-members of the UN have included Switzerland (which has never applied for UN membership), a number of micro-states, and dependent or non-self-governing territories. Many of these non-members are nevertheless involved in various aspects of the UN system, and some are members of specialized agencies. Other entities not members of the UN include Taiwan (which does not claim to be a state distinct from China, and was expelled from China's seat in the UN in 1971), Northern Cyprus (which is not regarded as a state except by itself and Turkey), and Western Sahara and Palestine (which have not had effective governmental control of most of their respective territories, but have received a degree of recognition by significant parts of the international community).

No member state has ever left the UN. However, for a short period in 1950 the Soviet Union refused to participate in the Security Council and other UN organs in protest against the UN's refusal to accept the government of the PRC as representative of China; and in 1965–6 Indonesia temporarily withdrew from the UN. In some cases the credentials of particular authorities to represent their state have not been accepted. South Africa, often treated as a pariah in the apartheid years, never ceased to be a UN member.

Near-universality of membership may be a necessary condition for the establishment of a general system of collective security, but it is not a sufficient one. Throughout its existence the UN has had difficulties in taking advantage of its large membership to exercise an effective security role. Indeed, one reason why states have been so consistently attracted by UN membership may be that it has in practice placed relatively few demands on them.

14.5. The Security Council Veto

The veto was created by the major powers in 1945 as a means of ensuring that the new organization could not act against their fundamental interests. Article 27 of the UN Charter, by giving each of the five permanent members the power to veto Security Council resolutions, made it more than doubtful whether the UN collective security system could be used against any of the five if it was considered to have threatened international peace; or indeed if any of them, for whatever reason, was against a proposed enforcement action. This constituted a major departure from the classical model of a collective security system. In a slight modification of the Charter scheme, in practice for a resolution to be vetoed one of the five has to vote against it (and not merely abstain).

The use of the veto by the five permanent members to prevent the passing of resolutions by the Security Council was often seen, especially during the Cold War years, as the main evidence of the incapacity of the UN to act in the field of international peace and security. In the whole period from 1945 to the end of 1994 vetoes were cast as shown in Table 14.1. These figures reflect the fact that a permanent member of the Security Council can avoid having to make direct use of the veto power if it is sure that the proposal in question will not in any event obtain the requisite majority. The Western states, in particular,

Table 14.1. Vetoes in the UN Security Council, 1945–1994

Years	China	France	UK	USA	USSR/Russia	Total
1946–55	1	2	0	0	75	78
1956–65	0	2	3	0	26	31
1966–75	2	2	8	12	7	31
1976–85	0	9	11	34	6	60
1986–94	0	3	8	23	2	36
Total	3	18	30	69	116	236

were frequently able to use this tactic in the early years of the UN, the Soviet Union in the 1970s and 1980s. To some extent the use of the veto has reflected a degree of diplomatic isolation of the vetoing state(s) on the particular issue. The ten non-permanent members are sometimes said to have a 'sixth veto' in that they can deny any resolution the nine votes it needs to pass. This has given them considerable power, which they have often used to modify the terms of resolutions.

The veto power in the hands of the five permanent members helps to explain why the Security Council had a marginal role over many decades in respect of a wide range of international security issues. The Council could contribute little to the amelioration of interventions and armed conflicts in which its permanent members were directly involved—as, for example, in Suez (1956), Hungary (1956), Vietnam (1946–75), the Sino-Vietnamese war (1979), Afghanistan (1979–88), and Panama (1991). Opposition by one or other of the permanent members also frequently prevented action in relation to other armed conflicts. For example, the Council did little in relation to the Iran–Iraq war (1980–88) until, by Resolution 598 of 20 July 1987, it demanded a ceasefire.

Following the end of the Cold War—a slow process culminating in the collapse of Communist regimes in Eastern Europe in 1989 and of the USSR itself in 1991—the Security Council developed what appeared to be a much-increased capacity to act. The period from 31 May 1990 to 11 May 1993 was the longest without use of the veto in the history of the UN. This was part of a broader process of increased activity. From 1945 to 1989 the average number of resolutions passed by the Security Council each year had been about fifteen. Figures for subsequent years are given in Table 14.2.

The veto system, much criticized for preventing UN action in many cases, has had complex effects, not all undesirable. On the positive side, it has played a part in getting, and keeping, major powers within the UN; and it may have saved the UN from being saddled with commitments which great powers were

Table 14.2. UN Security Council resolutions passed, and vetoed, 1990–1994

Year	Resolutions passed	Resolutions vetoed	Subject of vetoed resolutions
1990	37	2 (USA)	Panama; Israeli-occupied territories
1991	42	0	
1992	74	0	
1993	93	1 (Russia)	Peacekeeping costs in Cyprus
1994	77	1 (Russia)	Former Yugoslavia

not willing to support in practice. However, it has contributed to perceptions of the UN as a mere talking-shop; and to the tendency of states, large and small, to seek reinsurance in other security arrangements, including regional ones, where there was less risk of being outvoted or vetoed. As the Council's responses to the developing war in Yugoslavia from 1991 onwards showed, the substantial decline in use of the veto did not open the way to united and forceful policies to restore international peace and security. The failure to introduce a system of collective security has causes which go beyond the veto.

14.6. International Economic Sanctions and Arms Embargoes

Proposals for collective security have almost always involved a degree of reliance on means other than force. Sanctions are an important tool available to the Security Council in responding to conflicts and threats to international peace. They are envisaged in Article 41 of the UN Charter. They have collective security functions, i.e. against acts of aggression, but have also been initiated where other factors are present. They often seem a less controversial instrument than military force, but their use has been riddled with problems.

Cases of UN sanctions, fairly rare until 1990, have increased greatly since. General economic sanctions were applied to Rhodesia following its unilateral declaration of independence (1966–79); Iraq following its invasion of Kuwait (1990–); and Serbia and Montenegro (1992–). An arms and air traffic embargo was imposed on Libya (1992–), followed by more general sanctions in 1993. There were also embargoes on the supply of arms to South Africa (1977–94); former Yugoslavia (1991–); Somalia (1992–); Liberia (1992–); and Rwanda (1994). Arms and petroleum sanctions were imposed on Haiti (1993–4) and on the UNITA rebel movement in Angola (1993–).

The use of international economic sanctions, whether by states or groups of states, has always been controversial. There has been concern about their exact purposes, their effects, and their effectiveness.[4] As many of the cases in the UN era demonstrate, sanctions have symbolic functions, and are often used as a form of communication of international values. They can be a means of warning an adversary of the seriousness with which a particular matter is viewed, and of the prospect of more forceful action: however, where (as over Kuwait in 1991) their use is accompanied by a resort to armed force, there are bound to be arguments that sanctions should have been tried harder or for longer. Sanctions may also be used with the rather different purpose of assuaging domestic opinion in states taking part, often with the intention of avoiding military action or other unpalatable options. Further, sanctions may at one and the same time be completely effective and a total failure: they may stop the target country's international trade and hurt its citizenry, but fail to achieve the intended change of its policy. There can in some cases be serious questions about their compatibility with the human rights of the target state population. A UN report issued in 1995 expressed some of these concerns: 'Sanctions, as is generally recognized, are a blunt instrument. They raise the ethical question of whether suffering inflicted on vulnerable groups in the target country is a legitimate means of exerting pressure on political leaders whose behaviour is unlikely to be affected by the plight of their subjects.'[5] A further problem of sanctions is that they are sometimes seen to require near-universal support (and thus to be organized in a UN rather than regional framework) if they are to be in any way effective. Yet there are relatively few issues on which all countries agree to the point of being willing to take action. In short, for a collective action to work, sanctions are seldom enough: military means are therefore likely to be seen as necessary.

14.7. Failure to Provide Military Forces under Article 43

From the earliest years the Security Council has not in fact had armed forces at its disposal in the manner apparently envisaged in the UN Charter's Chapter VII. In 1946–7, in accord with Articles 43–8, the UN's Military Staff Committee was set up and asked to examine the question of contributions of armed forces to the Security Council. It duly published a report which reflected significant disagreements among the five permanent members about the size and composition of national contributions. The whole enterprise was abandoned.[6] This was part of a broader failure to implement the provisions of Chapter VII specifying an ambitious scheme for collective security.[7] In the first fifty years of the UN, agreements under Article 43 of the Charter, necessary to place national forces at the general disposal of the UN, have never been concluded.

The most obvious reason for the failure to implement the Charter provisions in the early years of the UN was the inability of the permanent members of the Security Council to reach agreement across the Cold War divide. However, there appears also to have been an underlying reluctance on the part of all states to see their forces committed in advance to participation in what might prove to be distant, controversial, and risky military operations without their express consent and command.

The failure to implement these parts of Chapter VII of the Charter has not led to anything like a complete abandonment of efforts to develop collective uses of armed force. On the contrary, the UN era has seen three striking variations on the collective security theme: regional alliances; UN authorizations of the use of force; and international peacekeeping forces. Each of these variations responds to difficulties in the pure idea of collective security.

14.8. Regional Alliances and Multilateral Military Interventions

Such actual international security arrangements as did emerge in the first decades of the UN's existence were centred less on the UN itself than on bilateral and regional security treaties. Many of these treaties referred to UN Charter principles and procedures, and reflected aspects of the Charter ethos, including emphasis on defence as the main legitimate use of force. These regional arrangements, which were often alliances against an external power rather than true cases of collective security, reflected the reality that states are generally willing to commit their forces for serious military action not on a universal basis, but in their own region, or in defence of countries with which there are ties of blood, commerce, religion, common culture, and political system. The development of nuclear weapons in the hands of a few powers reinforced the already existing tendency for alliances of one kind or another to take the place of the more ambitious UN scheme for collective security. The following examples suggest how widespread and varied regional arrangements have been in the post-1945 period, and how they have exposed difficulties in ideas of collective security.

Some regional organizations pre-dated both the UN and the development of nuclear weapons. The League of Arab States was established by a treaty signed in March 1945 in Cairo: this provided that in case of aggression by any country against a member, the League may decide, by unanimous vote, upon the measures necessary to repel the aggression. Although this provision has proved relatively ineffective in several crises, including in various Arab–Israeli wars and in the 1990–1 conflict over Kuwait, the Arab League has continued to have a role in authorizing certain uses of force—most notably the Arab Deterrent Force which the League Council established in October 1976 with the stated purpose of assisting the ending of hostilities in Lebanon.

In the Americas, the 1947 Inter-American Treaty of Reciprocal Assistance (Rio Treaty) was the first comprehensive convention on collective security to which all the American states became parties, being followed in 1948 by the Charter of the Organization of American States (OAS). The Rio Treaty involved a much stronger commitment to collective security than anything that can be found in the constitutive documents of certain other regional organizations, such as the Organization of African Unity (OAU), established in 1963, and the Association of South East Asian Nations (ASEAN), which originated in 1967. Yet OAS members have had profound disagreements about security issues, and cannot be said to have achieved a regional system of collective security.

In Western Europe and North America the 1949 North Atlantic Treaty (the Treaty of Washington), which established NATO, involved both an element of collective security and an attempt to make its provisions compatible with the UN Charter. As Article 5 stated:

The Parties agree that . . . if such an armed attack occurs, each of them, in exercise of the right of individual or collective self-defence recognized by Article 51 of the Charter of the United Nations, will assist the Party or Parties so attacked by taking forthwith, individually, and in concert with the other Parties, such action as it deems necessary, including the use of armed force . . .

Any such armed attack and all measures taken as a result thereof shall immediately be reported to the Security Council. Such measures shall be terminated when the Security Council has taken the measures necessary to restore and maintain international peace and security.[8]

In order not to circumscribe its freedom to take military action, NATO was deliberately presented as an organization to provide for the self-defence of the parties under Article 51 of the UN Charter, rather than as a regional arrangement under Chapter VIII.[9] It operated effectively as an alliance partly because it faced, for most of its existence, an identifiable threat; and partly because it consisted, with only a few exceptions, of relatively like-minded democratic states. The alliance as such was not, for the most part, drawn into the extra-European involvements of its various members. It was much more a regional military alliance than a collective security system.

The Western powers established a number of other regional bodies with some elements of collective security in their basic purposes. The 1951 security treaty between Australia, New Zealand, and the United States (the ANZUS Pact) was meant to be the first step towards a comprehensive security system in the Pacific. Operations under the New Zealand–US aspect of the treaty were curtailed in 1986, following New Zealand's insistence on assurances that US warships entering its ports were not carrying nuclear weapons—something the United States, as a matter of general policy, was unwilling to disclose.

In September 1954, under the Manila Treaty, the South-East Asia Treaty Organization (SEATO) was formed. It was intended partly to protect certain countries in the region that were not themselves members of SEATO, especially South Vietnam. Its creation reflected a US desire, in the aftermath of the Korean War, to share the burdens of collective security more widely in future. However, SEATO never functioned effectively. It did not play a significant part in assisting the US military involvement in the Vietnam War between the early 1960s and

1973. SEATO was formally abolished in September 1975, four months after South Vietnam came under Communist control.

In February 1955 the Baghdad Pact was signed between Iraq and Turkey, with Iran, Pakistan, and the United Kingdom joining in later in the year. This was intended to provide a framework for collective action only against a Communist power, not against other internal or external threats. The United States became an associate member in March 1958, but was never a full member. In 1959 Iraq withdrew from the Pact, which was then reincarnated in the form of the Central Treaty Organization (CENTO), with headquarters in Ankara. It never flourished, partly because of the absence of any regional consensus on security issues and the reluctance of Arab states to be marshalled into an anti-Soviet alliance. It became defunct when the remaining regional powers withdrew in 1979.

In May 1955 the Soviet Union and seven East European allies concluded a multilateral treaty in Warsaw (the Warsaw Pact) which consolidated their already existing bilateral military arrangements. Its Article 4 contained very similar provisions to those of Article 5 of the North Atlantic Treaty as quoted above.[10] Following the collapse of Soviet domination in Eastern Europe, with which the Warsaw Treaty was inextricably associated, the Treaty was annulled on 1 April 1991.

This pattern of regional alliances and other security arrangements had some successes; it also had some conspicuous failures, including SEATO, CENTO, and, eventually, the Warsaw Pact. In Europe during the Cold War years the Soviet Union often referred to the need for an all-European security system to replace the rival alliances of NATO and the Warsaw Pact: this led to the Helsinki Final Act of 1975, to which all European states except Albania subscribed, which set out important principles of international relations but did not purport to create a collective security system for Europe, nor to supplant the alliances.

Many regional alliances and organizations were associated with a tendency for uses of military force to have a multilateral character. Time and again, when states engaged in military interventions they did so with authorization by and assistance from a regional body. Such a tendency, not unknown in earlier decades and even centuries, became particularly marked in the decades after 1945. Thus the Soviet-led invasion of Czechoslovakia in August 1968 was under Warsaw Pact auspices and involved contingents from Bulgaria, East Germany, Hungary, and Poland. The Syrian role in Lebanon since 1976 has had the cooperation of Arab League members. The US-led invasion of Grenada in October 1983 had a degree of support from the Organization of Eastern Caribbean States. Such examples, which could be almost endlessly multiplied, might seem to be the tribute that vice pays to virtue: collective security acting as a facade for great power interests, and as a figleaf to conceal violations of Article 2(4) of the UN Charter, which prohibits 'the threat or use of force against the territorial integrity or political independence of any state'. However, in some cases the emphasis on collective purposes and multilateral participation probably helped limit the aims and activities of interventionists to those which were reasonably presentable.

Regional security arrangements can be seen as building-blocks for a general system of collective security, or as detracting from it. Since such a system was not a serious possibility anyway, perhaps the alliances that developed should be seen as the nearest approximation to collective security that was available in the harsh circumstances of international politics. Manifestly imperfect in many ways, they could never be a complete substitute for the idea of UN-based military force—an idea which was to assume two unanticipated forms.

14.9. UN Authorizations of Military Enforcement Activities

The UN's most explicit variation on the collective security theme has been its practice of authorizing certain uses of force by states or groups of states. This is distinct from the Charter conception of the Security Council having forces more directly under its authority. The practice has arisen because of the lack of real unanimity in the UN about the use of force, the failure of states to put forces at the disposal of the Security Council, and the need in military operations for an efficient system of intelligence and command.

The Korean War (1950–3) marked the beginning of the UN practice of authorizing the use of force by states. Following the invasion of South Korea by North Korean forces on 25 June, UN Security Council Resolution 83 of 27 June 1950 recommended that member states 'furnish such assistance to the Republic of Korea as may be necessary to repel the armed attack and to restore international peace and security in the area'. Subsequently, Resolution 84 of 7 July 1950 recommended 'that all military forces and other assistance be under a unified command under the USA'. It also authorized the unified command to use the UN flag— something that has never been repeated in UN-authorized enforcement actions.

Fifteen countries provided troops for the UN operations in Korea, and effectively saved South Korea from being completely overrun. The US management of the war was intensely controversial, especially the rapid advance by UN forces far north of the thirty-eighth parallel (the 1945 military boundary which marked the line between the two halves of Korea). When at the end of November 1950 UN forces reached almost to the Korea–China border, China intervened massively. The war ended only with the ceasefire of 27 July 1953, which established a new truce line close to the thirty-eighth parallel. Although a degree of success was achieved, the Korean War cost many lives and left a legacy of bitterness and recrimination, between allies as well as adversaries. To the extent that it could be seen as a collective security operation, it exposed some difficulties in the idea.

The initial Security Council resolutions on Korea could only be passed because, fortuitously, the Soviet Union was boycotting the Security Council at the time for its refusal to seat the PRC. When, later in 1950, the Soviet Union resumed its Security Council place it was able to use its veto to prevent the passing of any further substantive resolutions on Korea. The United States and its allies, which at that time could still view the General Assembly as a pliant body, then secured the passage of General Assembly Resolution 377 ('Uniting for Peace') of 3 November 1950:

If the Security Council, because of lack of unanimity of the permanent members, fails to exercise its primary responsibility for the maintenance of international peace and security in any case where there appears to be a threat to peace, breach of the peace, or act of aggression, the General Assembly shall consider the matter immediately with a view to making appropriate recommendations to Members for collective measures, including in the case of a breach of the peace or acts of aggression the use of armed force when necessary, to maintain or restore international peace and security. If not in session at the time the General Assembly may meet in emergency special session within twenty four hours of the request therefor. Such emergency special session may be called if requested by the Security Council on the vote of any seven members, or by a majority of the members of the United Nations.

This 'Uniting for Peace' procedure, which constituted a significant change in UN Charter arrangements, indicated that the Security Council veto need not be an insuperable obstacle to UN action. It was used against Britain and France in 1956 at the time of their Suez intervention. Apart from this, it has seldom been invoked, largely because in most cases on which action was stalled in the Security Council, there was not in fact enough consensus among General Assembly members about what action should be taken.

The *locus classicus* of Security Council authorization of the use of force to repel an act of aggression was the response to the Iraqi invasion of Kuwait of 2 August 1990. After numerous resolutions had imposed sanctions on Iraq and demanded its withdrawal from Kuwait, Security Council Resolution 678 of 29 November 1990 authorized 'Member States co-operating with the Government of Kuwait . . . to use all necessary means to uphold and implement resolution 660 (1990) and all subsequent relevant resolutions and to restore international peace and security in the area'. Significantly from the point of view of the theory of collective security, it did not call on all states to take military action (for which the term 'all necessary means' was to become a standard euphemism), but only those states already cooperating with the Kuwaiti government-in-exile.

This resolution was followed by intense military operations by a US-led 28-country military coalition, lasting from 16 January to 28 February 1991, and leading to the complete expulsion of Iraqi armed forces from Kuwait. There were sharp controversies about the conduct of the war, about US leadership, about the number of Iraqi casualties, and about the lack of UN control over military operations. However, the war was undeniably less catastrophic for the UN-authorized forces than the Korean War had been. The high degree of reliance on air power echoed the long-forgotten provision in Article 45 of the UN Charter that members should 'hold immediately available national air-force contingents for combined international enforcement action'. In the whole war, coalition armed forces suffered 466 killed—a far lower number than had been predicted by many critics of the military action.

The Iraqi invasion of Kuwait in 1990 had been uncharacteristic of the post-1945 era. It was the only case of a member state of the UN having the whole of its territory occupied and purportedly annexed by another state. Most wars and occupations have more complicated and ambiguous beginnings. Yet even in the unusually clear circumstances of Kuwait in 1990–1 many states and individuals expressed reservations of various kinds about the fact or the manner of the US-led military action. Although the overwhelming majority of states did take part in the sanctions against Iraq, the differences over the military action confirmed a weakness of collective security proposals, namely that they depend on more unanimity among states than actually exists.

In some of its authorizations of force from 1991 onwards, especially in northern Iraq, Somalia, Haiti, and Rwanda (each outlined below), the Security Council collectively, and its Western permanent members individually, were seen by many to be taking hesitant steps towards a new doctrine and practice of humanitarian intervention—that is, military intervention in a state, without the approval of its authorities, with the purpose of preventing widespread suffering or death among the inhabitants.[11] 'Humanitarian intervention' in this sense was not provided for in the Charter, and remains controversial under it.

The first case concerned the Kurds of northern Iraq. In the immediate aftermath of the 1991 war over Kuwait, and failed uprisings within Iraq, there were huge refugee outflows, leading to pressure on major states to do something to stop the exodus and enable the refugees to return. Security Council Resolution 688 of 5 April 1991 (which received only ten affirmative votes) insisted 'that Iraq allow immediate access by international humanitarian organizations to all those in need of assistance in all parts of Iraq'. However, this did not amount to a direct authorization to the United States or its allies to use force. Part of the legal justification for the US-led Operation Provide Comfort that followed lay in a view of what customary international law may be deemed to permit in a country whose government slaughters its own citizens, creating refugee problems that cause concern in neighbouring states. The operation has also to be seen partly in the special context of post-war actions by victors in the territory of defeated adversaries. Further, there were elements of Iraqi consent in the subsequent presence of UN guards in northern Iraq.

The UN explicitly authorized forceful interventions by US-led coalitions in Somalia and Haiti. In late 1992 Somalia faced vast problems: the collapse of government, civil war, widespread famine, conditions preventing the distribution of aid, and difficulties in getting a UN peacekeeping force in place. Security Council Resolution 794 of 3 December 1992 authorized the Secretary-General, the United States, and cooperating states 'to use all necessary means to establish as soon as possible a secure environment for humanitarian relief operations in Somalia'. An armed US-led military force, the Unified Task Force (UNITAF), then intervened, operating in Somalia between 9 December 1992 and 4 May 1993. It was then partially absorbed into a UN peacekeeping force, United Nations Operation in Somalia (UNOSOM II). In subsequent months the security situation in the capital, Mogadishu, deteriorated. In June UN peacekeeping forces were involved in incidents in which they both suffered and inflicted severe casualties. On 3 October some US Rangers, who were deployed in Mogadishu in support of the UNOSOM II mandate but were not under UN command or control, came under concentrated fire, in which eighteen were killed. Shortly thereafter, President Clinton announced that US forces would withdraw by 31 March 1994. The remaining contingents in UNOSOM II were nervous about both their security and their ability to achieve an end to the conflict in Somalia. They finally withdrew, under US protection, in March 1995. This collective action, a hybrid of enforcement and peacekeeping, thus achieved very mixed results, and was riddled with disagreements between different participants over the purposes of the operation and its command structure.

The crisis in Haiti following the September 1991 *coup d'état* which had toppled President Aristide led ultimately to the passing of Security Council Resolution 940 of 31 July 1994, which authorized the use of 'all necessary means to facilitate the departure from Haiti of the military leadership . . . and to establish and maintain a secure and stable environment'. This resolution is remarkable for its unequivocal call for action to topple an existing regime. Following this, a US-led force intervened in Haiti in September 1994. It did so only after a last-minute agreement providing a basis for a US military role in Haiti, signed in Port-au-Prince by Jimmy Carter and the Haitian President installed by the military, Emile Jonassaint. Thus even in this case, where the UN Security Council had authorized enforcement, there was hesitation in using force: some element of consent of the government in place was sought and obtained.

Rwanda marked the first explicit authorization for sending into a country a force under the leadership of a state other than the United States. Following war and genocide in Rwanda, which had reached a peak in April–May 1994, the UN failed to establish an effective peacekeeping force. Then, in Resolution 929 of 22 June 1994, the Security Council accepted an offer from France and other member states to establish a temporary operation there under French command and control. The Council stated that in doing so it was acting under Chapter VII of the Charter, and it authorized France to use 'all necessary means to achieve the humanitarian objectives' set out in earlier Security Council resolutions. This was the prelude to the French-led Operation Turquoise in western Rwanda in summer 1994. The UN encountered severe problems both before and after this operation in getting states to provide contingents for peacekeeping forces (which were separate from Operation Turquoise) either in Rwanda or in refugee camps on the country's borders.

These cases suggest that collective approaches to security are not necessarily limited to uses of force against 'aggression'. They also suggest that the very term 'humanitarian intervention' is an oversimplification. Military involvements may have more complex motives, purposes, and effects than the phrase implies, and their character may change markedly over time. Elements of the population of the target state frequently come to resent the impact of prolonged intervention on local decision-making, and to oppose the presence of foreign forces.

In addition to the above-mentioned cases, there have been several UN-based authorizations of force for more limited purposes: enforcing sanctions, air exclusion zones, and other restrictions on particular states and activities. In the case of Bosnia-Herzegovina, Security Council Resolution 836 of 4 June 1993 authorized member states, acting nationally or through regional organizations, to use air power to support the UN peacekeeping forces in and around the 'safe areas' which had earlier been proclaimed by the UN. Getting agreement on operations between NATO and the UN peacekeeping forces in former Yugoslavia proved to be extremely problematic, and illustrated some of the difficulties attached to collective attempts to authorize specific military actions, as well as the inherent difficulty of combining two distinct modes of action: peacekeeping and enforcement.

Despite the difficulties encountered, the arrangement whereby forces or missions are authorized by the Security Council but remain largely national or alliance-based in command may have advantages. It is slightly different from some of what was envisaged in the Charter, but has similarities to the practice of the allies in the Second World War. It reflects the reality that not all states feel equally involved in a given enforcement action. Moreover, military action requires an extremely close relation between intelligence-gathering and operations, a smoothly functioning decision-making machine, and forces with some experience of working together to perform dangerous and complex tasks. These things are more likely to be achieved through existing national armed forces, alliances, and military relationships than they are within the structure of a UN command. Further, action by one state or a group of states can be a valuable stopgap while the UN slowly cobbles together an international peacekeeping or other force. Finally, for the UN there may be risks in too-direct involvement in the management of military force: when terrible mistakes occur, as they inevitably do in military operations, they could reflect badly on the organization, and could threaten its universal character.

14.10. Peacekeeping Operations

Peacekeeping is the second major UN variation on traditional collective security ideas, and responds to a weakness at their heart. Most models of collective security are based on the idea of collective military enforcement actions in support of states which are victims of acts of aggression. However, in practice many international problems are not seen by states or indeed individuals in simple terms of 'aggression' versus 'defence'. Rather, they are viewed as more suitable for treatment by impartial efforts of various kinds. In conformity with this view, peacekeeping operations have evolved as the international community's principal form of collective military activity.

Peacekeeping operations, which may take a variety of forms ranging from unarmed military observer missions to armed peacekeeping units, are essentially an ad hoc mechanism developed by the UN. Although not envisaged in the Charter, such operations are compatible with the reference to 'other peaceful means' in Article 33. Peacekeeping forces, identified by their blue berets or helmets, generally consist of separate national contingents under a unified UN-appointed command. They must normally be authorized by the Security Council, but are directed on a day-to-day basis by the Secretary-General or his representative.

Peacekeeping forces have generally been expected to observe three principles which differentiate them sharply from the use of armed forces in enforcement mode, i.e. to resist aggression. First, they are supposed to be impartial as between the parties to a conflict. Secondly, until the early 1990s it was a fundamental principle that they were established and deployed only with the consent of states that were parties to the conflict: and this principle, although contested in the early 1990s both in theory and in practice, remains crucial. Lacking major enforcement power, UN peacekeeping operations have been generally seen as able to function effectively only with the cooperation of the parties directly concerned. Thirdly, avoidance of the use of force has been a basic principle of UN operations. In some of the early missions UN peacekeepers were permitted to use force only in self-defence. Since 1973 the understanding of self-defence has been broadened to allow the use of force against armed persons preventing fulfilment of the mandate, but in practice peacekeepers have seldom used force for this more sweeping purpose.[12]

The tasks of each UN peacekeeping operation, specified in the relevant authorizing resolutions, have traditionally included monitoring and enforcement of ceasefires; observation of frontier lines; interposition between belligerents; and, exceptionally, monitoring government and public order. Since the late 1980s such forces have been involved in monitoring and even running elections, as in Namibia, Angola, Cambodia, and Mozambique; and they have assumed major roles in assuring delivery of humanitarian relief during conflicts, especially in former Yugoslavia and Somalia.

By December 1994 (see Appendix at end of chapter) the UN had set up thirty-five bodies which it classified as peacekeeping operations. Thirteen were established between 1948 and 1978, the remaining twenty-two in the period from 1988. These operations have been used both in international conflicts (as between Israel and its neighbours, and on the Libya–Chad border) and in internal conflicts with international aspects. There have also been peacekeeping forces set up outside the UN, as for example the Commonwealth force in Zimbabwe in 1980.

UN peacekeeping has in several cases failed to prevent war and unilateral intervention. In 1967 Secretary-General U Thant felt obliged to accede to the Egyptian government's request for the withdrawal of UNEF, even though it was widely understood that this action was a prologue to the war between Israel and Egypt in June of that year. In Lebanon, the presence of UN forces failed to prevent either the country's slide into anarchy and communal warfare or the Israeli invasion in 1982. In Cyprus, the UN forces which existed to keep the peace between the Greek and Turkish communities could not prevent external involvement in that communal conflict, culminating in the 1974 Turkish invasion of northern Cyprus. In Angola in 1992, UN-monitored elections were followed by a new outbreak of the longstanding civil war.

The use of UN peacekeeping forces in situations of endemic intra-state conflict was already significant in the Congo in 1960–4, and in Cyprus from 1964 onwards. It increased markedly from about 1989, including in Angola, Cambodia, El Salvador, Georgia, Mozambique, Nicaragua, Rwanda, Somalia, and former Yugoslavia. In many of these cases there was not an effective ceasefire, nor even any clear front lines, and the problems confronting UN forces challenged the three traditional principles of peacekeeping outlined above: impartiality, consent, and non-use of force.

UN peacekeeping operations have sometimes, most notably in Cambodia, been involved in certain essentially governmental functions. Yet there has been little sign of willingness on the part of the UN or its leading members to accept some kind of formal trusteeship role as one possible consequence of taking on responsibilities in areas where order has broken down. The historical record of various forms of mandate, trusteeship, and international administration has been mixed. Yet collective uses of armed force may on some rare occasions require a clear conception of a quasi-imperial role.[13]

Since the end of the Cold War, and with the increase in the number of calls on UN peacekeeping, there have been hopes that the UN in general, and peace-keeping in particular, could have a more central role than before. Echoing such hopes, the first-ever Security Council summit, held in January 1992, led to the preparation of *An Agenda for Peace*, an outline of the UN's hoped-for security role in the post-Cold War world.[14] In practice, the UN has been compelled to confront the severe problems of peacekeeping in situations of endemic conflict and has had grave difficulty in coming up with answers. The problem is not just that the UN lacks a satisfactory command system capable of taking quick decisions and able to coordinate effectively the many different types of force and national contingents deployed. There is as yet little sign of the emergence of a satisfactory doctrine or practice regarding operations which have an essentially hybrid character, involving elements of both peacekeeping and enforcement. Above all, there are limits to what international peacekeeping can achieve in face of determined states and armed groups—especially in situations where troop-contributing states will make only a limited commitment to an operation, and have difficulties in achieving and holding an international consensus on its means and objectives.

In peacekeeping, as in collective security more generally, the UN cannot take on all possible tasks. In the 1990s there has been evidence of overload on the UN administrative system, and reluctance of troop-contributing countries to supply forces and funds for all operations. The UN has taken little action with regard to some crises, including that in Rwanda in 1994, and none in relation to others. In some conflicts, as in Georgia and Liberia from 1993 onwards, only small UN peacekeeping missions have been sent, with modest tasks, namely to verify the activities, in countries undergoing largely internal conflicts, of forces from neighbouring powers—Russia and Nigeria respectively.

UN peacekeeping is a significant innovation in the collective use of military force. It has helped to isolate certain conflicts from great power rivalry. In many cases the presence of peacekeeping forces has stabilized conflicts; but paradox-ically, in so doing it may have reduced pressure for long-term solutions. In some cases it has assisted solutions positively, especially through elections.

Peacekeeping has developed in response to realities which show that the col-lective security vision of international forces acting against aggression was too simple. Yet its practice has exposed many problems in collective military action, not the least of which are the huge number of crises which an international organization may be asked to address; the reluctance of states to provide the necessary financial, material, and human resources; the inherent limitations of a complex multinational system of decision-making and operational command; and the difficulty of engaging in enforcement at the same time as troops are widely dispersed in peacekeeping or humanitarian assistance mode.

14.11. The UN's Roles in the Security Field

In the period since 1945, the UN has had a peripheral role in many important security matters, including the following:

- in arms control talks, the most important of which were those held outside a UN framework, between the United States and the Soviet Union;
- in many crises, not just East–West ones but also such cases as the Indonesian invasion of the former Portuguese colony of East Timor in 1975, and the Iraqi attack on Iran in 1980 which led to eight years of war;
- in response to many terrorist activities, especially widespread from the early 1970s onwards, on which there were fundamentally different attitudes among states, deriving from their views of national liberation struggles.

Deprived, for much of its existence at least, of an effective security role, the UN has been deeply involved in advocacy of, and negotiations for, disarmament and arms limitation. In this field the UN Charter promised less than did the League Covenant, but it has helped to deliver more. Since the early 1960s there has been a large number of agreements, some of which have been negotiated in a UN framework. Such multilateral arms limitation treaties include the 1968 Treaty on the Non-Proliferation of Nuclear Weapons (Non-Proliferation Treaty or NPT), and the 1993 Convention on the Prohibition of the Development, Production, Stockpiling and Use of Chemical Weapons and on Their Destruction (Chemical Weapons Convention). More ambitious proposals for general and complete disarmament have frequently been advocated at the UN, especially from the 1960s to the 1980s, and have sometimes been accompanied by proposals for collective security arrangements to replace national armaments. However, these schemes have run into difficulties familiar from earlier eras of arms negotiations. Overall, the UN has had difficulty in developing a coherent vision of the place of arms limitation, including nuclear non-proliferation, in international politics.

As anticipated in certain provisions of the UN Charter, most states have sought their security less through the UN than through their own defence efforts or alliances. Yet many small or less powerful states, especially members of the Non-Aligned Movement which played a major role in the UN from the 1960s onwards, did perceive the international legal order in general, and the UN in particular, as providing an important buttress for their sovereignty and independence.

In the system that has emerged, multilateral uses of armed forces have had a more significant part than in any previous period. In its development of two practices—the authorization of the use of force by coalitions of states, and UN peacekeeping—the Security Council has been innovative, and has gone beyond the Charter scheme. Although these developments have been plagued by problems, the desire of many states to act within a UN framework remains strong.

For many, the successful conduct of the 1991 Gulf War contributed to a mood of optimism that the Charter's security scheme would be able to operate as its framers were believed to have intended. Many, not least in the United States, believed that the end of the Cold War could lead to a new era of collective security.[15] However, events after 1991 confounded these hopes. The Security Council was indeed unprecedentedly active, both in establishing peacekeeping operations and in ad hoc authorizations of uses of force by states; but its hectic activities involved much failure as well as some success, were highly reactive, and were not for long perceived as moving in the direction of a general system of collective security.

14.12. The Evolution of the Idea of Collective Security

The experience of the UN era confirms that of earlier periods: pure systems of collective security are hard if not impossible to achieve, especially on a global level. Despite a remarkable degree of collaboration on security matters in the Security Council since the late 1980s, the difficulties of collective security remain evident.[16] A symptom as much as a cause of this was the fact that by 1994 the United States was becoming increasingly reluctant to take on either the risks or the costs of peacekeeping and enforcement, especially in the light of its experience in Somalia. Many states, including the United States, were resisting paying their assessed dues for peacekeeping.

What, then, remains of the idea of collective security? Some have sought to preserve it, but within a larger framework entitled 'cooperative security' which also encompasses several other elements, including emphasis on UN peacekeeping, arms control agreements, and manifestly defensive military structures.[17] This approach has merits; yet in so far as it is still based on the idea of a general system of collective security, and presupposes fundamentally compatible security objectives of different states, it may suffer some of the defects of previous proposals.

It may be more fruitful to view collective security not as a full alternative security system, but in two other ways: first, as something that occasionally happens in response to a particularly egregious act, such as the North Korean attack on South Korea in 1950, or the Iraqi seizure of Kuwait in 1990; secondly, as one pole of a continuum, with purely unilateral use of force at the other end, and a vast and varied area to be explored in between. The first fifty years of the UN, and of the nuclear age, have seen unprecedented and unforeseen explorations of that area.

Nature is always richer than art. After the UN's first half-century, there is still no strong underlying unity of purpose of the five permanent members of the Security Council or of other major powers, nor a general collective security system. However, there is a more collaborative approach to security issues than in previous decades or even centuries. Collective approaches to security that remain in business, though problematic, include regional alliances and arrangements; international economic sanctions; uses of force by groups of states authorized by the Security Council; UN peacekeeping; and arms control. These variations on the theme of collective security may be more enduring, if less satisfying, than the idea of collective security itself.

Appendix: List of UN Peacekeeping and Observer Forces

This is a chronological list of the thirty-five UN peacekeeping and observer forces established up to the end of 1994. Their composition includes military or police units contributed for the purpose by member states. All were established on the basis of Security Council resolutions, except for UNEF-I and UNSF, which were set up by the General Assembly. This list does not refer to smaller special missions or deployments of UN guards; nor to UN-authorized forces under national control such as in Korea in 1950–3, the Gulf in 1990–1, Somalia in 1992–3 (UNITAF), and Rwanda and Haiti in 1994.

1. *UN Truce Supervision Organization (UNTSO)*, several areas in the Middle East, 1948–
2. *UN Military Observer Group in India and Pakistan (UNMOGIP)*, Jammu and Kashmir, 1949–
3. *UN Emergency Force (UNEF I)*, Suez Canal, Sinai, Gaza, 1956–67
4. *UN Observation Group in Lebanon (UNOGIL)*, Lebanon, 1958
5. *UN Operation in the Congo (Opération des Nations Unies pour le Congo = ONUC)*, Republic of the Congo, 1960–4
6. *UN Security Force in West New Guinea (UNSF)*, West Irian, 1962–3
7. *UN Yemen Observation Mission (UNYOM)*, Yemen, 1963–4
8. *UN Peacekeeping Force in Cyprus (UNFICYP)*, Cyprus, 1964–
9. *Mission of the Representative of the Secretary-General in the Dominican Republic (DOMREP)*, Dominican Republic, 1965–6
10. *UN India–Pakistan Observation Mission (UNIPOM)*, India–Pakistan border, 1965–6
11. *UN Emergency Force II (UNEF II)*, Suez Canal, Sinai, 1973–9
12. *UN Disengagement Observer Force (UNDOF)*, Golan Heights, 1974–

13. *UN Interim Force in Lebanon (UNIFIL),* southern Lebanon, 1978–
14. *UN Good Offices Mission in Afghanistan and Pakistan (UNGOMAP),* Afghanistan and Pakistan, 1988–90
15. *UN Iran–Iraq Military Observer Group (UNIIMOG),* Iran and Iraq, 1988–91
16. *UN Angola Verification Mission (UNAVEM I),* Angola, 1989–91
17. *UN Transition Assistance Group (UNTAG),* Namibia and Angola, 1989–90
18. *UN Observer Group in Central America (ONUCA),* Costa Rica, El Salvador, Guatemala, Honduras, Nicaragua, 1989–92
19. *UN Iraq–Kuwait Observation Mission (UNIKOM),* Kuwait–Iraq DMZ, 1991–
20. *UN Angola Verification Mission II (UNAVEM II),* Angola, 1991–
21. *UN Observer Mission in El Salvador (ONUSAL),* El Salvador, 1991–
22. *UN Mission for the Referendum in Western Sahara (MINURSO),* Western Sahara, 1991–
23. *UN Advance Mission in Cambodia (UNAMIC),* Cambodia, 1991–2
24. *UN Protection Force (UNPROFOR),* Bosnia-Herzegovina, Croatia, Macedonia, 1992–
25. *UN Transitional Authority in Cambodia (UNTAC),* Cambodia, 1992–3
26. *UN Operation in Somalia (UNOSOM I),* Somalia, 1992–3
27. *UN Operation in Mozambique (ONUMOZ),* Mozambique, 1992–4
28. *UN Operation in Somalia II (UNOSOM II),* 1993–5
29. *UN Observer Mission Uganda–Rwanda (UNOMUR),* Uganda–Rwanda border, 1993–4
30. *UN Observer Mission in Georgia (UNOMIG),* Georgia, 1993–
31. *UN Observer Mission in Liberia (UNOMIL),* Liberia, 1993–
32. *UN Mission in Haiti (UNMIH),* Haiti, 1993–
33. *UN Assistance Mission for Rwanda (UNAMIR),* Rwanda, 1993–
34. *UN Aouzou Strip Observer Group (UNASOG),* Chad–Libya border, 1994
35. *UN Mission of Observers in Tajikistan (UNMOT),* Tajikistan, 1994–

Chronology: UN Actions in Security Field

30 Oct. 1943	Moscow Four-Nation Declaration proposes general international organization for maintenance of peace and security
26 June 1945	UN Charter signed; enters into force 24 Oct.
16 July 1945	Atomic bomb first tested; used against Japan 6 and 9 Aug.
30 Apr. 1947	UN Military Staff Committee reports that it has failed to reach agreement on strength and composition of UN armed forces
15 July 1948	Security Council (SC) establishes first UN peacekeeping mission (UNTSO) (see Appendix)
27 June 1950	In response to N. Korean attack on S. Korea, SC authorizes use of force under US control

5 Nov. 1956	General Assembly establishes the first large peacekeeping force, UNEF I in Middle East; in 1957 it attained a maximum strength of 6,073
1961	Number of UN member states reaches 100
14 Mar. 1962	Eighteen-Nation Disarmament Conference opened in Geneva (re-named the Committee on Disarmament in August 1969)
31 Aug. 1965	UN Charter revised to take into account increased number of member states; number of non-permanent members of SC raised from six to ten
16 Dec. 1966	SC orders the first mandatory general economic sanctions, against Rhodesia
1 July 1968	Treaty on the Non-Proliferation of Nuclear Weapons signed
25 Oct. 1971	People's Republic of China admitted to UN membership
4 Nov. 1977	SC orders mandatory arms embargo against South Africa
8 Aug. 1988	Ceasefire ends the eight-year Iran–Iraq war, following extensive activities by SC and UN Secretary-General
6 Aug. 1990	In response to Iraqi attack on Kuwait, SC initiates economic sanctions against Iraq (6 Aug.)
29 Nov. 1990	SC authorizes use of force against Iraq
25 Sept. 1991	SC imposes arms embargo on Yugoslavia
Jan. 1992	Russia takes up former USSR seat as Permanent Member of SC; first Security Council summit held, issues statement about UN's security role.
Feb. 1992	SC establishes UN Protection Force in former Yugoslavia; this becomes its largest and most expensive peacekeeping operation ever
30 May 1992	SC imposes general economic sanctions on Serbia and Montenegro
3 Dec. 1992	SC authorizes US-led task force to operate in Somalia
13 Jan. 1993	Chemical Weapons Convention signed
1994	In response to war and genocide in Rwanda, UN succeeds in taking only limited action; number of UN member states reaches 185

Notes

1. On the recurrence of collective security practices and proposals over the centuries see Martin Wight, *Systems of States* (Leicester, 1977), 62, 149–50; F. H. Hinsley, *Power and the Pursuit of Peace* (Cambridge, 1963), esp. 309–21, 344–5; and R. N. Stromberg, 'The Idea of Collective Security', *Journal of the History of Ideas*, 17 (1956), 251.
2. For an enumeration of questions relating to collective security systems see Andrew Hurrell, 'Collective Security and International Order Revisited', *International Relations* (London), 11/1 (April 1992), 37–55.
3. A useful assessment is F. P. Walters, *A History of the League of Nations* (Oxford, 1960).
4. See generally Margaret Doxey, *International Sanctions in Contemporary Perspective* (London, 1987); David Leyton-Brown (ed.), *The Utility of Economic Sanctions* (New

York, 1987); David A. Baldwin, *Economic Statecraft* (Princeton, 1985); and Gary Hufbauer et al., *Economic Sanctions Reconsidered* (Washington, 1990).

5. 'Supplement to An Agenda for Peace: Position Paper of the Secretary-General on the Occasion of the Fiftieth Anniversary of the United Nations', UN doc. A/50/60 (3 Jan. 1995), para. 70.

6. Report of the Military Staff Committee, 'General Principles Governing the Organization of the Armed Forces Made Available to the Security Council by Member Nations of the United Nations', UN doc. S/336 (30 Apr. 1947).

7. See e.g. Fernand van Langenhove, *La Crise du système de sécurité collective des Nations Unies 1946–57* (The Hague, 1958).

8. The text of the 1949 North Atlantic Treaty is in *United Nations Treaty Series*, xxxiv. 243. There were also references to the UN Charter in Articles 1 and 7.

9. Dean Acheson's views during the negotiations for the North Atlantic Treaty, as cited in Escott Reid, *Time of Fear and Hope: The Making of the North Atlantic Treaty 1947– 49* (Toronto, 1977), appx. 3, 268.

10. The text of the 1955 Warsaw Treaty is in *United Nations Treaty Series*, ccxix. 3.

11. For general discussion of problems concerning the legitimacy of humanitarian intervention see R. Lillich (ed.), *Humanitarian Intervention and the United Nations* (London, 1973); Thomas Franck and Nigel Rodley, 'After Bangladesh: The Law of Humanitarian Intervention by Military Force', *American Journal of International Law*, 67 (1973), 275; Michael Akehurst, 'Humanitarian Intervention', in Hedley Bull (ed.), *Intervention in World Politics* (Oxford, 1984), 95–118; Nigel Rodley (ed.), *To Loose the Bands of Wickedness: International Intervention in Defence of Human Rights* (London, 1992); Laura Reed and Carl Kaysen (eds.), *Emerging Norms of Justified Intervention* (Cambridge, Mass., 1993).

12. See esp. Marrack Goulding, Under-Secretary-General for Political Affairs, 'The Evolution of United Nations Peacekeeping', *International Affairs*, 69/3 (July 1993), 453–5.

13. See Gerald B. Helman and Steven R. Ratner, 'Saving Failed States', *Foreign Policy*, 89 (Winter 1992–3), 3–20; Peter Lyon, 'The Rise and Fall and Possible Revival of International Trusteeship', *Journal of Commonwealth and Comparative Politics*, 31 (March 1993), 96–110.

14. Boutros Boutros Ghali, *An Agenda for Peace: Preventive Diplomacy, Peacemaking and Peace-keeping*, Report of the Secretary-General Pursuant to the Statement Adopted by the Summit Meeting of the Security Council on 31 Jan. 1992 (New York, June 1992). See also the much more sober 'Supplement' issued in Jan. 1995 (note 5 above).

15. For American explorations of collective security ideas as they relate to the post-Cold War world see Leon Gordenker and Thomas G. Weiss, 'The Collective Security Idea and Changing World Politics', in Weiss (ed.), *Collective Security in a Changing World* (Boulder, Colo., 1993), 3–18.

16. A well-argued attack on the capacity of international institutions to provide a collective security system in the post-Cold War world, and a warning of the pernicious effects of excessive reliance on institutional approaches, is John J. Mearsheimer, 'The False Promise of International Institutions', *International Security*, 19/3 (Winter 1994– 5), 5–49.

17. Janne E. Nolan (ed.), *Global Engagement: Cooperation and Security in the Twenty-first Century* (Washington, 1994). The Nolan volume presents 'cooperative security' as compatible with collective security (5–6). For advocacy of cooperative security by the Australian foreign minister see Gareth Evans, *Cooperating for Peace: The Global Agenda for the 1990s and Beyond* (St Leonards, New South Wales, 1993).

Further Reading

ARCHER, CLIVE (ed.), *International Organizations*, 2nd edn. (London, 1992). Very useful introduction to the role of the UN and other bodies.

ARMSTRONG, DAVID, *The Rise of the International Organisation: A Short History* (London, 1982). A new edition is due shortly.

BERRIDGE, GEOFF, *Return to the UN: UN Diplomacy in Regional Conflicts* (London, 1991). Examines the ways in which the UN has actually addressed certain regional conflicts.

DURCH, WILLIAM J. (ed.), *The Evolution of UN Peacekeeping: Case Studies and Comparative Analyses* (New York, 1993). Takes into account some post-Cold War cases.

HIGGINS, ROSALYN, *United Nations Peacekeeping*, 4 vols. (Oxford, 1969–81). An extremely useful legal analysis, including documents, from the early decades of UN peacekeeping. Includes also material on the Korean war.

JAMES, ALAN, *Peacekeeping in International Politics* (London, 1990). Relates peacekeeping activities to the broader political processes which they are intended to ameliorate.

ROBERTS, ADAM, and KINGSBURY, BENEDICT (eds.), *United Nations, Divided World: The UN's Roles in International Relations*, 2nd edn. (Oxford, 1993). Several chapters deal with security issues. *An Agenda for Peace* is reprinted as an appendix.

SIMMA, BRUNO (ed.), *The Charter of the United Nations: A Commentary* (Oxford, 1994). Encyclopaedic legal analysis of the legislative history, interpretation, and practical application of each Charter provision.

United Nations, *The Blue Helmets: A Review of United Nations Peace-Keeping*, 2nd edn. (New York, 1990). Useful factual survey of each operation.

—— *Yearbook of the United Nations* (New York, annually). An extremely useful reference work.

CHAPTER FIFTEEN

THE NORTH ATLANTIC TREATY ORGANIZATION: ALLIANCE THEORY

John Duffield

On 4 April 1949 the United States, Canada, and ten West European states signed the North Atlantic Treaty in Washington, DC. The heart of the treaty (Article 5) represented a classic alliance commitment, whereby the parties agreed to assist one another in the event of an armed attack. During the next two years the treaty framework was supplemented by an elaborate organizational structure, which effectively put the 'O' in NATO.

NATO has arguably been the most successful peacetime alliance in history. One manifestation of this success is the alliance's remarkable longevity. NATO endured some four decades of Cold War, and it remains the leading security organization in Europe, even though the most frequently cited reason for its existence, the threat posed by the Soviet Union, has disappeared. Few observers doubt that the alliance will be around to celebrate its fiftieth anniversary at the end of the century.

NATO has also proven to be a hugely popular alliance. Although the North Atlantic Treaty allowed for parties to withdraw after it had been in force for twenty years, no state has renounced its membership, and four states have joined the alliance since its inception. In the past few years, moreover, numerous Central and East European states, formerly in the Soviet bloc, have expressed a strong interest in membership.

Third, NATO has been characterized by an unusually high degree of security cooperation among its member states. In Article 3 of the treaty, the parties also

The author is grateful to Ngaire Woods and John Oneal for their comments on a draft of this chapter.

agreed 'by means of continuous and effective self-help and mutual aid, [to] maintain and develop their individual and collective capacity to resist armed attack'. To this end, the NATO countries have carried out detailed joint planning and training for the defence of Western Europe, stationed substantial numbers of troops on each other's territory, and even integrated their military forces to an exceptional extent, especially for a peacetime alliance. This cooperation has taken place primarily within the alliance's organizational structures for political consultation, joint policy-making, and integrated military planning and command. Such a high degree of institutionalization also makes NATO unique among consensual peacetime alliances.

15.1. Applying Alliance Theory

NATO and Alliance Theory

This chapter explores the ways in which—and the degree to which—alliance theory can be used to explain some of the main features of NATO and their evolution over time. NATO conforms easily to commonly used definitions of alliances and thus lends itself quite well to such an analysis.[1] Moreover, if any theory of alliances is to enjoy widespread acceptance, and certainly if it is ever to be considered of relevance to policy-makers, it must be able to explain significant cases, such as NATO.

The chapter focuses on two important aspects of NATO that are particularly conducive to theoretical analysis. The first is the alliance's emergence and persistence. Realist theorists, especially those who embrace balance-of-power theory, have traditionally regarded alliances as responses by states to the threats posed by powerful common adversaries. At first glance, NATO's evolution seems consistent with this approach. Both the creation of the alliance and its maintenance for the next forty years can be viewed as a Western reaction to the military power and ideological hostility of the Soviet Union. A more detailed examination of NATO history, however, finds that balance-of-power theory is not fully adequate as an explanatory device. It reveals a wider range of important motives than balance-of-power theory admits and thus suggests the need to modify and supplement the basic theory in several ways that yield a more satisfactory account of NATO.

Also important has been the way in which the burdens of alliance have been shared among the NATO states. Since the mid-1960s scholars have devised a number of economic theories to explain the relative military contributions of alliance members. In contrast to other areas of alliance theory, moreover, burden-sharing analysis has been developed almost entirely in reference to NATO, and, as a result of nearly three decades of effort, noteworthy progress has occurred. Nevertheless, no theoretical consensus has emerged among the economic theorists, prompting scholars to explore new analytical approaches to the problem.

The Warsaw Treaty Organization and Alliance Theory

Several attempts have also been made to apply alliance theory to NATO's former Eastern bloc counterpart, the Warsaw Treaty Organization (WTO).[2] Nevertheless, the WTO has received considerably less theoretical attention. One reason is that researchers have faced greater difficulties in obtaining reliable information about Soviet and East European activities, especially in the security realm. An even more inhibitory factor, however, has been the nature of the WTO itself, which raised questions about the very applicability of alliance theory.

Most analyses of alliances presume a high degree of autonomy on the part of alliance members. States are ultimately free to enter or leave alliances and to determine the nature and level of their participation, even if their actions are strongly influenced by external circumstances beyond their control. In contrast, most non-Soviet members of the WTO had little choice about membership in the alliance and only a limited amount of discretion in shaping other important aspects of their foreign and military policies, especially during the WTO's first decade. Indeed, the WTO was created by the Soviet Union largely as an instrument for maintaining control over Eastern Europe. Although definitions of alliances do not explicitly exclude relations of dominance, the presence of coercion blurs the distinctions between alliances, spheres of influence, and empires.

15.2. Explaining NATO's Formation and Persistence: Balance-of-power Theory

Why was NATO formed, and why has it persisted? Despite NATO's importance, scholars have made no systematic attempt to answer these questions in terms of alliance theory. Although historians have devoted considerable attention to the early years of the alliance, international relations theorists have seemingly taken the reasons for NATO's emergence and continued existence to be self-evident. Nevertheless, they have developed general theories of alliance formation and disintegration that promise to help us make sense of NATO.

Balance-of-power Theory and Alliances

The leading approach to explaining alliance patterns has long been balance-of-power theory. According to this theory, a state's behaviour is determined primarily

Table 15.1. Balance-of-power theory and alliances	
Causal variables	Hypotheses
Distribution of power; geographical proximity; offensive capabilities; intentions	The existence of a powerful, threatening state will prompt other states to ally. In the absence of such a state, other states will not ally, and existing alliances will dissolve.

by its external environment—especially the number of states in the international system and their relative power—rather than by its internal characteristics. The basic hypothesis of this approach is that states form alliances to protect themselves against powerful, threatening adversaries. By combining their capabilities, alliance members are better able to deter aggression and avoid war, to defend themselves successfully if deterrence fails, and more generally to prevent stronger powers from dominating them. Should the common threat greatly diminish or disappear, however, the alliance formed to address it is unlikely to endure for long (see Table 15.1).

Balance-of-power theorists have differed among themselves mainly on the issue of how states assess external threats. Structural realists such as Kenneth Waltz view the threat posed by a state to others as determined essentially by its capabilities. In contrast, Stephen Walt's 'balance of threat' theory considers a state's proximity to others, its offensive military capabilities, and its perceived intentions as well as its aggregate power.[3]

By viewing NATO as a Western response to the threat posed by an ideologically hostile and militarily powerful Soviet Union, balance-of-power theory does help to explain in a parsimonious manner the alliance's rise and persistence. Balance-of-power considerations clearly influenced the calculations of Western decision-makers in each of four important phases in NATO's evolution: (1) the origins of the alliance; (2) its subsequent militarization; (3) West Germany's accession in 1955; and (4) NATO's continued existence, to the surprise of many commentators, after the end of the Cold War in Europe, the dissolution of the WTO, and the break-up of the Soviet Union itself. A detailed inspection of these events, however, suggests that balance-of-power theory alone cannot satisfactorily explain them. Rather, it reveals a more complex picture of the motives of alliance members than the theory admits.

The Origins of NATO

Concern about Soviet power was certainly one consideration that motivated the authors of the North Atlantic Treaty. Following the Second World War, the Soviet

Union ranked easily as the most powerful country in Europe, the eastern half of which was controlled by its armies. Germany, previously the most plausible bulwark against expansion from the east, was now a power vacuum, having been militarily crushed and deprived of its sovereign rights. The countries of Western Europe, still recovering from the ravages of the war, were by no means prepared to erect an effective military counterweight. Thus the treaty was seen as helping to remedy the resulting power imbalance by more strongly linking the tremendous military power and potential of the United States to the Western half of the continent.

Nevertheless, the measures taken immediately after the treaty was ratified did little to enhance the prospects of deterrence or a successful defence of the region. The United States deployed no additional troops in Europe, it offered only a modest amount of military assistance to its allies, and it limited its participation in the alliance's initial defence planning bodies. As a result, few if any observers believed that NATO forces could prevent Western Europe from being overrun in the event of a determined Soviet attack.

In fact, during the deliberations preceding the signing of the treaty the possibility of Soviet aggression elicited surprisingly little concern. No Western leaders perceived an immediate Soviet military threat. Rather, they were animated primarily by two other considerations that fit much less easily, if at all, within the balance-of-power framework.[4]

First, many West European leaders were preoccupied with internal threats, especially in countries such as France and Italy where Communist movements remained a potent force. They feared that subversive elements, encouraged by Moscow, might seek to exploit prevailing economic hardships in order to promote instability, to undermine the political system, and, ultimately, to pave the way for a Communist seizure of power. Thus an alliance with the United States was seen as important less for balancing Soviet military power on the continent and deterring Soviet aggression than for restoring a general sense of security that would make it possible for governments to take effective measures against internal threats and enable the people of the region to approach the difficult tasks of economic and political reconstruction with confidence.

Secondly, an American security commitment was viewed in some quarters as a vital hedge against renewed German attempts at domination. French leaders in particular were as concerned about a possible resurgence of German power as they were about that of the Soviet Union. Germany remained occupied and demilitarized, but the United States and Britain regarded the economic revival of the three Western zones as necessary for the recovery of the region as a whole. Consequently, they pressed for the administrative merger of the three zones, their inclusion in the European Recovery Programme, the lifting of restrictions on German industrial production, and, as cooperation with the Soviet Union broke down, the establishment of a separate West German state. Faced with the possibility that they might soon have to deal once again with a sovereign and powerful Germany, the French demanded strong US guarantees in return for their acquiescence in these measures.

The Militarization of NATO

In contrast to the origins of NATO, the subsequent militarization of the alliance can be explained almost entirely in terms of balance-of-power theory. During the year following the signing of the treaty, two external events in particular caused NATO leaders to reassess Soviet intentions, leading them to conclude that the risk of aggression in Europe was considerably greater than they had previously assumed. The first Soviet nuclear test in the late summer of 1949, several years earlier than expected, prompted concerns that the leaders in the Kremlin would be increasingly emboldened to undertake risky actions that could lead to war as the Soviet Union narrowed the atomic lead of the United States. Any remaining uncertainties about the need to strengthen Western Europe's defences were swept away by the outbreak of the Korean War in June 1950. There was little doubt in the West that the Soviet Union had instigated the North Korean attack. Consequently, most allied leaders concluded that Moscow would henceforth be more willing to use force to achieve its aims around the globe.

This reassessment of Soviet intentions precipitated a four-pronged effort to erect a strong conventional defence in Western Europe that would help to balance Soviet military power on the continent and, the allies hoped, to deter aggression. Both the United States and Britain substantially augmented the military forces they deployed in the region; the other European allies stepped up their rearmament efforts with the help of a fivefold increase in US military assistance; the alliance established an integrated military command and planning structure to ensure the most efficient use of the assigned national forces; and the NATO countries agreed in principle to pursue a German military contribution.

German Membership of NATO

Turning to West Germany's accession to NATO in 1955, however, we find once again that a state's motives for joining the alliance do not conform neatly to the expectations of balance-of-power theory. To be sure, the German government saw alliance membership as enhancing its country's security *vis-à-vis* the Soviet Union. Germany obtained formal NATO security guarantees and a say in Western defence plans. But the security benefits of membership can be exaggerated and were largely offset by other costs and risks. West Germany already enjoyed de facto security guarantees by virtue of the presence of Western forces and defence pledges made by the occupying powers as early as 1950. Some Germans, moreover, feared that joining NATO would foreclose the possibility of unification and, in conjunction with German rearmament, might even precipitate a preventative Soviet attack. In addition, rearmament threatened to be a costly proposition that, in the worst case, risked reviving German militarism.

Obtaining greater protection from the Soviet threat was but one of several reasons for joining the alliance. Another was to strengthen Germany's ties with the West in order to ensure the establishment of strong democratic institutions and values in Germany. Also, Chancellor Konrad Adenauer used German leverage in the negotiations over membership in first the European Defence Community and then NATO to attain a number of additional important objectives. These included terminating the occupation regime, restoring German sovereignty, eliminating all non-voluntary restrictions on German policy, and obtaining commitments of Western support for unification. Thus Germany's accession to NATO occurred only after several years of hard bargaining, during which its partners made significant concessions on these issues.[5]

NATO's Persistence after the Cold War

Balance-of-power theory is least helpful for understanding NATO's persistence after the Cold War. In view of the profound changes that occurred in the Soviet bloc between 1989 and 1991, resulting in a drastic decline in the former threat, one might well expect the theory to predict that NATO would wither away. Yet the alliance remains Europe's leading security institution and continues to enjoy the strong support of its members.

Of course, one of NATO's functions continues to be the traditional one of balancing the not insubstantial residual military power of Russia, especially its large nuclear arsenal, and hedging against a revival of hostile Russian intentions toward the West. But the alliance's persistence owes at least as much to its ability to address a variety of other security concerns that are not easily captured by the balance-of-power framework.[6]

Since 1990 NATO members have increasingly viewed the alliance as having an important role to play in dealing with crises and conflicts that may arise in Central and Eastern Europe, even when such developments do not threaten them directly. More profoundly, the alliance works to prevent regional crises and conflicts from occurring in the first place by stabilizing the countries of the former Soviet bloc. It does so primarily in two ways: by promoting political reform in the new democracies, in part by exposing their leaders to Western models of civil–military relations; and by enhancing their security *vis-à-vis* possible external threats. To this end, NATO has created new frameworks for meaningful security cooperation, the North Atlantic Cooperation Council (NACC) and the Partnership for Peace (PfP), that include the countries of Central and Eastern Europe.

Finally, NATO's rarely noted internal function of smoothing relations among its members has assumed greater relative importance following the decline of the Soviet threat and German unification. By fostering a common identity, promoting joint defence planning, integrating national forces to a significant extent, and facilitating American involvement in European security affairs, the continued existence of the alliance reassures its European members that they have nothing to fear from one another. In addition, NATO's elaborate consultative mechanisms constitute the principal instruments of transatlantic dialogue, understanding, and influence.

Modifying and Supplementing Balance-of-power Theory

In sum, NATO's formation and persistence, at least until the end of the Cold War, conform fairly well to the expectations of balance-of-power theory. But the motives of member countries for joining and maintaining the alliance have clearly not been limited to that of protecting themselves against the most serious external threat, that posed by the Soviet Union. Indeed, for some countries at certain critical moments, other considerations were equally if not more important.

There are at least four ways in which balance-of-power theory might be modified and supplemented to yield a more satisfactory account of this aspect of NATO. First, greater explanatory power could be gained by making explicit provision for the possibility of multiple threats. Formulations of balance-of-power theory tend to treat alliance formation as a response to a single external danger, be it a threatening state or an opposing alliance. The origins of NATO, however, suggest that states may ally at least in part to address distinct threats. Such a modification would be consistent with Walt's refined version of balance-of-power theory, since differences in location are likely to cause potential allies to perceive the threats posed by possible adversaries differently.

Secondly, our understanding of NATO is enhanced if we consider the role that internal threats may play in motivating ruling regimes to form alliances with other states. Valuable work along these lines has been done in recent years through the study of alignments in the Third World.[7] NATO's early history shows that domestic threats can also be a principal motive for alliance formation in developed but temporarily weakened countries.

Thirdly, students of NATO would also do well to consider the impact of ideology. Indeed, the existence of NATO may provide at least as much support for the theory that ideological affinity determines alliances as it does for balance-of-power theory. At a minimum, ideology has been an important factor shaping threat perception, since Western views of the Soviet Union were difficult to dis-entangle from the East–West ideological conflict. NATO's continued existence even after the collapse of the Soviet Union implies, moreover, that liberal states based on democracy, political pluralism, and the rule of law may be inclined to maintain (if not to form in the first place) alliances even in the absence of a compelling external threat, since they are much less likely to perceive one an-other as dangerous.

Finally, NATO's institutional character has probably contributed to the alliance's persistence. The concept of institutional inertia is a familiar one, although exactly how much influence it should have on alliance longevity remains to be hypo-thesized. But the study of other types of international institutions suggests that participating states will not readily dispense with them even after the conditions that gave rise to the institutions have been altered.[8] In addition, NATO includes large international bureaucracies, the International Staff/Secretariat and the Supreme Headquarters Allied Powers Europe, whose top officials enjoy consider-able autonomy. These supranational bodies and the individuals who head them have almost certainly helped the alliance to adapt to changing external circum-stances by defining new tasks, identifying ways to achieve them, forging com-promises, and otherwise providing leadership.

15.3. Explaining Allied Military Contributions: Economic Theories of Alliances

A second important aspect of NATO has been the size, in both relative and absolute terms, of its members' contributions to their common security. The sum total of these contributions has critically shaped whether the alliance could reliably deter aggression and, should deterrence have failed, mount a successful defence of its members. Perceptions of the fairness with which the burdens of common security have been distributed, moreover, have greatly affected the tenor of intra-alliance relations, if not NATO's very cohesiveness.

Not surprisingly, controversies over burden-sharing and the adequacy of NATO's military preparations have arisen repeatedly within the alliance.[9] Typically, the United States has judged the contributions of its allies to be insufficient and has pressed them to do more, although the issue has appeared in numerous guises over the years. In the early and mid-1950s most disputes revolved around conven-tional force levels, as the European allies struggled to achieve the goals that had been agreed upon at the beginning of the NATO military build-up. In the 1960s and early 1970s the focus of the debate shifted to whether the Europeans should—

Table 15.2. Economic theories of alliances

Wave	Assumptions	Dependent variables	Independent variables	Hypotheses
First wave: public goods theory	Public nature of defence outputs; independent decision-making	Relative defence burdens (ME/GNP); optimality of defence output	Number of alliance members; relative size (GNP)	The much greater size of the United States results in disproportional defence burdens (free-riding by its allies) and suboptimal defence spending
Modifications of the second wave: the joint product model	Mixed nature of defence outputs: public, private, and impurely public	Relative defence burdens	Distribution of defence outputs as influenced by alliance strategy and military technology	Shift to impurely public outputs (protective weapons) causes disproportionality in defence burdens to decline
Third-wave modifications	Cooperative decision-making and intra-alliance bargaining		Emphasis on private benefits of military spending; threat perception	Persistence of disproportionality, despite some decline in magnitude over time

and how they could—offset the foreign exchange losses incurred by the United States in stationing troops in Europe. And in the late 1970s and 1980s attention turned to levels of defence spending, as the United States insisted that its partners achieve the annual real increases in military expenditures agreed upon at the 1977 NATO summit.

Largely independently of these transatlantic debates, a number of scholars have attempted to explain the level and distribution of defence burdens within NATO, devising several so-called economic theories of alliances to do so. This literature has been developed in three successive waves, beginning in the mid-1960s and, as noted above, almost entirely in reference to NATO (see Table 15.2).[10] In part because most conceptual advances have built on previous analyses, moreover, it has made notable progress.

The First Wave: Public Goods Theory

The earliest economic theorists, Mancur Olson and Richard Zeckhauser, sought to address two questions. First, why did the larger members of NATO, especially the United States, tend to spend disproportionately more on defence than did the smaller allies? In 1964, for example, the United States had ranked first within the alliance in both GNP and the percentage of GNP spent on defence. Britain and France had ranked third and fourth, respectively, in both categories, and Germany, with the second largest economy, had devoted the sixth highest percentage of its GNP to defence even though it had not yet completed the expensive process of rearming. Secondly, why had the alliance repeatedly failed to provide the forces that its members themselves had described as necessary?

To answer these questions, Olson and Zeckhauser made the assumption that the security resulting from the combined military efforts of alliance members can be regarded as a public good having the properties of non-exclusion and non-rivalness. No member of a group producing a public good can be prevented from enjoying the good, and one member's consumption of the good does not significantly diminish the supply available to others. As a result, members acting independently will seek to 'free-ride' on others' contributions. The authors also assumed that most alliances are 'privileged' groups, in which at least one member has an incentive to see that the public good is provided, even if it has to bear the full burden of providing the good.[11]

From these assumptions Olson and Zeckhauser derived two hypotheses about alliance behaviour. First, members that place a higher absolute value on the public good—typically the 'larger' members—will make disproportionately large contributions. Smaller members will have little or no incentive to contribute, since the larger members will provide for most if not all of their security needs. Secondly, and consequently, alliance members will collectively tend to make suboptimal contributions to the public good.

The data available at the time seemed to confirm both of these hypotheses. Few analysts would have disputed that the overall size of NATO's military preparations was suboptimal, since the alliance had consistently failed to achieve its goals for ground forces in Western Europe. Moreover, using military expenditure (ME) as a measure of each state's contribution to the public good and GNP as a proxy for the value each state places on the public good (since larger states would presumably desire greater amounts), Olson and Zeckhauser found a statistically significant positive correlation between GNP and defence burden, defined as the percentage of GNP devoted to defence (ME/GNP), for NATO countries in 1960 and 1964. In other words, larger alliance members clearly did shoulder disproportionately heavy defence burdens in those years.[12]

Despite its elegance, Olson and Zeckhauser's analysis suffered from at least two shortcomings. One problem concerned the definition of suboptimality. NATO force goals, always the subject of heated intra-alliance debate, never constituted an objective standard of optimality, nor could a meaningful alternative be easily fashioned. Consequently, subsequent work in this area has focused on the question of disproportionality. A second and more serious shortcoming was the fact that Olson and Zeckhauser considered data from just two years. Later longitudinal studies showed a significant temporal decline in the correlation between defence burden and GDP. Thus, for example, although the US share of NATO's combined GDP declined by a mere 3 per cent, from 59 per cent to 56 per cent, between 1960 and 1975, its share of alliance defence spending dropped by 6 per cent, from 73 per cent to 67 per cent, during the same period.[13]

The Second Wave: The Joint Product Model

This apparent failure of public goods theory prompted a second wave of theorizing in the late 1970s and early 1980s. In order to account for the perceived decline in disproportionality, theorists relaxed the assumption that alliance defence spending results primarily in public goods. Instead, they proposed a 'joint product model', according to which military spending generates purely private and impurely public as well as public outputs. Private benefits include the use of armed forces for domestic purposes or for the pursuit of national interests outside the alliance area. Impurely public goods consist of weapons systems with important protective, as opposed to purely deterrent, functions, such as missile defences and conventional forces. Protective weapons may be subject to spatial rivalry, since they cannot defend all areas of the alliance at once, and even to exclusion.[14]

The joint product model predicts that defence burdens are influenced by the nature and distribution of the benefits of military spending as well as by GNP. As the percentage of defence spending resulting in private and impurely public outputs rises, the incidence of disproportionality—and suboptimality—in defence spending will decline, since each alliance member must increasingly rely on its own efforts to achieve security. In the limiting case, a state's defence burden will be entirely a function of the benefits it derives from its own expenditures.

Proponents of the joint product model argued that NATO had come to place greater reliance on protective weapons, causing disproportionality in burden-sharing to diminish. They attributed this shift primarily to the change in alliance strategy from massive retaliation to flexible response that occurred in the late 1960s. Flexible response emphasized the ability to make non-nuclear responses to Soviet aggression and thus increased the need for strong conventional forces. At the same time technological developments, especially the advent of precision-guided munitions, made it possible for NATO to neutralize the Warsaw Pact's traditional non-nuclear advantages, providing a further rationale for increased spending on conventional forces. Finally, they maintained that such increases by one country might actually induce its allies to spend more rather than less because of a presumed ' complementarity' of defence goods under flexible response.[15]

Analyses based on the joint product model went largely unchallenged until the late 1980s, when they encountered a barrage of criticism. Although the model seemed to account for the decline in free-riding, the underlying causal explanation did not square with reality. In particular, the critics argued, the alleged shift in NATO strategy had been greatly overstated. The fundamental objective of the alliance and the military efforts of its members remained security through deterrence. The purpose of flexible response had been to buttress the credibility of US extended deterrence, not to replace it with a strategy of defence, especially as far as the European allies were concerned. In addition, the presumed impact of flexible response on defence spending and the significance of technological developments had been exaggerated. The countries of Western Europe had made little effort to field conventional forces adequate to defend the region against a determined attack, as evidenced by adverse trends in the European military balance and a significant decline in NATO Europe's combined military expenditures as a percentage of Soviet defence spending.[16]

The Third Wave

As a result of these challenges, the late 1980s and early 1990s witnessed a number of further attempts to develop a satisfactory explanation of allied defence burdens that built upon the existing economic models. These efforts refocused attention on the transatlantic differences in burden-sharing that endured even as the relative US contribution to NATO declined, while seeking to account for departures from the behaviour of the European allies as predicted by public goods theory.

Third-wave analyses introduced three particularly productive theoretical refinements. First, they paid more attention to identifying and segregating the purely private benefits of defence spending. Although the joint product model included private outputs, second-wave applications had concentrated instead on what was seen as the increasingly impure nature of the public outputs of military spending as NATO placed greater emphasis on defence. Later studies showed, however, that much of the apparent decline in free-riding could be attributed to the fact that a substantial proportion of the defence spending of several alliance members was devoted to the pursuit of purely private goods.[17]

Some third-wave studies also modelled the impact on defence burdens of changes in threat perceptions. Although realist theory would suggest a strong link between fears of aggression and military effort, this relationship had been absent from previous economic models of alliances. Yet by explicitly incorporating threats, one could explain more parsimoniously than with the joint product model why the defence burdens of large and small allies might rise or fall in unison.[18]

Finally, third-wave analyses challenged Olson and Zeckhauser's assumption that national decisions about defence spending are made in a purely independent and non-cooperative manner. Instead, they argued, defence policy-making, at least within NATO, is characterized by a high degree of strategic interaction. Intra-alliance bargaining results in smaller members increasing their military contributions in order to cement the vital security commitments of their larger partners. Also, increasing interdependence and cooperation among European members of the alliance may have resulted in greater coordination of defence policy among them and thus a convergence in the size of their defence burdens.[19]

The general thrust of this third wave was to reconfirm the central insight of public goods theory—that the largest member of an alliance is likely to bear a disproportionately large defence burden. In particular, it established the continued existence of a strong relationship between defence burden and GDP in the 1970s and 1980s within NATO. As one representative study concluded, 'NATO is still best characterized as a uniquely privileged group that provides a relatively pure, inclusive public good.'[20]

New Approaches to the Study of Burden-sharing

Recent years have also seen new approaches to the study of burden-sharing within NATO. One of these, although itself an economic theory at heart, challenges the assumption of previous analyses that alliances produce only a single public good, namely military security. Rather, it adopts a broader definition of burden-sharing, arguing that alliance members contribute to their common security through the provision of multiple public goods. These include foreign aid, research and development, and efforts at monetary stabilization as well as the benefits of military expenditures. It posits, moreover, that alliance members may specialize in the provision of these goods according to their comparative advantage. Preliminary analyses using this more comprehensive approach have found less free-riding among members of the Western alliance (including Japan) and a more optimal provision of security by them overall than a narrower application of public goods theory would predict.[21]

In contrast, a second new approach represents a complete break with economic theories. It attempts instead to explain allied military contributions in terms of international regimes, which consist of norms and rules governing state behaviour in particular issue areas. The regime approach establishes the existence of a set of rules regarding the provision of conventional forces by NATO members, especially in the Central Region of Europe, and argues that alliance conventional force levels have indeed been strongly influenced by these rules.

The overall effect of this regime has been to promote stability in the size of NATO's conventional forces. Thus from the mid-1960s until 1990 the overall level of conventional forces in the Central Region, as measured in terms of divisions, brigades, and military personnel, varied for the most part within a range of less than 10 per cent, and the contributions of individual countries with forces in the region were almost as stable. The influence of the regime has been particularly marked when changes in the Soviet threat or shifts in the distribution of military potential among the NATO countries might have been expected to result in altered national force contributions but did not.[22]

15.4. Conclusion

This survey suggests that alliance theory can shed considerable light on important aspects of NATO. Balance-of-power theory shows how NATO's formation and persistence can be understood at least in part as a response by its members to the threat posed by an ideologically hostile and militarily powerful Soviet Union. Economic theories of alliances reveal how the relative size of the NATO countries, and the degree to which the outputs of their military spending can be characterized as public goods, influence the magnitude of their respective defence efforts.

Nevertheless, the chapter also suggests that existing analytical approaches do not yet yield fully satisfactory explanations of NATO. More work needs to be done before we can pronounce them as adequate. Balance-of-power theory fails to capture some of the main motives of member countries for joining and maintaining the alliance. Consequently, we may gain a fuller understanding of NATO's formation and persistence if we modify and supplement the basic theory by making explicit provision for the possibility of internal and multiple external threats and by considering the impact of ideology and the alliance's institutional character.

Likewise, the economic approaches merit further development. Promising independent variables, such as how differences in per capita GNP and threat perception may affect the willingness of alliance members to contribute to the public good, remain to be explored. A more careful disaggregation, based on thorough empirical analysis, of the public and private components of defence outputs is called for. Furthermore, as suggested above, much of the literature has been characterized by a surprisingly superficial treatment of the details of NATO history, raising questions about the reasonableness of its assumptions and thus the soundness of its conclusions. Greater care in its application to NATO is required.

Chronology: Development of NATO

1948	Negotiations for a transatlantic security pact begin
1949	North Atlantic Treaty signed
1950	Outbreak of the Korean War triggers NATO military build-up
1951	Integrated military structure established; United States deploys additional troops in Europe; negotiations on a German military contribution begin
1954	German rearmament approved; NATO adopts 'New Look' strategy (MC 48)
1955	Germany joins NATO and Western European Union
1961	Berlin crisis prompts strengthening of NATO's forces
1966	France completes its withdrawal from NATO's military structures
1967	Harmel Report calls for pursuit of detente as well as deterrence; NATO adopts flexible response strategy (MC 14/3)
1971–3	Mansfield amendments calling for US force reductions in Europe defeated
1977	Long-term defence programme initiated; goal of 3% real increases in defence spending established
1979	Dual-track long-range theatre nuclear force (LRTNF) decision
1982	Debate over 'no first use' begins
1983	NATO deploys first intermediate-range nuclear forces (INF)
1984	Nunn amendment proposing possible US force withdrawals defeated
1987	INF treaty signed
1990	German unification; Germany allowed to remain in NATO
1991	NATO's first post-Cold War strategic concept and force structure adopted; North Atlantic Cooperation Council established
1992	NATO forces enforce UN arms blockade on the former Yugoslavia and monitor UN flight ban over Bosnia
1993	NATO forces enforce Bosnian no-fly zone
1994	Partnership for Peace established; NATO forces fire first shots in anger, downing Serb aircraft and conducting air strikes in Bosnia

Notes

1. Particularly influential is Stephen Walt's definition of an alliance as 'a formal or informal arrangement for security cooperation between two or more sovereign states'. Also useful is Glenn Snyder's formulation of alliances as 'formal associations of states for the use (or non-use) of military force, intended for either the security or the aggrandizement of their members, against specific other states'. See Stephen M. Walt, *The Origins of Alliances* (Ithaca, NY, 1987), 12, and Glenn H. Snyder, 'Alliance Theory: A Neorealist First Cut', *Journal of International Affairs*, 44 (1990), 104.

2. See esp. Harvey Starr, 'A Collective Goods Analysis of the Warsaw Pact after Czecho-slovakia', *International Organization*, 28 (1974), 521–32, and William M. Reisinger, 'East European Military Expenditures in the 1970s', *International Organization*, 37 (1983), 143–55.

3. Kenneth N. Waltz, *Theory of International Politics* (Reading, Mass., 1979); Walt, *The Origins of Alliances*.

4. See e.g. Timothy P. Ireland, *Creating the Entangling Alliance* (Westport, Conn., 1981), esp. ch. 2.

5. For further discussion of German objectives see Robert McGeehan, *The German Rearmament Question* (Urbana, Ill., 1971).

6. For a detailed analysis, see John S. Duffield, 'NATO's Functions after the Cold War', *Political Science Quarterly*, 109 (1994–5), 763–88.

7. Steven R. David, *Choosing Sides* (Baltimore, 1991); Michael A. Barnett and Jack S. Levy, 'Domestic Sources of Alliances and Alignments', *International Organization*, 45 (1991), 369–95.

8. See e.g. Stephen D. Krasner (ed.), *International Regimes* (Ithaca, NY, 1983); Robert O. Keohane, *After Hegemony* (Princeton, NJ, 1984).

9. For an overview see Simon Duke, *The Burdensharing Debate* (New York, 1993).

10. In addition to the works on the WTO cited above, principal exceptions are Wallace Thies, 'Alliances and Collective Goods', *Journal of Conflict Resolution*, 31 (1987), 298–332, and John A. C. Conybeare and Todd Sandler, 'The Triple Entente and the Triple Alliance', *American Political Science Review*, 84 (1990), 1197–1206.

11. Mancur Olson, Jr., and Richard Zeckhauser, 'An Economic Theory of Alliances', *Review of Economics and Statistics*, 48 (1966), 266–79. For the more general theory on which the article is based see Mancur Olson, *The Logic of Collective Action* (Cambridge, Mass., 1965; repr. 1971).

12. Most subsequent studies have used Gross Domestic Product (GDP) instead of Gross National Product (GNP).

13. See esp. Bruce Russett and Harvey Starr, 'Alliances and the Price of Primacy', in Russett, *What Price Vigilance?* (New Haven, Conn., 1970); Todd Sandler and John F. Forbes, 'Burden Sharing, Strategy, and the Design of NATO', *Economic Inquiry*, 18 (1980), 425–44 at 439.

14. In addition to Sandler and Forbes, 'Burden Sharing', these ideas are developed in Todd Sandler and Jon Cauley, 'On the Economic Theory of Alliances', *Journal of Conflict Resolution*, 19 (1975), 330–48, and Todd Sandler, 'Impurity of Defense', *Kyklos*, 30 (1977), 443–60.

15. The concept of complementarity is presented in James C. Murdoch and Todd Sandler, 'A Theoretical and Empirical Analysis of NATO', *Journal of Conflict Resolution*, 26 (1982), 237–63, and Murdoch and Sandler, 'Complementarity, Free-Riding, and the Military Expenditures of NATO Allies', *Journal of Public Economics*, 25 (1984), 83–101.

16. See esp. John R. Oneal and Mark A. Elrod, 'NATO Burden Sharing and the Forces of Change', *International Studies Quarterly*, 33 (1989), 435–56. Evidence that the alliance had in any case begun to shift away from the strategy of massive retaliation as early

as the late 1950s is presented in John S. Duffield, 'The Evolution of NATO's Strategy of Flexible Response', *Security Studies*, 1 (1991), 132–56.

17. John R. Oneal, 'The Theory of Collective Action and Burden Sharing in NATO', *International Organization*, 44 (1990), 379–402; William R. Gates and Katsuaki L. Terasawa, 'Commitment, Threat Perception, and Expenditures in a Defense Alliance', *International Studies Quarterly*, 36 (1992), 101–18.

18. Gates and Terasawa, 'Commitment'; John R. Oneal, 'Testing the Theory of Collective Action', *Journal of Conflict Resolution*, 34 (1990), 426–48.

19. Glenn Palmer, 'Alliance Politics and Issue Areas', *American Journal of Political Science*, 34 (1990), 190–211, and 'Corralling the Free Rider', *International Studies Quarterly*, 34 (1990), 147–64; Oneal, 'Testing the Theory of Collective Action', and 'The Theory of Collective Action'. The last point may be criticized, however, on the grounds that most defence policy coordination among the European members of NATO continued to take place within the alliance, not within other, purely European bodies.

20. Oneal, 'Testing the Theory of Collective Action', 445. The most comprehensive third-wave analysis is John R. Oneal and Paul F. Diehl, 'The Theory of Collective Action and NATO: New Empirical Tests', *Political Research Quarterly*, 47 (1994), 373–96.

21. Mark A. Boyer, 'Trading Public Goods in the Western Alliance System', *Journal of Conflict Resolution*, 33 (1989), 700–27, and *International Cooperation and Public Goods* (Baltimore, 1993).

22. John S. Duffield, 'International Regimes and Alliance Behavior', *International Organization*, 46 (1992), 819–55.

Further Reading

The best general overviews of NATO are:

KAPLAN, LAWRENCE S., *NATO and the United States* (Boston, 1994);
KUGLER, RICHARD L., *Commitment to Purpose* (Santa Monica, Calif., 1993);
POWASKI, RONALD E., *The Entangling Alliance* (Westport, Conn., 1994).

Several books provide more detailed analysis of NATO's military posture. Two that discuss nuclear issues are:

DAALDER, IVO H., *The Nature and Practice of Flexible Response* (New York, 1991);
SCHWARTZ, DAVID N., *NATO's Nuclear Dilemmas* (Washington, 1983).

The role and capabilities of NATO's conventional forces are the focus of

DUFFIELD, JOHN S., *Power Rules* (Stanford, Calif., 1995).

Two useful, if increasingly dated, surveys of the theoretical literature on alliances are:

HOSLTI, OLE, HOPMANN, P. TERRENCE, and SULLIVAN, JOHN D., *Unity and Disintegration in International Alliances* (New York, 1973);
WARD, MICHAEL DON, *Research Gaps in Alliance Dynamics* (Denver, 1982).

CHAPTER SIXTEEN

ARMS CONTROL: A FORMAL APPROACH

George Downs and Peter Barsoom

This chapter introduces the reader to how non-cooperative game theory can be used to study arms control and attempts to see what light it can shed on the evolution of arms control since 1945. Like those analysts who use more conventional case-study methods and quantitative approaches, formal modellers are interested in understanding the extent to which arms control has achieved or is likely to achieve its classic goals of reducing the likelihood and destructiveness of war and the magnitude of military expenditures. The difference between the approaches lies in the method by which they go about arriving at these estimates and in the relative attention they devote to assessing the strengths and limitations of different arms control strategies.

Case-study and quantitative researchers, for their part, rely on historical data and either intuition or a regression equation to form a counterfactual estimate of what would have occurred in the absence of an arms control agreement. They then estimate the effects of arms control by comparing this to what did in fact occur. Formal modellers, by contrast, use a game to evaluate logically the extent to which the incentives and information embodied in an arms control agreement have reduced the attractiveness of two undesirable strategies: initiating conflict and increasing defence spending.[1] This method produces no more than a rough estimate of the effects of any arms control agreement, but it more easily addresses issues of strategy, for example, what a state should do if it suspects a violation.[2]

As is the case in many policy areas, part of the rationale for applying formal models to arms control issues lies in the difficulties encountered by a more empirical approach. Even the most skilled historian is likely to be frustrated in her attempt to paint an accurate picture of the motives and expectations underlying an agreement concluded decades ago, and estimates of the counterfactual tend to be quite controversial. Whereas it is easy to argue that the Washington Naval Accord of 1922 did little to blunt growing Japanese ambitions and the likelihood of eventual confrontation with the United States, it is far more difficult to provide an authoritative estimate of its effect on the growth of the US navy or on US–British relations. Determining the impact of the more recent ABM or non-proliferation treaties is no less difficult.

The political scientist who applies quantitative methods to a large number of cases is no better off. Measurement problems abound in connection with control variables such as relative power and 'level of hostility', and arms control agreements, the units of analysis, are unlikely to be statistically independent of one another. Most daunting of all, many of the variables that are of greatest interest, such as the kind of strategy that a state employs to induce its rival to agree to an arms control agreement and the strategy it uses to maintain that agreement, are 'endogenous' (see Chapter 3 in this volume): that is, a state chooses a strategy based on expectations of its effectiveness under a specific set of conditions. This means that any attempt to compare the effectiveness of two strategies inevitably runs the risk of simply being a comparison of how two different sets of conditions influence effectiveness. Overcoming this problem requires removing the effect of each of these sets of conditions; but simple, statistical controls are usually not enough to do the trick.

16.1. Simple Games with Important Implications

Many of the most recent applications of formal models to arms control were spurred by developments in game theory that took place during the 1980s. These innovations married the strategic equilibrium calculations of non-cooperative game theory with situations characterized by ongoing interaction between parties (i.e. repeated as opposed to single-play games) and uncertain information about the motives and/or behaviour of the states involved (i.e. incomplete information). This makes it possible for formal modellers to work with more realistic assumptions about the knowledge available to decision-makers and permits them to explore the implications of the uncertainty often associated with verification, the development of new weapons systems, and political changes within states. Most important for the policy-maker, the formal modeller is now able to provide some modest assistance in evaluating the utility of various policy options. For example, models can be used to assess 'signalling' strategies intended to reveal a state's peaceful intentions or its unwillingness to tolerate futher treaty violations.

Until relatively recently, formal modellers were inclined to look at arms races and arms control agreements as homogeneous phenomena. They have come to

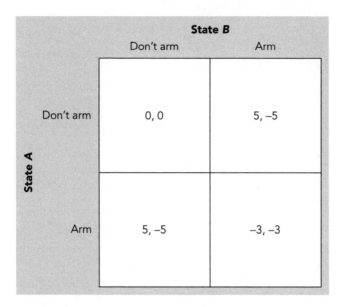

Fig. 16.1. Prisoner's Dilemma or mixed-motive game

appreciate, however, that different patterns of incentives drive different types of arms races and that this should affect the choice of arms control strategy. To understand how this works, let us begin by looking at four simple, archetypical games that both logic and history suggest are associated with arms races and arms control.

Fig. 16.1 depicts the pay-offs associated with the classic Prisoner's Dilemma. If the game is to be played only once, the sole Nash equilibrium is for both parties to choose the 'defect' option and engage in an arms build-up. This is the case despite the benefits of mutual cooperation because regardless of what one party expects the other to do, the other can improve her lot by defecting.

Rational cooperation, in the sense of being consistent with the self-interest of each party, is possible only if the players believe the game will played an indefinite number of times and if each party can devise and somehow communicate a strategy that convinces the other that the short-term benefit gained through defection will lead to a lower expected benefit for the game as a whole.[3] The SALT I Treaty is a good example. While either the Soviet Union or the United States might have derived a modest benefit from violating the treaty in any given period, the prospect that such a move would provoke an equivalent or greater counter-violation (and intensify an already expensive and politically problematic arms race) made such a move unattractive.

Fig. 16.2 depicts the game called Deadlock. Again, the only equilibrium is an

	State B	
	Don't arm	Arm
Don't arm	0, 0	5, 10
Arm	10, 5	8, 8

Fig. 16.2. Deadlock

arms build-up or mutual defection; but in Deadlock, unlike in the Prisoner's Dilemma, neither party would be better off if mutual cooperation were somehow possible. Shifting the context from a single-play game to a repeated game that will be played an infinite or indefinite number of times offers no help.

Fig. 16.3 depicts a pure coordination game in which the only two equilibria call for cooperation. Treaty 1 offers the higher pay-offs, but Treaty 2 is none the less a Nash equilibrium since neither party can improve its pay-off if it expects the other to choose it. The 'Hot Line' Agreement is one such agreement. While one can imagine the United States and Soviet Union agreeing to any one of a number of different versions of the treaty, there was every incentive for both states to agree to *some* version and no reason for either to defect from whatever version was finally signed. Unlike the Prisoner's Dilemma and like Deadlock, repeating the game promises no change in outcome unless the parties somehow begin by coordinating on Treaty 2 and decide to switch to Treaty 1 after mutual consultation.

The game shown in Fig. 16.4 is more interesting. It is called Battle of the Sexes because it was originally designed to depict the coordination problems of a man and a woman who want to spend the evening together but who have different preferences about what they should do. As in the case of the coordination game, both sides would be better off cooperating than defecting, but unlike the coordination game there are significant distributive benefits to be bargained

State A \ State B	Treaty 1	Treaty 2
Treaty 1	10, 10	0, 0
Treaty 2	0, 0	5, 5

Fig. 16.3. Coordination game

State A \ State B	Treaty 1	Treaty 2
Treaty 1	10, 7	0, 0
Treaty 2	0, 0	7, 10

Fig. 16.4. Battle of the Sexes game

over. For example, State A would like to see Treaty 1 enacted or be compensated in some fashion for agreeing to Treaty 2. State B feels the same way except that it prefers Treaty 2.

Simple games like these can help us understand and even 'narrate' the history of arms control. They suggest, for example, that the easiest sorts of arms agreements to achieve and sustain are those driven by coordination games. All things being equal, such agreements should constitute the most prevalent and stable kind of arms control. The Chronology at the end of the chapter bears out this expectation. Many of the agreements are basically variations of either 'pure' coordination games or the Battle of the Sexes variety. In addition to the 'Hot Line' Agreement of 1963 and its amendments, these include the 'Accident Measures' Agreement of 1971, the 'Incidents at Sea' Agreement of 1972, the Convention on the Physical Protection of Nuclear Material of 1980, the Ballistic Missile Launch Notification Agreement of 1988, the Agreement on the Prevention of Dangerous Military Activities of 1989, the Major Strategic Exercises Agreement of 1989, and, at least with respect to the preferences of states that possess nuclear weapons, the Non-Proliferation Treaty of 1970.

One common critique of coordination-type arms control agreements is that such treaties cannot contain the sort of calculated aggression that precedes major wars and are unlikely to produce significant reductions in arms expenditures.[4] While the critique is correct, the agreements should probably not be judged so harshly. History is an unreliable guide to estimating the value of agreements designed to deal with technologies that did not exist until the latter half of the twentieth century. Moreover, because coordination game agreements are almost always easier to achieve than mixed-motive or Prisoner's Dilemma game agreements, they tend to predominate in *every* sphere of international relations.[5]

Conversely, advocates of arms control should not overestimate the achievement that coordination game agreements represent. There is no reason to believe, for example, that the solution of a coordination game portends the solution of mixed-motive arms games in which there is a significant incentive to defect. This would be analogous to believing that because two shrimp fleets have agreed on procedures for entering and exiting a harbour or for handling emergencies, they should trust each other to abide by an agreement to refrain from overfishing.

Solutions to coordination games almost invariably precede solutions to mixed-motive games only because they are easier to reach. They do not prepare the way in any causal sense for the settlement of games in which there is a significant incentive to defect. Similarly, the high compliance rate of coordination games indicates nothing more than the absence of an incentive to violate the agreement. Indeed, a major message of game theory is that the only thing that really builds a state's confidence that another state will resist a given temptation is the demonstrated ability to do so.

The Chronology does, of course, contain agreements that appear to be solutions to Prisoner's Dilemma or mixed-motive games. These include the Antarctic Treaty of 1959, the Outer Space Treaty of 1967, the Seabed Arms Control Treaty of 1971, the SALT I Agreement of 1972, the ABM Treaty of 1972, the SALT II Treaty of 1979, and the various INF and START Agreements. These are distinguished from the treaties cited previously in that at least one state, and often both the United States and the Soviet Union, would have been likely to violate the agreement had it been structured as a single-play game. Thus the maintenance of the agreement and the likely motivation behind its creation lay in the expectation that the game would be repeated an indefinite number of times and that the rival state would punish defections so severely that the expected benefits of breaking the treaty were not worth the costs.[6]

Yet, in respect of a treaty's capacity to overcome a substantial incentive to defect, the game theorist, like many critics of arms control, would argue that the achievement of most of these treaties is quite modest. There is little to be gained from defecting from treaties like SALT I or SALT II, which more or less represent the status quo. It is also far from clear whether an unpunished violation of the Antarctic Treaty or Outer Space Treaty would have been worth the financial costs of carrying it out at the time the treaties were signed. It is not trivial for states to assure each other through a treaty that they each view the exploitation of a given environment as too costly since it can prevent the waste of resources. However, it represents as much coordination as it does serious cooperation. As we have already noted, a state does not signal much about its true intentions by engaging in a cooperative agreement when there is little incentive not to do so. More arms cooperation may come, but there is no reason for a rational state to expect that it will.

In fact, the formal theorist is likely to worry about the future viability of these agreements. When the incentive to defect is so modest, the size of the expected punishment for defection is unlikely to have played much of a role in bringing about the decision to cooperate. There were not many expected benefits that needed to be offset by retaliation. This can pose a problem if technology or domestic politics change in a way that makes defection significantly more attractive. A state that wants to maintain the agreement under such circumstances will have to start virtually from scratch to make credible its willingness to implement a punishment as large as the benefit the other state now expects to obtain.

The Non-Proliferation Treaty provides a good example of this dynamic. It began as a coordination treaty between states that possessed nuclear technology; expected punishment for defection played an almost negligible role at the time it was created. Over time, however, the profile of a potential defector shifted. Where it had once been a state that possessed the technology and had relatively little incentive to see it diffuse more widely, it came to include states like North

Korea that were developing the technology more or less endogenously and felt they had a great deal to gain from violation. Such states can only be dissuaded from defecting by the expectation of a significant punishment; and, given the absence of any precedent for inflicting punishment in the coordination-orientated history of the NPT regime, this simply does not exist. Moreover, such problems are likely to continue unless credible commitment to costly punishment is somehow established.

16.2. More Complicated Problems and Arms Control Strategies

These simple games are valuable for clarifying the ecology of arms control and providing a clear rationale for not inferring too much from confidence-building gestures. Their contribution to developing a deeper understanding of strategic issues is modest, however. Their assumptions are simply too restrictive to enable formal reasoning to display its power or to demonstrate the corresponding limitations of intuition. For either to occur we have to introduce some (more realistic) complications. For example, we might permit states to choose from a continuum of arms production rates, or introduce imperfect information about verification and the ambitions of rival states. These are the kinds of environments in which intuition becomes a less reliable guide and in which formal models thrive—although, predictably, at the price of more complicated models and mathematics.

More complicated models can provide us with insights into the strategies that states might employ to establish and maintain cooperative equilibria (there are often a number of them). They can also enable us to specify the conditions under which such cooperation will break down. Not surprisingly, the reasoning underlying the strategies is reminiscent of deterrence logic. A state committed to preserving arms stability must find a way to convince its rival that any violation of the arms equilibrium will be met by a response that is at least as costly as any expected benefit. This is the expectation that sustained the SALT agreements when they were first created: the very modest benefit of exceeding the arms limitations on strategic weapons was offset by the mutual expectation that any violation would only lead to a resumption of the arms race.

The emphasis on deterring violations and the signals that must be sent to create the appropriate expectation do not mean that positive incentives do not have a role to play. To convince a rival to take arms control negotiations seriously, a state must convince that rival that it is worth paying the typically substantial bargaining costs (including the domestic political costs) connected with negotiating an agreement and that it is unlikely to defect at the first opportunity. Such expectations are best established by some 'costly signal' such as Gorbachev's withdrawal of troops from Germany and Eastern Europe or the United States' unilateral decision to destroy its stocks of biological weapons.

Formal models that focus on signals to establish positive and negative expectations bridge the gap between the rational choice approach to arms control and the growing emphasis in the security literature on employing unilateral initiatives and tacit bargaining as an alternative to formal negotiations.[7] Formal models differ in that they establish *specific* conditions under which gestures of different magnitudes are likely to be employed and when they will be successful in fostering or maintaining cooperation.

For example, formal models suggest that unilateral gestures of the magnitude that Gorbachev made in 1988 are as rare as they are because states have no rational grounds for believing that the gesture will be reciprocated. Indeed, in one model, if the estimated probability that the rival will ignore a cooperative gesture reaches 55 per cent the optimal strategy is to make no gesture at all, not even a small one. If that probability is less than 55 per cent but doubts about the likelihood of the other state's reciprocating still exist, the model predicts that the gesture will be small or relatively modest, such as declaring a moratorium on nuclear testing after a series of tests has been completed.[8] These less costly signals are less risky, but they are also less convincing. Almost invariably, such ambiguous gestures spark political controversy in the rival state about their significance and generate doubts about the motives behind them.

Different considerations limit the effectiveness of a Tit-For-Tat or TFT. This is the strategy of reciprocity embedded in treaties in other areas such as trade (via GATT) that has received so much attention since the publication of Axelrod's *Evolution of Cooperation* in 1984.[9] One problem with TFT is that it does a poor job coping with imperfect information. If State A mistakenly believes that State B has violated the treaty, it will punish B which will respond by punishing A back (it has no way of knowing whether A has made a mistake or is being exploitative), and so forth. This 'echo' will continue for ever.

A further problem with TFT stems from the relationship between the arms benefit sacrificed under arms control and the size of the sanction necessary to maintain the treaty. In situations where arms control is feasible but an incentive to cheat exists, the temptation to cheat is likely to rise more rapidly than the benefits of cooperation.[10] This increase in the ratio of the benefits of cheating to the one-period benefit of the treaty means that increasingly severe punishments are necessary to deter defection as the benefits of the treaty and corresponding restrictiveness of its requirements increase.

This relationship means that harsher strategies can enforce more cooperative treaties than TFT can. Although this claim is difficult to test there is some fragmentary evidence that bears on the issue. Mauer argues that Churchill forced

Germany to accept a naval arms equilibrium in 1908 with a variation of Britain's 'two for one standard'. That is, Churchill threatened and then carried out the threat to build at least two capital ships in response to each that Germany built.[11] In this instance the coercive advantage that this very aggressive punishment provided appears to have made the difference between success and failure.

In short, formal models demonstrate that the relevant criterion for choosing a sanction to apply for cheating is that the punishment must offset what the transgressor gained by the violation. This is not a requirement that a given level of arms overproduction be punished by an equal overproduction (TFT). Nor is it equivalent to prescribing that the transgressor must be punished at least as much as its violation hurt the other party. Both of these standards have aspects of fairness associated with them that many of us find attractive, but neither is relevant to supporting the treaty equilibrium or obtaining an agreement in the first place. Justice must take a back seat to applying the appropriate disincentive: the costs of cheating must offset the gains of defection.

This is not to imply (as deterrence theorists sometimes do) that the threat of ever larger punishments provides ever greater confidence that a treaty will not be violated—at least, not for the formal modeller. Rather, the concept of 'renegotiation-proofness' places a limit on what ever larger punishments can accomplish. It has a number of technical definitions, all involving the dimension of credibility that springs from assessments of a state's motivation rather than simply its capacity to carry out a particular threat.

Assume that two states have learned the lesson that the level of cooperation that can be maintained in a mixed-motive game is related to the level of punishment used to enforce it and that they agree to punish violations of an anti-ballistic missile treaty by abrogating the treaty for ever. Suppose that by some unexpected sequence of events (e.g. the leader of one of the states momentarily overestimates the prospects of a new technology), one side violates the treaty. In response, the other state declares the treaty null and void and resumes deployment of its anti-ballistic missile system. After a significant time period has passed, the president of the state that violated the treaty communicates to the other state's leader that while he appreciates their mutual pledge to defect for ever in the face of a violation, the new arms race has already cost him more than what his state gained by breaking the treaty. 'We have paid the price for our mistake. To continue the race any further will hurt us both. Let's (re)negotiate a new treaty.'

This is the logic of renegotiation. When a punishment strategy is vulnerable to such an offer, it is said not to be renegotiation-proof. As a practical matter, think of it as restricting the credibility of punishment for an arms violation to a level no greater than the benefit that the violator has obtained by cheating.

Although we noted one of the problems that imperfect intelligence can cause when we were discussing TFT, we have for the most part been assuming that verification information on both sides is perfect and instantaneous. Yet, even in an age of satellite reconnaissance, this standard is often not met. In the 1980s US estimates of Soviet underground test yields (made in connection with the Threshold Test Ban Treaty) were uncertain because of differences in the test site geologies of the respective countries.[12] Allegations of Soviet violations of SALT I, which prohibits the deployment of mobile radars that can be used to support ABM systems, were also based on uncertain information. It was known that the Soviets had constructed a radar that *could* be placed on a truck, but no one came forth with evidence that one had actually been moved or even placed on wheels. Even had there been such evidence, the problem of assessing the significance of the violation would have remained. Was this a violation of marginal consequence or something more? Does it matter how certain we are about the benefit represented by the violation?

These uncertainties that spring from the imperfections in the quality of information about verification have implications both for how cooperation should be enforced and for the level of cooperation that can be achieved. In order to cope with errors in observation (and mistakes about the implications of supposed violations for a rival's capability), states need an enforcement strategy that is at once less aggressive than a full information strategy but also not so slow to react that it creates an incentive to cheat under the cover of noise (bad information). To this end, formal modellers have developed a class of strategies called 'trigger strategies'.[13] These operate on the basis of a kind of significance test. That is, they prescribe the initiation of punishment when the likelihood that a violation has occurred reaches some specific level. Both parties announce in advance what their trigger level is and also the magnitude of the punishment that they plan to implement when the trigger is tripped. The strategies will be in equilibrium if neither side has an incentive to produce more than the treaty amount during cooperative periods.

Cooperation among states will also be affected by estimates of the degree to which verification is uncertain. This is because the existence of 'noise' or bad information in the system means that false positives are inevitable. Apart from having to accept the idea of a good treaty with a less than 100 per cent compliance rate, the fact of this expectation means that when information is less than perfect states must balance the benefits that the threat of a marginally greater sanction provides against the costs of having to apply it periodically. This will inevitably reduce the size of the optimal sanction, which will in turn reduce the level of cooperation that can take place.[14]

A further sort of uncertainty involves state preferences. Security theorists in the realist tradition do not worry too much about goal uncertainty because they see state aspirations as a fairly straightforward function of resources filtered through capability. If, however, we take the liberal position seriously and assume that state aspirations are more complicated than a simple function of resources, we need to think about how the level of goal uncertainty affects the strategies we use to obtain an agreement and then to ensure treaty compliance. Certainly such uncertainty does seem to matter. During the 1920s uncertainty about Japanese ambitions led the United States to view Japanese violations of the Washington Naval Treaty accord in a different light from those of Britain, and goal uncertainty appears to have had an impact on US strategy with regard to North Korean violations of NPT.

Formal analysis suggests that preference uncertainty matters, but in an un-expected way. It appears that if State *B* is not sure whether State *A* is friendly or aggressive, State *B* should punish State *A* as if it were aggressive. Renegotiation-proofness, which usually bounds the severity of the punishment, loses its appli-cability: State *A* may suggest that State *B* renegotiate the punishment downward, but *B* has no way of telling whether *A* is relatively unaggressive and telling the truth or aggressive and trying to trick it into punishing too little. Since game theory tells us that both types of states will, in this instance, act in the same way (i.e. we have a 'pooled' equilibrium), *B* must punish *A* as if it were the worst possible adversary. In this instance at least, utility uncertainty requires that we deal with a liberal world in a realist way.

16.3. Conclusion

To date, formal modelling arrives at an overall assessment of arms control similar to that of the majority of analysts employing other methods.[15] Both generally agree on the following points:

1. Coordination agreements such as those establishing the Hot Line, handling incidents at sea, and providing for notification of nuclear accidents have probably enhanced crisis stability by reducing the chances of accidents and misinterpretation.
2. While the Non-Proliferation Treaty and the secret agreement controlling the diffusion of missile control technology have proven unable to stop states from developing these technologies within their borders, they have enabled advanced industrial states to work together to slow the spread of these technologies to less developed states.
3. Agreements like the SALT I ABM treaty and SALT II have modestly increased each side's assessment of the other's reasonableness and desire to avoid an intense and expensive arms competition.
4. INF, CFE, and START have been factors in reducing specific expenditures and quite probably have lowered, in the absence of any unexpected crisis, the public's

tolerance of major increases in total military expenditures. They may also have further improved crisis stability.

5. Arms control has not succeeded in reducing the likelihood of a war brought about by the kind of calculated ambition that produced two world wars and dozens of smaller ones in this century; nor has it reduced the level of destruction that would accompany a large-scale conflict.

Any determination of the net contribution of these achievements to preserving peace very much depends on one's assessment of three counterfactuals: the dangers posed by nuclear accidents without the coordination agreements; the diffusion of nuclear technologies without NPT; and total military expenditures in the absence of INF, CFE, and START. Neither formal theory nor more empirical methods provides a reliable guide to estimating any of these.

Formal modellers have yet to link arms control models convincingly to the conditions under which deterrence is sustainable.[16] This has prevented them from speculating about the ultimate potential of arms control for reducing the probability of intentional (as opposed to accidental) war. In the absence of this integration of arms control and deterrence models, the special contribution of formal modelling to arms control will probably continue to lie in advising decision-makers how they can best bring about meaningful arms agreements and maintain them. This advice, which is rarely advanced in the more empirical literature of arms control, includes suggestions such as the following:

1. Sanctions to punish arms violations (such as a limited resumption of an arms race) should be designed to inflict a cost on the violator that completely offsets the expected benefit. This standard is unrelated to any standard of fairness such as punishing the violator to an extent that compensates the loss suffered by the victim, and the sanction may have to be considerably more severe than that prescribed by reciprocity or Tit-For-Tat.

2. There is no reason to expect arms agreements that solve coordination games (e.g. the Hot Line Agreement) to lead to cooperation in areas where the incentive to defect is much larger (e.g. arms limitation, research and development). A corollary of this is that a state that has entered such an agreement should not believe that it has adequately signalled its willingness to cooperate further.

3. Sanctions for the violations of arms agreements involving an undeveloped technology (e.g. the ABM Treaty) have to increase as the underlying technology improves.

4. When there is doubt about the magnitude of the benefit that a rival state has derived from a violation, it should be punished as if it had received the maximum.[17]

5. When intelligence about the existence of violations is imperfect—as it will often be—a trigger strategy should be used that will systematically discount the 'noisy' information. Under these conditions a decision-maker will have to choose between the twin perils of accepting the domestic political consequences

for not punishing some number of apparent violations or of following a sub-optimal enforcement strategy.

Obviously, this strategic side of arms control does not have the summary weight of such questions as: 'To what extent did arms control operate to stabilize US–Soviet relations during the Cold War?' or 'Does arms control work?' Yet because such prescriptions are based on what are often dramatic differences in relative effectiveness, they may have a great deal to contribute to the future of arms control.

Chronology: Arms Control and Related Treaties and Agreements

17 June 1925	Geneva Protocol signed; entered into force 8 Feb. 1928
1 Dec. 1959	Antarctic Treaty signed; entered into force 23 June 1961
20 June 1963	'Hot Line' Agreement signed and entered into force
5 Aug. 1963	Limited Test Ban Treaty signed; entered into force 10 Oct. 1963
27 Jan. 1967	Outer Space Treaty signed; entered into force 10 Oct. 1967
14 Feb. 1967	Treaty of Tlatelolco signed; entered into force 22 April 1968
1 Apr. 1968	Protocol II to the Treaty of Tlatelolco signed; ratified by USA 8 May 1971
1 July 1968	Non-Proliferation Treaty signed; entered into force 5 March 1970
11 Feb. 1971	Seabed Arms Control Treaty signed; entered into force 18 May 1972
30 Sept. 1971	'Accident Measures' Agreement, signed and entered into force; 'Hot Line' Modernization Agreement signed and entered into force
10 Apr. 1972	Biological Weapons Convention signed; entered into force 26 March 1975
25 May 1972	'Incidents at Sea' Agreement signed and entered into force
26 May 1972	SALT I Interim Agreement signed; entered into force 3 Oct. 1972. ABM Treaty signed; entered into force 3 Oct. 1972
29 May 1972	Declaration of Basic Principles of Relations between the USA and USSR signed and entered into force
23 June 1973	Prevention of Nuclear War Agreement between USA and USSR signed and entered into force
3 July 1974	ABM Treaty Protocol signed; entered into force 24 May 1976; Threshold Test Ban Treaty signed; entered into force 11 Dec. 1990
1 Aug. 1975	Helsinki Final Act signed and entered into force
28 May 1976	PNE Treaty signed; entered into force 11 Dec. 1990
18 May 1977	ENMOD Convention signed; entered into force 5 Oct. 1978
26 May 1977	Protocol I to the Treaty of Tlatelolco signed; ratified by USA 19 Nov. 1981

18 June 1979	SALT II Treaty signed (never entered into force)
3 Mar. 1980	Convention on the Physical Protection of Nuclear Material signed
17 July 1984	'Hot Line' Expansion Agreement signed and entered into force
19 Sept. 1986	Stockholm Accord adopted
15 Sept. 1987	Nuclear Risk Reduction Centers Agreement signed and entered into force
8 Dec. 1987	INF Treaty signed; entered into force 1 June 1988
12 May 1988	INF Diplomatic Note on 'Weapons Delivery Vehicle', INF Agreed Minute signed, entered into force 1 June 1988
31 May 1988	US–USSR Ballistic Missile Launch Notification Agreement signed and entered into force
24 June 1988	'Hot Line' MOU Modification Agreement signed and entered into force; INF Inspection Procedures Agreement signed and entered into force
20 Dec. 1988	INF Special Verification Commission MOU signed and entered into force
17 Feb. 1989	Treaty of Tlatelolco IAEA Safeguards Agreement signed; entered into force 6 April 1989
9 June 1989	INF Continuous Monitoring Inspection Procedures Agreement signed and entered into force
12 June 1989	US–USSR Agreement on the Prevention of Dangerous Military Activities signed; entered into force 1 Jan. 1990
23 Sept. 1989	US–USSR Major Strategic Exercises Notification Agreement signed and entered into force; START Trial Verification and Stability Measures Agreement signed and entered into force; START ICBM Verification Agreement signed and entered into force; CW Verification and Data Exchange MOU signed and entered into force
21 Dec. 1989	INF Verification Implementation MOU signed and entered into force
1 June 1990	US–USSR CW Destruction Agreement signed; agreement has not yet entered into force
12 Sept. 1990	2 Plus 4 Treaty signed; entered into force 3 Oct. 1990
17 Nov. 1990	The Vienna Document 1990 adopted; entered into force 1 Jan. 1991
19 Nov. 1990	CFE Treaty signed; entered into force 9 Nov. 1992
4 Apr. 1991	Amendment I to MOA on INF Verification signed and entered into force; Amendment II to the MOA on INF Verification signed and entered into force
11 Dec. 1991	Amendment III to the MOA on INF Verification signed and entered into force; Amendment IV to the MOA on INF Verification signed and entered into force
31 July 1991	START Treaty signed; not yet entered into force
4 Mar. 1992	The Vienna Document 1992 adopted
24 Mar. 1992	Treaty on Open Skies signed; not yet entered into force
23 May 1992	Lisbon START Protocol signed
5 June 1992	Oslo Final Document on CFE Implementation signed and entered into force

17 June 1992	US–USSR Joint Understanding on Strategic Offensive Arms signed; Open Lands MOU, signed and entered into force; Korean Nuclear Non-Proliferation Statement dated; US and Russian Agreement on Transportation and Destruction of Weapons Proliferation signed and entered into force; Fissile Material Containers Agreement signed; not yet entered into force; Armoured Blankets Agreement signed and entered into force; Emergency Response Equipment and Training Agreement signed and entered into force
18 June 1992	Joint Understanding Side Letter on Strategic Offensive Arms signed and entered into force
10 July 1992	CFE 1A Concluding Act signed; entered into force 17 July 1992
30 July 1992	US DOD and Russian President's CW Committee Agreement on CW Destruction, Transport, or Storage signed and entered into force
28 Aug. 1992	US DOD and Russian MINATOM Agreement on Cargo and Guard Railcar Conversion Kits for Transportation of Nuclear Weapons and Material signed and entered into force; US and Russian Agreement on Disposition of HEU initialled; not yet entered into force
6 Oct. 1992	US DOD and Russian MINATOM Agreement on Technical Assistance for Storage Facility Design for Fissile Material signed and entered into force
22 Oct. 1992	US and Belarussian Agreement on Emergency Response and Prevention of Proliferation of Weapons of Mass Destruction signed; Emergency Response Equipment and Training Agreement, signed and entered into force; Export Control Systems Agreement signed and entered into force
3 Jan. 1993	START II Treaty signed; not yet entered into force
13 Jan. 1993	Chemical Weapons Convention signed; not yet entered into force
15 Jan. 1993	Continuous Communications Link Agreement signed and entered into force

Notes

1. Characterizing the formal modelling approach to arms control is perilous since it encompasses many different types of axiomatic models that address an equally diverse number of policy issues. This essay will sacrifice variety in order to focus on the logic of formal enquiry. The range of formal applications to arms control is well exemplified by Huber and Avenhaus or Isard. See R. K. Huber and R. Avenhaus (eds.), *International Stability in a Multipolar World: Issues and Models for Analysis* (Baden-Baden, 1993); W. Isard, *Arms Races, Arms Control, and Conflict Analysis* (New York, 1988).

2. The distinctions made here reflect the current state of the art in both approaches, but they are anything but absolute. Case-study and quantitative researchers need models to transform data into counterfactual estimates, and there is nothing to prevent them from using formal ones. Conversely, the specifications used by formal modellers are inevitably shaped by knowledge drawn from case studies and behavioural data.

3. The theory of repeated games supplies a technology that can be used to evaluate the strategic implications of such situtations. To understand this technology the reader should consult any one of the excellent textbooks that have recently been published. A good place to begin is with J. Morrow, *Game Theory for Political Scientists* (New York, 1994). Readers comfortable with axiomatic reasoning should consider D. Fudenberg and J. Tirole, *Game Theory* (Boston, 1992).

4. Colin S. Gray, *House of Cards* (Ithaca, NY, 1992).

5. There are times when the distributive benefits at stake in a Battle of the Sexes-type game can lead to substantial bargaining delays.

6. The requirement that the players expect the game to be repeated means, of course, that neither side can believe it likely that the acquisition of a given weapon systems will end the arms race through victory at war or capitulation.

7. See K. Adelman, 'Arms Control With and Without Agreements', *Foreign Affairs*, 63 (1984), 240–62; G. W. Downs and D. M. Rocke, *Tacit Bargaining, Arms Races, and Arms Control* (Ann Arbor, 1990); B. Ramberg, *Arms Control Without Negotiation* (Boulder, Colo., 1993).

8. Downes and Rocke, *Tacit Bargaining*.

9. See R. Axelrod, *The Evolution of Cooperation* (New York, 1984).

10. Downes and Rocke, *Tacit Bargaining*, 138.

11. J. H. Mauer, 'The Anglo-German Naval Rivalry and Informal Arms Control', *Journal of Conflict Resolution*, 36 (1992), 284–308.

12. R. J. Smith, 'Administration at Odds over Soviet Cheating', *Science*, 228 (1985), 695.

13. E. J. Green and R. H. Porter, 'Noncooperative Collusion under Imperfect Price Formation', *Econometrica*, 52 (1984), 87–100; R. H. Porter, 'Optimal Cartel Trigger Price Strategies', *Journal of Economic Theory*, 29 (1983), 313–38; A. R. Ghosh and P. R. Masson, *Economic Cooperation in an Uncertain World* (Cambridge, Mass., 1994).

14. From a technical standpoint, this is because the benefits of an arms agreement are likely to increase linearly while the temptation to defect probably increases non-linearly. This is justified intuitively by the idea that every decrease in the rate of arms building produces roughly the same savings, whereas the danger of falling behind an opponent in an arms race grows at a progressively increasing rate.

15. See Mauer, 'Anglo-German Naval Rivalry'.

16. There has been a recent tendency to call any strategy Tit-For-Tat if it prescribes a sanction in response to a violation. Such an elastic definition is exceedingly dangerous because it renders the results of analysis prescriptively meaningless. The success of a large sanction like Churchill's says nothing about the likely success of a smaller one.

17. See Smith, 'Administration at Odds'.

Further Reading

BERKOWITZ, BRUCE D., *Calculated Risks* (New York, 1987). This book contains both a critique of classic arms control arguments and an analysis of what kind of arms control agreements work and what kind fail. It provides one of the most compact introductions to the subject that is available.

CARNESDALE, ALLEN, and HAAS, RICHARD (eds.), *Superpower Arms Control: Setting the Record Straight* (Cambridge, Mass., 1987). A helpful attempt to assess what arms control between the United States and Soviet Union has and has not accomplished.

DOWNS, GEORGE W. and ROCKE, DAVID M., *Tacit Bargaining, Arms Races, and Arms Control* (Ann Arbor, 1990). One of the relatively few attempts to examine arms control problems using game theory and simulation. Much of the emphasis is on how states interested in maintaining arms control but fearful of exploitation should respond to real or suspected violations.

GRAY, COLIN S., *House of Cards* (Ithaca, NY, 1992). A passionate and almost uniformly negative evaluation of arms control and the reasoning of arms control advocates. Supporters of arms control will find Gray's argument and aggresssiveness maddening, but he raises numerous issues that deserve attention.

SCHELLING, THOMAS C., and HALPERIN, MORTON H., *Strategy and Arms Control* (New York, 1961). One of the two 'classic' attempts to analyse the strategic role that arms control can play. The other is Hedly Bull's *The Control of the Arms Race: Disarmament and Arms Control in the Missile Age* (New York, 1965).

INDEX

Note: The term 'post-war' means 'post-Second World War'; page numbers in *italics* denote figure or box.